D1031823

The Untilled Garden

Natural History and the Spirit of Conservation in America,
1740–1840

This book traces the origins of conservation thinking in America to the naturalists who explored the middle-western frontier between 1740 and 1840. Their inquiries yielded a comprehensive natural history of America and inspired much of the conservation and ecological thinking we associate with later environmental and ecological philosophy. These explorers witnessed one of the great environmental transformations in American history, as the vast forests lying between the Appalachian Mountains and the Mississippi River gave way to a landscape of fields, meadows, and pastures. In debating these changes, naturalists translated classical ideas such as the balance of nature and the spiritual unity of all species into an American idiom. This book highlights the contributions made by the generation of natural historians who pioneered the utilitarian, ecological, and aesthetic arguments for protecting or preserving nature in America.

Richard W. Judd is the Col. James C. McBride Professor of History at the University of Maine and editor of the journal *Maine History*. He is the author of *Natural States: The Environmental Imagination in Maine, Oregon, and the Nation* (2003); *Common Lands, Common People: The Origins of Conservation in Northern New England* (1997); and *Maine: The Pine Tree State from Prehistory to the Present* (1995). His current research includes a survey of New England's environmental history.

Studies in Environment and History

Editors
Donald Worster, University of Kansas
J. R. McNeill, Georgetown University

Other Books in the Series

Donald Worster   *Nature's Economy: A History of Ecological Ideas, second edition*

Kenneth F. Kiple   *The Caribbean Slave: A Biological History*

Alfred W. Crosby   *Ecological Imperialism: The Biological Expansion of Europe, 900–1900, second edition*

Arthur F. McEvoy   *The Fisherman's Problem: Ecology and Law in the California Fisheries, 1850–1980*

Robert Harms   *Games Against Nature: An Eco-Cultural History of the Nunu of Equatorial Africa*

Warren Dean   *Brazil and the Struggle for Rubber: A Study in Environmental History*

Samuel P. Hays   *Beauty, Health, and Permanence: Environmental Politics in the United States, 1955–1985*

Donald Worster   *The Ends of the Earth: Perspectives on Modern Environmental History*

Michael Williams   *Americans and Their Forests: A Historical Geography*

Timothy Silver   *A New Face on the Countryside: Indians, Colonists, and Slaves in the South Atlantic Forests, 1500–1800*

Theodore Steinberg   *Nature Incorporated: Industrialization and the Waters of New England*

J. R. McNeill   *The Mountains of the Mediterranean World: An Environmental History*

Elinor G. K. Melville   *A Plague of Sheep: Environmental Consequences of the Conquest of Mexico*

Richard H. Grove   *Green Imperialism: Colonial Expansion, Tropical Island Edens, and the Origins of Environmentalism, 1600–1860*

Mark Elvin and Tsui'jung Liu   *Sediments of Time: Environment and Society in Chinese History*

Robert B. Marks   *Tigers, Rice, Silk, and Silt: Environment and Economy in Late Imperial South China*

Thomas Dunlap   *Nature and the English Diaspora*

Andrew C. Isenberg   *The Destruction of the Bison: An Environmental History*

Edmund Russell   *War and Nature: Fighting Humans and Insects with Chemicals from World War I to Silent Spring*

Judith Shapiro   *Mao's War Against Nature: Politics and the Environment in Revolutionary China*

Adam Rome   *The Bulldozer in the Countryside: Suburban Sprawl and the Rise of American Environmentalism*

Nancy J. Jacobs   *Environment, Power, and Injustice: A South African History*

Matthew D. Evenden   *Fish versus Power: An Environmental History of the Fraser River*

Myrna I. Santiago   *The Ecology of Oil: Environment, Labor, and the Mexican Revolution, 1900–1938*

Frank Uekoetter   *The Green and the Brown: A History of Conservation in Nazi Germany*

The Untilled Garden

Natural History and the Spirit of Conservation in America, 1740–1840

RICHARD W. JUDD

University of Maine

CAMBRIDGE
UNIVERSITY PRESS

CAMBRIDGE UNIVERSITY PRESS
Cambridge, New York, Melbourne, Madrid, Cape Town, Singapore, São Paulo, Delhi

Cambridge University Press
32 Avenue of the Americas, New York, NY 10013-2473, USA

www.cambridge.org
Information on this title: www.cambridge.org/9780521729840

© Richard W. Judd 2009

First published 2009

Printed in the United States of America

A catalog record for this publication is available from the British Library.

Library of Congress Cataloging in Publication data
Judd, Richard William.
The untilled garden : natural history and the spirit of conservation in America,
1740–1840 / Richard W. Judd.
p.   cm. – (Studies in environment and history)
Includes bibliographical references and index.
ISBN 978-0-521-50998-5 (hardback) – ISBN 978-0-521-72984-0 (pbk.)
1. Nature conservation – United States – History – 18th century.   2. Nature
conservation – United States – History – 19th century.
3. Human ecology – United States – History – 18th century.   4. Human ecology – United
States – History – 19th century.   5. United States – Environmental conditions.
I. Title.   II. Series.
QH76.J83   2009
333.720973'09033 – dc22   2008053973

ISBN   978-0-521-50998-5 hardback
ISBN   978-0-521-72984-0 paperback

Contents

Contents

Preface

The title of this book derived from John Winthrop's observation that "the whole earth is the lords Garden & he hath given it to the sonnes of men," but its beginnings are linked to a search for alternatives to the term *wilderness*, which had very different connotations in the early nineteenth century. The garden reference took on new meaning as I worked through the literature on continental exploration and discovered that scientists described nature as much as a process as a constellation of plants and animals – a process brought to consummation by the Western settler. *Wilderness*, when they used the term, described an expectation: a point in a trajectory that began with Native inhabitants and continued through stages of settlement to what they considered a higher form of civilization. This trajectory – from untilled to tilled – explained a great deal about how early naturalist-explorers thought about nature.

Yet there was, I noticed, a subtle shift in this expectation after the turn of the nineteenth century, by which the untilled garden – a state of becoming – became a Garden of Eden – a state of being. In this sense, the pages to follow explore ways in which nature gained intrinsic value. This shift in thinking took three forms. Scientists first learned that certain trees, plants, and animals provided practical benefits to humankind, and on these terms they should be conserved. Second, they learned that all aspects of nature are interconnected, and these ecological connections should be maintained – perhaps even celebrated. Finally, scientists contributed to the growing popular appreciation for natural beauty that came to fruition in the mid-nineteenth-century Romantic movement.

In tracing these conservation ideas, I also became interested in how these wandering scientists brought together a natural history of America.

To convey their enthusiasm for this epic endeavor, I have relied heavily on the language of the journals, field books, taxonomies, texts, and correspondence they themselves produced, because this faithfully represents the flavor, mood, and symbolic meaning of their work in progress. I trust this reproduction also preserves the conditional and tentative nature of their forays into a natural history of America.

I represent these excerpts as faithfully as possible, but on occasion I have modernized punctuation when archaic forms were confusing. In another sense, I have not been exactly true to the original texts: I use the terms *ecology* and *scientist*, as do many historians, to explain methods of thinking evident in the early nineteenth century, even though the terms were not coined until later. Less anachronistic alternatives are neither graceful nor economical. Likewise, *naturalist* is used expansively to include all those interested in nature from a professional or amateur point of view. This, as I explain in Chapter 2, covers a broad canvas. I have included scientific names in parentheses where local designation might be confusing. Finally, in conceiving this study, I made some arbitrary geographic, chronological, and topical demarcations. Although naturalists wrote voluminously about Native Americans, I resolved early on that I could not do justice to this aspect of their work while concentrating on the relation between science and conservation. Hence, I commend this largely unexplored body of knowledge to others. Also, I have made no attempt to follow these explorers beyond the Mississippi River, partly again for reasons of space and time and partly because I see the fundamental principles of American natural history already in place when these surveys moved beyond the Mississippi. And, for similar reasons, I have not ventured into or beyond the Darwinian revolution.

This book has been a relatively solitary quest, which may account for its faults. However, I would like to thank editors Adam Rome and Mark Cioc and their external readers for comments on a synopsis of this work published in *Environmental History* (Vol. 11, January 2006). Frank and Deborah Popper helped me put the relationship between agricultural decline and conservation in broader perspective. Don Worster and John McNeal commented on an earlier draft of this manuscript, and their valuable insights guided me through final revisions. I am especially indebted to the American Philosophical Society, the Library Company, and the Pennsylvania Historical Society, all in Philadelphia, for their generous financial assistance, and I owe thanks to Roy Goodman at the APS for his valuable and innumerable suggestions about research materials and his encouragement on the project. Valerie-Anne Lutz was likewise helpful at the APS as was James Green at the Library Company. Scott See read and commented helpfully on portions of the text, and my colleagues at the University of Maine listened patiently to presentations of this material in various venues and asked good questions, as did colleagues at Bowdoin College and Colby College. Pat and Lily helped in numerous ways that would be difficult to specify in a brief acknowledgment, but I am especially thankful for Lily's help in surmounting the last few hurdles in this project.

Introduction

Imagination and Nature, 1808

In early fall 1808, English adventurer Thomas Ashe arrived in Philadelphia and began preparing for a trip across the Appalachians and down the Ohio River on one leg in a journey of some ten thousand miles across North America. His account of this experience, published two years later in a volume titled *Travels in America*, presents a strange mix of travelogue, autobiography, natural history, and romance based on an amazing set of experiences that began in England and continued through Ireland, Switzerland, France, Prussia, Portugal, Holland, Corsica, the Isle of Man, and North America. Ashe's leaps from country to country and from occupation to occupation, as he tells it, were prompted by escapades with women inconveniently related to his superiors: Melanie, the daughter of his merchant-boss; Nora, the mistress of an English earl; Seline, "one of the fairest daughters of Vevay in Switzerland." Destitute at the end of this exhausting train of new places and occupations, Ashe, like so many others, turned to America as his "future lot."

From Baltimore, he traveled west in 1799, purchased a "wretched farm" and a black woman named Faveen, and launched into another new life as an American pioneer. He was afflicted by fevers, attacked by a panther, harassed by Indians, and bitten by a rattlesnake, thereby conforming, as he said, "to the customs and manners of an ordinary frontier settler." Faveen bore him two children but, after a few years, Ashe grew tired of his life as "a mere demi-savage" and once again abandoned his mistress and his occupation. He moved to Washington and then to Montreal, where he met Canadian naturalist Sir John Johnstone. Fascinated by Johnstone's cabinet of curiosities, Ashe adopted a new occupation, inquiring into the "earth, its animals, vegetables, minerals, and other productions." He hunted the fields and shores around Montreal for shells and fossils, and in less than six months he could expatiate upon "every instance in which the hand of the Deity was conspicuous." Soon, he thought, his name would be "known throughout all the nations of the earth," and this is why he set his sights on the Ohio Valley in 1808.[1]

While in Canada, Ashe had come across a publication by Charles Willson Peale, owner of the Philadelphia Museum, who, with his sons, had recently exhumed the bones of a mammoth in the bogs of upper New York. This consummate natural curiosity captured Ashe's imagination: Here was evidence of a monstrous beast that roamed the woods a thousand years ago, an animal as "cruel as the bloody panther, swift as the descending eagle, and terrible as the angel of night," Ashe wrote, pirating his material from Peale's museum pamphlet. Having fixed on a new goal, he set out for Big Bone Lick near the mouth of the Kentucky River, where according to reports, hundreds of mammoth bones could be gathered with relatively little effort.[2]

From Philadelphia, he traveled westward by horseback and, in early October, once again found himself mingling with the backcountry folk of the American West. His assessment of this pioneering society was harsh but not uniform. "I assure you," he wrote, "that when I expressed the supreme disgust excited in me by the people of the United States, the ladies were by no means included in the general censure." At one stop, the daughter of the tavern keeper showed him to his room after the evening meal, and Ashe entreated her to tarry: "Her person was tall and elegant; her eyes were large and blue; her features regular and animated and expressive of a pride and a dignity which the meanest clothing... could neither destroy nor conceal." In the tradition of the traveling naturalist, he queried her about the "natural curiosities in the neighbourhood, the face of the country, manners, books, &c." and, in the tradition of the traveling raconteur, he posed the equally foreseeable question: "By what accident has one so lovely in person, so improved in understanding, and so delicate in mind, become the inhabitant of these... gloomy woods?" His companion explained that her father was an Irish nobleman who took refuge in America and in his abominably provincial situation took

---

[1] Thomas Ashe, *Confessions of Captain Ashe,... Written by Himself* (London, 1815), Vol. 2, pp. 54, 56, 64–9, 105–6, 109, 111–15, 120–9, 133–8, 191–6, 201.

[2] Ashe, *Confessions*, Vol. 2, pp. 196–200; Thomas Ashe, *Travels in America, Performed in 1808, for the Purpose of Exploring the Rivers Alleghany, Monongahela, Ohio, and Mississippi* (Newburyport, 1808), p. 4. See "Skeleton of the Mammoth Is Now to Be Seen at the Museum," Broadsides, American Philosophical Society (hereafter APS), 1801.

to drinking. His wife died of a broken heart and this, in turn, condemned the well-bred but lonely daughter to a life of "unmerited misery" in the Pennsylvania backcountry.[3] This exchange confirmed Ashe's judgment that wilderness living was incompatible with true civilization.

A few days after this encounter, Ashe was overtaken by nightfall on an Allegheny ridge, "where the road was narrow and bounded by frightful precipices." The way ahead, he wrote in his *Travels*, promised only "a sudden and rapid death" but to go back seemed no less perilous: "wolves, panthers, and tiger cats were at hand to devour me." Faced with this Hobson's choice, he bedded down on the mountain, there being "less of fatal certainty in it." As he hunkered down beside his horse, "clouds of owls" rose from the valleys and "flitted screaming" about his head, and the distant howls of the wolf "reverberated from mountain to mountain." Startling images flooded his mind. "Every tree, shrub, plant, and vegetable harboured some thousands of inhabitants, endowed with the facility of expressing their passions, wants, and appetites in different tones and varied modulations." When the howling finally stopped, he imagined a scenario unfolding down the canyon: a deer, perhaps hearing the hellish cries of the wolf at hand, "turns, stops, and trembles; his eyes fill; his flanks heave; his heart bursts, and he dies the moment before the monster rushes upon him." Toward daybreak, a new specter broke upon Ashe's sleepless mind: a panther, lurking in the brush, would "never . . . be . . . heard till in the act of springing on his victim, when he utters a horrid cry." Somehow Ashe survived this nocturnal ordeal, and day dawned with the sound of a whippoorwill. The "noisy . . . world now withdrew and left to Nature a silent solemn repose."[4]

Ashe's English readers no doubt found these sublime flights of fancy compelling, but Americans were not much amused by his clouds of owls and lurking panthers. Although his *Travels in America* was widely read, American reviewers uniformly dismissed it as an "extravagant episode" written by a man with a "natural appetite for the marvelous." Geographer John Bristed, writing in 1818, enumerated the various writers who fell short of his own precise descriptions and insisted that "the silliest of these" was the "*soi-disant* military officer" Thomas Ashe. Another pronounced *Travels* nothing more than "prejudice and invective," and still another

---

3 "Travellers in America," *Niles' Weekly Register* 2 (April 18, 1812): pp. 94, 114; Ashe, *Travels*, pp. 12–13; Ashe in Henry T. Tuckerman, *America and Her Commentators, with a Critical Sketch of Travel in the United States* (New York, 1864), p. 204.
4 Ashe, *Travels*, pp. 15–18.

found his account so "void of truth as to deprive him of all claim to veracity." Christian Schultz, who passed through the Ohio Valley in 1810, decided after reading Ashe's work that it was, in his opinion, concocted wholesale from *The Pittsburgh Navigator*, a pilot's guide to the Ohio River; "nor does he [Schultz] believe that any such person ever travelled the route pretended to be described." In fact, Schultz was at least partly wrong, because another critic discovered Ashe subsequently tutoring children in French in Cincinnati under the name of Arville. This, he added, "is the same man, who afterwards, to the astonishment of those who knew him at Cincinnati, published three volumes of *Travels*, which have become in America almost proverbial for their extraordinary and gratuitous lies."[5]

Ashe's next moves are something of a mystery. A decade or so earlier, Cincinnati's most prominent gentleman-naturalist, Dr. William Goforth, spent four days at the nearby Big Bone Lick collecting a wagonload of fossil bones and teeth, which George Turner of the American Philosophical Society thought to be the remains of "no less than six nondescript quadrupeds, most of them gigantick!" Hoping to sell the collection, Goforth shipped it upriver to Pittsburgh, where a representative from the American Academy of Arts and Sciences described it in 1793 in terms much like Turner's. In 1804, the collection caught the eye of Thomas Jefferson, who was then engaged in a debate with European naturalists over the relative size and vigor of American and European fauna. In a show of national pride, Jefferson instructed Meriwether Lewis to stop at Big Bone Lick on his way west to the Louisiana Territory to gather more mammoth bones. Jefferson stored Lewis's bones in the East Room of the White House and dispatched American Philosophical Society President Casper Wistar and later University of Pennsylvania Professor Benjamin Smith Barton to Pittsburgh to procure those gathered by Goforth. However, by then, according to the *American Quarterly*, Goforth's collection had "attracted the attention of a foreign swindler named *Thomas Arville*, alias *Ashe*, who obtained permission of the owner to ship them to Europe for exhibition." The doctor apparently never heard from Ashe again.[6]

---

[5] Tuckerman, *America and Her Commentators*, p. 203; John Bristed, *The Resources of the United States of America* (New York, 1818), p. 4; John Palmer, *Journal of Travels in the United States of North America, and in Lower Canada, Performed in the Year 1817* (London, 1818), pp. iii; 293n; Christian Schultz, *Travels on an Inland Voyage Through the States of New-York, Pennsylvania, Virginia, Ohio, Kentucky, and Tennessee* (New York, 1810), Vol. 1, p. v. See *North American Review* 3 (July 1816): p. 230.

[6] American Academy of Arts and Sciences *Memoirs* 1 (Part 1, 1793): p. 119; Thomas Jefferson to Benjamin Smith Barton, October 10, 1796, Benjamin Smith Barton Papers, Correspondence, Pennsylvania Historical Society; *American Quarterly* in *North American*

Ashe stowed his "grand collection of stupendous bones" in the hold of a river vessel and continued down the Ohio. He explored the Wabash, Mississippi, and Missouri rivers gathering more natural curiosities, among them the remains of a "huge carnivorous animal" that was clearly, in Peale's borrowed words, as "cruel as the bloody panther, swift as the descending eagle, and terrible as the angel of night." Ashe next stopped in Natchez, hoping to sell his augmented collection for $10,000. Samuel Brown, another American Philosophical Society member, rushed to the city to negotiate but, by this time, the collection was on its way to New Orleans. Brown proceeded southward but sent a message east to Philadelphia: "Send one of the . . . Peales or some other confidential person to the Big Bone Lick where I am confident a most valuable collection might be procured at a trifling expense."[7]

From New Orleans, Ashe shipped out for Liverpool but, on his arrival, the customs-house officials imposed a steep duty on his collection and refused to allow it ashore. Short of funds, Ashe was forced to consign his six tons of "first-rate curiosities" to William Bullock, a well-known Liverpool museum proprietor, "for the . . . contemptible sum of two hundred pounds." The indomitable explorer continued to capitalize on his collection by delivering public lectures at the Liverpool museum. On the mammoth bones he noted some teeth marks, clearly indicating that nature had "formed some huge carnivorous animal" capable of subduing even this enormous beast. He displayed the remains of the great predator he procured on his western travels: a creature of "inexpressible grandeur and sublimity," some sixty feet long and twenty-five feet high, whose clawed foot, "possibly of the order of *ferae*," suggested a predator, he told his enraptured audience, "cruel as the bloody panther, swift as the descending eagle, and terrible as the angel of night." Having unveiled this ultimate curiosity of nature, Ashe retired to a garret to compose a memoir far more curious than any set of mammoth bones tucked away in a Liverpool museum.[8]

Review 3 (July 1816): p. 230; *Monthly American Journal of Geology and Natural Science* 1 (October 1831): pp. 161–2; Zadok Cramer, *The Navigator; Containing Directions for Navigating the Monongahela, Allegheny, Ohio, and Mississippi Rivers* (Pittsburgh, 1811), pp. 117–18; Palmer, *Journal of Travels*, p. 100; William Newnham Blane, *An Excursion Through the United States and Canada During the Years 1822–23* (London, 1824), p. 132.

[7] Ashe, *Travels*, p. 42; Samuel Brown to Thomas Jefferson, n.d., Caspar Wistar Papers, APS; Joseph Kastner, *A Species of Eternity* (New York, 1977), p. 129.

[8] *Monthly American Journal of Geology and Natural Science* 1 (October 1831): pp. 161–2; Ashe, *Travels*, pp. 7–8, 4–44; Ashe, *Confessions*, pp. 204–5, 210, 215–16; Palmer, *Journal of Travels*, p. 100.

The reasons for Ashe's flights of fancy are hard to fathom: Was he, as some suggested, a compulsive liar? Did he embellish his natural history to attract readers? Was he exaggerating these wilderness terrors to discourage emigration from England? Perhaps it was Ashe, who collected much of his data from locals, who was gullible, a possibility suggested by his relation to a Native American named Cuff, who guided him through the Ohio Valley. Each night before bedding down, Cuff, who was obliged to call Ashe "master," would find a way to turn the campfire conversation to rattlesnakes, a creature Ashe feared more than any other in America, adding details "sufficient to appal the stoutest heart." A child of the Enlightenment, Ashe ridiculed the "sorcery and supernatural power [that] gains great dominion over every savage mind" – a perspective he no doubt shared with Cuff – but he was fully prepared to believe that Indians like his companion could establish a "tyranny . . . over rattle-snakes" through supernatural means. Each night after Cuff expounded on his favorite bedtime topic, Ashe would command him to perform "certain rites and incantations, in the manner of his country, and which had the faculty of checking the advances of snakes." Cuff readily obliged, inscribing a circle around the campsite with a stick and dropping a precise number of carefully chosen leaves on the circle. He concluded with three "infernal yells" and then, "under a decided impression . . . of safety," fell asleep beside the fretful Ashe.[9]

The Search for Meaning in Nature

Whether fantasy or fabrication, Ashe's account brings into focus the gap between nature as it was and nature as the early nineteenth-century naturalist saw it. Ashe is one of many scientific travelers who crossed the eastern continent between 1730 and 1850. Some, like Ashe, were mere dilettantes, whereas others dedicated their lives to understanding nature. Eclectic observers, they commented on everything from antiquities to zoology, including, as with Ashe, the human condition in this wilderness environment. Mark Catesby, John and William Bartram, François-André Michaux, Henry Schoolcraft, Alexander Wilson, Charles Lyell, Thomas Nuttall, John James Audubon, and, of course, Meriwether Lewis are only the best known among hundreds of like-minded explorer-naturalists, and each interpreted the natural landscape according to a combination of detached observation, scientific speculation, and unlicensed imagination.

---

[9] Ashe, *Travels*, pp. 136–7, 243.

Ashe's tale was extravagant, but no account was free of what New York's Gouveneur Morris called "the influence of exaggerated description." According to Morris, the encounter with unexplored landscapes could easily unhinge the intellect: "Those awful forests which have shaded through untold ages a boundless extent," he wrote, invariably "dazzled the eye of reason and led the judgment astray." Even Schultz, so disparaging of Ashe's night on the Appalachian ridge, found himself trembling at the "distant howlings" of the wolves in circumstances similar to those Ashe experienced. At one point, he and his companions found the wolves "becoming such near neighbours that we began to recollect all the dreadful tales and disasters which we had heard upon our travels." He cut himself a "good cudgel" and spent the night banging on a log to "make as much noise as we could, in order to let the wolves know we were not afraid of them." Accounts like these highlight the difficulty of separating science and imagination in the era of continental exploration. In the light of day, the Appalachian forest looked different to Ashe and Schultz, and to another generation, traveling under less threatening circumstances, the American wilderness would look different yet again.[10]

If these first scientific encounters with nature in America so dazzled the eye and bewildered the judgment, why should we take them seriously today? This was a question that nagged Charles Sprague Sargent in 1889 as he composed his thoughts for an introduction to the collected works of America's great pre-Darwinian botanist, Asa Gray. "The value of these papers . . . is historical only," Sargent wrote. "All that they contain of permanent usefulness has already been incorporated in standard works upon the science." The rest, he implied, had been eclipsed by the convulsion in thinking brought on by publication of Darwin's *Origin of Species* in 1859. In a period "marked by the gradual change of ideas among naturalists upon the origin and fixity of the species," Sargent concluded, Gray's scientific insights, so novel and exciting when he wrote them down in the 1850s, were either stale scientific truisms or blatant error.[11]

In fact, there are important reasons for returning to these early naturalists, even though their works are tinged by imagination and outdated by the Darwinian revolution. First, their achievements constitute an

---

[10] Gouveneur Morris, *Notes on the United States of America* (Philadelphia, 1806), p. 22; Schultz, *Travels on an Inland Voyage*, p. 162. See Calvin Colton, *Tour of the American Lakes and Among the Indians of the North-West Territory in 1830* (London, 1833), p. 33.

[11] Asa Gray, *Scientific Papers of Asa Gray*, compiled by Charles Sprague Sargent (Boston, 1889), pp. iv–v.

important benchmark in our national experience. In the years between Mark Catesby's explorations in the 1730s and those of John James Audubon a century later, scientists produced the first detailed account of the state of nature in America – its rocks, minerals, climates, plants, animals, birds, insects, fish, and diseases, among other things. Although laced with imagination, this was the foundation for our scientific – and popular – understanding of the continent. It summarizes America's search for meaning in nature and, given the complexity of this continental field of study, it was no mean accomplishment. Ashe's claim to have traveled some ten thousand miles by foot, horse, and boat was not as extravagant as some of his boasts and, in a saner moment, he reflected that "whoever dares to compose the history of nature [in America] should first pass a night where I did; he would ... there learn that though gifted with a thousand years of life, and aided by ten thousand assistants, he still would be hardly nearer to his purpose."[12] Not only was the West scientifically uncharted, but in 1808 it also was unmapped and often dangerous. More than clouds of owls and lurking panthers awaited these footsore naturalists in the western wilderness.

Although we fancy our love of nature to be a modern development, its origins lie in the myth-laced scientific tomes left by these explorer-scientists. These were the writers who fixed the idea of nature in the American mind and placed it at the core of our national consciousness. Their taxonomies revealed the tremendous diversity of this vast continental wilderness, and their journals interpreted its economic and cultural significance. Their explorations helped forge what historian Clarence Glacken called a "feeling for nature" – a people's understanding of the natural environment communicated through art, literature, and other public venues.[13] The art and literature of the Romantic period were important statements of this feeling, but it was the scientific explorer in the trans-Appalachian West who provided the imaginative appraisal that set the tone for these cultural expressions.

Second, the science that emerged from this assessment was far more enduring than Sargent would have us believe. These naturalists absorbed the great imaginative ideas of the pre-Darwinian age – the balance of nature, the transforming sublimity of the primeval landscape, the purpose,

[12] Ashe, *Travels*, p. 17.
[13] Clarence J. Glacken, *Traces on the Rhodian Shore: Nature and Culture in Western Thought from Ancient Times to the End of the Eighteenth Century* (Berkeley, 1969), pp. 27, 173.

order, and unity inherent in creation – and made them American. These ideas satisfy a deep-seated need to understand our relation to nature, and their application to the American landscape was an important development in our cultural history. "The idea that nature is orderly, that its order is rational and effective, that it is for the most part a stable, self-equilibrating order, is the most precious idea modern science has given us," environmental historian Donald Worster wrote.[14] Clearly, it is important to understand how this idea became part of the national idiom.

Finally, and most important for our purposes, this search for meaning in nature takes us to the roots of the American conservation movement. At the turn of the twentieth century, America emerged as a leader in forest, wildlife, and wilderness conservation, having created the world's first national parks, its first public game refuges, its first national forests, and its first full-blown preservationist and conservationist ideologies. Despite the global importance of these achievements, the history of American conservation is poorly represented. Its chronology is usually reduced to a few obvious benchmarks involving well-known literary and artistic figures like Henry David Thoreau, Ralph Waldo Emerson, James Fenimore Cooper, and George Catlin, and a handful of conservation pioneers like George Perkins Marsh, Gifford Pinchot, and John Muir. Yet this litany of a few dozen careers in conservation begs the question: Can such a world-shaping idea flow from such a thin national tradition? It seems unlikely, but if we add to this the early naturalists who voiced a collective concern for the natural landscape in the first half of the century, a fuller story emerges. Conservation, as it turns out, is more deeply embedded in American history than we might imagine.

America's conservation giants drew upon three essential ideas that first took shape in the minds of their early nineteenth-century predecessors: a practical concern for protecting those species of birds, animals, and trees deemed useful to human society; a romantic appreciation for the beauty of natural form and primitive landscape; and a close understanding of the complex biological interdependencies that sustain all natural systems. These themes – commercial utility, romantic attraction, and ecological necessity – became the foundation for turn-of-the-century conservation, and they are so ingrained in our environmental consciousness today that we hardly give them a second thought. To understand their origins and

---

[14] Donald Worster, *Nature's Economy: A History of Ecological Ideas* (New York, 1977), p. ix.

evolution, we must turn to the pre-Darwinian era, where they were formulated and popularized as part of the process of creating a natural
history of America.

Environmental historians have all but ignored this corpus of pre-
Darwinian scientific literature, partly because it *is* pre-Darwinian and
partly because they often fail to see beyond the simple taxonomical compilations so common to this era. Roderick Nash's *Wilderness and the
American Mind*, the most significant modern survey of the American
idea of nature, hardly mentions natural history apart from Thoreau, and
Donald Worster's *Nature's Economy* likewise relies on Thoreau to represent the American pre-Darwinian naturalist tradition. The reasons for this
neglect have to do with the widespread impression that pre-Darwinians
saw the world as frozen in time and compartmentalized in arrangement –
as a list of parts rather than as a set of organic relations. Natural history
was a cataloging exercise, its goal being "simply to describe, name and
classify the diverse riches of nature," as historian Martin Rudwick puts
it. Raymond Stearns notes in his sweeping *Science in the British Colonies
of America* that early naturalists pursued three primary objectives: collection, classification, and nomenclature.[15] In this view, scientific exploration was little more than an epic quest to fill out the list of American
species.

Absent the environmental historian, these early naturalists have been
left largely to literary biographers, who typically focus on one individual
and examine a personal and subjective relationship to nature, an exercise
that tells us much about the inner geography of the explorer but little
about the physical or cultural geography through which the explorer
traveled. Scientific biographers, also active in this field, tell us more about
the physical and intellectual milieu, but they seldom take the explorer's
subjectivity seriously. Most assume a positivist framework that locates the
individual in a general transition from natural philosophy to empirical
science. Like Sargent, these biographers see the scientist emerging out of
the shell of the "old-style, romantic naturalist" and dismiss the shell as a
matter of mere "historical" interest. As science moves inevitably toward

---

[15] Martin Rudwick, "Minerals, Strata, and Fossils," in N. Jardine, J. A. Secord, and
E. C. Spary, *Cultures of Natural History* (Cambridge, 1996), p. 269; Raymond
Phineas Stearns, *Science in the British Colonies of America* (Urbana, 1970), p. 6. See
Ella M. Foshay, *Reflections of Nature: Flowers in American Art* (New York, 1984),
pp. 29, 30–1; James P. Ronda, "Dreams and Discoveries: Exploring the American
West, 1760–1815," *William and Mary Quarterly* 3rd ser. 46 (January 1989): pp. 145–
62, 146.

the Darwinian revolution and the experimental standard, this imaginative description of nature falls away, the chaff of history.[16]

However, this linear flow is not the world the naturalists knew: They searched for meaning in a landscape of shadows and shades, of myths and metaphors, and they bounded across this landscape in great leaps of imaginative logic. Ashe's clouds of owls and prowling panthers would have no place in the post-Darwinian, lab-based understanding of nature, but his night on the Appalachian ridge, despite the skeptical reaction, resonated in the soul of America. To judge pre-Darwinian science against a fixed scientific standard denies this cultural agency – and natural history's transcendent qualities.

Individual biographies leave our picture of natural history incomplete. "To follow a single thread or an individual career in isolation would be to ignore the cross-fertilization that was constantly going on," Paul Brooks once said about the world of science. If we are to understand the context for this imaginative grasp of nature, we must note the explorer's dialogue with the rest of the scientific community and with the overall idea of nature that emerged from their discoveries. This is best accomplished through a collective intellectual biography that values the individual discoveries of each naturalist as part of a broader view of nature. It must also weigh equally the subjective and the objective – the facts and hypotheses along with the fears, frustrations, and anticipations this deep-woods experience generated.[17] These scientific assumptions were, of course, dynamic and fluid, and to fix them across the span of a century is somewhat artificial, but there are consistencies enough to speak of American natural history as a system. This was the composition that gave America a first impression of its natural landscape and inspired the conservation movement that came together at the end of the century.

Nature and Purpose

For all their confusion amid clouds of owls and prowling panthers, naturalists found an underlying logic in the arrangement of mountains, the

---

[16] On literary biography, see for example Amy R. W. Meyers and Margaret Beck Pritchard (eds.), *Empire's Nature: Mark Catesby's New World Vision* (Chapel Hill, 1998), p. 34; N. Bryllion Fagin, *William Bartram: Interpreter of the American Landscape* (Baltimore, MD, 1933); Wayne Franklin, *Discoverers, Explorers, Settlers: The Diligent Writers of Early America* (Chicago, 1979); Thomas P. Slaughter, *The Natures of John and William Bartram* (New York, 1996). Scientific biographies are too numerous to mention.

[17] Paul Brooks in Daniel J. Philippon, *Conserving Words: How American Nature Writers Shaped the Environmental Movement* (Athens, 2004), p. 4.

flow of the rivers, the endlessness of the forests, and the bounty of animals and birds they encountered. Approaching a subject as complex as
this, they were often inconsistent in their conclusions, but they did agree
on some basic assumptions. Most important, they believed that nature
was purposive and interconnected, a "well governed state" in which each
plant, animal, rock, mineral, tree, bird, river, and mountain existed –
had to exist – as a necessary part of a greater whole.[18] "Every part of
nature, from the largest to the smallest, from the planet to the atom,"
Henry Colman wrote, is "bound together by a reciprocity of dependence
and advantage." Well versed in classical and Christian thinking, they saw
the perfect adaptation of species to environment as a reflection of divine
thought. Secularized in the late nineteenth century, this idea of unity
among diversity became an argument for conservation and a standard
for beauty in nature.[19]

Because they saw the farmer as the agent of completing this harmonious natural landscape, early scientists condoned the pioneering assault
on the trans-Appalachian forest. Yet, like Ashe, they scrutinized this settler society closely, assessing its relation to the wilderness around it,
and like Ashe they were critical and at times blunt in their pronouncements about this society. Sensing the flow of cause and effect across the
natural landscape, they grew anxious about the degree to which nature
was diminished by the settlers' drive to cut it down and use it up. John
Bartram, writing as early as the 1750s, cautioned about the delicate links
among trees, soils, and streams, and later naturalists saw reason to be
concerned about deteriorating climates, desiccated lands, disappearing
birds and animals, and multiplying insects. By the time Vermont conservationist, George Perkins Marsh, presented his impressive research on
forests in the fabric of nature in 1864, naturalists had already developed
a sophisticated ecological critique of human modifications to the natural world. Writing in 1967, Clarence Glacken noted that "the sources
of... environmental theory are both in the philosophical and scientific
theory of the Greeks and in conclusions drawn from practical life and
common observation." They are part of the Western European tradition

---

[18] Christopher Christian Sturm, *Beauties of Nature Delineated*, compiled by Thaddeus
  M. Harris (Charlestown, 1801), pp. 48–9. See *American Journal of Science* 11 (No. 2,
  1826): p. 218.
[19] Henry Colman, *Agriculture of the United States* (Boston, 1840), p. 5. See W. Bingley,
  Animal Biography, or Popular Zoology (London, 1813), Vol. 1, pp. 3–4; *Advocate of
  Science and Annals of Natural History* 1 (No. 1, 1834), p. 27; Katie Whitaker, "The
  Culture of Curiosity," in Jardine, Secord, and Spary, *Cultures of Natural History*, p. 76.

but were reconstituted in each place and era. How they became real for Americans is a question of consuming importance.[20]

This book is divided into three sections. The first begins in the colonial period and surveys the transformation of the scientific community from a scattered collection of naturalist-explorers, largely dependent on European patronage and European ideas, into a cohesive body of scholars and collectors with a common national identity. The second section describes the natural world as these scientists saw it during the first decades of the nineteenth century, from its geological underpinnings to the ends and purposes of each species of plant and animal. The third section concentrates on how and why these ways of looking at nature changed in the first half of the century, particularly in view of the ecological transformations in the Ohio Valley and the unforeseen difficulties of sustaining the agricultural republic in the Northeast.

Doing justice to the men and women who made up this history is more than an academic exercise; it brings to light a rich and viable conservation tradition with roots as deep as the republic itself. Conservation was not simply the brainchild of a few enlightened and outspoken men; it was embedded in the very idea of nature in America. The fundamental thought that all of nature is connected and that all Americans are morally bound to maintain these connections derives from these writings, and it is important to remember, as we adjust this old idea to new circumstances, just how long this has been a part of American history. Each generation rethinks its practical, aesthetic, and ecological connection to the natural world, and history provides the forum for assessing this process of renovation and rediscovery.[21] Although laced with prejudice, fantasy, dread, and moral bearing, these early scientific ideas spawned a compelling argument for conservation. It seems proper to begin here as we adjust these ideas to our new global circumstances.

---

[20] Glacken, *Traces on the Rhodian Shore*, p. 117.
[21] Gilbert Chinard, "The American Philosophical Society and the Early History of Forestry in America," *APS Proceedings* 89 (1945): pp. 448–9.

PART ONE

FORGING A SCIENTIFIC COMMUNITY

"A Country Unknown"

Utility and Romance in the Colonial Idea of Nature

In words chosen carefully to emphasize the rewards of western wilderness travel, imperial administrator Thomas Pownall wrote in his 1776 *Topographical Description of the Dominions of the United States of America* that an exciting field of discovery awaited those willing to endure the rigors of scientific exploration. "When one travels . . . along the rivers," he announced, "from reach to reach, at each turning of the courses, the imagination is in a perpetual alternative of curious suspense and new delight." Pownall presented this western country as a magnificent bounty and an exciting adventure. Banks along the rivers bore shoulder-high grasses in soils "so rich that they could be tilled repeatedly for centuries." These and other images of a lush, untilled garden attracted and intrigued Pownall's generation and gave America its first record of a land where each turning of the courses opened a new page in the book of nature.[1]

Pownall's careful wording glossed over his general confusion about this exciting new world. His Enlightenment vision of creating order in the wilderness was inspired by the exhilarating achievements of the previous century – the Age of Exploration, the rise of capitalism, and the ascendancy of the empirical method. These events heralded an optimistic view of nature as a complex system of mechanical laws that could be understood and employed to meet the needs of humankind. Yet, an equally powerful strain of Enlightenment thinking saw nature as aimless, chaotic,

---

[1] Thomas A. Pownall, *Topographical Description of the Dominions of the United States of America* (Pittsburgh, 1949 [c. 1776]), pp. 23, 31.

and vicious, and in the colonial mind, these darker images left the more lasting impression.[2]

Explorers like Pownall were philosophically unprepared for the western wilderness. "The whole design of American nature seemed unsettling," historian David Scofield Wilson writes. Beyond the Appalachians, the comforting vision of an orderly and hierarchical world no longer pertained, and as long as nature would remain mysterious, it remained unconquered. "A country unknown, must, if a paradise, still continue a desart," John Bartram cautioned in 1769. This, then, was the challenge that awaited Pownall and those he urged to take up the banner of science in America: to name and give meaning to the wilderness, as part of the narrative of conquest in North America.[3]

These early explorers allayed their confusion by ascribing to a single structuring theme. As Pownall and Bartram suggested, the land was incredibly bountiful – a paradise – but its gifts made sense only when juxtaposed against the needs of the new American civilization. Explorers of Pownall's generation did not study nature for its own sake. Theirs was an instrumental and imperial view, and nature – the untilled garden – was the object of improvement. "The heart melt[s]," Pownall wrote, "while one views the [river] banks where rising farms, new fields, or flowering orchards" would soon grace the countryside. These anticipations arranged and clarified the unfamiliar landscapes he encountered at each turning of the courses.[4] To impose order, prioritize, and, above all, anticipate the needs of a future civilization: these were the impulses that linked the world that colonial naturalists explored to the civilization they left behind. Where nature and expectation conjoined, we find the colonial explorer's mandate.

The Colonial Naturalist in British North America

This mandate was clear in the earliest European appraisals of the continent. Sailing under French patronage, Florentine explorer, Giovanni da

---

[2] Donald Worster, *Nature's Economy: A History of Ecological Ideas* (New York, 1977), p. 47.

[3] David Scofield Wilson, "Introduction," in Gene Wise (ed.), *In the Presence of Nature* (Amherst, 1978), p. xv; John Bartram, *A Description of East-Florida*, William Stork (ed.), (London, 1769), p. xi. See Brian Morris, "Changing Conceptions of Nature." *Ecologist*, 11 (May–June 1981), p. 132; Thomas R. Cox, "Americans and Their Forests: Romanticism, Progress, and Science in the Late Nineteenth Century." *Journal of Forest History* 29 (October 1985), p. 156; Pamela Regis, *Describing Early America: Bartram, Jefferson, Crevecoeur, and the Influence of Natural History* (Philadelphia, 1992), p. 78.

[4] Pownall, *Topographical Description*, p. 31.

Verrazano, arrived on the Carolina coast in 1524, sailed north to Nova Scotia inventorying the natural riches along the shore, and returned to France with accounts of a wondrous land of valuable plants and trees and obliging native inhabitants. Verrazano established the quest for commercial riches as one key theme in early American natural history, whereas the experiences of Englishman David Ingram, an ordinary sailor, gave voice to another: natural history as fantasy. In 1565, Sir John Hawkins put Ingram and several other sailors ashore on the coast of Mexico and left them to march several thousand miles over Indian trails to Cape Breton, where they were rescued three years later. Ingram's version of this journey became the first in a long line of wilderness narratives enlivened by stories of fantastic plants and creatures.[5] Captain John Smith's tales of Virginia and New England with their well-known mix of romance and astute commercial insight were unusual only for the ebullience of the prose and the audacity of the hyperbole.

Early descriptions of British and French North America were often styled after European herbaria and bestiaries that dated back to classical times, but they differed in three ways. First, they weighed the visual record more than they trusted to classical canon, and their emphasis on first-hand description founded American natural history on a more empirical methodology. Second, colonial natural history was cast in promotional terms, dedicated as it was to attracting merchant-backers or migrants to America. This made American science more fanciful and more popular. It also encouraged a third characteristic of New World natural history: a set of images and associations linking America with primitive virtues and natural abundance. The title alone of Gabriel Thomas's 1698 *Historical and Geographical Account of the Province and Country of Pensilvania* [sic]; *and of West-New-Jersey in America. The Richness of the Soil, the Sweetness of the Situation, the Wholesomeness of the Air, the Navigable Rivers, and Others, the Prodigious Encrease* [sic] *of Corn . . . the Strange Creatures, as Birds, Beasts, Fishes and Fowls, with the Several Sorts of Minerals, Purging Waters, and Stones . . .* sums up much of the empirical, promotional, and Edenic intent of this early science – the means by which colonial naturalists hoped to change a country unknown into a paradise.[6]

[5] Elsa Guerdrum Allen, *The History of American Ornithology Before Audubon,* hereafter APS *Transactions* (Philadelphia, 1951), pp. 401, 443, 445–6; Richard H. Grove, *Green Imperialism: Colonial Expansion, Tropical Island Edens, and the Origins of Environmentalism, 1600–1860* (New York, 1995), p. 39; Ella M. Foshay, *Reflections of Nature: Flowers in American Art* (New York, 1984), pp. 18–19.

[6] Gabriel Thomas, *An Historical and Geographical Account of the Province and Country of Pensilvania* [sic]; *and of West-New-Jersey in America* (London, 1698), pp. 8–9, 17.

The record of this exotic land coincided with important changes in European science. Partly under the influence of worldwide explorations like those in America, natural history shifted from Aristotelian codifications to a more empirical approach, systematically comparing plants and animals from all corners of the globe. With the spread of literacy in Europe, naturalists wrote more frequently in vernacular and offered public lectures, profiting from a growing popular taste for the natural and the exotic.[7] Thus, American natural history merely accented trends already underway in Europe. Explorers found themselves with more lavish patronage and more precise systems of taxonomy, and they found new ways to describe nature and assess its importance to the European settlements on the eastern shores.

The first detailed account of nature in British North America was William Wood's *New England Prospect*, written in 1634. More litterateur than naturalist, Wood was far from precise in his descriptions. His somewhat florid and stylized descriptions of American plants, animals, and birds, including the "princely Eagle," the "swift wing'd Swallow," and the "bellowing Bitterne," were heavily promotional, but his interest in birds and beasts extended beyond their use as food and, in that sense, he differs from maritime explorers like Verrazano. John Josselyn's *Account of Two Voyages to New-England* and his *New-England's Rarities Discovered*, published in 1674 and 1675, respectively, were similarly detached and even more precise in their observations.[8]

The early eighteenth century saw several studies of the southern colonies. Among these was Robert Beverley's *History and Present State of Virginia*, which appeared in London in 1705. In true scientific fashion, Beverley began by criticizing his predecessors as producing books "stuff'd with Poetical Stories," and thus he set the mandate for an empirical methodology. "For my part, I have endeavour'd to hit the likeness, though, perhaps, my colouring may not have all the life and beauty I cou'd wish." His work was based on the 1680 *Catalogus plantarum in Virginia obervatarum*, left unfinished by English missionary and botanist

See Hans Huth, *Nature and the American: Three Centuries of Changing Attitudes* (Berkeley, 1957), p. 4; Angela Miller, *The Empire of the Eye: Landscape Representation and American Cultural Politics, 1825–1875* (Ithaca, 1993), p. 12.

7   Paula Findlen, "Courting Nature," in N. Jardine, J. A. Secord, and E. C. Spary, *Cultures of Natural History* (Cambridge, 1996), pp. 60, 71, 73; Allen G. Debus, *Man and Nature in the Renaissance* (Cambridge, 1978), p. 38.

8   William Wood in Allen, *History of American Ornithology*, p. 452; Stearns, *Science in the British Colonies of America*, pp. 139, 144. See Stearns, *Science in the British Colonies of America*, pp. 77–9; Allen, *History of American Ornithology*, p. 449.

John Banister when he died. Yet, even with Banister's work before him, Beverley admitted that the task was "very copious" for one untutored in natural history.[9] Beverley focused his efforts, as did earlier coastal explorers, on narrating his voyage of discovery; he proceeded descriptively up the James, York, Rappahannock, and Potomac Rivers listing the soils, trees, and plants as they appeared off the bow of his boat, casting these aggregations in promotional terms. Various earths were useful for healing, cleaning, potting, or brick-making; wild fruits and berries promised a feast "as delicious as any in the world, and growing almost every where in the woods and fields." These and an "infinite . . . number of other valuable vegetables of every kind" would greet the Virginia settler. Laboring under his scientific inadequacies, Beverley set out what would become the major themes in colonial natural history: an emphasis on empirical understanding, a strong promotional cant, and a fascination with the Edenic qualities of the untilled garden.[10]

John Lawson, fur-trader, land speculator, and surveyor-general of South Carolina, arrived in Charleston in 1700 and explored the backcountry until he was killed by Tuscarora Indians near the Neuse River in 1711. He spent these years compiling a "faithful account" of the province's natural history, combining his own observations with those of the trappers, traders, and Indians he met in the upland. Like Beverley, he ordered this vast landscape by composing it as a travel narrative: a canoe trip into the interior in the company of three Englishmen, three Indian men, and an Indian woman, wherein he discussed each new species as it appeared en route. The narrative account, typical in natural histories of the period, reflects the ad hoc cataloging arrangements in the decades before Swedish naturalist Carolus Linnaeus established a standard binomial nomenclature. Naturalists discussed species in order of appearance or commercial value rather than by taxonomical affinities. Because turtles laid eggs, Lawson ranked them among the insects; "I did not know well where to put them." Palmettos were trees with leaves "growing only on the top . . . , in the shape of a fan, and in a cluster, like a cabbage." The wood, he related, was porous and stringy, but the leaves made fine hats, baskets, and boxes.[11]

9   Robert Beverley, "Preface," in History and Present State of Virginia, in Four Parts (London, 1705), n.p. See Frederick Brendel, "Historical Sketch of the Science of Botany in North America from 1635 to 1840," The Naturalist 13 (November 1879): pp. 755–6.
10 Beverley, History and Present State of Virginia, pp. 2–6, 13–15, 26.
11 William Martin Smallwood in collaboration with Mabel Sarah Coon Smallwood, Natural History and the American Mind (New York, 1941), pp. 21–2; John Lawson, The History of Carolina (London, 1714), pp. 4–5, 7.

Lawson's *New Voyage to Carolina*, published in 1709, profiles nicely the advances in American natural history in his day. Like Beverley, he was selective in his specimens, but he was also surprisingly detailed. His bird descriptions included life span, nesting habits, time of incubation and fledgling, food, and "musicall notes & cryes," and he often compared these species to European varieties. Aware of a growing European interest in useful New World plants, he listed those that would grow in his homeland and sent seeds across the Atlantic. Although including much in the way of hearsay, he relied heavily on his own travels, reflecting a preference for firsthand description.[12]

Like Lawson, John Clayton represents a trend toward precision and firsthand observation. While serving as clerk in a Virginia county court, Clayton collected birds and plants until his death in 1773. He cultivated a botanical garden, corresponded with naturalists like Linnaeus and Johann Friedrich Gronovius of Holland, and published an account of Virginia in the London-based *Miscellanea Curiosa*. Like Lawson, Clayton shows a progression toward the minutely detailed observations that characterized American natural history after the turn of the century. He described, for instance, three types of woodpeckers: one with "blackish brown feathers and a large scarlet tuft on the top of the head"; another with variegated green, yellow, and red head-feathers; and a third with "spotted black and white [features], most lovely to behold."[13] In 1739–43, Gronovius revised and published Clayton's larger manuscript under his own name as *Flora Virginica*, apparently without Clayton's knowledge. Although unethical, the effort was timely because servants destroyed parts of Clayton's collection while he was indisposed by a "gripping of the guts," and the rest was consumed by fire shortly after his death. As late as 1812, Clayton's work was regarded as the most authoritative source of southern plants.[14]

Equally influential was John Brickell, whose *Natural History of North Carolina*, published in 1737, was copied uncredited from Lawson with additional anecdotes and critical notes. Although not entirely original, Brickell offers some valuable insights into colonial-era natural history. Writing before the adoption of standardized taxonomy, he described the country's curious and useful creatures in somewhat random order, placing

[12] Lawson in Stearns, *Science in the British Colonies of America*, pp. 310–11; Lawson, *History of Carolina*, pp. 79, 310–11; Allen, *History of American Ornithology*, p. 461.

[13] John Clayton, *Miscellanea Curiosa: Containing a Collection of Some of the Principal Phaenomena in Nature* (London, 1708), Vol. 3, pp. 301, 325, 327–9.

[14] Benjamin Smith Barton, *Flora Virginica* (Philadelphia, 1812), p. vi. See Stearns, *Science in the British Colonies of America*, pp. 556–8.

the bat "amongst the beasts, tho' it partakes of both Natures, of the Bird and the Mouse kinds."[15] Like others, he confined his taxonomy to "such only as I can perfectly remember, and whose qualities are best known." For those "inclined to live in these parts," he delved deeply into the nature of the soils, some "stiff" and others "light," and the climate, which was "sometimes extremely hot, at other times subtle and piercing."[16] Plants, too, he ordered according to their uses. Red-dock, swamp lily, golden-rod, mayapple, sunflower, Indian fig, and prickly pear drew his attention because Indians or "common people" found them to be curatives. A powder of grasshoppers with pepper helped with colic or "difficulty of urine," and hog lice (*Haematopinus suis*) cured "French pox and many other stubborn and lingering disorders." Earwigs boiled in oil and applied to the temples and wrists stopped convulsions by causing a fever. Of Spanish fly (*Lytta vesicatoria*), the "uses and virtues are so well known, that it wou'd be needless to trouble the reader about them." From colonial woodworkers, he gathered an equally detailed knowledge of each tree's properties and arranged them according to use, beginning with the lofty chestnut oak (*Quercus prinus*), the region's largest and most valuable tree. In a rambling summary, he described the colony's "pleasant savannas" and "wholsome pure air," along with a veritable cornucopia of wild fruits and nuts.[17] Effusive praise and Edenic allusions like these foreshadowed the mid-nineteenth-century romantic reinterpretation of nature.

As historian John Gatta writes, nature and theology seemed "to occupy separate spheres" in the colonial era: piety was not prominent in colonial natural history, and nature was not common in colonial religion. Cotton Mather was among the few who showed interest in both. Best known for his Puritan sermons, Mather also wrote communications to the Royal Society of London, and these were preserved in his *Curiosa Americana* and *The Christian Philosopher*, published, respectively, in 1712–24 and 1721. Historian Raymond Stearns saw in these writings a measure of "self-delusion, self-conceit, arrogance, and passion for public recognition" but, for all his ideological rigidness, Mather was an important transitional figure in colonial science. Whereas naturalists like Lawson and Clayton compiled factual descriptions based on their fieldwork, Mather turned to antiquity to understand the deeper logic in natural

[15] John Brickell, *The Natural History of North-Carolina, with an Account of the Trade, Manners, and Customs of the Christian and Indian Inhabitants* (Dublin, 1737), p. 132.
[16] Brickell, *Natural History of North-Carolina*, pp. 13, 132–3, 251.
[17] Brickell, *Natural History of North-Carolina*, pp. 23, 59, 69, 158–60, 253.

FIGURE I.I. Most early naturalists described the country's curious and useful creatures in random order, compiling whatever information came to hand through personal observation or hearsay. This cursory understanding was apparent in early natural histories, which included a heady mix of empirical fact, promotional bias, romantic exaggeration, and fantasy. John Brickell, *The Natural History of North-Carolina* (1737). Courtesy of the American Philosophical Society.

events. "Would it not be proper," he wrote, "to lay down those Laws of Nature, by which the Material World is governed, and which, ... we have in the Rank of Second Causes, no further to go?" After considering all "mechanical accounts," the Christian philosopher would naturally reason upward to "the Glorious God Immediately." Mather's intense otherworldly focus left him outside the mainstream of colonial natural history, but his conviction that nature moved according to certain fundamental laws challenged the next generation of American naturalists to seek broader interpretations.[18]

As a classical scholar, Mather helped draw American natural history back to its Aristotelian roots and to the idea of perfect harmonies so prominent in this classical literature. Like the Scholastics, he arranged his discourses according to the way natural history topics were taken up in Aristotelian texts, beginning with the heavenly bodies and moving on to terrestrial phenomena. Also in the scholastic tradition, his work was derivative; he began each discussion by citing biblical and ancient authority, then introduced modern naturalists, and, in some instances, his own observations.[19] His lack of field experience was evident. The rattlesnake, he thought, was "such a venomous wretch, that if he bite the edge of an axe, we have seen the bit of steel that has been bitten, come off immediately, as if it had been under a putrefaction." He classified earthworms with serpents and divided his ornithology into rapacious birds with hooked beaks and long talons, climbing birds with strong thighs and legs, and swimming birds with fin-toes. He constructed these classifications primarily to show how marvelously providence had formed each species to its purpose, borrowing from classical tradition the understanding that each species fit perfectly into its own special place in nature. "How conveniently are the legs of birds curved, for their easy perching, and roosting and rest!" In his appreciation for divine planning, he introduced the ideas of adaptation and harmony into American natural history. Because he believed that God fit this universe together at creation, his approach was static, but his exposition on how nature's parts fit together pioneered the ecological approach to nature in America.

Mather's main accomplishment, as Winton U. Solberg points out, was the study of purposes. His thinking was teleological: "every particular part of the plant has its astonishing uses," he wrote; "the roots give

---

[18] John Gatta, *Making Nature Sacred: Literature, Religion, and Environment in America from the Puritans to the Present* (New York, 2004), p. 17; Cotton Mather, *The Christian Philosopher: A Collection of the Best Discoveries in Nature, with Religious Improvements* (London, 1721), p. 8.

[19] Stearns, *Science in the British Colonies*, 403–4, 415. *Christian Philosopher* was completed in 1715, although it bears a 1731 imprint. See Solberg, "Science and Religion in Early America," p. 75; Frank N. Egerton, "Changing Concepts of the Balance of Nature," *Quarterly Review of Biology* 48 (June 1973): pp. 322–50.

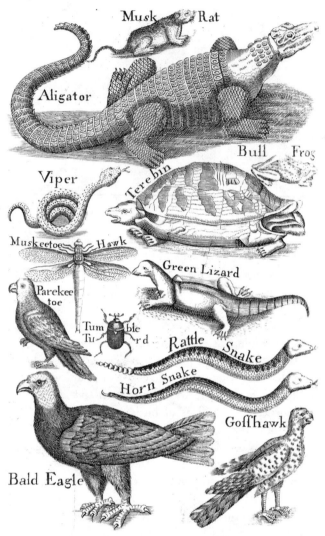

FIGURE 1.2. Puritan thinkers bequeathed to the American scientific community a theological structure for arranging the animal kingdom, beginning with the lowest order, the reptiles, and mounting progressively to humankind. This hierarchy presumed a reason for every organism. This purpose, assigned according to Divine wisdom, elevated each species in importance beyond its immediately useful properties. John Brickell, *The Natural History of North-Carolina* (1737). Courtesy of the American Philosophical Society.

it a stability, and fetch the nourishment into it, which lies in the earth ready for it. The fibres contain and convey the sap which carries up the nourishment." Nature was mechanical but also a reflection of God's perfect plan. To explain the earth's hydrological cycles, he drew from English clergyman John Ray's widely read *Wisdom of God Manifested in the Works of Creation* the idea that clouds were a "sort of hanging seas, that serve to temper the air, break the fiery rays of the Sun, and water the Earth when it is too dry." They operated according to Newton's physics but also reflected God's wisdom and love. "What hand was able to hang over our heads those great reservatories of Waters! What hand takes care never to let them fall, but in moderate showers!" Clouds were "so carried about by the winds . . . as to be so equally dispersed, that no part of the Earth wants convenient Showers, unless when it pleases God, for the Punishment of a sinful People, to withhold Rain, by a special interposition of his Providence." Mather articulated, for the first time in America, an argument for higher design in nature.[20]

Puritan thinkers like Mather also bequeathed to the American scientific community a theological means of ordering the species randomly mentioned in the naturalist narrative. Like all Puritan theologians, Mather arranged these species according to their importance in the overall design of the universe. This hierarchical structure, derived largely from England's eighteenth-century neo-Platonists, presumed a reason for every organism, some as predators and others as prey.[21] In explaining this *scala naturae*, Mather introduced Americans to another classical premise: the balance of nature.

That the Numbers of insects and vermin may not be too offensive to us, Providence has ordained many Creatures, especially such as are in superior orders, to make it their business to destroy them, especially when their increase grows too numerous and enormous. As in the Indies, where they are sometimes exceedingly punished with ants, there is the *Ursus formicarius* [brown bear], whose very business is to devour them. Hideous Armies of worms do sometimes visit my country, and carry whole fields of corn before them, and climbing up trees, leave them as bare as the

---

[20] Mather, *Christian Philosopher*, pp. 1–2, 53–4, 125, 129, 166–9, 184, 192, 213–14; Solberg, "Science and Religion in Early America," pp. 74–8, 90; Ernst Mayr, "The Idea of Teleology," *Journal of the History of Ideas* 53 (January–March 1992), pp. 118–19; Maxine Van De Wetering, "Moralizing in Puritan Natural Science: Mysteriousness in Earthquake Sermons," *Journal of the History of Ideas* 43, No. 3 (1982), pp. 417–18; Gatta, *Making Nature Sacred*, pp. 36, 38. On John Ray, see Egerton, "Changing Concepts of the Balance of Nature," p. 330–2.

[21] Solberg, "Science and Religion in Early America," p. 76; Holbrook, *Jonathan Edwards*, pp. 26, 38–40.

middle of winter. Our wild pidgeons [sic] make this the season of their descent, and in prodigious flocks they fall upon these robbers, and clear the country of them.[22]

Although not the first American to find unifying links in nature, Mather was the first to formulate a philosophical system for examining them. Whereas most colonial taxonomies were based on commercial use, he placed his species in a larger analytical framework, revealing the laws "by which the Material World is governed." Although seldom credited as a natural historian, Mather played a crucial role in American science: giving natural history a theological problematic helped liberate Americans from their status as "mere field agent[s] for European scientists in the New World."[23] The idea of nature as an ecological system owes much to his Puritan way of thinking.

"Strangers That Keep Journals": Late-Colonial Visiting Naturalists

As Mather's work suggests, colonial natural history depended heavily on European influences. Scientific explorers were generally trained (if at all) in Europe, and some spent relatively little time in the New World. Yet, if their sojourns were brief, they provided important methodological and philosophical models for their successors. Certainly, the most significant European visitor was Mark Catesby. Born in England in 1679, Catesby arrived in Virginia in 1712, and in the colony's capital he enjoyed the company of leading landowner and merchant families, many of them with at least a passing interest in natural history. "I soon imbibed a passionate desire of viewing...the animal [and]...vegetable productions in their native countries," he wrote later. Aware of European interest in New World plants, he sent specimens to several noted botanists, pointing out that "a forest of a thousand miles in length, extending twenty degrees in latitude from north to south...must afford a plentiful variety of trees and shrubs that may be usefully employed to inrich [sic] and adorn our woods ..., or to embellish and perfume our gardens." Back in England in 1719, he found a dozen patrons eager to finance another excursion to the colonies.[24] He returned in 1722, explored the Savannah River,

[22] Mather, *Christian Philosopher*, p. 161.

[23] Mather, *Christian Philosopher*, pp. iv, 8, 187; Stoll, *Protestantism, Capitalism, and Nature*, p. 75; Solberg, "Science and Religion in Early America," pp. 76, 90.

[24] Mark Catesby, *The Natural History of Carolina, Florida, and the Bahama Islands* (London, 1731–43), pp. i, iii–ix. See William Jackson Hooker, "On the Botany of

and then passed overland into Georgia and Florida. In the uplands, he began to sense the botanical geography of the land: a change in vegetation corresponding to changes in elevation and latitude. Drawn onward by this "succession of new vegetable appearances," he grew ever more sensitive to the relationship between land and vegetation. Catesby returned to England and completed his *Natural History of Carolina, Florida, and the Bahamas* between 1726 and 1732.[25]

Being the last in a line of explorers working without benefit of Linnaean taxonomy, Catesby has long stood in the shadow of more scientific or artistic naturalists. He held his own illustrations in low regard, hoping that his "flat, tho' exact manner may serve the purpose of natural history better in some measure than in a more bold and painter like way." Compared to later illustrators, his subjects seem stylized, but given the wilderness conditions under which he worked, he was surprisingly true and his inventory reasonably complete: a valuable beginning for those seeking cognitive mastery over this unknown country. No less important, his *Natural History* established an American tradition of illustrating subjects in their natural surroundings. Unlike his predecessors, Catesby often drew birds or animals with the plants and trees they lived in, or the insects they ate, arranging them according to what he called "affinities." Later, ornithologists elaborated this technique to produce rich ecological compositions that linked their birds to the web of nature.[26]

Linnaeus's scientific classification, finished in the mid-eighteenth century, increased the accuracy of species description throughout the world, and it was fitting that the next important European naturalist to visit America was a direct disciple of the Swedish taxonomist. Like Catesby, the European Peter Kalm was attracted to North America by the prospect

America," *American Journal of Science* 9, No. 2 (1825): pp. 263–4; George Frederick Frick and Raymond Phineas Stearns, *Mark Catesby: The Colonial Audubon* (Urbana, 1961), pp. ix, 11–12, 19, 36; Amy R. W. Meyers and Margaret Beck Pritchard (eds.), *Empire's Nature: Mark Catesby's New World Vision* (Chapel Hill, 1998), pp. 2–3.

[25] Catesby, *Natural History of Carolina*, pp. iii–ix. See Mark Catesby to John Bartram, May 20, 1740, Edmund Berkeley and Dorothy Smith Berkeley, *The Correspondence of John Bartram, 1734–1777* (Gainesville, 1992), p. 132.

[26] Catesby, *Natural History of Carolina*, p. xi; Frick and Stearns, *Mark Catesby*, pp. x, 62; Allen, *History of American Ornithology*, pp. 467–8; Stearns, *Science in the British Colonies*, p. 321. See Joyce E. Chaplin, "Mark Catesby: A Skeptical Newtonian in America," in Meyers and Pritchard, *Empire's Nature*, pp. 46–7, 64; Joseph Kastner, *A Species of Eternity* (New York, 1977), pp. 16–17; William Darlington, "Progress of Botany in North America," William Darlington (ed.), *Memorials of John Bartram and Humphry Marshall* (New York, 1967 [1849]), p. 19.

of finding species of plants and trees useful in his own country. Born in 1716 and educated at Abo and Uppsala, he was an outstanding student and quickly adopted the system constructed by his colleague Linnaeus, who around 1745 began sending students to some of the most remote corners of the world to classify new species.[27] For North America, he chose Kalm.

One of the earliest professional naturalists to visit America, Kalm arrived in Delaware Bay in September 1748 and spent three years, mostly in the Philadelphia area, gathering seeds and plants and sending them to England and Sweden. Recognizing that a complete botany would be impossible, he limited his list to commercial and medicinal species suitable for cultivation in Sweden. He, too, categorized his specimens according to use. Spruce provided a "healthful and agreeable small beer," and fir, with its bark of sap blisters, contained a "clear, liquid turpentine [that could be] tapped off and used for various purposes in medicine." However, like Mather, he saw these species as part of a larger system. Aware that European gardeners would need instructions for transplanting his specimens, he carefully noted their natural context. The sassafras tree grew best in "dry loose ground, of a pale brick colour, which consists of for the greatest part of sand, mixed with some clay.... The mountains round Gothenburgh, in Sweden, would afford many places rich enough for the sassafras to grow in, and I even fear they would be too rich."[28] This practical concern for relations among plants, soils, and climate hint at the ecological associations later naturalists discovered in the landscapes they explored.

[27] Peter Kalm, *Travels into North America, Containing its Natural History, and a Circumstantial Account of its Plantations and Agriculture in General,* John R. Foster (trans.), (Warrington, England, 1753–61), Vol. 1, p. vi; Kalm, "Pehr Kalm's Description of Maize, How It Is Planted and Cultivated in North America, Together with the Many Uses of this Crop Plant," Esther Louise Larsen (trans.), *Agricultural History* 9 (April 1935): pp. 99–101; Lisbet Koerner, "Carl Linnaeus in His Time and Place" in Jardine, Secord, and Spary, *Cultures of Natural History,* pp. 151–2.

[28] Kalm, *Travels,* Vol. 1, p. viii, x, 10–11, 76–7, 82–3, 85–6, 146–7; Vol. 2, p. 134; Kalm, "Pehr Kalm's Observations on the Natural History and Climate of Pennsylvania: Excerpts from his Letter of October 14, 1748," translated by Larsen, *Agricultural History* 17 (July 1943): p. 172; Kalm, "Peter Kalm's Short Account of the Natural Position, Use, and Care of Some Plants," translated by Larsen, *Agricultural History* 13 (January 1939): pp. 35, 37; Allen, *History of American Ornithology,* p. 510; Brooke Hindle, *The Pursuit of Science in Revolutionary America, 1735-1789* (Chapel Hill, 1956), p. 34; Allen, *History of American Ornithology,* p. 510; Henry T. Tuckerman, *America and Her Commentators, with a Critical Sketch of Travel in the United States* (New York, 1864), p. 295.

Kalm drew much of this information from other naturalists and from farmers and Indians, and his queries were often demanding. He asked New York botanist, Cadwallader Colden, for a "catalogue of all the quadrupeds you have any knowledge of to be here in North America, both wild and tame" and volleyed several more questions: "Is there more than one sort of panther? Wild cat?...Is there any opossum so far to Norse [sic] as where you lives?...Seals in Hudson's River; more than one sort of porcupine? Wolf? Bear? Bat? Rat-kind, Deer?...Have you heard anything of the 'Mouse- [Moose] Deer'?" And, finally: "What is your opinion why people so loose their teeths in this country?" To all of this Colden doggedly replied. One "never hears of more than one kind of wolf," he explained, except for the Indian dog. He had "often heard of the mouse deer," and as to the teeth, he attributed this "entirely to the Scurvy of which scarce one family in this Country is free."[29]

Kalm often failed to credit these obliging sources and, for this and for a number of disparaging remarks about the colonies, he was not well received among colonial literati. Sweden's long-standing alliance with France also put distance between Kalm and his British-American hosts. Finally, American-born naturalists were sensitive to distortions in his record. His tale of frogs that outran Indians did little to enhance his reputation.[30] Benjamin Franklin once complained in a letter that Kalm's work was "full of idle stories, which he pick'd up among ignorant people, and either forgetting of whom he had them, or willing to give them some authenticity, he has ascrib'd them to persons of reputation who never heard of them till they were found in his book." Franklin was "asham'd to meet with some mention'd" as coming from him. It was dangerous, he concluded, "conversing with these strangers that keep journals." Still, Kalm was an influential figure in American science. Being on intimate terms with Linnaeus, he urged the *Systema Naturae* on all he met. His professional deportment and his zeal inspired American naturalists, who had relatively few such models to emulate in the colonies.[31]

---

[29] Peter Kalm to Cadwallader Colden, January 4, 1751, in Colden, *The Letters and Papers of Cadwallader Colden* (New York, 1917–22), Vol. 1, pp. 251–2. Colden to Kalm, January 4, 1751, ibid., p. 261; Colden to Kalm, January 4, 1751, ibid., p. 261.

[30] Allen, *History of American Ornithology*, p. 508; Kalm, *Travels*, Vol. 3, p. iii; David Colden to Benjamin Franklin, November 30, 1772, Colden, *Letters and Papers of Cadwallader Colden*, Vol. 6, p. 184.

[31] Benjamin Franklin to David Colden, March 5, 1773, Colden, *Letters and Papers of Cadwallader Colden*, Vol. 6, p. 185. See Regis, *Describing Early America*, p. 49; Benjamin Smith Barton, *Observations on Some Parts of Natural History* (London, 1787), p. 7; Stearns, *Science in the British Colonies*, p. 530; Peter Kalm to Cadwallader Colden,

Encouraged by Kalm and by Linnaeus himself, New York's Cadwallader Colden became the first American naturalist to employ the new binomial nomenclature. Born of Scottish parents in 1688, Colden was educated in Edinburgh and moved to Philadelphia in 1710. In 1718, he joined the New York colonial office, became the province's first surveyor-general, and eight years later bought a country estate near the Hudson River. Given his official duties and the threat of war with France and its Indian allies, he had no time to explore, so he indulged his "philosophical amusements" by examining plants in his own neighborhood. Inspired by a visit from Kalm, he arranged a list of three hundred local plants according to Linnaeus, at a time when only a handful of scientists understood the system.[32]

Colden's career exemplifies the position of the colonial naturalist in the transatlantic scientific world. Isolated by the obscurity of his scientific interests, he relied on his overseas contacts to give meaning to his work. "I shall... indeavour to collect for you all the specimen's [sic] which you desire," he wrote to Johann Friedrich Gronovius. He passed along his philosophical reflections as well, for "the approbation of those Gentlemen to whose Judgment it is submitted."[33] Although he gained a measure of confidence from these contacts, he was inclined to self-doubt. "I am so sensible of my want of skill in the botanical science," he wrote to Linnaeus, "that I can no way deserve the praises you are pleased to bestow on the little performances I have made."[34] He was marginalized as well by his pressing administrative duties. In 1754, Franklin complemented Colden's resolution to pass the "remainder of life in philosophical retirement" but, by 1761, Colden was lieutenant-governor of New York. He retired to Long Island in 1775 and died the following year.[35]

September 29, 1748, James Edward Smith, *A Selection of the Correspondence of Linnaeus, and Other Naturalists, from the Original Manuscripts* (London, 1821), Vol. 2, p. 77; Colden to Linnaeus, February 1, 1750–1, ibid., pp. 457–8.

[32] Cadwallader Colden to Peter Kalm, January 4, 1751, Colden, *Letters and Papers of Cadwallader Colden*, Vol. 4, pp. 258–60. Colden to Kalm, January 4, 1751, ibid., pp. 258–60; Colden to Johann Friedrich Gronovius, December 1744, ibid., Vol. 3, p. 84; Hindle, *Pursuit of Science*, pp. 41–2.

[33] Cadwallader Colden to Johann Friedrich Gronovius, December 1744, Colden, *Letters and Papers of Cadwallader Colden*, Vol. 3, p. 84; Colden to John Frederic Gronovius, October 1, 1755, ibid., Vol. 5, p. 29.

[34] Cadwallader Colden to Carl Linnaeus, February 9, 1748–9, Smith, *Selection of the Correspondence of Linnaeus*, Vol. 2, p. 451.

[35] Benjamin Franklin to Cadwallader Colden, September 14, 1754, Colden, *Letters and Papers of Cadwallader Colden*, Vol. 4, p. 343; Colden to Johann Friedrich Gronovius, October 1, 1755, ibid., Vol. 5, p. 29. See Colden to John Fothergill, October 18, 1757,

Philadelphia naturalist Benjamin Barton later remarked that Colden was a "man but little talked of," although his "botanical services were not inconsiderable, at a time when this amiable science was hardly known in America." Colden's reputation as pioneer in Linnaean classification was circumscribed by his own self-doubts, by his administrative duties, and by his awkward position as a Tory lieutenant-governor in a revolutionary situation. His accomplishments should have brought him greater acclaim.[36]

Thomas Pownall's fate was similar. Like Colden, Pownall was a provincial governor at a time when war threatened along the western borders. When peace was restored in 1763, he was transferred from Massachusetts to South Carolina, and in 1776, despite his pressing responsibilities, he published his *Topographical Description of the Dominions of the United States of America*. He intended this as a guide for prospective settlers, but he was also conscious of the growing popular interest in natural history in America and abroad. "It will be curious in a few years," he wrote, "as the face of the country ... is totally altered, to ... read in this description, what it was in its natural state." The first natural history to span more than one or two colonies, *Topographical Description* provided a summary of eastern landforms, including the Appalachian ridges, the rivers that coursed between them, and the way in which these rivers "interlocked" with those of the St. Lawrence and Mississippi, making military or commercial movement between New England and New France possible with "very short portages."[37]

In Pownall's war-torn world, science bent to commercial and military needs. An astute observer, he combined a sensitivity to landscape features with close attention to their strategic importance. "I was particular in my observations and inquiries into the courses and nature of the currents of the several rivers, their falls and fords, ... the passes and gaps in the mountains, and especially the places where [out]posts ... might give a command in the country." Naturalists like Pownall demonstrate the

ibid., Vol. 5, p. 204; J. Bevis to Peter Collinson, August 10, 1755, ibid., Vol. 5, p. 23; Colden to Linnaeus, February 9, 1748–9, Vol. 4, pp. 95–6; Colden to Peter Kalm, January 4, 1751, ibid., Vol. 4, p. 258; "Preface," ibid., Vol. 1, pp. v–viii; Colden to Carl Linnaeus, February 9, 1748–9, Smith, *Selection of the Correspondence of Linnaeus*, p. 455; Kastner, *Species of Eternity*, pp. 5–6.

36 Benjamin Smith Barton, Journals and Notebooks, 1785–1806, APS, n.p.; "Preface," Colden, *Letters and Papers of Cadwallader Colden*, Vol. 1, pp. i, v–viii; Colden to Peter Kalm, January 4, 1751, ibid., Vol. 4, pp. 258–60.

37 Pownall, *Topographical Description*, pp. 10, 23, 29, 62. See Mulkearn, "Preface" in ibid., p. 23.

strengths and weaknesses of the emerging field in America: an almost irrepressible curiosity satisfied only by confronting nature in the field, and yet narrowed by the difficult demands of colonial life.[38] Their observations were circumscribed by a provincial culture and filtered through a practical lens but, even in this limiting intellectual milieu, it is possible to see signs of the ecological consciousness that would become a core element of American natural history in the next century.

"No Stranger to America": Client–Patron Relations in the Colonial Era

European patronage helps explain how colonial naturalists transcended these practical concerns. The Royal Society of London, founded in 1662, did much to encourage colonial scientific enterprise, but even more important was the relation between individual European botanists and gardeners and their clients in America.[39] John Fothergill's missive to Pennsylvania botanist, Humphry Marshall, in 1767 reflects the combination of business arrangement, apprenticeship, and friendship that often cemented these transatlantic arrangements. "I should be glad if thou would proceed to collect the seeds of . . . American shrubs and plants, as they fall in thy way," Fothergill wrote coyly,

and if thou meets with any curious plant or shrub, transplant it at a proper time into thy garden, let it grow there a year or two; it may then be taken up in autumn, its roots wrapped in a little moss, and laid in a coarse box, just made close enough to keep out mice, but not to exclude the air.

If thou knows of any plant possessed of particular virtues, and that is known by experience to be useful in the cure of diseases, this I should be glad to have in particular, both the parts used, and seeds of the same.

I accept thy offers to collect for me the curious animals of your country, very readily; and, as I may, shall readily make such acknowledgments as may be agreeable: and in doing this, I shall take it kind, if thou will just point out in what manner I can render thee most service.[40]

Americans responded to this entreatment in many ways. Some pursued their own scientific interest and sent extra seeds and plants overseas,

---

[38] Pownall, *Topographical Description*, p. 66; Frick and Stearns, *Mark Catesby*, p. ix.

[39] Janet Browne, "Biogeography and Empire" in Jardine, Secord, and Spary, *Cultures of Natural History*, p. 306; Frick and Stearns, *Mark Catesby*, p. ix; Stearns, *Science in the British Colonies*, p. 115.

[40] John Fothergill to Humphry Marshall, March 2, 1767, Darlington, *Memorials of John Bartram and Humphry Marshall*, p. 495.

expecting a return in European specimens or suitable scientific recognition. Others received financial support from one or more patrons, and some gardeners, seedmen, and taxidermists collected in anticipation of selling their specimens. The result was a flood of New World species crossing the Atlantic. In 1741, Peter Collinson told Colden that his garden contained more American plants than any other in England, "from seed & growing plants sent me by my friends in ye world." Although he had never crossed the Atlantic, he was, as he put it, "no stranger to America."[41]

This overseas demand for plants and information challenged American naturalists. "Pray have you thought or can you give a conjecture how America was peopled or was it a separate creation," Peter Collinson asked Colden. "Most of your vegetables & many of ye animals are different from ours, and yet you have some exactly like ours." Questions like these forced American correspondents to think deeply about what they discovered. Gronovius gave Colden a copy of his *Flora Virginica* and some works by Linnaeus and instructed the American neophyte to read them "over and over." Patrons funded and instructed their clients and legitimized field study at a time when few Americans would have done so.[42] This relationship could be overbearing as well as instructive. Boston naturalist, Manasseh Cutler, courted a British colleague in 1787 by promising to exchange information on American and European plants. The patron sent Cutler a list of more than two hundred American species for identification. Inquiries like this may have discouraged domestic exchanges; both Cutler and Colden pledged to direct their correspondence overseas, and in this way European synthesizers reaped the benefits of American fieldwork.[43] Later American naturalists objected to this division of labor, insisting that the essence of a species could be captured only by descriptions made in the field but, in these formative years, European tutelage played an important part in the maturation of American science.

[41] Peter Collinson to Cadwallader Colden, March 7, 1741–2, Colden, *Letters and Papers of Cadwallader Colden*, Vol. 2, p. 246. See John Fothergill to Humphry Marshall, April 23, 1771, Darlington, *Memorials of John Bartram and Humphry Marshall*, p. 506; Browne, "Biogeography and Empire," p. 307; Colden to Collinson, June 1744, Colden, *Letters and Papers of Cadwallader Colden*, Vol. 3, p. 60; Colden to Johann Friedrich Gronovius, December 1744, ibid., Vol. 3, p. 83.

[42] Peter Collinson to Cadwallader Colden, March 7, 1741–2, Colden, *Letters and Papers of Cadwallader Colden*, Vol. 2, p. 246; Johann Friedrich Gronovius to Colden, September 9, 1743, ibid., Vol. 3, p. 31. See Colden to Peter Collinson, November 13, 1742, in ibid., Vol. 2, p. 281.

[43] Manasseh Cutler to Monsieur Le Roi, November 24, 1787, Cutler to Monsieur Le Roi, November 24, 1787, Manasseh Cutler Papers, APS.

John Bartram epitomized this patron–client relationship. As a colonial naturalist, he worked amid other pressing responsibilities, viewed nature in utilitarian terms, and depended heavily on European patronage. As a pioneering American scientist, he valued his intimate relation to nature and allowed his curiosity to range beyond economic considerations. Bartram was born in 1699 in Delaware and raised in a Quaker family. As a farmer on the banks of the Schuylkill below Philadelphia, he developed a passing interest in medicinal herbs and began collecting native species for a botanic garden in 1730. When he died in 1777, he was the country's most prominent naturalist, a member of the Royal Society of London and the Swedish Academy and, with Benjamin Franklin, a founder of the American Philosophical Society, the country's first successful scientific academy.[44] Bartram's greatest accomplishment was his garden, a median between the tangled world of the backcountry and the scientist's neatly arranged catalog of species. Not only did the garden represent his own ambitious collecting forays, but he also benefited from exchanges made throughout the colonies. Addressed variously as "the philosopher," "the botanist," or the "master gardener," he received hundreds of queries, including some from Europe's greatest botanists.[45]

Bartram's skills as a naturalist were brought to fruition through the patronage of Peter Collinson, who initiated a working friendship in the 1730s and introduced Bartram to others who subscribed to his collecting efforts. As Bartram's tutor, Collinson encouraged strict standards and broadened Bartram's sense of curiosity. Fossils, he wrote, were "stones, found all the world over, that have either the impressions, or else the regular form of shells, leaves, fishes, fungi, teeth, sea-eggs, and many other productions.... What use the learned make of them, is, that they are evidences of the Deluge." In return for patronage, Bartram quickened the flow of New World species across the Atlantic, adding in one shipment a "barrel...of our bull frogs for ye king," explaining that they would propagate in the parks and "surprise & divert all ye adjacent inhabitants of London."[46]

44 William Bartram, "Some Account of the Late Mr. John Bartram, of Pennsylvania," *Philadelphia Medical and Physical Journal*, part 1, Vol. 1, section 2 (1804): p. 116; Ernest Earnest, *John and William Bartram: Botanists and Explorers, 1699–1777; 1739–1823* (Philadelphia, 1940), p. 6; Tuckerman, *America and Her Commentators*, pp. 372–4.

45 See, for instance, Thomas Orde to John Bartram, "Master Gardener at Philadelphia," n.d., Vol. 4, File 94, Bartram Family Papers, PHS; Wayne Hanley, *Natural History in America: From Mark Catesby to Rachel Carson* (New York, 1977), p. 16.

46 Collinson to Bartram, March 20, 1736, Darlington, *Memorials of John Bartram and Humphry Marshall*, p. 74; John Fothergill to Bartram, n.d., ca. 1772, ibid., p. 344;

Barton's curiosity about "undescript" species explains much of his interest in botany, but his choice of career bears closer scrutiny because there was so little in his cultural environment to encourage ambitions like this. Most accounts repeat a story told by J. Hector St. John de Crèvecoeur in which Bartram, plowing a field one day, was struck by the fact that he had spent his years "in tilling the earth and destroying so many flowers and plants without being acquainted with their structures and their uses." Bartram's son William confirms this without casting the notion as epiphany: "While engaged in ploughing his fields, and mowing his meadows, his inquisitive eye and mind were frequently exercised in the contemplation of vegetables; the beauty and harmony displayed in their mechanism; the admirable order of system, which the great Author of the universe has established throughout their various tribes." As William intimates, Bartram's decision was incremental, and it was influenced by his work in the field and his Quaker appreciation for God's creations. In addition, he occasionally used herbs to treat neighbors' illnesses, and a constant parade of admirers through his garden no doubt encouraged his passion for expanding his plant and tree inventory.[47]

Equally important was Bartram's relation to European naturalists. Although he never explicitly related his own version of this life-transforming decision, he did give some account of his interest in a letter to an English patron: "I have had, ever since I was twelve years of age, a great inclination to botany and natural history; but could not make much improvement therein for want of books or other instructions, until I entered into correspondence with my good friend Peter Collinson, who engaged, first Lord Petre, then, Philip Miller, and the Dukes of Richmond and Norfolk to subscribe thirty guineas, in order to enable me to travel...to search for forest seeds, roots, and plants to adorn their gardens."[48] As with Colden, Bartram received a great deal of

---

Collinson to Bartram, March 12, 1735–6, in ibid., p. 72; Bartram to John Fothergill, November 26, 1769, Berkeley and Berkeley, *Correspondence of John Bartram*, p. 725. See Hindle, *Pursuit of Science*, p. 1; Collinson to Bartram, March 12, 1735–6, Darlington, *Memorials of John Bartram and Humphry Marshall*, p. 73; Collinson to Bartram, March 14, 1736–7, ibid., p. 93; Benjamin Gully to John Bartram, January 1768, Bartram Family Papers, PHS; Catesby to Bartram, ca. March 1741–2, Berkeley and Berkeley, *Correspondence of John Bartram*, p. 183; Earnest, *John and William Bartram*, pp. 24, 35, 39–40, 44, 50; Kasner, *Species of Eternity*, pp. 18.

[47] Bartram, "Some Account," pp. 116–17; Earnest, *John and William Bartram*, pp. 14–16; Crevecoeur in Franklin, *Discoverers, Explorers, Settlers*, p. 48.

[48] John Bartram to Alexander Catcot, May 26, 1742, Darlington, *Memorials of John Bartram and Humphry Marshall*, p. 324.

encouragement from these European patrons, who funded his travels, validated his speculations, and boosted his confidence and his reputation abroad. Bartram considered their missives "a great incouragement," and their financial patronage was essential because the Bartram family included nine children, and the patriarch felt keenly his duty to provide for them.[49]

In July 1743, Bartram set out from Philadelphia with fellow explorer Lewis Evans for New York's upper Susquehanna drainage. Marching through the "hollows and steep ascents and over many boggy rotten places," he kept a journal he later published as *Observations on the Inhabitants, Climate, Soil, Rivers, Productions, Animals, and other Matters Worthy of Notice*. The volume suggests the intense and broad-ranging curiosity that drew Bartram and others like him into these wild and remote corners of America. "No feature or phase of nature seems to escape him," a biographer wrote. "He notes the earth beneath, the vegetation around, and the sky above; fossils, insects, Indian ceremonies, flowers; the expanse of the 'dismal wilderness,' the eels roasted for supper, and the moss and fungus as well as locusts and caterpillars." Like several before him, Bartram arranged these seemingly unrelated features in narrative form, describing each element of the landscape as it appeared in his line of travel.[50] This decision to describe species in situ – in order of appearance rather than by taxonomic relations – resulted in a transect sampling of those aspects of nature he thought valuable or "curious." In this way, he ordered an inchoate landscape; his scientific eye swept the alluvial soils of the Genesee country and fell on the many springs of pure water, the limestone bedrock, the "spacious level of middling land" suitable for farming, and the steep and stony ridges that would produce only a crop of trees.[51] The narrative included the plants and animals that

[49] John Bartram to Peter Collinson, n.d., Bartram Family Papers, Folder 14, Vol. 1, PHS; Tuckerman, *America and Her Commentators*, pp. 374–5; Bartram to Alexander Catcot, May 26, 1742, Darlington, *Memorials of John Bartram and Humphry Marshall*, p. 324; Bartram to John Fothergill, December 7, 1745, Berkeley and Berkeley, *Correspondence of John Bartram*, p. 267.

[50] Tuckerman, *America and Her Commentators*, p. 376. See William Bartram, *The Travels of William Bartram*, Francis Harper (trans.) (New Haven, 1958), p. 18–19, 28, 25–7, 37; John Bartram to Peter Collinson, ca. September, 1743, Berkeley and Berkeley, *Correspondence of John Bartram*, p. 223; Franklin, *Discoverers, Explorers, Settlers*, p. 49.

[51] John Bartram, *Observations on the Inhabitants, Climate, Soil, Rivers, Productions, Animals, and Other Matters Worthy of Notice*, Kalm, Peter (ed.), (London, 1751), p. 11.

inhabited each of these landscapes, and thus hints at his interest in the way these various features fit together. Flocks of wild turkeys, snakes, gnats, wild grass, and tree species appeared and disappeared in a succession of swamps, ridges, hollows, and plains, each a part of a larger community.

The travel narrative was a popular vehicle for late-eighteenth-century science, conveying important information while capturing the thrill of discovery. Although it lacked the precision of a scientific catalog, it was attuned to interdependencies, and in his correspondence, Bartram demonstrated that these connections were not lost on him. As with Kalm, requests for instructions on growing his plants encouraged Bartram's sensitivity to ecological relations. The sugar birch (*Betula lenta*), he wrote to Collinson, "delights to grow on cold north sides of hills where there is springs or river . . . or . . . at the bottom of hills tho it often times grows in the cliffs of rocks & no growth can be so stoney for them. I have walked for an hour . . . upon nothing but great stones & no soil to be seen yet these trees and white pine growed finely."[52]

Bartram continued his collecting trips until confined by the frontier wars of the 1750s and 1760s. In 1764, at the end of the French and Indian War, he ventured down the Ohio River and overland to the Potomac. On the entire journey, as he later wrote, he observed "not . . . one tree or shrub but what I have growing on my own land except a vine very dramatick which is very curious." A year later, Collinson had Bartram appointed as the king's official botanist for North America, an honor that came with an annual stipend of fifty pounds. Added to his income from collecting, this allowed him to "range widely at the expense of his farming," as Collinson phrased it.[53]

In 1766, Bartram began his most important exploration: a journey into the East Florida interior along the St. John's River – a "ravishing place for a curious botanist." As he did in New York, Bartram arranged his observations in a narrative format and, again like New York, he prioritized them according to economic considerations.[54] Trees were valuable for

[52] John Bartram to Peter Collinson, n.d., Bartram Family Papers, Folder 16, Vol. 1, PHS See William Bartram, "Some Account," p. 120.

[53] J. M. Edelstein, "America's First Native Botanists," *Library of Congress Quarterly Journal of Current Acquisitions* 14 (February 1958), p. 54; John Bartram to Peter Collinson, October 18, 1741, Bartram to (brother) William Bartram, February 5, 1764, Bartram Family Papers; Hanley, *Natural History in America*, p. 16; Peter Collinson to John Bartram, April 9, 1765, Darlington, *Memorials of John Bartram and Humphry Marshall*, p. 268.

[54] John Bartram to Peter Collinson, May 10, 1762, Berkeley and Berkeley, *Correspondence of John Bartram*, p. 558. See B to [obscured], ibid., p. 622; "Introduction,"

masts, planks, timbers, resin, pitch, tar, tanbark, or construction; and soils for various crops: "hammocky ground" for corn and pumpkin; "pine-lands" for corn, potatoes, and cotton; "palmetto ground" for corn and indigo; savannahs for pasture; and cypress swamps for lumber. Florida soils were arranged in layers, he found: a "thin mould" covering a thicker stratum of sand with a third and fourth layer of white clay and fused shells. This was the key to Florida's fecundity. The impermeable clay and shell layers prevented the rains from "sinking away from the roots of the plants and trees," while the natural churning of these limey sediments fertilized the soil layers that lay above them. He ended on a promotional note: Farmers would find East Florida far more productive than common prejudice suggested.[55]

Despite his wide-ranging correspondence and his explorations, Bartram remained a provincial scientist. He yearned to travel to England to show Collinson and others how to care for the specimens he sent abroad, but he found it impossible to leave his family and his garden: "I have many small children & none yet growd up to take care of business, & servants in this country strives to do as little work [in] . . . as much time as they can." Nor were his expeditions as frequent as he might have wished. When Collinson asked him to collect in the Ohio country, he agreed, but with reservations: "If the barbarous Indians . . . hinder me and if I die a martyr to Botany, God's will be done."[56] Colden, somewhat more bookish than his Philadelphia counterpart, considered Bartram a won-derful observer but lacking in the "principles of Botany as a Science," and Bartram himself sensed this. Nature was subject to higher causes but explaining these "obtuse phanomenia" seemed like "shooting arrows against a rock; thay all fly back again at my face." His own acquain-tances, he admitted, expressed "very little taste for these amusements" and thus he explored alone, "passing over rivers, climbing over moun-tains and precipices, amongst the rattlesnakes, and often obliged to fol-low the track, or path, of wild beasts for my guide through these desolate and gloomy thickets."[57] Despite these limitations, Bartram did much to

Bartram, *Description of East-Florida*, pp. 14–17, 19, 33; Edelstein, "America's First Native Botanists," p. 54.
[55] Bartram, *Description of East-Florida*, pp. 14–17, 34; William Stork in ibid., pp. i, 4; Tuckerman, *America and Her Commentators*, pp. 372–3. See Bartram, "Some Account," pp. 122–3.
[56] John Bartram to Peter Collinson, June 21, 1743, Bartram Family Papers, Vol. 1, PHS; Bartram in Kastner, *Species of Eternity*, p. 64.
[57] Cadwallader Colden to Peter Collinson, November 13, 1742, Colden, *Letters and Papers of Cadwallader Colden*, Vol. 2, p. 280; Colden to Collinson, June 1744, ibid., Vol. 3,

unveil this country unknown, and his speculations about connectedness, although limited, inspired a trend that would later inform the conservation movement. In his thirty years of travel, he informed John Hope in 1764, he had "acquired a perfect knowledge of most, if not all of the vegetables between New England and Georgia, and from the sea-coast to Lake Ontario and Erie."[58] At the time, no other scientist could make that boast.

Nature and Adventure on the Western Frontier

Whereas French and Spanish missionaries, military officers, and traders explored deep into the interior of the continent, British colonials seldom left the seaboard. Lawson, one of the few early naturalists to travel west of the mountains, complained that those who frequented the backcountry – traders, hunters, and skin-dealers – seemed "uncapable of giving any reasonable account of what they met withal in those remote parts, tho' the country abounds with curiosities." He himself traveled the region apprehensively. The highlands were haunted by "the dismall'st and most hideous noise that ever pierc'd my ears," produced, his Indian friends told him, by "endless numbers of panthers, tygers, wolves, and other beasts of prey." Beyond the mountains, Brickell added, "you have a prospect only of large woods, savannas, dismal swamps and forests, being as is supposed, the habitation of savage Indians and wild beasts of various kinds." These fearful and dismissive tones underscore the dilemma of the British-colonial naturalist, who was both intrigued and repelled by these terrifying unknowns.[59] Late in the colonial period, a few explorers parted this dark shroud to reveal a land of enormous promise and, gradually, a sense of wonder supplanted these feelings of consternation. The emotions aroused by this uncharted territory blossomed into a romantic discourse among the next generation of explorers.

p. 61; Bartram, "A Journey to Catskill Mountains with Billy, 1753," Bartram Family Papers, Vol. 1, PHS. See Collinson to John Bartram, April 9, 1765, Darlington, *Memorials of John Bartram and Humphry Marshall*, p. 325; Collinson to Bartram, April 9, 1765, ibid., p. 325.

[58] John Bartram to John Hope, October 4, 1764, Darlington, *Memorials of John Bartram and Humphry Marshall*, p. 433. See Stearns, *Science in the British Colonies*, p. 589.

[59] Lawson, "Preface," *History of Carolina*, n.p.; ibid., p. 26; Brickell, *Natural History of North-Carolina*, p. 43. On madness and wilderness, see Robert D. Arner, "Pastoral Patterns in William Bartram's *Travels*," *Tennessee Studies in Literature* 18 (1973), p. 141.

The blend of promotion, romance, and exaggeration in this western
literature was apparent in Jonathan Carver's *Travels*, based on his expedition to the Mississippi headwaters in the mid-1760s. Born in Connecticut
in 1732, Carver joined a Connecticut militia regiment in 1757 and, after
his company disbanded, he was placed at the head of a survey party traveling to the Mississippi to examine the commercial possibilities of the newly
won region. He traveled to Michilimackinac, at the head of Lake Huron,
then left for Green Bay and, via the Fox and Wisconsin Rivers, reached
the Mississippi. He spent 1766 and 1767 exploring portions of the headwaters region as far north as the falls of St. Anthony. Although short of
his objective, he mapped out the "sources of four great waterways" at
the heart of the continent: the Red River flowing north to Hudson Bay;
the Great Lakes discharging into the Atlantic; the Mississippi sending its
waters to the Gulf; and the Minnesota stretching to the West, which he
thought would take him to the illusive "River Oregon" and the Pacific.[60]
Carver left for England in 1768, and before Parliament he championed
the idea of a northern passage to the West; however, before he could
broker a return trip, war broke out between England and America, and
Parliament's waning interest in the Northwest left him without patronage. Impoverished and stranded between two hostile nations, he died in
poverty at age 48 in 1780.[61]

Carver's *Travels*, which appeared in 1778, contained a wealth of information about the lakes, rivers, portages, plants, animals, and Indians of
the Northwest. As a military man, he freighted his ethnography with
concerns about potential enemies or allies, and his cartography stressed
the importance of strategic military or commercial travel routes. Yet,
along with these practical interests, he conveyed a variety of subjective
judgments. The country around the Falls of St. Anthony he described
as "extremely beautiful," with its "many gentle ascents, which in the
summer are covered with the finest verdure, and interspersed with little
groves that give a pleasing variety to the prospect." The "Shining Mountains" to the west received their name from the "infinite number of crystal
stones, of an amazing size, with which they are covered, and which, when

---

[60] Jonathan Carver, *Three Years Travels Through the Interior Parts of North-America*
(Philadelphia, 1796), pp. xix, 23, 30, 34, 41, 43, 55, 60, 67. See Edward D. Neill,
"Capt. Jonathan Carver, and his Explorations," Minnesota Historical Society *Collections* 1 (1872), pp. 351-2, 355-6, 360; Henry R. Schoolcraft, *Summary Narrative of an
Exploratory Expedition to the Sources of the Mississippi River, in 1820* (Philadelphia,
1855), p. 21; Allen, *History of American Ornithology*, p. 526.
[61] Neill, "Capt. Jonathan Carver," p. 361; Schoolcraft, *Summary Narrative*, p. 21.

the sun shines full upon them, sparkle so as to be seen at a very great distance."[62]

Despite the wealth of personal observations Carver collected in his two and a half years in the wilderness, his journal is riddled with plagiarism. Critics speculate that he sketched out his recollections at Michilimackinac or Detroit, and when the British government refused to subsidize a return trip, he pawned these sparse notes to a bookseller who may have combined Carver's sketches with earlier French accounts. Plagiarism was not unusual; other explorers, or their editors, borrowed heavily to ready a journal for public consumption. And whether compiler or observer, Carver left a fascinating document that stimulated great interest in the West. His *Travels* circulated widely in Europe and America, bringing the natural history of the upper Mississippi before an audience increasingly interested in the romance of the frontier.[63]

In Carver, the West became a vision of wealth, beauty, mystery, and dread – a country unknown. Over time, a new generation of explorers softened these glaring images into a romantic pastel, piecing together a synthesis of older myths and newer observations at once more scientific and more romantic. Despite the preoccupations with cataloging and classifying under the Linnaean regimen, these naturalists speculated widely and described poetically. Where earlier explorers had focused on the practical uses of nature's bounty, this generation, driven by an irrepressible combination of awe and curiosity, wove their observations into a new system of categories based on the picturesque, the majestic, and the sublime: tools for describing a paradise.

William Bartram's Romance with Nature

William Bartram demonstrates the blend of utility and romance that characterized the emerging philosophical perspective on the American wilderness. Born on his father's estate in 1739, Bartram grew up in a world of exotic plants and curious people. He died in his father's garden in 1823 as the nation's most accomplished botanist. His *Travels Through North*

---

[62] Carver, *Three Years Travels*, pp. 33, 42, 179.

[63] Schoolcraft in Edward Gaylord Bourne, "The Travels of Jonathan Carver," *American Historical Review* 11 (January 1906): 287–8, 291–5, 298–9, 300, 301–2; N. Bryllion Fagin, *William Bartram: Interpreter of the American Landscape* (Baltimore, 1933), p. 39. See John Thomas Lee, "Captain Jonathan Carver: Additional Data," State Historical Society of Wisconsin *Proceedings* (Madison, 1913): pp. 88, 90–1, 95, 99, 102–4; Tuckerman, *America and Her Commentators*, pp. 386–8.

and South Carolina, Georgia, East and West Florida, published in 1791, remains the best-known natural history in America prior to the writings of John James Audubon and Henry David Thoreau. A man of deep religious conviction and wide-ranging interests, Bartram, like his father, folded his natural history observations into a firm belief in providential design. This blend of science and spirituality was by no means uncommon at the end of the colonial period, but Bartram brought to perfection the use of emotive and pietistic reaction as a means of comprehending nature. John Bartram, despite his vast knowledge of plants, was a reluctant scholar, unassuming in his correspondence and largely factual in his journals. William, familiar with classical and Christian imagery, wrote brilliantly, bridging the gap between Enlightenment science and Romantic literature. He was, in William Martin Smallwood's words, America's premier "poet-naturalist."[64]

Bartram's decision to follow in his father's footsteps was not instinctive. In 1755, the elder Bartram explained in a letter to Peter Collinson that "Billy," now age 16, would have to find "some way . . . to get his liveing by." In the Quaker manner, John Bartram envisioned a life of honest labor for his son: "I don't want him to be what is commonly called a gentleman. I want to put him to some business by which he may with care & industry get a temperate resonable living." William sampled life as a printer, a farmer, and a merchant but, as his father said, he did not "make out so well as he expected."[65] In 1765, he acquired a run-down estate on the St. John's River and pursued a hermit-like existence as an indigo planter, driving his father to "great straits." He endured this solitary existence for a year or so, "a gentle, mild young man, no wife, no friend, no companion, no neighbour, no human inhabitant within nine miles of him," but was salvaged when his father, appointed America's royal botanist and given orders to explore Florida, instructed William to "sell of[f] all thy good[s] at a publick venue" and meet him in St. Augustine.[66] From 1766 to 1770, William explored with his father and, in 1773, he

[64] Regis, *Describing Early America*, pp. 41, 46–7; Smallwood, *Natural History*, p. 35. See Hanley, *Natural History in America*, p. 24; Earnest, *John and William Bartram*, p. 3; Francis Harper, "Introduction," in William Bartram "Travels in Georgia and Florida, 1773–74: A Report to Dr. John Fothergill," annotated by Harper, APS *Transactions*, n.s., 33 (1943): p. 128.

[65] John Bartram to Peter Collinson, April 27, 1755, Berkeley and Berkeley, *Correspondence of John Bartram*, p. 384; Caroline Bartram Kelly, address, June 8, 1893, Bartram Family Papers, Miscellaneous Manuscripts, PHS, pp. 10–12 (Bartram quote from p. 12).

[66] Bartram in Earnest, *John and William Bartram*, p. 104; Thomas Lamboll to John Bartram, August 31, 1765, Darlington, *Memorials of John Bartram and Humphry*

once again left for Florida at the request of English botanist John
Fothergill. It was this "lonesome pilgrimage," a series of explorations
lasting until 1777, which provided materials for his *Travels*.[67]

Bartram returned occasionally to the settlements to forward his collections to Fothergill and for updates on Indian–white relations. Bound
to explore the province "at all events," he purchased a small canoe on
the St. John's and set out for the interior. Despite the threat of warfare,
his Quaker background served him well; Indians responded to his gentle
manner by proclaiming him "Puc-Puggy," or Flower Hunter.[68] In 1778,
a year after his father died, Bartram returned to Philadelphia and for the
rest of his life remained anchored to the garden on the Schuylkill, where he
cultivated and dispensed seeds with his brother John. Late in life, the University of Pennsylvania offered him a chair of botany, which he declined
because of age and infirmity. For the same reason in 1803, he declined
Jefferson's invitation to travel with what would become the Lewis and
Clark expedition. Having missed the defining natural history event of the
century, he turned down a second expedition to the Red River a year
later.[69] Bartram understood the significance of his decisions and wistfully
imagined himself a younger man. "When, as I frequently perceive . . . the
vast, boundless, diversified field for contemplation & researches in Natural History westward beyond the elevated mountains for the ingenious
of future generations, [I] am almost ready to wish that the appointed
time of my existence here had been postponed to that day," he wrote to
his friend Henry Mühlenberg. "But then, I consider the [sentimentality?]
of such a desire, & suppress the imagination, being content that God
Almighty orders all events for the best."[70]

     Marshall, pp. 439–40; John Bartram to William Bartram, July 7, 1765, Bartram Family
     Papers, PHS.

[67] Bartram, *Travels*, pp. 1, 216; Smallwood, *Natural History*, p. 41; Charlotte M. Porter,
     The Eagle's Nest: Natural History and American Ideas, 1812–1842 (Tuscaloosa, 1986),
     pp. 5–7.

[68] Billy Bartram to John Bartram, March 27, 1775, Bartram Family Papers, PHS; Fagin,
     William Bartram, pp. 30–1.

[69] Harper, "Introduction," in Bartram, *Travels*, pp. xvii–xviii, xx, xxviii; John Hope to
     William Bartram, ca. March 1765, Bartram Family Papers, PHS; Dr. Nutenreith to
     Bartram, ca. 1795, Bartram Family Papers, Folder 11, Vol. 1, PHS; Kerry S. Walters,
     "The 'Peaceable Disposition' of Animals: William Bartram on the Moral Sensibility of
     Brute Creation," *Pennsylvania History* 56 (No. 3, 1989): p. 157; Fagin, *William Bartram*,
     p. 12; Benjamin Smith Barton to William Bartram, November 30, 1805, Benjamin Smith
     Barton Papers, APS; Barton to Bartram, August 1803, Bartram Family Papers, PHS.

[70] William Bartram to Henry E. Mühlenberg, November 29, 1792, Henry E. Mühlenberg
     Manuscripts, PHS. See Edelstein, "America's First Native Botanists," p. 56; Fagin,
     William Bartram, p. 72.

A literary as much as a scientific accomplishment, *Travels* was well regarded by American, French, and English romantics, who drew inspiration from his intensely personal and emotional engagement with nature, his evocative landscape descriptions, and his allusions to classical literature. Despite his literary flourish, scholars accept his descriptions as "painstakingly precise" across a broad range of interests – plants, birds, animals, landscapes, geological formations, Native Americans, and settlers. Like his father, he was heavily influenced by his Quaker upbringing, and his belief that nature expressed the goodness of God appealed to an age that was beginning to seek evidence of divinity in the works of nature. "Even in the visible... parts of... creation," he wrote to Mühlenberg, "we... behold with inexpressibly pleasing love & veneration the majesty, power, and goodness of God the Creator thereof." This graceful connection between nature and religion provided a desideratum for American science that lasted through several generations. Bartram's enduring spirituality and his quest for connections in nature had enormous impact on his American colleagues.[71]

"A Country Unknown Must, If a Paradise, Still Continue a Desart"

Naturalists like Bartram seldom used the term *wilderness*, but their descriptions of this country unknown carried much of the ambivalence later Americans imparted to the concept. Their view of nature was based partly on Puritan suspicions of a savage and immoral land and partly on European romantic fantasies of natural innocence and primitive virtue. They saw the forest as incredibly diverse yet endlessly monotonous. It was empty yet, when literary needs dictated, filled with settlers, hunters, and Indians. Most often, it was a place of anticipations, an unfinished land awaiting the hand of the pioneer, the missionary, the builder.

Naturalists were equally ambivalent about the land's original inhabitants. From William Wood forward, they understood how Indians used fire to manage the forests, but they rarely allowed for this influence in their representations of the western woods. They derived a wealth of geographical information from Native guides, but seldom acknowledged this

---

[71] William Bartram to Henry E. Mühlenberg, September 8, 1792, Mühlenberg Manuscripts, PHS; Huth, *Nature and the American*, p. 21; Edelstein, "America's First Native Botanists," pp. 56–8; Gatta, *Making Nature Sacred*, p. 49; Fagin, *William Bartram*, pp. 21, 26, 37; Walters, "'Peaceable Disposition' of Animals," p. 157; Smallwood, *Natural History*, pp. 35, 38, 40; Porter, *Eagle's Nest*, p. 296; Foshay, *Reflections of Nature*, p. 26.

contribution, partly because colonial readers remained suspicious of Indians wandering about "the heads of their own rivers," as John Bartram put it. Naturalists drew heavily on Indian legends about formidable creatures in the western forests, but they often used these stories only to accent the fact that the land was "unknown." They saw evidence of brilliant social and religious organization and artistic endeavor in the mysterious mounds of the Ohio Valley but preferred to imagine this civilization built by Celtic, Chinese, or Norwegian voyagers blown off course in their seafaring adventures.[72] Presuming a connection between wilderness and depravity, naturalists rarely challenged prevailing stereotypes about Indians. They acknowledged Native sources of herbal cures because they believed that all local diseases had local remedies and that original inhabitants were familiar with these cures, but they balanced this assumption against the idea that "primitive" knowledge was inherently superstitious. "Scarcely two of them will tell you the same story," one naturalist complained.[73]

In general, naturalists had good reason to acknowledge the Indians' presence in their explorations. As an example of primitive culture and passive interaction with the land, Indians were useful in contrasting the country unknown with the paradise that would come with a better understanding of nature.[74] "Mighty kingdoms will emerge from these wildernesses," Carver predicted in the preface to his *Travels*, "and stately palaces and solemn temples, with gilded spires reaching the skies, supplant the Indian huts, whose only decorations are the barbarous trophies of their vanquished enemies."[75] However, naturalists had equally good reason to write the Indians out of their natural landscapes because the idea of an

---

[72] Bartram, *Observations on the Inhabitants*, p. 15; Brickell, *Natural History of North-Carolina*, pp. iii, iv, 110; E[phrian] G[eorge] Squier, *Observations on the Aboriginal Monuments of the Mississippi Valley* (New York, 1847), p. 75; David Hosack, "A Biographical Memoir of Hugh Williamson," New York Historical Society *Collections* 3 (1821): p. 164.

[73] George William, Featherstonhaugh *A Canoe Voyage Up the Minnay Sotor* (London, 1847), pp. 172, 284; Christian Schultz, *Travels on an Inland Voyage* (New York, 1810), p. 146; Arnold Henry Guyot, *The Earth and Man: Lectures on Comparative Physical Geography in its Relation to Mankind*, C. C. Felton (trans.), (Boston, 1850), p. 216; Lawson, *History of Carolina*, pp. 10–11; Benjamin Smith Barton, *Collections for an Essay towards a Materia Medica of the United-States* (Philadelphia, 1801), p. 27; Alexander Wilson and Charles Lucian Bonaparte, *American Ornithology: or, the Natural History of the Birds of the United States* (Philadelphia, n.d.), p. 248.

[74] William Byrd, *History of the Dividing Line and Other Tracts from the Papers of William Byrd*, T. H. Wynne (ed.), (Richmond, 1866), Vol. 1, p. 32.

[75] Carver, *Three Years Travels*, p. xix.

empty land helped justify their own scientific explorations and the idea
of manifest destiny. Late in the colonial period, these ethnographic representations absorbed the Rousseauian veneration of the primitive that
would mark the coming Romantic era, but a more generous assessment
of the indigenous westerner awaited that moment.

The idea of nature that took shape amid these conflicting impulses
was both practical and philosophical. Typically, colonial accounts began
with a straightforward presentation of factual topography known as the
face of the country: a picture of the landscape as it would appear in the
eye of the beholder. It ranged from soil and plant life to topography,
and it aimed at describing useful features in the country unknown. The
face of the country was stylized and static, leaving the higher meanings
"to those who have more leisure and disposition for speculation."[76] John
Drayton's 1802 *View of South Carolina* began typically by describing
the configurations of the coast, with its maze of inlets, creeks, marshes,
and islands, and placing on this factual foundation "small pines and bay
trees, live oak, cedar, ... palmetto, silk grass, myrtle, cassena, wild olive,
tooth-ache tree, [and] prickly pear." His Savannah River was "bold and
deep," navigable to the first falls for boats of seventy tons. He measured out South Carolina in three north-to-south bands, the first being
a low, flat, woody coastal plain blessed with fertile soil; the second, a
"middle country" demarcated by undulating sand hills; and the third,
beginning at the first falls of the rivers, a hilly frontier region characterized by stony soils, rocky ridges, and good land along the rivers. These
three "departments" provided a framework for ordering his complicated
field observations on geology, botany, zoology, and climate; often, this
division was the highest level of abstraction reached in a "face of the
country."[77]

This descriptive construct best represented colonial natural history's
practical bent. Eyes fixed on the coming colonial paradise, naturalists
described plants in terms of culinary and medicinal uses, trees according to their structural properties, and topographical features in light of
military and commercial advantages. Visions of use and improvement
prioritized nature and held together the scientific narration. Red oak was
suitable for rails and fences; Spanish oak for clapboards; bastard oak for

---

[76] *American Journal of Science* 22 (1832): 205–8; Oliver Goldsmith, *An History of the Earth and Animated Nature in Four Volumes* (Philadelphia, 1795), pp. 19–20.

[77] John Drayton, *A View of South Carolina, as Respects Her Natural and Civil Concerns* (Charleston, 1802), pp. 6, 8–11, 30.

fencing; and live oak, the most durable of all, for framing: "a nail once driven therein, 'tis next to an impossibility to draw it out."[78] With details pieced together from direct observation and personal conversation, naturalists compiled a surprisingly sophisticated practical understanding of this unknown country.[79]

Colonial natural history was also shaped by military needs. Compact settlement strategies left the British colonies vulnerable to Spanish and French influences on their western flanks, and no colonials were more sensitive to this than those who traveled for scientific reasons. Spanish and French explorers had mastered the art of combining scientific examination and military exploration, William Byrd complained, but after more than 130 years of settlement, British Americans "hardly know any thing of the Appalachian Mountains."[80] The French and Indian Wars highlighted this liability, creating a demand for topographical information about the West. Virginia physician and botanist, John Mitchell, published his *Map of the British and French Settlements in North America* in 1750 and 1755 to highlight the Ohio Valley's natural barriers, boundaries, roads, and rivers. In 1755, Lewis Evans explored the same region to compile his *General Map of the Middle British Colonies in North America*. Both carefully indicated where rivers and streams were navigable and where portages could be made from one drainage to the next. The French dominated the St. Lawrence, Lewis observed, because they fortified the strategic straights of Niagara: "those in power see at last its consequence." In his 1765 *Concise Account of North America*, Major Robert Rogers likewise warned that colonial officials, "so distant from the

---

[78] Lawson, *History of Carolina*, pp. 79–80, 85–6, 91–2, 95; Brickell, *Natural History of North-Carolina*, p. 12; Hanley, *Natural History in America*, p. 6. See Benjamin Lincoln, *A Description of the Situation, Climate, Soil, and Productions of Certain Tracts of Land in the District of Maine, and Commonwealth of Massachusetts* (Philadelphia, 1793), p. 6.

[79] See William Strickland, *Journal of a Tour in the United States of America, 1794–1795* (New York, 1971), p. 138; Clayton, *Miscellanea Curiosa*, pp. 285–7, 301–2, 324; Thomas, *Historical and Geographical Account*, p. 7; Lincoln, *Description of the Situation*, pp. 4–8; Pownall, *Topographical Description*, pp. 27–9.

[80] Byrd, *History of the Dividing Line*, Vol. 1, p. 152. See Daniel Coxe, "Preface," *A Description of the English Province of Carolana* (London, 1722), n.p.; Clayton, *Miscellanea Curiosa*, pp. 312–13; Carver, *Three Years Travels*, pp. xvii–xix; Byrd in Dorothy Anne Dondore, *The Prairie and the Making of Middle America: Four Centuries of Description* (Cedar Rapids, 1926), p. 99; Franklin, *Discoverers, Explorers, Settlers*, p. 48; Lawson, *History of Carolina*, pp. 85–6; Smallwood, *Natural History*, p. 122; Richard Blome, "Preface," *The Present State of His Majesties' Isles and Territories in America* (London, 1687), n.p.

seat of empire," would be well served to take their geography seriously, and John Bartram justified his own travels in New York and Florida on military grounds.[81]

Describing a land both useful and exotic, colonial natural history was also distinctively popular in its appeal compared to Europe's more erudite and gentlemanly science. This vernacular tone reflected the common origins and amateur status of American naturalists, the impulse to promote the West among prospective settlers, and the immense popular appeal of America's exotic plant and animal life. Appealing to popular curiosity, naturalists accented the most curious features of the American landscape. Bullfrogs produced a "roaring noise, hardly to be distinguished from that...of the beast from whom it takes it [name] sake," and skunks emitted a smell "ten times stronger and more offensive" than the European polecat. When a skunk encountered a dog, Brickell related, "they piss on their Tails and sprinkle it on him, by which means he shall smell a month or more, so that he is not to be suffered to come into the houses."[82] Opossums, with their "false bellies," prehensile tails, and curious sexual anatomy, were equally inviting: "the male's pizzle is placed retrograde; in time of coition, they differ from all other animals turning tail to tail."[83] Brickell described fiendish "tygers" on the far side of the mountains, with shining eyes and sharp teeth, ready to devour "man . . . or beast to satisfie their hunger," and Lawson insisted that American bears could seize a hunting dog and "blow his skin from his flesh, like a bladder, and often kill him."[84] Reports like these were irresistible to readers of all classes,

---

[81] Edmund Berkeley and Dorothy Smith Berkeley, *Dr. John Mitchell: The Man who Made the Map of North America* (Chapel Hill, 1974), pp. 175–6; Lewis Evans, *Geographical, Historical, Political, Philosophical, and Mechanical Essays* (Philadelphia, 1755), p. iii; Robert Rogers, *A Concise Account of North America, Containing a Description of the Several British Colonies on that Continent* (London, 1765), p. iii; Bartram, *Observations*, p. iii; William Stork, "Preface," Bartram, *Description of East-Florida*, p. vi. See Thomas Hallock, *From the Fallen Tree: Frontier Narratives, Environmental Politics, and the Roots of a National Pastoral, 1749–1826* (Chapel Hill, 2003), p. 30.

[82] Gabriel Thomas, *Historical and Geographical Account*, p. 16; Brickell, *Natural History of North-Carolina*, p. 118.

[83] Lawson, *History of Carolina*, p. 121; Brickell, *Natural History of North-Carolina*, p. 123. See Anon., *The Book of Nature* (Boston, 1826), pp. 43–4; Anon., *A Compendious Description of the Thirteen Colonies, in British-America* (London, 1777), pp. 17–18; Thomas, *Historical and Geographical Account*, pp. 13–16; Clayton, *Miscellanea Curiosa*, p. 338.

[84] Brickell, *Natural History of North-Carolina*, pp. 114–15; Lawson, *History of Carolina*, pp. 116–17; Peter Kalm in Gilbert Chinard, "Eighteenth-Century Theories on America as a Human Habitat," *APS Proceedings* 91 (February 1947): p. 33.

and this popular appetite for curiosities of nature fueled a tendency to present the American wilderness as a romantic mystery.

This nascent romanticism also drew on the adventure of wilderness travel. Endless forests, swollen rivers, terrifying storms, distressing heats, biting flies, concealed rattlesnakes, debilitating fevers, and unneighborly Indians laced the explorer's depiction of the West, even while their promotional instincts lent their descriptions an enthusiastically positive tone. William Bartram related several stories that highlighted nature's malignancy. "I was attacked on all sides," he wrote about one encounter with alligators; "two very large ones... rush[ed]... up with their heads and part of their bodies above the water, roaring terribly and belching floods of water over me. They struck their jaws together so close to my ears, as almost to stun me, and I expected every moment to be dragged out of the boat and instantly devoured." Swamps, with their thick vegetation, black organic soils, and loathsome or terrifying creatures, added more texture to the adventure. Brickell described the roar of the alligator in its den as akin to "some diabolical Spirit breaking through the bowels of the earth."[85] Bartram bolted out of his sleep one night as the "terrifying screams of Owls" reverberated through the swamp "in dreadful peals." As he drifted between dream and reality, he imagined a crocodile "dashing my canoe against the roots of the tree, endeavouring to get into her for the fish," and he later dreamt of the crocodile dragging him into the river. He awoke to find "the monster on the top of the bank,... not above two yards distant." Violence bound together a nightmarish world of predator and prey; creatures interacted, as Catesby's biographer puts it, by devouring one another.[86]

Despite these hardships, naturalists also found occasion to present nature, even in its primitive state, as a paradise; Bartram's writings in particular included rumors of lost Edenic civilizations, fragrant bowers of orange and date trees, and allusions to redemption.[87] Yet, his descriptions were never one-dimensional. Describing a wolf that stole into his camp

---

[85] Bartram, *Travels*, p. 76; John Bartram to Peter Collinson, February 21, 1756, Berkeley and Berkeley, *Correspondence of John Bartram*, p. 400; Bartram to Peter Templeman, July 6, 1761, ibid., p. 525; Lawson, *History of Carolina*, p. 26; Brickell, *Natural History of North-Carolina*, p. 137.

[86] Bartram, *Travels*, p. 86; Chaplin in Meyers and Prichard, *Empire's Nature*, pp. 69–70.

[87] Bartram, *Travels*, pp. 117–18. See Strickland, *Journal of a Tour*, p. 131; John Bartram to Alexander Garden, March 25, 1762, Darlington, *Memorials of John Bartram and Humphry Marshall*, p. 398; Kastner, *Species of Eternity*, p. 36; Kalm, *Travels*, Vol. 1, p. 133; Brickell, *Natural History of North-Carolina*, pp. 91, 93–4; Arner, "Pastoral Patterns," p. 138; Franklin, *Discoverers, Explorers, Settlers*, p. 60.

one night and dragged off several fish hanging from a tree, he revealed his ambiguity about nature in the new land. The wolf was clearly a threat, but its decision to forego a greater evil seemed evidence of a curious moral choice:

How much easier . . . might it have been for him to have leaped upon my breast in the dead of sleep, and torn my throat . . . and then glutted his stomach for the present with my warm blood, and dragged off my body, which would have made a feast afterwards for him and his howling associates; . . . than to have made protracted and circular approaches, and then after, by chance, espying the fish over my head, with the greatest caution and silence rear up, and take them off the snags one by one, then make off with them, and that so cunningly as not to awaken me until he had fairly accomplished his purpose.[88]

The wolf's forbearance puzzled Bartram, and he was not alone in finding both violence and benevolence in natural law. Lawson noted the bounty of deer, turkey, and partridge along the banks of the Cape Fear River but, without so much as a break in sentence, he passed on to a darker reflection: "We likewise heard several wolves howling in the woods, and saw where they had torn a deer in pieces."[89]

On his journey through Florida, Bartram discovered a deep, clear pool fringed by orange, palm, and magnolia trees that, like the story of the wolf, suggested both the brighter and darker sides of nature. "The balmy air vibrates the melody of the merry birds, tenants of the encircling aromatic grove," he wrote. In the pool were fish of various sizes and species, all moving about "peaceably and complaisantly" in the crystal waters. This "free and unsuspicious intercourse" intrigued him: the fish – predator and prey – seemed oblivious to the enemies in their midst. Still, Bartram reminded his readers, this "peaceable and happy state of nature" was an illusion. The pool offered no cover, no possibility of ambush, and the pellucidity of the waters made the predator's stealth impossible. "The trout freely passes by the very nose of the alligator and laughs in his face, and the bream by the trout." Bartram was clearly attracted to nature's Edenic possibilities, but he was never completely convinced of its essential goodness.[90] Fearsome creatures still roamed the transmontane wilderness.

---

[88] Bartram, *Travels*, p. 101. See William Bartram in Earnest, *John and William Bartram*, p. 114; Edelstein, "America's First Native Botanists," p. 56; Grove, *Green Imperialism*, p. 32; Fagin, *William Bartram*, p. 38.

[89] Lawson, *History of Carolina*, pp. 67–8.

[90] Bartram, *Travels*, pp. 104–5. See Bartram in Arner, "Pastoral Patterns," p. 137.

Each turning of the courses, as Thomas Pownall put it, was to be dreaded as well as relished. Yet, if naturalists were uncertain about what the wilderness was, they were absolutely sure about what it would become. This was clear in the changing tone of Pownall's narrative when, after weeks of travel in the Connecticut backcountry, he emerged from the thick woods, stood atop a hill above the town of New Haven, and saw before him a template for understanding the confusing and chaotic land to the west. In a rush of lyrical prose, he described the pleasing geometric forms New Haven's founders had sculpted from the woods and hills. The town was centered on a square, "from the angles of which go off, in right lines, eight streets." To the north lay the "great vale" of the Connecticut, equally exquisite in its arrangement of "woods & rivulets, amidst cleared & cultured lands teeming with abundance." Here, nature's exuberant primal energies were controlled and cultivated and the meaning of the landscape was made clear.[91] A half-century later, western explorer Caleb Atwater paused on a hill overlooking the Ohio River, fixing in his mind a similar panorama of nature and civilization that would order his interpretation of the wilderness that lay to the westward:

Looking [back] towards the East,... you behold a beautiful country of hill and dale spread out before you, divided into convenient and well-cultivated farms, intersected by glittering streams, meandering through them towards the Ohio. You hear the lowing of numerous herds..., the shrill matin of the songsters of the forests, and the busy hum of the industrious husbandman; you see here and there a clump of trees interspersed among the cultivated parts of the country; you see the comfortable dwelling house, the substantial barn, and hear the rumbling noise of the mill."[92]

Cartographer John Mitchell once summarized the complicated moral and physical landscapes of the West as "one continued and thick forest," thus avoiding the colossal ambiguities in a landscape that shifted abruptly, in a single turning of the courses, from one meaning to its opposite.[93] In these decades, Mitchell's forest world was best understood in simple terms as an antipode, an untilled garden awaiting the hand of the settler and husbandman. However, even in this starkly practical era, explorers

---

[91] Pownall, *Topographical Description*, pp. 58–9, 102. See Brickell, *Natural History of North-Carolina*, pp. 10–11.

[92] Caleb Atwater, "Notice of the Scenery, Geology, Mineralogy, Botany, &c. of Belmont County, Ohio," *American Journal of Science* 1 (1818): p. 226.

[93] John Mitchell and Arthur Young, *American Husbandry: Containing an Account of the Soil, Climate, Production of the British Colonies in North-America and the West-Indies* (London, 1775), Vol. 1, p. 58.

were beginning to see nature in its own light, and as they later penetrated this thick forest and parsed its many levels of meaning, they described a complicated but delightful new-world panorama. Regarding nature on more intimate terms, they saw it less as a prelude to civilization and more as a refuge from civilization's ills. The untilled garden was also a paradise: a land worth considering – and preserving – as an end in itself.

2

Rambles in Eden

In Spring 1808, at the end of a wearying transatlantic voyage, 22-year-old Yorkshire native, Thomas Nuttall, stood at the bow of a ship and gathered in his first impression of the brooding American forest stretching back from the Delaware capes. More than three decades later, the sense of expectancy and wonder was still palpable as he wrote about the experience in a preface to his natural history of American trees: "My eyes were riveted on the landscape with intense admiration," he related. "All was new! – and life, like that season, was then full of hope and enthusiasm. The forests, seemingly unbroken in their primeval solitude and repose, spread themselves on either hand as we passed placidly along. The unending vista of dark pines gave an air of deep sadness to the wilderness."[1] Admiration and anticipation, sadness and solitude, and, above all, the exhilarating prospect of a primeval woods – these were the impressions that stayed with Nuttall and shaped his record of nature as he crossed and recrossed America on his scientific rambles.

Thomas Nuttall's reflections help explain the personal expectation explorers held going into the American backcountry.[2] The challenge was formidable. When Thomas Jefferson asked Meriwether Lewis to lead a

---

[1] Thomas Nuttall, *The North American Sylva* (Philadelphia, 1842), Vol. 1, p. ix. See Jeannette E. Graustein, *Thomas Nuttall: Naturalist Explorations in America, 1808–1841* (Cambridge, 1967), p. 2.

[2] Patricia Tyson Stroud, *The Emperor of Nature: Charles-Lucien Bonaparte and His World* (Philadelphia, 2000), p. 54; Thomas Hallock, *From the Fallen Tree: Frontier Narratives, Environmental Politics, and the Roots of a National Pastoral, 1749–1826* (Chapel Hill, 2003), p. 6.

scientific expedition through the Louisiana Territory in 1803, he wrote in confidence to University of Pennsylvania Professor Benjamin Barton, remarking that he had been "many years wishing to have the Missouri explored, & whatever river heading with that, runs into the Western ocean," but he deemed it futile to proceed without a scientist to record the natural wonders along the way. Finally, he selected Captain Lewis, relying on the Virginia frontiersman to guide the party through the western wilderness and on his Philadelphia friends to tutor Lewis in the fundamentals of natural history. He explained to Barton:

It was impossible to find a character who is a compleat [authority]... in botany, natural history, mineralogy & astronomy, joined [with] the firmness of constitution & character, prudence, habits adapted to the woods, & a familiarity with the Indian manners & character, requisite for this undertaking. All the latter qualifications, Capt. Lewis has[,] altho' no regular botanist.... He will be with you in Philadelphia in two or three weeks, & will... receive thankfully... any verbal communication which you may be so good as to make to him. I make no apology for this trouble, because I know that the same wish to promote science which has induced me to bring forward this proposition, will induce you to aid in promoting it.[3]

Coached by Barton and his colleagues, Lewis performed credibly as naturalist to the Corps of Discovery in 1804–5, but the question implicit in Jefferson's letter remained unanswered: Could America muster a corps of explorers with the wilderness savvy and the scientific acumen necessary to complete the natural history begun by Lewis and Clark? Nuttall, whose career ranged from the halls of Harvard to the wilderness West, provides some insights into how this challenge was met.

Born in 1786 in a Yorkshire village, Thomas Nuttall was apprenticed to an uncle in 1800 to learn printing. Intrigued by the idea of America, he left for Philadelphia in 1808 and began botanizing in the woods and fields around the city. When he discovered a small vine he was unable to identify, he visited Benjamin Barton, who offered the enthusiastic young Englishman a brief instruction and sent him out on two collecting trips, the first to the Chesapeake Bay marshes and the second to the southern shores of Lakes Erie and Ontario. Nuttall proved an excellent field naturalist: enthusiastic, at home in the wilds, oblivious to danger, and eager to discuss his business with strangers who might provide information.[4]

[3] Thomas Jefferson to Benjamin Smith Barton, February 27, 1803, Benjamin Smith Barton Papers, Correspondence, Pennsylvania Historical Society (hereafter PHS).
[4] Joseph Kastner, *A Species of Eternity* (New York, 1977), pp. 129, 256–7.

Casting his gaze westward, Nuttall joined a fraternity of scientists dedicated to garnering knowledge by rambling: a form of scientific travel best described as part aimless wandering and part planned expedition. With a vast field of "undescript" species before them and no set plan of travel, they trusted to serendipitous discovery, obliging local contacts, and an eclectic technique devoted to observing virtually anything new and curious that crossed their path. In 1810–11, Nuttall accompanied a band of Astor Company traders to the Mandan country on the upper Missouri and fell in with Scottish naturalist, John Bradbury. In 1818–20, he traveled the Arkansas and Red River region and in 1822 became curator of Harvard's botanical garden. He remained in Cambridge for eleven years, publishing botanical and ornithological manuals. However, as historian John Moring points out, his "burning curiosity" could "only be quenched by plunging into the field" and, in 1834, he resigned his chair and set off again for the West, this time on Captain Nathaniel J. Wyeth's expedition to the Pacific Ocean. After a year in the Pacific Northwest, he sailed to the Sandwich Islands and returned to prepare specimens at the Academy of Natural Sciences in Philadelphia. By then one of the great field naturalists of his generation, Nuttall became embroiled in an argument with Asa Gray, who held the chair at Harvard that he had vacated.[5] In 1842, he inherited a small estate near Liverpool, but the terms of the bequest required him to remain in England. Tired of wandering and perhaps alienated from academic botanists like Gray, he accepted the conditions. In England, he prepared a three-volume appendix to François-André Michaux's *North American Sylva*. Aside from one trip back to the United States in 1847–8, he spent the rest of his life on his estate, where he died in 1859.[6]

Well before 1808, scientists were beginning to piece together the natural history of America, but it was left to Nuttall's generation to fill the significant gaps and interpret nature on its own terms rather than as a material base for an expanding empire. Given the vast natural

[5] John Moring, *Early American Naturalists: Exploring the American West, 1804–1900* (New York, 2002), p. 58. See Thomas Nuttall, *Journal of Travels into the Arkansa* [sic] *Territory, During the Year 1819* (Philadelphia, 1821), p. vi; Frederick Brendel, "Historical Sketch of the Science of Botany in North America from 1635 to 1840," *The Naturalist* 13 (November 1879): p. 766; Reuben Gold Thwaites, "Introduction," in John Bradbury, *Travels in the Interior of America, in the Years 1809, 1810, and 1811* (Cleveland, 1904 [c. 1819]), p. 12; Graustein, *Thomas Nuttall*, pp. 128–9, 131.
[6] Kastner, *Species of Eternity*, p. 260, 308; *North American Review*, n.s., 59 (July 1844): p. 193.

differences across the continent, from Florida's palm-studded plains to the rolling hardwood hills of the Middle West and the spruce forests of the North, this was no small undertaking, and those who responded occupied a unique place in the history of American science, combining the adventuresome spirit of Meriwether Lewis and the keen scientific curiosity of Lewis's mentor, Benjamin Barton.[7] Their arrival was timely; they explored the West at a point when fire, ax, and musket were altering its landscapes dramatically, and their scientific interpretations of this momentous change set the stage for an American conservation tradition.

Thomas Nuttall was the archetypal American naturalist, but the true contemporary model for these scientific adventurers was Prussian naturalist, Alexander von Humboldt, whose wide-ranging travels and expansive interpretations epitomized early nineteenth-century science.[8] Humboldt represents the best of two European scientific personalities: the explorer and the *philosophe*. The latter tradition, a deductive science bent on uniting the truths emerging from every branch of knowledge in this Enlightened age, was introduced into natural history by George-Louis Leclerc, Comte de Buffon, director of the Jardin du Roi in Paris. As the world's first modern natural scientist, Buffon was immensely influential in separating natural history from biblical and classical dogma and establishing the basis for modern deductive inquiry. His forty-four-volume *Histoire naturelle*, begun in 1749, combined cosmological speculations about the origin of the earth with a rigorous interpretative logic applied to even the smallest details of life on the planet.[9] An archetypical philosopher, Buffon was a synthesizer and logician of the first order but hardly an explorer. Humboldt was both: he gathered his facts firsthand and deduced from these observations a systematic understanding of the universe.

In 1799, Humboldt received patronage from the Court at Madrid to map out the physical and botanical geography of the Spanish possessions in America. While there, he ascended the slopes of Ecuador's 18,000-foot Mount Chimborazo, keeping a careful record of changes in elevation, electrical tension, humidity, atmospheric composition, light intensity and refraction, geology, botany, and gravity. Based on comprehensive observations like these, he devised, among many other things, methods for

---

[7] Nuttall, *North American Sylva*, p. x.

[8] Michael Dettelbach, "Humboldtian Science," in N. Jardine, J. A. Secord, and E. C. Spary, *Cultures of Natural History* (Cambridge, 1996), p. 291; Stroud, *Emperor of Nature*, p. 55.

[9] David R. Oldroyd, *Thinking About the Earth: A History of Ideas in Geology* (Cambridge, 1996), pp. 89, 90.

mapping and defining life zones and isothermal lines.[10] He returned from the Americas a scientific hero and spent the next twenty-two years in Paris publishing the results of his travels in some thirty volumes. He finished his *Cosmos*, the great summary explanation of all these experiences, at age 90, two months before his death in 1859. Humboldt's example was powerful because he observed so broadly and speculated so boldly. His true genius was generalizing – discovering principles and associations that were "everywhere the same," as he continually assured his readers. For those who followed in Humboldt's footsteps, the ideal in science would be the connection: the general law that brought together insights from across the disciplines and ultimately combined all natural dynamics into a single system.[11] This dialectic of observation and speculation brought many facets of nature together into a single system that connected everything the naturalist observed to everything else. Thus, the naturalist's ramble was a beginning point for ecological thinking in America.

Naturalists in the Early Republic

Inspired by Humboldt and following in the footsteps of Nuttall, literally hundreds of naturalists crossed the Appalachian Mountains in the early decades of the century, fanning out into the American West to explore, discover, and explain. Aside from their shared curiosity, their wanderlust, and their passion for connections, they were a diverse lot. Some were trained scientists; others, a subgroup of the upper-class European tourist on the Grand Tour of North America. Their commitment to rigor varied but, at their best, they provided a running commentary on all aspects of nature and frontier life in America. Following a few of the most important into the middle-western wilderness helps explain why they traveled so extensively and what they saw as important in the changing panorama of nature and settlement in the West.

Apart from Nuttall, the most influential was André Michaux. Born at Satory, France, in 1746, Michaux developed a passion for botany and moved to Paris to be near the Jardin du Roi and its chief botanist, the Comte de Buffon. Here, he became interested in exotic species that might enrich his home country and, with this in mind, he contracted with the

---

[10] Dettelbach, "Humboldtian Science," pp. 290–1; Louis Agassiz, *Address Delivered on the Centennial Anniversary of the Birth of Alexander von Humboldt* (Boston, 1869), pp. 6, 8–12, 15.

[11] Agassiz, *Alexander von Humboldt*, pp. 12, 26, 28–9.

French government in 1782 to travel first to the Mediterranean and then to North America.[12] Michaux was undoubtedly aware of English botanist John Evelyn's *Discourse of Forest-Trees and the Propagation of Timber in His Majesty's Dominions*, first published in 1664, and enlarged in 1776–86 by Alexander Hunter. Convinced that understanding trees was vital to their preservation, Evelyn studied and inventoried those in Europe, and Hunter expanded his list with species from North America. Influenced by France's landmark Forest Ordinance of 1669, Michaux acted on similar concerns in his country.[13]

Arriving in New York in September 1785, Michaux established nurseries in New Jersey and South Carolina and, with his son François André, collected specimens from Hudson Bay west to the Mississippi. In all, he shipped home more than sixty thousand plants and forty boxes of seeds. For his grandest adventure, he hoped to cross the Rocky Mountains to the Pacific, and with this in mind, he laid his plans for an expedition before Secretary of State Thomas Jefferson, who passed his proposition to the American Philosophical Society (APS). The Society procured a subscription and offered Michaux a contract that became a prototype for the Lewis and Clark expedition, launched by Jefferson in consultation with the APS a decade later. Society president, Caspar Wistar, advised Michaux to "find the shortest & most convenient route of communication between the U.S. & the Pacific ocean,... & to learn such particulars as can be obtained of the country through which it passes." Michaux was to record the names and customs of the Indian nations and to watch for mammoths.[14] His plans, however, were cut short when French ambassador Edmond Charles Genêt recruited him to help carry out a complicated scheme designed to draw western settlers into France's war with

---

[12] Kastner, *Species of Eternity*, p. 114; Henry Savage, Jr., and Elizabeth J. Savage, *André and François André Michaux* (Charlottesville, 1986), pp. 9, 11, 34–5.

[13] John Evelyn, *Sylva: Or, A Discourse of Forest-Trees and the Propagation of Timber in His Majesty's Dominions*, annotated by A. Hunter (New York, 1786), pp. 2–3, 69; Clarence Glacken, *Traces on the Rhodian Shore: Nature and Culture in Western Thought from Ancient Times to the End of the Eighteenth Century* (Berkeley, 1967), p. 491.

[14] Charlotte M. Porter, *The Eagle's Nest: Natural History and American Ideas, 1812–1842* (Tuscaloosa, 1986), p. 22; Brendel, "Historical Sketch," pp. 760–1; *North American Review*, n.s., 59 (July 1844): pp. 192–3; Savage and Savage, *André and François André Michaux*, pp. 126–30; Thomas Jefferson to Benjamin Smith Barton, December 2, 1792, Barton Papers, Correspondence, PHS; "Instructions from the American Philosophical Society to Andrew [sic] Michaud for Exploring the Country along the Missouri and thence Westwardly to the Pacific Ocean," Caspar Wistar Papers, no. 27, American Philosophical Society (hereafter APS).

England and Spain. When Genêt's plan disintegrated, Michaux abandoned his Pacific expedition project and set out for the Great Lakes in 1795. He returned to France in 1796 but found that his nurseries at Rambouillet had been neglected during the country's political turmoil. Frustrated in his plans for reforesting France, he turned to writing. In 1801, he published *Oaks of North America*, then ventured on a collecting expedition to Madagascar, where he died of fever in 1802, leaving his most significant work, *Flora boreali-americana*, unfinished.[15]

In October 1801, Michaux's son, François-André, crossed the Atlantic to complete his father's work. His own rambles took him across the Appalachians and down the Ohio through some 1,800 miles of wilderness. Along the way, he gathered information about trees and their uses from carpenters and shipbuilders and, back in France in 1810–13, he combined his father's manuscripts with his own findings and published *North American Sylva*.[16] "No tree [is] so generally useful as the oak," he began this great work. "It is everywhere the most highly esteemed in the construction of houses and of vessels, and is commonly selected for implements of husbandry. It seems, also, to have been multiplied by nature in proportion to its utility." *Silva* was translated into English in 1819 and enhanced by the supplemental volumes produced by Nuttall in 1842–9.[17]

André and François-André Michaux contributed immeasurably to American taxonomy. Like Evelyn, they compiled their knowledge as a first step in conserving trees, and they included in their taxonomies ecological considerations like soil and moisture requirements, growth habits, succession, and recommendations for cultivation. Although they were seldom openly critical of American forest practices, they highlighted the need to preserve certain valuable species.[18] As the younger Michaux put

[15] Savage and Savage, *André and François André Michaux*, pp. 4, 65, 135, 184; *Medical Repository*, 2d ser., 2 (1805): 406–8; Kastner, *Species of Eternity*, p. 118.

[16] Francois-André Michaux, *Travels to the West of the Allegheny Mountains, in the States of Ohio, Kentucky, and Tennessea* [sic], ... *Undertaken in the Year 1802* (London, 1805), pp. 23–4; Savage and Savage, *André and François André Michaux*, pp. 217, 224, 227, 231, 356; Elias Durand, "Biographical Memoir of the Late Francois Andre Michaux," *American Journal of Science*, n.s., 24 (November 1857): pp. 161–5; François André Michaux, *Prospectus: The North American Sylva, 1817*, Broadsides, APS.

[17] Francois André Michaux, *The North American Sylva* (Philadelphia, 1871), pp. 13, 24.

[18] *Medical Repository*, 2d ser., 2 (1805): pp. 394–5; Darlington, "Progress of Botany in North America," in William Darlington, *Memorials of John Bartram and Humphrey Marshall* (New York, 1967 [c.1849]), p. 24; William Jackson Hooker, "On the Botany of America," *American Journal of Science* 9 (no. 2, 1825): p. 268; Jacob Richard Schramm,

it, "I am of opinion, that a bad tree ought not to be suffered to exist in a soil, where a better one could grow; and there is no country, where it is more important to make a choice, than in America." *North American Sylva* provided Americans with a first thorough understanding of their trees, and for this it remains an important benchmark in American conservation.[19]

If the Michaux gave birth to American forestry, Alexander Wilson fathered the American study of birds. Born in Scotland in 1766, Wilson left school at an early age, apprenticed with a weaver in Paisley, and traveled as a journeyman across the Highlands, writing poetry to express his love of the land. After emigrating to Philadelphia in 1793, he grew despondent as a country schoolmaster and sought solace from William Bartram, who recommended nature study as a way of relieving his depression. After consulting several published works on American birds, he turned "from these barren and musty records to . . . the Grand Aviary of Nature" and resolved to compile his own ornithology.[20] In 1805, he wrote to Thomas Jefferson that he found an "innocent and delighfull retreat from the sometimes harassing business of life in . . . drawing many of these charming songsters of the grove with a view at some future day of publishing . . . all the birds resident in . . . the United States."[21] When he had completed around a hundred drawings, he found a publisher, and the first volume appeared in September 1808.

Confident that he could fill the gaps left by Catesby and others, Wilson toured the northeastern states in 1810 collecting birds and book subscriptions.[22] He bought an open skiff in Pittsburgh and set out on the Ohio, and at Lexington chanced upon John James Audubon at work in his

"Influence – Past and Present – of François-André Michaux on Forestry and Forest Research in America," *APS Proceedings* 101 (no. 4, 1957): pp. 337–8.

[19] Francois André Michaux, *Prospectus, The North American Sylva, 1817*. See Schramm, "Influence – Past and Present – of François-André Michaux," p. 337.

[20] Alexander Wilson to Thomas Crichton, November 2, 1790, in Clark Hunte (ed.), *The Life and Letters of Alexander Wilson* (Philadelphia, 1983), pp. 47–9, 62–70, 137; Wilson, *American Ornithology* (Philadelphia, 1878), pp. xi–xvii, li; Henry T. Tuckerman, *America and Her Commentators, with a Critical Sketch of Travel in the United States* (New York, 1864), pp. 199–200; Elsa Guerdrum Allen, *The History of American Ornithology Before Audubon* (Philadelphia, 1951), p. 554; "Wilson, the Ornithologist," pp. 361–2; Wayne Hanley, *Natural History in America: From Mark Catesby to Rachel Carson* (New York, 1977), p. 48; Kastner, *Species of Eternity*, p. 162.

[21] Alexander Wilson to Thomas Jefferson, September 30, 1805, in Hunter, *Life and Letters of Alexander Wilson*, p. 245; "Wilson, the Ornithologist," p. 363.

[22] Alexander Wilson to George Ord, June 23, 1820, in Elliott Coues (ed.), "Private Letters of Wilson, Ord, and Bonaparte," *Penn Monthly* 10 (June 1879), pp. 443–55; Wilson,

store. In an encounter made mythical by biographers of both parties, Wilson displayed his two volumes and asked Audubon to take a subscription. Audubon, by his own account, was agreeable but was dissuaded by his business partner, who proclaimed Audubon's own unpublished sketches the better of the two. Audubon's weak financial situation was probably the more important consideration.[23] While Wilson continued his rambling, *American Ornithology* took form. Ambitious and expensive, it put the country's commitment to natural history to the test. "We should feel a degree of . . . mortification, if an undertaking of such beauty and extent should be discontinued through the failure of patronage," New York naturalist Samuel Mitchell wrote in his *Medical Repository*. Mitchell reported in 1811 that "with a spirit that does honour to our country," subscribers had underwritten the subsequent volumes. Wilson, however, died of tuberculosis in 1813, and the last volumes were completed by Philadelphian George Ord.[24]

Despite its cost, *Ornithology* launched a new era in American natural history. Appealing directly to a nonscientific readership of farmers, country gentlemen, amateur naturalists, and women of leisure, Wilson was an important force in bringing nature before the American public. He described each bird's habits, color, shape, song, migration pattern, and behavior in graceful prose and included anecdotes from his travels. A critic wrote in 1812 that Wilson's manner, "although sometimes . . . perhaps too colloquial for a work of science, has about it an originality and a stamp of truth, which is of far greater importance." His casual but authoritative style and his warm sense of affection for his subjects appealed to an emerging romantic temperament. "I believe," he once wrote, "a Scotsman [is] better fitted for descriptions of rural scenes than those of any other nation on earth. His country affords the most picturesque and striking scenery; his heart and imagination [are] warm and animated, . . . his taste is highly improved by the numberless pathetic

American Ornithology, pp. xxv, xlv–xlviii, li, lxxi; *North American Review*, n.s., 24 (January 1827): p. 116.

23 Wilson, *American Ornithology*, p. lxxii, lxxviii–lxxix; Alexander Wilson to George Ord, June 23, 1820, in Coues, "Private Letters of Wilson, Ord, and Bonaparte," pp. 450–1; Richard Rhodes, *John James Audubon: The Making of an American* (New York, 2004), p. 67; Robert Buchanan, *The Life and Adventures of John James Audubon, the Naturalist, Edited from Materials Supplied by his Widow* (London, 1868), pp. 20–1; Allen, *History of American Ornithology*, p. 562.

24 *Medical Repository*, 2d ser., 6 (1809): pp. 157–8; ibid., 3d ser., 2 (1811): p. 47; Kastner, *Species of Eternity*, p. 169; Allen, *History of American Ornithology*, pp. 563–4; *North American Review*, n.s., 24 (January 1827): p. 116.

ballads and songs handed down from generation to generation."[25] Wilson's great horned owl was a "ghostly watchman" who warned him of morning's approach by "sweeping down and around my fire, uttering a loud and sudden Waugh O! Waugh O! sufficient to have alarmed a whole garrison." Alone in the forest, he found these "nocturnal solos" melodious and entertaining, even though they resembled the "half-suppressed screams of a person suffocating or throttled." Wilson's mix of empirical observation and romantic imagination set a new standard for American natural history.[26]

Following closely in Wilson's footsteps, John James Audubon likewise displayed the prerequisites outlined in Jefferson's letter: intense scientific curiosity, love of the wilds, and a passion for sharing discoveries with others. Audubon was born in Santo Domingo in 1785. His father owned a small fleet of trading vessels and land in Santo Domingo, Louisiana, and later at Mill Grove northwest of Philadelphia. His mother, the captain's mistress, died six months after his birth, and when the boy was three, his father took him to France, where he grew up under his foster mother's care. At age 18, Audubon moved to the Mill Grove estate and, with his dog Zephyr, explored the countryside and honed his skills as hunter and marksman.[27] In 1806, he became engaged to Lucy Bakewell, who lived nearby, and after a short merchant apprenticeship in New York City, he married Lucy, and together they traveled down the Ohio to Lexington, where he and his friend Ferdinand Rosier established a store.[28]

While Rosier stuck to the counter in Lexington, Audubon roamed the woods with his hunting companions and accumulated a portfolio containing some two hundred life-size illustrations. In 1810, Audubon and Rosier moved their store down river to Henderson, Kentucky, and when this location proved no more promising, they ended their partnership,

[25] *Port Folio* 8, 2d ser. (July 1812): pp. 1–2, 7. See James Ellsworth De Kay, *Anniversary Address on the Progress of Natural Sciences in the United States* (New York, 1826), pp. 37, 43; *Medical Repository,* 2d ser., 6 (1809): pp. 155–7; Allen, *History of American Ornithology,* pp. 558, 560; Alexander Wilson to Charles Orr, July 15, 1802, in Hunter, *Life and Letters of Alexander Wilson,* pp. 193–4.

[26] Alexander Wilson and Charles Lucian Bonaparte, *American Ornithology: or, the Natural History of the Birds of the United States* (Philadelphia, n.d.), p. 94; Wilson in Whitfield J. Bell, Jr., et al., *A Cabinet of Curiosities: Five Episodes in the Evolution of American Museums* (Charlottesville, 1967), p. 73; *Port Folio* 8, 2d ser. (July 1812): pp. 1–2, 7.

[27] Buchanan, *Life and Adventures of John James Audubon,* pp. 1–2, 16; Rhodes, *John James Audubon,* p. 4; Kastner, *Species of Eternity,* 207.

[28] Francis Hobart Herrick, *Audubon the Naturalist: A History of His Life and Time* (New York, 1917), Vol. 1, pp. 302, 110, 171–2; Buchanan, *Life and Adventures of John James Audubon,* pp. vi–vii, 3–7, 17–19; Kastner, *Species of Eternity,* pp. 210–13.

and Audubon entered a series of unrewarding ventures with his brother-in-law Thomas Bakewell. In 1819, he moved to Cincinnati to prepare specimens at the newly founded Western Museum and, after showing his drawings to several naturalists, he set out, like Wilson, to depict every bird in America – an audacious undertaking for an émigré with little formal training in art, no background in natural history, and no funds or patronage. Over the next five years, Audubon crisscrossed the West, surviving as a portrait painter and art and fencing instructor while Lucy tutored children near New Orleans and raised their two boys.[29]

Adrift geographically and socially, Audubon, like Wilson, developed his own techniques for illustration. Where earlier naturalists represented specimens in profile, Audubon often drew birds in groups, using multiple perspectives against a background that told much about their habitat. Early on, he developed a technique for passing wires through a freshly killed specimen to manipulate its position into characteristic poses and, using this device, he mastered the foreshortening, dramatization, and attitude necessary to make his illustrations seem, as one biographer said, "more lifelike than life itself."[30]

In April 1824, Audubon exhibited his drawings in Philadelphia, and although he garnered a few encouraging comments, no engraver was willing to attempt his life-size renditions. In part, this lukewarm reception resulted from his outsider status as the "American woodsman" – a self-designation that set him apart from the academy naturalists – and, in part, it reflected his own somewhat self-centered and abrasive personality.[31] Audubon also suffered at the hands of a few key members of the Philadelphia establishment, notably George Ord. Wealthy, privileged, and known for his rudeness, Ord built his reputation around editing the eighth volume of Wilson's *American Ornithology*, and he took upon himself the task of defending Wilson against Audubon's claims as America's leading ornithologist. As Audubon's work gained stature, enemies like Ord lost ground, but while he labored over his early volumes, he received little support from the scientific community.[32]

[29] Herrick, *Audubon the Naturalist*, Vol. 1, pp. 198, 236–7, 245, 254, 301, 303.
[30] Kastner, *Species of Eternity*, p. 223.
[31] Buchanan, *Life and Adventures of John James Audubon*, p. vi.
[32] Allen, *History of American Ornithology*, p. 564; Herrick, *Audubon the Naturalist*, Vol. 1, pp. 5, 231–2, 363, 439; Stroud, *Emperor of Nature*, pp. 52, 56; Rhodes, *John James Audubon*, p. 221. See Edmund Berkeley and Dorothy Smith Berkeley, *George William Featherstonhaugh: The First U.S. Government Geologist* (Tuscaloosa, 1988), p. 95; Hanley, *Natural History in America*, p. 68; George Ord in Stroud 1992,

Finding American printers unreceptive, Audubon exhibited in Edinburgh, where he caught the attention of William Lizars, a well-known engraver who offered to publish the drawings. Thus began one of the most ambitious natural history projects ever attempted. Over the next twelve years, between 1826 and 1838, Audubon, Lizars, and Robert Havell oversaw the production of more than one hundred thousand individually colored plates.[33] Striving for perfection, Audubon examined each of the early plates "at great leisure" and returned those with faults. He hoped to see them, as he wrote to Lucy, "finished in such superb style as to eclipse all of the kind in existence." Published in four massive volumes, *Birds of America* remains America's greatest monument to ornithology.[34] Audubon next published his *Ornithological Biography*, a textual accompaniment to the illustrations, and finally he collaborated with Charleston's eminent zoologist, John Bachman, on *The Viviparous Quadrupeds of North America*, a work that owes more to Bachman than to Audubon.[35] This being his last major publication, Audubon retired to his farm on Manhattan Island, where he died in 1851.

In 1835, Audubon wrote to his son Victor that *Birds of America* would "be the standard of American Ornithology," and in a letter to Bachman written that same year, he proclaimed that he had "done rather more towards the completion of . . . [America's] ornithology than ever Alexr Wilson!"[36] Biographers still debate the relative merits of the two ornithologists. Despite Audubon's advantage in outliving Wilson by

pp. 260–1; *Monthly American Journal of Geology and Natural Science* 1 (April 1832): pp. 460–1.

[33] *Monthly American Journal of Geology and Natural Science* 1 (April 1832): p. 459. See Hanley, *Natural History in America*, p. 69; Patricia Tyson Stroud, *Thomas Say: New World Naturalist* (Philadelphia, 1992), p. 200; Herrick, *Audubon the Naturalist*, Vol. 1, p. 358, 389; ibid., Vol. 2, pp. 86–7; Kastner, *Species of Eternity*, pp. 216–19, 223, 228.

[34] John James Audubon to Lucy Audubon, December 1826, in John James Audubon, *Letters of John James Audubon, 1826–1840*, edited by Howard Horward Corning, (Boston, 1930), Vol. 1, p. 18. See Audubon to Robert Havell, Jr., June 29–30, 1830, in ibid., Vol. 1, p. 112; Hanley, *Natural History in America*, pp. 70–1; *Monthly American Journal of Geology and Natural Science* 1 (April 1832) p. 459; ibid., 1 (September 1831): p. 136; Herrick, *Audubon the Naturalist*, Vol. 2, p. 177.

[35] Lester D. Stephens, *Science, Race, and Religion in the American South: John Bachman and the Charleston Circle of Naturalists, 1815–1895* (Chapel Hill, 2000), pp. 17, 39, 41, 43, 49. See *North American Review*, n.s., 50 (April 1840): pp. 137, 403; *American Journal of Science* 39 (October 1840): p. 350; Rhodes, *John James Audubon*, p. 352.

[36] Kastner, *Species of Eternity*, p. 310; John James Audubon to Victor Audubon, January 14, 1834, in Audubon, *Letters of John James Audubon*, Vol. 2, p. 5; Audubon to John Bachman, December 1, 1835, in ibid., Vol. 2, p. 102.

nearly four decades, contemporaries considered Wilson the better scientist, as some do today. Wilson was more consistently engaged in scientific discourse, taking on renowned European naturalists who denigrated American fauna, and it was indeed Wilson's thoroughness, precision, and accuracy in arguing the superiority of American birds that won him the title "father of American ornithology."[37] Still, Audubon probably did more to shape popular impressions of nature. A contemporary found his prose more expressive: "he has not the solemn enthusiasm of Wilson, who . . . lived in a world of his own. Audubon's passion for the science, is . . . more easy, graceful, and such as others know better how to share."[38] At a time when naturalists were wooing the American public, this was an important distinction.

Nevertheless, it was Audubon's illustrations, not his prose, which captured popular attention. Audubon overwhelmed his readers with his huge folios, and he had better engravers and better technology, and thus the benefit of more faithful copies. His backgrounds were often drawn by others more expert in plants or insects than he was, but he lavished attention on every detail – color, configuration, proportion – and he was a master at conveying bird emotions. His illustrations, moreover, included sufficient botanical context to show "where the birds build and disport in their native woods."[39] Wilson drew his birds against a simpler background, a point that drew criticism from reviewers. Yet, if Audubon was the more facile illustrator, Wilson was the pioneer, both in his ornithology and in his wilderness travels. Thus, Audubon had "the path broken before him," as a reviewer commented; in many ways, he simply carried forward the illustrative and literary techniques innovated by Wilson.[40] Although the debate continues, it is important to look at them together as a benchmark in bringing nature before the American public. Despite

[37] Hans Huth, *Nature and the American: Three Centuries of Changing Attitudes* (Berkeley, 1957), p. 25; Kastner, *Species of Eternity*, p. 190; Hanley, *Natural History in America*, p. 52; Allen, *History of American Ornithology*, p. 553.

[38] *North American Review*, n.s., 41 (July 1835): p. 230.

[39] *Monthly American Journal of Geology and Natural Science* 1 (September 1831): p. 137. See *North American Review*, n.s., 50 (April 1840): p. 404; ibid., n.s., 41 (July 1835): pp. 195–6; John Bachman in Herrick, *Audubon the Naturalist*, Vol. 2, p. 63; Kastner, *Species of Eternity*, p. 237; William Martin Smallwood in collaboration with Mabel Sarah Coon Smallwood, *Natural History and the American Mind* (New York, 1941), pp. 116–17, 187.

[40] *Medical Repository*, 2d ser., 6 (1809): p. 162; Herrick, *Audubon the Naturalist*, Vol. 1, p. 207; *North American Review*, n.s., 41 (July 1835): pp. 195–6. See Smallwood, *Natural History and the American Mind*, p. 187.

their differences, they shared an uncommon skill at conveying their passion for birds, teaching Americans "to observe, to examine, and to love [the]... works of nature."[41] Both epitomized the romance of American natural history, demonstrating how the American people developed a stronger appreciation for nature in the middle decades of the century.

Not all naturalists were wanderers, of course. John Brickell of Savannah, who was terrified of serpents and "violent heats," traveled no farther than the neighboring forests but found an astonishing variety of new species. Jacob Bigelow collected within ten miles of Boston for his *Florula Bostoniensis*, on the assumption that his plants were typical of New England; and Henry Mühlenberg, pastor of the Lancaster Lutheran Church and a nationally respected botanist, collected more than eleven hundred plants within three miles of his home.[42] "Let others so the same," he urged, "and after collecting materials for a dozen of years a *Flora americae septintoralis* may be written."[43] Mühlenberg's dream of patching together a botany of America was not unrealistic; almost every state or region had its own naturalist. Harvard professor Samuel Williams published a *Natural and Civil History of Vermont* in 1794 and 1809, and although he was not an explorer, his careful observations and experiments were influential nationwide. Zadock Thompson, who traveled little but corresponded a great deal, added to Williams's work a three-volume *Natural, Civil, and Statistical History of Vermont*, published between 1838 and 1842. Jeremy Belknap's history of New Hampshire (1812), Benjamin Trumbull's history of Connecticut (1818), William D. Williamson's history of Maine (1839), Samuel P. Hildreth's *Contributions to the Early History of the North-West* (1863), and Daniel Drake's several studies of Cincinnati were compilations of local knowledge gained through similar correspondence.[44]

---

[41] *North American Review*, n.s., 50 (April 1840): p. 404.

[42] John Brickell to Benjamin Smith Barton, August 8, 1807, Barton Papers, Vol. 2, APS; John Brickell to Henry E. Mühlenberg, February 7, 1802, Henry E. Mühlenberg Manuscripts, PHS. (This is not the naturalist John Brickell of 1710?–1745 but rather an Irish physician who immigrated in Georgia and died in 1809); Jacob Bigelow, *Florula Bostoniensis: A Collection of Plants of Boston and Its Environs* (Boston, 1814), p. vi; Paul Anthony Wilson Wallace, "Henry Ernest Mühlenberg," *APS Proceedings* 92 (no. 2, 1948): pp. 107, 109; C. Earle Smith, "Henry Mühlenberg – Botanical Pioneer," *APS Proceedings* 106 (no. 5, 1962): p. 443.

[43] Henry Mühlenberg to Manasseh Cutler, April 11, 1791, Manasseh Cutler Papers, APS. See Graustein, *Thomas Nuttall*, p. 27; Bartram *Travels*, p. xxxi.

[44] Zadock Thompson, *Natural History of Vermont: An Address Delivered at Boston, Before the Boston Society of Natural History* (Burlington, 1850), pp. 3–5; Samuel

The local naturalist who most endeared himself to the American public was John Godman of Philadelphia. Godman studied medicine at the University of Maryland, practiced in various western towns and in New York City, then returned in 1822 to Philadelphia, where he died in 1830. As a country doctor, he inspected nature a few steps from the dooryard, and like England's Gilbert White, his morning walks on the outskirts of Philadelphia became a "source of great delight." He was best known for his *Ramblings of a Naturalist*, a book of essays on the natural history of the outer Philadelphia neighborhoods published in 1833.[45] In one of his typical walks, he found in the turf below a fence a series of burrows, each a "subterranean road, along which the inhabitants could securely travel at all hours without fear of discovery," and in the hillocks of excavated earth thrown up in an abandoned lot, he explored the headwaters of a "delightful brook" inhabited by crayfish. Moving along a stream bank, he discovered a horde of beautiful shells and wondered why nature would lavish such exquisite ornamentation on creatures "destined to pass their lives in and under the mud." Intrigued by these curiosities, Godman returned again and again to the lane, finding grist for the inquiring mind within a few miles of home.[46]

American naturalists found ample opportunity for exploration and discovery. Whereas some crossed the continent, others consolidated their activities in a single locale and drew on a wealth of experiences gained by others in the surrounding area. Thus, the accumulation of natural history proceeded, as Mühlenberg envisioned, ramble by ramble, locale by locale.

Williams, *The Natural and Civil History of Vermont* (Burlington, 1809), Vol. 1, pp. 5, 25, 54, 101, 124, 127; John Andrew Graham, *A Descriptive Sketch of the Present State of Vermont* (London, 1797), p. 7; George P. Merrill, *The First One Hundred Years of American Geology* (New Haven, 1924), p. 248; Zadock Thomson to L. W. Parmaden?, November 29, 1854, Miscellaneous Collection, APS; Samuel P. Hildreth, *Contributions to the Early History of the North-West* (Cincinnati, 1864), pp. 5, 15–16; Daniel Drake, *Pioneer Life in Kentucky: A Series of Reminiscent Letters from Daniel Drake, M.D., to his Children*, edited by Charles D. Drake (Cincinnati, 1870), pp. 121–9; Adolph Waller, "Daniel Drake as a Pioneer in Modern Ecology," *Ohio State Archaeological and Historical Quarterly* 56 (No. 4, 1947): pp. 362–73; Henry D. Shapiro, "Daniel Drake: The New Western Naturalist," *Bartonia* No. 54 (1988): pp. 39, 40–5; S. D. Gross, *A Discourse on the Life, Character, and Services of Daniel Drake* (Louisville, 1853), pp. 18–19; Charles D. Meigs, *A Biographical Notice of Daniel Drake, M.D., of Cincinnati* (Philadelphia, 1853), pp. 12–13, 19–20.

[45] John D. Godman, *Rambles of a Naturalist* (Philadelphia, 1833), pp. 37–8, 43; Thomas Sewall, *An Eulogy on Dr. [John D.] Godman, Being an Introductory Lecture* (Washington, 1830).

[46] Godman, *Rambles of a Naturalist*, pp. 38–9, 40–5, 50, 58–9, 65.

The land was rich enough everywhere to satisfy the adventuresome or the merely curious with the rewards of original discovery.

Adrift on the Bosom of Nature: Settlers and the Western Wilderness

Those who took their natural history in broad geographical swaths – Nuttall, Wilson, Audubon – were not wandering alone in the West. Hundreds of thousands of migrants from the eastern states and the villages and towns of Europe were traveling the same turnpikes and trails, and although naturalists devoted most of their attention to plants, animals, and rocks, they also took note of this immense demographic movement and its effects on the natural environment.[47]

Their interpretation of this event was subject to powerful cultural associations that took form in Europe in the Age of Discovery and traveled to the young nation without much alteration. A half-century before Nuttall set foot on American soil, the great French naturalist, Comte de Buffon, reviled the unimproved wilderness as a nightmarish repetition of aimless growth and decay that, without human intervention, was barren of purpose. The primeval forest, he wrote, was

covered or rather bristling in all the higher parts with thick and dark woods, trees without bark and without tops, curved, broken, falling with age, [with] many more lying... rotting on the already rotted heap, suffocating, burying seeds ready to sprout.... The earth... offers... only an overcrowded space, filled with old trees loaded with parasitic plants, lichens, fungi, the impure fruits of corruption; in all the lower parts, dead and stagnant waters... which nourish only venomous insects and serve as a den for foul animals.

According to biographer Jacques Roger, Buffon considered the conquest of nature part of the "long march toward the accession to the kingdom of God." On similar grounds, American naturalists welcomed the pioneer into the wilderness world, but their assessment of this primitive society was ambivalent. Weighing the social chaos of the western settlements against the harmonies they began to see in nature, they reassessed the logic of Buffon's priorities.[48]

Suppression of the Native uprisings collectively known as Pontiac's Rebellion at the end of the French and Indian War in 1763 augured for

---

[47] See Gregory H. Nobles, "Breaking into the Backcountry: New Approaches to the Early American Frontier," *William and Mary Quarterly* 46 (October 1989): p. 642.

[48] Buffon in Jacques Roger, *Buffon: A Life in Natural History* (Ithaca, 1997), pp. 236–7, 403. On American views, see Thomas R. Cox, "Americans and Their Forests: Romanticism, Progress, and Science in the Late Nineteenth Century," *Journal of Forest History* 29 (October 1985): p. 156.

British settlement of the West, but imperial authorities left the territory to Britain's Native allies, an arrangement formalized by the 1773 Proclamation Line that proscribed, however ineffectively, Anglo-American settlement west of the Appalachians. Indian resistance continued after the Treaty of Paris in 1783, forcing settlers to cluster around outlying forts and along military roads, but in subsequent decades this resistance was overwhelmed by a flood of white settlers.[49] The Ohio Company's Rufus Putnam founded the first permanent Anglo-American town in the Ohio Valley at the mouth of the Muskingum in 1788, named Marietta after Marie Antoinette, and the following year John Cleves Symmes from New Jersey settled at the confluence of the Great Miami and the Ohio. In the peace that followed General Anthony Wayne's 1795 Treaty of Greenville, the packhorse trail across the Alleghenies was rebuilt as a wagon road, and taverns along the way became villages and towns.[50]

Emigrants traveled over these primitive roads in canvas-covered wagons, light enough to be wrestled out of quagmires and shouldered over rocks and stumps, yet large enough to bear a load of bedding, utensils, and provisions. The most northerly route followed the Hudson River to Albany and the Mohawk River to Buffalo. A second route took emigrants over the Allegheny ridges to Pittsburgh, where they sold their wagons, boarded a scow, and, with a copy of the *Ohio Pilot* or *Pittsburgh Navigator*, set sail for the West.[51] Settlers from Virginia, the Carolinas, and Georgia followed the Wilderness Road through the Cumberland Gap. Thus, three streams of immigrant traffic converged on the Ohio Valley, heralding a new civilization, as the bumptious Daniel Boone put it, that would "in all probability,... rival the glory of the greatest on earth."[52]

---

[49] Charles Joseph Latrobe, *The Rambler in North America* (London, 1835), Vol. 1, p. 95; Eric Hinderaker and Peter C. Mancall, *At the Edge of Empire: The Backcountry in British North America* (Baltimore, 2003), pp. 123–4; Dana, *Geographical Sketches*, p. 6.

[50] John W. Monette, *History of the Discovery and Settlement of the Valley of the Mississippi* (New York, 1846), Vol. 2, pp. 311–12.

[51] Francois Alexandre Liancourt, sur de La Rochefoucault, *Travels Through the United States of North America* (London, 1799), Vol. 2, p. 220; David Thomas, *Travels Through the Western Country in the Summer of 1816* (Auburn, 1819), p. 24; Henry R. Schoolcraft, *Narrative Journal of Travels Through the Northwestern Regions of the United States* (Albany, 1821), p. 74; Jacob Ferris, *The States and Territories of the Great West* (New York, 1856), pp. 100–3; James Flint, *Letters from America*, edited by Reuben Gold Thwaites (Cleveland, 1904), pp. 77, 96, 184–5.

[52] "Appendix: The Adventures of Col. Daniel Boon [sic]; Containing a Narrative of theirs of Kenuucke," in John Filson, *The Discovery, Settlement, and Present State of Kentuckie* (Wilmington, 1784), p. 50. See William Newnham Blane, *An Excursion Through the United States and Canada During the Years 1822–1823* (London, 1824), pp. 86–7; John

Pittsburgh was clearly America's gateway to the West. Here, the Monongahela joined the Allegheny to form the Ohio and the starting point for an epic journey that carried settlers past nine hundred miles of prime settling land on the Ohio, Kentucky, and Indiana shores and on to the Mississippi. A river of islands, sandbars, and deadheads, the Ohio was tricky to navigate but not particularly dangerous. Its striking natural beauty, its meandering course through towering forests, its high banks of deep, rich loam, and its convenience as a pathway to the West drew enthusiastic comment.[53] Benjamin Harding, who expected a dark and tangled wilderness west of Pittsburgh, was "struck with surprise at the beauty of the county"; soils that produced forests like these, he thought, boded well for a coming frontier civilization. Thomas Ashe described a sense of exhilaration mixed with melancholy; the currents carried him westward with a kind of inescapable certainty into a land "pregnant with danger, vicissitude, and death."[54]

The ease of travel in high water made the Ohio the most popular route west for settler families, and naturalists followed this human tide down the river, observing not only the forests along the shores but the effect of human ambition on these woods as well. Harding described the "almost incredible" number of boats carried by the currents – a floating town, according to Ashe. Stacks of hay, with horses and cows feeding on them, along with plows, wagons, pigs, children, and poultry, gave the shipboard scene a sense of permanence. One included a "respectable looking old lady" knitting in a chair and another bent over a washtub. Here, the observer mused, was "honest Jonathan, surrounded with his scolding, grunting, squalling, and neighing dependants," moving westward "with as much complacency as if they had been in 'the land of steady habits.'"[55]

Lewis Peyton, *Over the Alleghanies and Across the Prairies: Personal Recollections of the Far West One and Twenty Years Ago* (London, 1869), p. 21.

[53] Palmer, *Journal of Travels*, p. 56; Zadok Cramer, *The Navigator* (Pittsburgh, 1811), pp. 24–5; Andrew R. L. Cayton, *The Frontier Republic: Ideology and Politics in the Ohio Country, 1780–1825* (Kent, 1986), p. 1; Michaux, *Travels to the West*, p. 69; Thomas Hulme, "A Journal Made During a Tour in the Western Countries of America: September 30, 1818–August 7, 1819," in Gold Thwaites, *Early Western Travels*, pp. 38–9; Nuttall, *Journal of Travels into the Arkansa*, p. 26.

[54] Benjamin Harding, *A Tour Through the Western Country* (New London, 1819), p. 4; Thomas Ashe, *Travels in America, Performed in 1806, for the Purpose of Exploring the Rivers Allegheny, Monongahela, Ohio, and Mississippi* (Newburyport, E. M. Blunt, 1808), p. 77.

[55] Harding, *Tour Through the Western Country*, pp. 4–5; Ashe, *Travels in America*, p. 38; Hall, *Letters from the West*, pp. 87–8. See Maria R. Audubon, *Audubon and His Journals* (New York, 1960 [c. 1897]), Vol. 2, p. 206; Nuttall, *Journal of Travels into*

Those adrift on the Ohio were anything but steady. André Michaux saw these travelers as supremely opportunistic, "abandoning themselves to the mercy of the stream." Borne along in this liquid landscape, they relished their rootlessness, aware that they might strike up a homestead beside any small stream, and then, "wearying of continuous residence and having their eyes always on a better land in the West, embark... upon the capacious bosom of the flat [boat]." Limitless opportunity, the lure of new beginnings, and the seductiveness of the westward-flowing waters beckoned them onward. Audubon, who made the trip in a skiff with his wife and infant son, recorded mixed feelings about this mesmerizing flow of water and people. "We glided down the river, meeting no other ripple of the water than that formed by the propulsion of our boat..., gazing all day on the grandeur and beauty of the wild scenery around us.... We foresaw with great concern the alterations that cultivation would soon produce along those delightful banks."[56]

At Louisville, the river, a mile and a quarter wide, fell twenty-two feet in a span of two miles, marking the Falls of the Ohio. Never one to understate his adventures, Ashe described the accelerating current that drew his craft toward the din of the falls. As he and his pilot advanced, a thunderstorm "burst at once in heavy peals," and through this furious cacophony of rain, wind, thunder, and rushing water, they raced the "rock-lined chute" past a threatening vortex that appeared to the wide-eyed Ashe the very "residence of death." All this was over before he had time to make his amends, and once again the craft floated on a calm sheet of water.[57] Others described the falls as "nothing more than an inclined plane of... [water] which in fact produces no other effect than that of rendering the current more rapid." In 1808–10, engineers constructed a canal around the falls, anticipating by one year the advent of steamboat service on the river.[58]

Below the falls, settlers encountered a different landscape. The hills were more rounded, and the forests shaded into maple, hickory, oak, walnut, beech, ash, cherry, mulberry, and magnolia. Beyond the Wabash,

the *Arkansa*, p. 41; Hulme, "A Journal Made During a Tour in the Western Countries," p. 39.

[56] Michaux, *Travels to the West*, p. 72; Dorothy Anne Dondore, *The Prairie and the Making of Middle America: Four Centuries of Description* (Cedar Rapids, 1926), p. 180; Audubon, *Audubon and His Journals*, pp. 204–5.

[57] Ashe, *Travels in America*, pp. 238–9; Gilbert Imlay, *A Topographical Description of the Western Territory of North America* (London, 1792), p. 51. See Hall, *Letters from the West*, pp. 84–6; Wilson, *American Ornithology*, p. lxxx; Flint, *Letters from America*, p. 160; Nuttall, *Journal of Travels into the Arkansa*, p. 36.

[58] Ashe, *Travels in America*, p. 239; Beltrami, *Pilgrimage in Europe and America*, p. 78.

an "inexhaustible pasture" dominated the landscape, provided by providence, one naturalist thought, for the region's vast herds of grazing animals. Some settlers were intimidated by this relentless openness, but once they understood the productivity of the prairie soils, they began edging westward, then continued on to the plains of Illinois and southern Michigan, the rolling hills of Missouri, or the bottomlands along the White, Arkansas, and Red Rivers. "We read advertisements that a thousand persons are shortly to meet at St. Louis to form a company to cross the Rocky Mountains, with a view to select settlements on the Oregon," Timothy Flint noted in 1832.[59]

In the first three decades of the nineteenth century, the outward edge of the settlement frontier passed down the Ohio Valley and out of the great eastern forest. Before the 1795 Treaty of Greenville, François-André Michaux found only thirty families on the upper river; when he retraced his route in 1802, he found farms every two or three miles down its entire length. The following year, Ohio, with some 45,000 residents, became a state and, by 1810, its population had grown to more than 230,000.[60] In the span of a single generation, the pulse of settlement and land-clearing had passed beyond the Ohio but, while it lasted, this demographic movement and its accompanying environmental changes fascinated America's traveling scientists. The lessons they learned as they explored this changing landscape left an indelible impress on the natural history of America.

Explorers in a Changing Land

With their own bundles of baggage and equipment, scientific travelers followed these pioneer families up the Mohawk, through the Cumberland Gap, or over the Pittsburgh Pike. The latter route was popular with naturalists because the point of debarkation, Philadelphia, was the scientific center of the nation. Heading west on the Pike, they advanced through well-cultivated farmland along the Susquehanna to Lancaster and continued on a rougher road to Harrisburg. There, they turned west up the

---

[59] Timothy Flint, *The History and Geography of the Mississippi Valley* (Cincinnati, 1832), p. 186.

[60] Michaux, *Travels to the West*, p. 108; William Henry Harrison, "A Discourse on the Aborigines of the Valley of the Ohio," Historical and Philosophical Society of Ohio *Transactions* 1 (1839): p. 222; Edward W. Watkin, *A Trip to the United States and Canada: In a Series of Letters* (London, 1852), p. 57; Monette, *History of the Discovery and Settlement of the Valley*, Vol. 2, pp. 193, 195.

brawling Juniata into the heart of the Alleghenies. Here, at the fringes of Pennsylvania's settled country, the land assumed a wilder appearance; the road became rougher, the terrain more uneven, and the farms less frequent.[61] After climbing for a day, travelers reached a series of high ridges separated by valleys some twenty miles wide – a land known for its "picturesque ruggedness." Traveling in March, Benjamin Barton found the spring retarded in these highlands, and the barren trees, festooned with parasitic mosses, gave the appearance of a vast, dead forest. The more romantic Alexander Wilson noted "a kind of fearful sublimity," whereas Thomas Nuttall found the scenery tedious rather than sublime. "Most of the climes, terraces, and piles of rocks lose their effect beneath the umbrageous forest which envelopes them, and which indeed casts a gloomy mantling over the whole face of nature."[62]

By the 1820s, the journey could be accomplished by stagecoach as far as Pittsburgh, but even along this well-traveled route, the country-side seemed stark and primitive, with few farms to relieve the relentless forest canopy. The stagecoach itself was an ungainly vehicle resting on heavy leather slings.[63] When the uneven terrain tired the horses, travelers continued on foot, or the stage came to a halt. On rougher roads, passengers would "trim the coach" when the driver bellowed "To the right, gentlemen! – Gentlemen, to the left!" In particularly rough spots, male passengers were obliged to get out and "hold up the stage for the ladies," Susan Fenimore Cooper remembered. "Often the coach is upset; frequently coach, passengers, and all sink into the slough to an alarming depth, when rails are taken from the fences to 'pry the stage out,' but, by dint of working with good will, . . . the whole part generally contrives to reach its destination in a better or worse condition."[64]

---

[61] Dondore, *Prairie and the Making of Middle America*, p. 163; Finch, *Travels in the United States*, pp. 83, 86–7; Jacob Burnet, *Notes on the Early Settlement of the Northwestern Territory* (New York, 1847), p. 33; Michaux, *Travels to the West*, p. 27; Cuming, *Sketches of a Tour*, pp. 29, 34.

[62] American Academy of Arts and Sciences *Memoirs* 2 (no. 1, 1793), p. 119; "Large Crossings," Barton Papers, PHS; Alexander Wilson to George Ord, June 23, in Coues, "Private Letters of Wilson, Ord, and Bonaparte," p. 450; Nuttall, *Journal of Travels into the Arkansa*, p. 14.

[63] Palmer, *Journal of Travels*, pp. 11–12; Flint, *Letters from America*, pp. 50, 81; Robert Barclay Allardice, *Agricultural Tour in the United States and Upper Canada* (Edinburgh, 1842), p. 30. See Thomas Twining, *Travels in America 100 Years Ago, Being Notes and Reminiscences* (New York, 1893), p. 65.

[64] Susan Fenimore Cooper, *Rural Hours* (New York, 1850), p. 380; Palmer, *Journal of Travels*, pp. 38, 41; Peyton, *Over the Alleghanies*, p. 23.

THE AUTHOR IN HIS TRAVELLING DRESS.

FIGURE 2.1. With their baggage and equipment, scientific travelers followed the American pioneer up the Mohawk, through the Cumberland Gap, and over the Pittsburgh Pike. Scientific rambling embedded the observer in the natural world, while the act of sorting out eclectic observations en route promoted a sensitivity to ecological connections. With the arrival of steamboats and railroads, touring became extensive rather than intensive, and the nature of scientific observation – and the science itself – changed appreciably. Patrick Campbell, frontispiece, *Travels in the North America* (1793). Courtesy of the Historical Society of Pennsylvania.

West of the Alleghenies, the road passed over Laurel Hill, a steep-sided limestone ridge that marked the descent into the Ohio basin. Its crest offered a first glimpse of the immense western valley and during the descent, the hemlock, spruce, and white pine gave way to white oak, chestnut, pitch pine, mountain laurel, rhododendron, and magnolia. These lowland woods promised a richer soil, and the air, cold and raw on the ridge tops, grew mild and then warm as travelers descended into the headwaters of the Ohio. Timothy Flint, a young Massachusetts missionary-naturalist with an unaffected enthusiasm for the West, found his spirits lifted as he traveled along a mountain stream leading into the valley, with "the breeze sweeping down the sloping forest,... the screaming of the jay and the dash of the water, rolling rapidly along its rocky bed . . . under the shade of laurels."[65]

For the naturalist, settlement of the upper Ohio closed a frontier of another sort. The classic scientific tour of the Ohio Valley took place between 1795, at the end of Indian resistance, and the 1830s, when travel became possible by rail or steamboat. Exploration by foot, stage, open boat, or horseback involved an intimate engagement with the landscape and close attention to the nuances of each particular region's human and natural character. It offered time for reflection and journal-keeping and reinforced what one naturalist called the "wild poetic cast" of the passage. In company with others in a canal barge, a railroad car, or steamboat, the traveler's descriptive powers focused on personalities rather than landscapes.[66] Geologist George Featherstonhaugh, commissioned to explore the Mississippi headwaters in 1837, began his journey on a boat traveling the Chesapeake and Ohio Canal. He disembarked to inspect the strata along the canal in the first few miles but quickly found the boat's interior more inviting. "We now, all seated in the comfortable cabin of our nice floating hotel, proceeded to discuss a cold collation consisting of a great many good things; some very choice old Madeira not being wanting to crown our repast. We all got very merry, and began singing songs as we guided along the pleasant canal." Hoping to disembark and inspect the geology along a cut bank, he asked a jovial Virginia Quaker when they would reach the next lock: "Thee may'st put it down in thy book, that it will take us just two bottles of Madeira to get there." With the arrival of steamboats and railroads, touring became extensive rather than intensive, and commentary focused on points of departure and destination rather than the landscapes between.[67] The western travel experience had been transformed, and the age of the pedestrian ramble was over.

---

[65] Ashe, *Travels in America*, p. 38; Flint, *History and Geography of the Mississippi Valley*, p. 19. See Tuckerman, *America and Her Commentators*, pp. 401–4.

[66] Cuming, *Sketches of a Tour*, p. 25. See John R. Stilgoe, "Landschaft and Linearity," in Stilgoe (ed.), *Landscape and Images* (Charlottesville, 2005); Palmer, *Journal of Travels*, p. 42; Twining, *Travels in America*, p. 76; Charles Augustus Murray, *Travels in North America During the Years 1834, 1835, & 1836* (London, 1839), pp. 189, 193, 199.

[67] Berkeley and Berkeley, *Featherstonhaugh*, pp. 153–4; George William Featherstonhaugh, *A Canoe Voyage Up the Minnay Sotor* (London, 1847), pp. 5–6, 9, 15. See *American Journal of Science* 31 (January 1837): p. 2; William Edward Baxter, *America and the Americans* (London, 1855), pp. 5–6.

"A Delightful Entertainment"

The naturalists who made this arduous journey were obviously attracted to the unknown, but they were not always specific about their motives. Sensitive perhaps to the pragmatic and skeptical instincts of the young nation, many justified their scientific wanderlust on therapeutic grounds. Botanist Thaddeus Harris hoped to dispel a "wasting sickness" that kept him from his academic duties, and Estwick Evans sought to divest himself of "the factitious habits, prejudices, and imperfections of civilization; to become a citizen of the world."[68] Others, again stressing the practical, held out the prospect of discovering valuable resources. Yale geologist, Benjamin Silliman, pronounced the West "a treasure but just opened" and issued a challenge to fellow naturalists to bring these riches to light: "There can be little doubt that a vast number of...[useful] substances...remain for future inquirers to discover."[69]

Although these practical considerations were paramount in the scientist's apologia, most found simple curiosity a more compelling reason to ramble. To be considered curious – drawn to the rare, the novel, the surprising, the beautiful, or the mysterious, independent of any particular intellectual goal or economic consideration – was a high compliment in scientific circles. Unfocused and eclectic, this drive generated an enormous fund of undigested "curiosities of nature" as part of the scientific record. In a journal of his 1743 trip to New York, John Bartram mentioned that he and his companion left their canoe to "look for curiosities, but found none; the rock consisted of a dark coloured shelly stone. Then we diverted our selves with swimming." It is difficult to fathom what exactly Bartram was looking for but, in other places, his curiosity was piqued by fossils, rare plants, good and bad soils, various tree species, an "enraged rattlesnake," water gushing from the side of a hill, and other

---

[68] Thaddeus Mason Harris, "The Journal of a Tour into the Territory Northwest of the Allegheny Mountains," in *Early Western Travels, 1748–1846*, edited by Reuben Gold Thwaites (Cleveland, 1904), p. 313; Lewis Evans, *Geographical, Historical, Political, Philosophical, and Mechanical Essays* (Philadelphia, 1755), pp. 102–3.

[69] *American Journal of Science* 1 (1818): p. 6. See Drake in Meigs, *Biographical Notice of Daniel Drake*, p. 17; Bigelow, *Florula Bostoniensis*, pp. vi–vii; Moses Greenleaf, *A Statistical View of the District of Maine* (Boston, 1816), p. 169; Samuel Kramsch to Humphrey Marshall, July 25, 1789, in Darlington, *Memorials of John Bartram and Humphrey Marshall*, p. 574.

phenomena both rare and common.[70] Other naturalists were drawn to caves, natural bridges, Indian mounds, boiling springs, flammable pools, whirlpools, and balanced or "rocking" boulders, and they made detailed scientific investigations of these phenomena. Jacob Moore learned of a huge rock in New Hampshire so perfectly balanced that the wind would move it, but three or four years before he arrived on the scene, a group of Portsmouth men dislodged it with levers. This, Moore reported, was a "barbarous curiosity, of which it is hoped the persons concerned are now ashamed!" John Godman's natural history of bats included their curious mode of voiding excrement while hanging upside down in a cave.[71]

On a continent not yet fully explored, the line between curious and sensational was not always clear. An article in the *American Journal of Science* weighed the evidence for unicorns and mermaids, and the New York Lyceum presented a paper in 1828 on the "History of Sea Serpentism" following a sighting off Marblehead and Cape Ann.[72] Curiosities like these furthered no particular theoretical point; in fact, it was the lack of theoretical context that made them curious. Yet, because all nature's works were linked in some fashion, each curiosity would eventually prove

[70] John Bartram, *Observations on the Inhabitants, Climate, Soil, Rivers, Productions, Animals, and Other Matters Worthy of Notice*, edited by Peter Kalm (London, 1751), p. 17; Courtney Robert Hall, *A Scientist in the Early Republic: Samuel Latham Mitchill, 1764–1831* (New York, 1934), pp. 5, 63; Katie Whitaker, "The Culture of Curiosity," in Jardine, Secord, and Spary, *Cultures of Natural History*, pp. 75–6; Anthony Pagden, *European Encounters with the New World: From Renaissance to Romanticism* (New Haven, 1993), p. 10; Andrew Ellicott to Benjamin Smith Barton, November 30, 1795, Barton Papers, APS.

[71] Jacob B. Moore, "On a Rocking Stone in Durham, New Hampshire," *American Journal of Science* 6 (No. 2, 1823): p. 244; John D. Godman, *American Natural History – Mastology* (Philadelphia, 1826), Vol. 1, p. 54. See Rebecca Bedell, *The Anatomy of Nature: Geology & American Landscape Painting, 1825–1875* (Princeton, 2001), p. 29; James Mease, *Geological Account of the United States* (Philadelphia, 1807), pp. 444, 447, 472, 473–5.

[72] "Some Observations on the Sea-Serpent," American Academy of Arts and Sciences *Memoirs* 4 (Part 1, 1818): pp. 86, 91. See Whitaker, "Culture of Curiosity," p. 81; Mease, *Geological Account*, p. 444; J. Macloc, *New, Complete, and Universal Natural History of All the Most Remarkable Quadrupeds, Birds, Fishes, Reptiles, and Insects, in the Known World* (Philadelphia, 1818); J. F. Laterrade, "An Attempt to Prove the Existence of the Unicorn," *American Journal of Science* 21 (No. 1, 1832): p. 123; Brooke Hindle, *The Pursuit of Science in Revolutionary America, 1735–1789* (Chapel Hill, 1956), p. 11; Hall, *Scientist in the Early Republic*, pp. 90–91; *Just Arrived!!! A Great Serpent* (1818), Broadsides, APS; Michael Brown Chandos, "A Natural History of the Gloucester Sea Serpent: Knowledge, Power, and the Culture of Science in Antebellum America," *American Quarterly* 42 (September 1990): pp. 402–15.

important to the overall matrix; further examination would make these links clear, and the curiosity would be assigned its place according to the laws of nature.[73]

Curiosity took the rambling naturalist in almost any direction. Crèvecoeur was drawn to the American hummingbird, the "most irascible of the feathered tribe," simply because he admired its character. Where, he wondered, did such passions "find room in so diminutive a body?" William Priest found his first experience with frogs equally captivating. Their performance, he wrote,

was *al fresco*, and took place . . . in a large swamp, where there were at least ten thousand performers; and I really believe not two exactly in the same pitch, if the octave can possibly admit of so many divisions . . . Treble is performed by the tree-frogs, the smallest and most beautiful species. . . . The next in size are our counter tenors; they have a note resembling the setting of a saw. A still larger species sing tenor; and the under part is supported by the bull-frogs; which are as large as a man's foot, and bellow out the bass in a tone as loud and sonorous as that of the animal from which they take their name.[74]

Indians excited a great deal of curiosity as well. The ancient mounds in the Ohio Valley were part of every scientific tour of the West, and as they wandered among these mysterious formations, some of them nearly four miles square, explorers marveled at the variety of the worked metals and stones, the meaning of the temples, and the devotional preoccupation that made the ruins possible.[75] Mammoth and mastodon bones were the ultimate curiosities of nature, combining scientific mystery with the sublime. "The emotions experienced, when . . . we behold the giant relics of this great animal are those of unmingled awe," John Godman wrote.

We cannot avoid reflecting on the time when this huge frame was clothed with its peculiar integuments, and moved by appropriate muscles; when the mighty

---

73 Pagden, *European Encounters*, p. 11; Herbert Leventhal, *In the Shadow of the Enlightenment: Occultism and Renaissance Science in Eighteenth-Century America* (New York, 1976), p. 223.

74 J. Hector St. John de Crèvecoeur, *Letters from an American Farmer and Sketches of Eighteenth-Century America*, edited by Albert E. Stone (New York, 1986 [c. 1782]), p. 184; Priest, *Travels*, pp. 48–50. See Pamela Regis, *Describing Early America: Bartram, Jefferson, Crevecoeur, and the Influence of Natural History* (Philadelphia, 1992), pp. 110, 250; Drake, *Pioneer Life in Kentucky*, pp. 123–4; Barton, *Discourse on Some of the Principal Desiderata*, pp. 39, 40–1; *American Journal of Science* 22 (1832): p. 122; John Melish, *Travels in the United States of America, in the Years 1806 & 1807, 1810, & 1811* (Philadelphia, 1812), Vol. 1, pp. iii–iv.

75 Ephrian George Squier, *Observations on the Aboriginal Monuments of the Mississippi Valley* (New York, 1847), p. 46.

heart dashed forth its torrents of blood through vessels of enormous caliber, and the mastodon strode along in supreme dominion over every other tenant of the wilderness.... Looking at its ponderous jaws, armed with teeth peculiarly formed for the most effectual crushing of the firmest substances, we are assured that its life could only be supported by the destruction of vast quantities of food.[76]

Mammoths stirred the scientific imagination because they were initially considered unique to America and thus an object of national pride. They also triggered profound philosophic questions: Why would God create such magnificent creatures simply to destroy them as a race? And being elephants, why were they found in such northern latitudes? Many, including Jefferson, Barton, and Michaux, were convinced the animals still wandered the unexplored territories of the Northwest.[77] America offered thousands of creatures equally as curious, if not as formidable, and this understanding was a primary impulse for exploration. Those blessed with a curious nature, as Peter Collinson put it, would find "the wasts & wilds which to others appear dismal... a delightful entertainment."[78]

The Rigors of Scientific Exploration

In the years before the railroad and riverboat, the scientific ramble was a true expedition, and naturalists took pride in the rigors of their pursuit of knowledge. Speaking for his peers, Philadelphia's Benjamin Barton laid out the dictum that a "correct theory of the earth is not to be attained... in a cabinet of little fragments of stones, of earths, and of

---

[76] Godman, *American Natural History*, Vol. 2, p. 208. See John Bartram to Peter Collinson, August 15, 1762, in Edmund Berkeley and Dorothy Smith Berkeley, *The Correspondence of John Bartram, 1734–1777*, p. 568; Bartram to Collinson, August 15, 1762, in ibid., p. 568; Benjamin Smith Barton, *Archaeologiae Americannae Telluris Collectanea et Specimina* (Philadelphia, 1814), p. iv; Godman, *American Natural History*, Vol. 2, p. 207; Thomas Ashe, *Memoirs of Mammoth* (Liverpool, 1806); Francois Auguste Rene, Vicomte de Chateaubriand, *Travels in America and Italy* (London, 1828), Vol. 1, p. 163; John Palmer, *Journal of Travels in the United States of North America, and in Lower Canada* (London, 1818), p. 98.

[77] Bedell, *Anatomy of Nature*, p. 10. See Godman in Samuel G. Goodrich, *Peter Parley's Tales of Animals* (Boston, 1832), p. 111; Kastner, *Species of Eternity*, pp. 143–4; Barton, *Archaeologiae Americannae*, p. 12; Humphrey Marshall, *The History of Kentucky* (Frankfort, 1812), pp. 6–7; Williams, *Natural and Civil History of Vermont*, Vol. 1, pp. 124–5; André Michaux, *Journal of Travels into Kentucky, July 15, 1993–April 11, 1796*, edited by Reuben Gold Thwaites (Cleveland, 1904), pp. 36–7; John Drayton, *A View of South Carolina, as Respects Her Natural and Civil Concerns* (Charleston, 1802) 1802, pp. 42–5.

[78] Peter Collinson to Cadwallader Colden, August 23, 1744, Colden, *The Letters and Papers of Cadwallader Colden* (New York, 1917–1922), Vol. 3, p. 68.

metals. Nature . . . will not answer us unless we interrogate her in all the wild and majestic scenery of her works." New York's Stephen van Rensselaer noted that the totality of a plant, animal, or mineral – its natural history – could be assessed only in situ. Geologists, he explained, were "compelled to traverse every stream of water, to search out every naked cliff, to descend into every cavern, [and] to examine wells, water raceways and ditches . . . before we . . . dare trust our views before the doubting public."[79] Inhabited by Native people and a few whites, the West was not totally unexplored but, aside from the main-traveled routes, the roads were, as Michaux put it, choked with a "thousand common-place obstacles" impossible to foresee. Water was a preferable medium of transportation, but it was often dangerous. On Lake Superior in a Mackinaw boat, Louis Agassiz mused that the sudden changes in weather and icy water made it easy to see why his guides hugged the coastline, but the prospect of a forced retreat "through this rugged, gameless, fly-possessed region" made the thought of reaching the shore only slightly more welcoming. Geologist James T. Hodge, perched in a frail birchbark canoe amid the Penobscot River's tumbling waters, expressed similar concerns that the traveling naturalist "must keep himself perfectly cool amid dangers, trusting to the skill of his aboriginal navigator for safe deliverance." Many persons, he added for emphasis, "lose their lives in those waters."[80]

Hodge's geological survey of Maine's Mount Katahdin suggests other challenges. Scrambling up the boulder fields that skirted the mountain, he and his crew reached timberline at a surprisingly low elevation, and further ascent became "exceedingly laborious, owing to large overhanging rocks, which were covered with moss, and, being wet, were very slippery." Caught in a sudden squall, they pressed onward as the driving wind froze their wet clothes to their bodies. They consummated their scientific mission, finding "an abundance of rounded diluvial boulders of grau-wacke

---

[79] Benjamin Smith Barton, *A Discourse on Some of the Principal Desiderata in Natural History, and on the Best Means of Promoting the Study of This Science, in the United States* (Philadelphia, 1807), p. 55; Stephen Van Rensselaer, *A Geological and Agricultural Survey of the District Adjoining the Erie Canal, in the State of New-York* (Albany, 1824), pp. 8–9.

[80] Michaux, *Travels to the West*, p. 24; Louis Agassiz, *Lake Superior: Its Physical Character, Vegetation, and Animals, Compared with Those of Other and Similar Regions* (Boston, 1850), p. 53; James T. Hodge in Charles T. Jackson, *Second Annual Report on the Geology of the Public Lands, Belonging to the Two States of Maine and Massachusetts* (Augusta, 1838), pp. 7–8. See Flint, *Letters from America*, p. 79; Joseph Whipple, *A Geographical View of the District of Maine* (Bangor, 1816), p. 27; Greenleaf, *Statistical View*, pp. iii–iv, vi–vii, 83.

and compact limestone, filled with impressions of marine shells." Their clothes encrusted with snow, they slid carefully down the rock face until darkness brought a halt to the descent. After an uncomfortable night, they awoke "so enfeebled . . . by hunger, privations, and fatigue, that . . . every now and then, our knees would give way beneath us, and cause us to fall upon the ground." Revived by a meal of chokecherries and blueberries, they returned to the river with specimens in hand.[81]

In his southern travels, William Bartram was plagued by biting flies so thick that they obscured distant objects. Like Hodge, he remained steadfast in his pursuit of science, describing in surprising detail the taxonomy of his tormentors. The largest, a horsefly (*Hippobosca equina*), was

armed with a strong sharp beak or proboscis, shaped like a lancet, and sheathed in flexible thin valves; with this beak they instantly pierce the veins of the creatures, making a large orifice from whence the blood springs in large drops, rolling down as tears, causing a fierce pain or aching for a considerable time after the wound is made; there are three or four species of this genus of less size but equally vexatious, as they are vastly more numerous, active and sanguineous; particularly, one about half the size of the first mentioned, the next less of a dusky colour with a green head; another yet somewhat less, of a splendid green and the head of a gold colour; the sting of this last is intolerable, no less acute than a prick from a red-hot needle, or a spark of fire on the skin; these are called the burning flies.[82]

Science and expressions of extreme discomfort intermixed in these accounts, the experience of place forming a context for the analysis of nature.

Even along the well-traveled routes, there were trials sufficient to test the explorers' resolve. An awkward meeting of culture and country, taverns unsettled many European explorers. James Flint, whose expectations proved wildly out of line with frontier conditions, took an instant dislike to sleeping in a bed with one or more fellow travelers and to the fact that there were no "menials accustomed to move at the signal of the stranger." Morris Birkbeck slept on the floor in one tavern after being assured it was "too damp for fleas." Travelers were besieged by "idle and impertinent" questions: "Whence did you come? – Where are you going? – What is your name? – Where do you live? – and why do you travel?"[83] Even the

---

[81] James T. Hodge in Jackson, *Second Annual Report*, pp. 17–21.

[82] Bartram, *Travels*, p. 243. See Thaddeus William Harris to John L. Le Conte, September 10, 1851, John Le Conte Papers, APS.

[83] Flint, *Letters from America*, pp. 161–2; Birkbeck, *Notes on a Journey*, p. 141. See William Dalton, *Travels in the United States of America, and Part of Upper Canada* (Appleby, 1821), pp. 18–19; Featherstonhaugh, *Canoe Voyage Up the Minnay Sotor*, p. 23; Blane, *Excursion Through the United States*, pp. 82, 84–5; Isaac Weld, *Travels*

genial Ben Franklin was put off by this widespread country habit. Obliged to answer questions before he could obtain food and drink, he resolved the matter:

The moment he went into any of these places, [he] inquired for the master, the mistress, the sons, the daughters, the men servants and the maid-servants; and having assembled them all together, he began in this manner. "Worthy people, I am B. F. of Philadelphia, by trade a____, and a bachelor; I have some relations at Boston, to whom I am going to make a visit: my stay will be short, and I shall then return and follow my business, as a prudent man ought to do. This is all I know of myself, and all I can possibly inform you of; I beg therefore that you will have pity upon me and my horse, and give us both some refreshment."

Under these conditions, many travelers preferred to sleep in the open in good weather.[84]

When naturalists were not vexed, they were often confused. Jacob Bigelow described the White Mountains as a "loose, irregular, disconnected heap of rocks of all shapes and dimensions, . . . lying confusedly one above another." Only at great distance did such mountains resolve into "one great range of highlands," Ebenezer Emmons explained.[85] Rivers were disorienting as well. The current, Thomas Ashe found, held steady to one side for miles, then for no apparent reason shifted to the opposite bank, "as if to enjoy, for a certain time, the beauties of the opposite shore." Air currents moving from side to side added to the confusion. Against this capricious flux and flow, the land itself seemed less fixed.[86]

Unable to find solid ground in this incoherent landscape, naturalists relied on their own shifting moods as a baseline for scientific description; emotion became a way of understanding or predicting. Emerging from the relentless Appalachian woods, Birkbeck felt his spirits lifted when he reached the broad Ohio River: "The view of that noble expanse was like

Through the States of North America, and the Provinces of Upper and Lower Canada, During the Years 1795, 1796, and 1797 (London, 1799), pp. 76–7.

[84] Benjamin Franklin in Andrew Burnaby, *Travel Through the Middle Settlements in North-America, in the Years 1759 and 1760, with Observations Upon the State of the Colonies* (London, 1775), pp. 143–4; Flint, *Letters from America*, p. 73.

[85] Jacob Bigelow, *Some Account of the White Mountains of New Hampshire* (Boston, 1816), p. 11; Emmons, *Report of the Survey of the Second Geological District,* pp. 10–11. See Francis Hall, *Travels in Canada, and the United States, in 1816 and 1817* (Boston, 1818), p. 151; Jeremy Belknap, *History of New-Hampshire* (Dover, 1812), Vol. 3, p. 32; *American Journal of Science* 26 (No. 2, 1834): pp. 220, 224; Greenleaf, *Statistical View,* pp. 51, 54.

[86] Ashe, *Travels in America,* pp. 115–16.

the opening of bright day upon the gloom of night, to us who had been so long buried in deep forests."[87] Audubon traveled up Florida's St. John's River a few decades after John and William Bartram had explored this botanical paradise and discovered a land of orange trees and calm, clear air. However, because he had lost a chance to shoot ibises that day, his mood was somber. He described the scene before him:

Here I am then in the Floridas, thought I, a country that received its romantic name from the fragrant odors wafted from the orange groves,... which from my childhood I have consecrated in my imagination as the garden of the United States. A garden where all that is not mud, mud, mud, is sand, sand, sand; where the fruit is so sour that it is not eatable, and where in place of singing birds and golden fishes, you have a species of ibis that you cannot get when you have shot it, and alligators, snakes, and scorpions.[88]

Scientists used their feelings to give meaning to a land that carried no established cultural associations and where nature itself seemed formless and confusing. Their emotional reactions accented the wildness of the landscape but, as they learned to ignore the biting flies and let these confusing features sort themselves out, the language of emotion became a way of conveying the beauty and majesty of the western wilderness. The reader saw with the naturalist "the arm of Omnipotence laid bare" in the sublime mysteries of nature.[89] In a more predictable land, naturalists became romantics.

Acquisition of Knowledge

Working across this largely uncharted continent in the decades before steamboats, railroads, and canals, the curious traveler used a variety of means to order this inchoate landscape. Although they were observers par excellence, they were also good listeners, and their willingness to consult with Indians, settlers, guides, and local amateur naturalists demonstrates the collectivity of scientific discovery in the era. German botanist Frederick Pursh remembered that his "first object" on arriving in America was to "form an acquaintance with all those interested in the study of Botany." In Pennsylvania, he visited Henry Mühlenberg, the aged Humphrey

---

[87] Birkbeck, *Notes on a Journey*, pp. 38, 132–3.

[88] John James Audubon in *Monthly American Journal of Geology and Natural Science* 1 (June 1832): pp. 535–6.

[89] *Niles' Weekly Register* 2 (April 11, 1812): p. 94; Edward Hitchcock, *First Anniversary Address Before the Association of American Geologists* (New Haven, 1841), p. 45.

Marshall, William Bartram, and Benjamin Barton.[90] British geologist I. Finch carried a letter of introduction to Governor DeWitt Clinton, who then wrote similar letters to his scientific friends at Troy, who in turn wrote introductions for Finch as he traveled farther west.[91] Alexander Wilson composed a letter typical of these introductions: "This will be handed to you by Mr. [André] Michaux, a gentleman of an amiable character and a distinguished naturalist, who is pursuing his botanical researches through North America and intends visiting the Cataract of Niagara. The kindness I received from your family in 1804 makes me desirous that my friend, Mr. Michaux, should reside with you during his stay at Niagara; and any attention paid to him will be considered as done to myself."[92] William Darlington, who specialized in the flora of Westchester Borough in Pennsylvania, considered exchanges between traveling and local naturalists necessary to "obtaining the materials for that great desideratum, a complete American Flora," and, with this in mind, he and others readily yielded up information when outsiders passed through.[93]

As Darlington suggested, untutored local authorities were often crucial to the completion of this natural history. "In most every town there is a farmer or mechanic who has addicted himself to some kind of knowledge very remote from his occupation," James Parton explained. "Here you will find a shoemaker . . . who has attained celebrity as a botanist. In another village there may be a wheelwright, who would sell his best coat for a rare shell; and, not far off, a farmer, who is a pretty good geologist." Farmers, mechanics, and shoemakers were ready to share their knowledge, and naturalists were willing listeners. "I like these Western men," Tyrone Power wrote. "Their off-hand manner makes you at once at your ease with them; they abound in anecdote growing out of the state in which

90 Frederick Pursh, *Flora Americae Septentrionalis; or, A Systematic Arrangement and Description of the Plants of North America* (London, 1814), Vol. 1, pp. vi, viii; J. F. D. Smyth, *A Tour in the United States of America* (London: G. Robinson, 1784), Vol. 1, p. 3; Michaux, *Travels to the West*, pp. 27–8; Henry E. Mühlenberg to John Brickell, March 1, 1804, Miscellaneous Collection, APS; John Brickell to Henry E. Mühlenberg, February 7, 1802, Mühlenberg Manuscripts, PHS.

91 Finch, *Travels in the United States*, pp. 69–70, 105–6, 309–10. See Johannes Genais to Andrew Williamson, April 18, 1775, Bartram Family Papers, PHS; Murray, *Travels in North America*, p. 182; Joseph Banks to Benjamin Smith Barton, December 31, 1802, Barton Papers, APS.

92 Wilson, *American Ornithology*, p. xlix. See Pursh, *Journal of a Botanical Excursion*, pp. 18–19.

93 William Darlington, *Flora Cestrica: A Catalogue of the Phaenogamous Plants, Native and Naturalized* (Westchester, 1826), p. 2.

they live, full of wild frolic and hardy adventure, and they recount these adventures with an exaggeration of figure quite Oriental, in a phraseology peculiar to themselves, and with a manner most humorous." Westerners were "as ready to give information as to ask for it."[94]

Locals, especially Indians, were well versed in neighborhood botany. After visiting a Mohawk village, Benjamin Barton wrote in his journal that "the principal Indian chief . . . , whom I have formerly known in Philadelphia, received me with kindness, and treated me with hospitality." He carefully recorded Indian uses for plants and scrutinized totemic and origin stories seeking scientific information about geology or climate.[95] Settlers were equally forthcoming. In Lancaster, Michaux detoured to the Patrick Archibald farm, where he was "kindly received" in a "miserable log-house about twenty feet long" and shown an extraordinary azalea growing nearby. Near Pittsburgh, he met a French expatriate who had "very correct ideas concerning the western country," and at Wheeling, he "stopped at the hut of one of the inhabitants of the right bank, who shewed us, about fifty yards from his door, a palm-tree [sycamore] . . . the trunk of which was swelled to an amazing size." Near Knoxville, he talked with a farmer, who "in his leisure hour, . . . busies himself in chemistry."[96] J. Hector St. John de Crèvecoeur, a botanist as well as a farmer and essayist, described his local guide's expertise in awed tones: "He follows the ancient blazed trees with a sagacity and quickness of sight which have many times astonished me," he recalled. "Next he judges of the soil by the size and the appearance of the trees; next he judges of the goodness of the timber by that of the soil. The humble bush which delights in the shade, the wild ginseng, the spignet, the weeds on which he treads teach him all he wants to know."[97] Alexander Wilson showed his illustrations

94 James Parton in *Burlington Free Press*, December 28, 1868; Tyrone Power, *Impressions of America During the Years 1833, 1834, and 1835* (London, 1836), Vol. 1, p. 297; Bradbury, *Travels in the Interior*, p. 292.

95 Benjamin Smith Barton Papers, Correspondence, pp. 97–8, PHS.

96 Michaux, *Travels to the West*, pp. 47–8, 50, 73, 86–7, 136, 205. See Thomas Nuttall, "Nuttall's Travels into the Old Northwest: An Unpublished 1810 Diary," edited by Jeannette E. Graustein, *Chronica Botanica* 14 (1950–1951), pp. 31–32, 50–1, 58, 65; Nuttall, *Travels into the Arkansa*, pp. 32, 58.

97 Crèvecoeur, *Letters from an American Farmer*, p. 255. See Charles Daubeny, *Sketch of the Geology of North America, Being the Substance of a Memoir Read Before the Ashmolean Society* (Oxford, 1839), p. 189n; Liancourt, *Travels Through the United States*, Vol. 2, p. 228; Birkbeck, *Notes on a Journey*, pp. 154, 158; Schoolcraft, *Narrative Journal of Travels*, pp. 35–6; Savage and Savage, *André and François André Michaux*, p. 37.

to "a very extraordinary character between 80 and 90 years of age," and the old trapper enlivened his *Ornithology* with "anecdotes [for]...the greater part of the first volume, & some of the second." His journals and those of others are replete with passive-construction introductory phrases – "I am informed"; "I am told" – suggesting informants who fleshed out their understanding of local flora, fauna, and geology.[98] For his natural history of New Hampshire, Jeremy Belknap made personal observations, corresponded with "gentlemen of public character," and consulted with those whose life experiences – logging, fishing, hunting, trapping, surveying, farming, woodworking, trading – made them particularly intimate with nature. Housewives, Vermont naturalist Zadock Thompson wrote, "by their habits of careful discrimination in the process of cooking, obtain so accurate a knowledge of various animals used for food as might sometimes enable them to put the professed comparative anatomist to the blush for his ignorance." Naturalists accepted what historian Thomas R. Dunlap calls "folk-biology" because this was often the only knowledge available in the new country.[99]

A drawback to these conversations with Indians and other country folk was a certain amount of misinforming, and nothing illustrates this better than the natural history of the beaver. Because beavers had become rare east of the Mississippi, naturalists received their information secondhand from westerners, and these overextended lines of communication left a record of distortion. Benjamin Barton published an article in the American Philosophical Society's *Transactions* on the "Facts and Observations Relative to the Beaver," which he collected by correspondence with Moravian missionary John Heckewelder, who took his facts from I. Pemaholend, a "famous beaver-trapper," who in turn interviewed "aged and respected" Delaware Indians who remembered when beaver inhabited the Susquehanna drainage. More of Heckewelder's story came from a

---

[98] Alexander Wilson to Alexander Lawson, February 22, 1810, Coues, "Private Letters of Wilson, Ord, and Bonaparte," p. 448. See Liancourt, *Travels Through the United States*, Vol. 1, p. xix.

[99] Belknap, *History of New-Hampshire* (Dover, 1812), Vol. 3, p. iii; Zadock Thompson, *Natural History of Vermont: An Address Delivered at Boston, Before the Boston Society of Natural History* (Burlington, 1850), p. 27; Thomas R. Dunlap, *Nature and the English Diaspora: Environment and History in the United States, Canada, Australia, and New Zealand* (New York, 1999). See Franklin B. Hough, *A History of Jefferson County in the State of New York, From the Earliest Period to the Present Time* (Albany, 1854), p. 3; Amos Eaton, *Geological and Agricultural Survey of Rensselaer County, in the State of New York* (Albany, 1822), p. vi.

French trader at Detroit who had been recommended to him by another "as a person of credit." The trader, in turn, had gathered his stories while living among the Chippewa on Lake Heron. Heckewelder's beaver history appears reasonably accurate by modern standards, but this was rare for information gathered in so extensive a net. Samuel Hearne, who actually kept beavers as pets, described the accounts written by others as outlandish. "Little remains to be added... beside a vocabulary of their language, a code of their laws, and a sketch of their religion."[100]

Why beavers were subject to such fantasies is difficult to say. Italian naturalist Giacomo Beltrami traveled on the upper Mississippi with several Chippewa guides, who might have found these anthropomorphic accounts an amusing way to pass time in a canoe with a credulous foreigner. John Godman noted that fur-traders and Indians were often "jealous... of all those who are too inquisitive about their particular concerns." When questioned about beaver, he noted:

they take a malicious pleasure in palming, with truly Indian gravity and patience, the most false and marvellous relations upon their auditor.... We have been informed by an early witness on one such occasion that he was astonished to hear a trader giving a long account, full of the most extraordinary and interesting particulars, of the habits of the beaver to an ardent inquirer who was writing it down with great delight. As soon as the collector of notes on natural history had retired, ... the other inquired of the trader how it happened that he never had before given this information.... The answer to this question was a roar of laughter, and an assurance that there was not a word of truth in the whole statement.[101]

Although "country people" provided a fund of useful information, naturalists found it difficult to separate out the legends, fantasies, and outright inventions, and America's natural history retained these fanciful notions until a slower and more focused process of systematic field observation replaced them. In the meantime, folk science spiced the record, legitimized popular lore, and prepared the ground for a romantic interpretation of nature at midcentury.

---

[100] John Heckewelder, "Facts and Observations Relative to the Beaver of North America, Collected by Mr. John Heckewelder, in Answer to Queries Proposed by Professor Barton," *APS Transactions* 6 (1809): pp. 209–12; Hearne in Bell, *Cabinet of Curiosities*, p. 130. See Williams, *Natural and Civil History of Vermont*, pp. 116–20; Jonathan Carver, *Three Years Travels Through the Interior Parts of North-America* (Philadelphia, 1796), pp. 186–7.

[101] Godman, *American Natural History*, Vol. 2, pp. 39–40, 48, 50–1.

An "Entertaining and Instructive Species of Reading"

Typically, naturalists arranged their conversations and observations about complex and unfamiliar landscapes into a travel narrative, a format that was accessible to most readers and still satisfied the scientist's deep-seated need for orderly composition. A literary form as old as Homer, travel narratives were widely read in Europe, and the scientist who used this genre was likely to reach a popular audience. The naturalist's ramble was thus rendered as a travelogue, and the arcane scientific observations made along the way transformed into adventure and aesthetic instruction. It presented, John Melish wrote, "a *living picture* of the state of the country through which [the naturalist]... passes," making natural history an "entertaining and instructive species of reading."[102]

The naturalist's narrative borrowed from two traditions. It was a conventional technique used by explorers worldwide, dating back to the epic transatlantic voyages of the early 1500s. In these global explorations, ship captains, as historian Bruce Greenfield puts it, "restricted themselves to reporting on what they themselves actually saw and experienced; they told their stories from the observer's point of view; they focused on regions that were 'unknown' to their readers; they organized their narratives around a journey; and they held out the advancement of scientific knowledge as a concern transcending their more immediate practical goals."[103] The nineteenth-century narrative found its specific form in a genre of tourist literature then in great vogue. Early in the century, as travelers became "tourists," many took up natural history as a means of positioning themselves in the adventure of discovery in America. A serious pursuit but not so serious as to be considered work, natural history provided relief from the round of grand hotels and watering holes.[104] It was tastefully modern, but its interpretive framework was compatible with most religious assumptions of the day. Trained in the classics and conversant with modern science, the tourist-naturalist shared much in

[102] Melish, *Travels in the United States*, p. iii. See Angela Miller, *The Empire of the Eye: Landscape Representation and American Cultural Politics, 1825–1875* (Ithaca, 1993), p. 15; Robert D. Arner, "Pastoral Patterns in William Bartram's *Travels*," *Tennessee Studies in Literature* 18 (1973): p. 133; Regis, *Describing Early America*, pp. 5, 11; Bedell, *Anatomy of Nature*, pp. 17–18.

[103] Bruce Greenfield, *Narrating Discovery: The Romantic Explorer in American Literature, 1790–1855* (New York, 1992), p. 71.

[104] Dona Brown, *Inventing New England: Regional Tourism in the Nineteenth Century* (Washington, 1995), p. 33.

common with the more dedicated explorer, who in turn employed the tourist's polite literary devices – wit, irony, sensitivity, variety, contrast, wonder, curiosity – to draw readers into their own world.[105]

Some scientists remained aloof from these genteel tourist conventions. John Haywood confined his *Natural and Aboriginal History of the Tennessee* to those discoveries "conducive to the advancement of science," and Amos Eaton emphasized that fieldwork should not be considered a "sport." In contrast, some tourists refused to look at nature scientifically. Philadelphian James Hall, who wrote about the West in a series of letters to the literary magazine *Port Folio*, insisted that he loved nature and delighted in gazing "upon her beauties," but he contemplated these natural forms "as I do those of a lovely female, without the least curiosity to pry into matters which lie beyond the surface." Arrayed along the broad spectrum between empirical method and undisciplined curiosity, the scientific narrative was sufficiently flexible to accommodate almost any level of interest in nature.[106] This mix of science and tourism gave natural history its popular audience and its distinctive romantic cast.

The travel narrative also shaped the way naturalists thought about nature. In an era before fixed scientific disciplines, naturalists celebrated their eclecticism. Peter Kalm's descriptive narrative moved from polecats to pine tar, pitch, and rice, and from a dissertation on cockroaches to American marriage customs, toothache remedies, and Indian hunting techniques, all in a few score pages.[107] In the preface to his *Travels in the Central Portions of the Mississippi Valley*, Henry Schoolcraft promised information on all branches of natural history, committed to paper by the light of his campfire. There, literally in the wilderness he described, he drew narrative connections among rocks, plants, birds, climates, and civilizations – past, present, and yet to come. In an age of scientific eclecticism, the travel narrative was an appropriate vehicle for moving from botany to entomology to geology as quickly as the observer's eye moved from

---

[105] See William Chambers, *Things As They Are in America* (Philadelphia, 1854), p. 1; *American Journal of Science* 11 (No. 2, 1826): p. 219; Oldroyd, *Thinking About the Earth*, pp. 133–4; Temple, *American Tourist's Pocket Companion* pp. 9–10; Whitaker, "Culture of Curiosity," p. 84; Watkin, *Trip to the United States*, p. viii.

[106] John Haywood, *The Natural and Aboriginal History of the Tennessee* (Nashville, 1823), p. ii; Amos Eaton, *Geological Text-Book, Prepared for Popular Lectures on North American Geology* (Albany, 1830), p. iv; Hall, *Letters from the West*, p. 180.

[107] Peter Kalm, *Travels into North America, Containing Its Natural History, and a Circumstantial Account of Its Plantations and Agriculture in General*, John R. Foster (trans.), (Warrington, 1753–1771), Vol. 1, pp. 278–9; Vol. 2, pp. 13–16, 27–30, 33–5, 39–43.

forest to insect to bedrock ledge, and the narrative account helped bring these landscape elements together. Recording observations in sequence, observers situated each plant, animal, or mineral in a broader ecological context that included soil and forest types, topographical features, climate, and latitude. Where taxonomy removed specimens from their environment, narrative embedded them, arranging specimens and species in situ and suggesting a holistic perspective where trees, shrubs, and flowers melded into forests, swamps, meadows, or uplands.[108]

The flexible format of the narrative record also encouraged a blend of empiricism and speculation that raised natural history to a philosophical level. According to English writer, Oliver Goldsmith, scientific exploration had two goals. The first involved describing new species according to the taxonomical system devised by Linnaeus in the mid-eighteenth century. This task he found "systematical, dry, mechanical, and incomplete." The second involved describing the relation these species bore "to us and to each other." This, he thought, was "more amusing" because it exhibited "new pictures to the imagination, . . . by widening the prospect of nature around us." American naturalists embraced both goals. Thus, while much of the taxonomical record was indeed systematical and dry, the travel narrative encouraged broad philosophical speculations that connected the various species naturalists described.[109]

The narrative of discovery also incorporated sight, sound, smell, touch, and even taste into the scientific assessment of nature. The technique of sensual observation dated from colonial times when specimens sometimes served as food as well as objects of scientific contemplation. John Brickell reported in 1737 that "the shag [*Phalacrocoras auritus*] is somewhat like the cormorant, but . . . the flesh is black, ill-tasted, and hard of digestion." John Clayton wrote that muskrats looked like European water rats but had a "curious musky scent," which he experienced firsthand when a captive he kept in his room sickened and died. Boston's Jacob Bigelow chewed his plant specimens to determine their chemical properties and possible medical applications.[110] All forms of comprehension were

---

[108] Henry Rowe Schoolcraft, *Travels in the Central Portions of the Mississippi Valley* (New York, 1825), p. 11. See Wilson, *Lyell in America*, p. 142; Temple, *American Tourist's Pocket Companion*, p. 9; Smallwood, *Natural History and the American Mind*, pp. 30, 338; N. Bryllion Fagin, *William Bartram: Interpreter of the American Landscape* (Baltimore, 1933), pp. 80, 84.

[109] "Preface," Oliver Goldsmith, *An History of the Earth and Animated Nature in Four Volumes* (Philadelphia, 1795), Vol. 1, n.p.

[110] Brickell, *The Natural History of North-Carolina*, p. 212; Clayton, *Miscellanea Curiosa*, Vol. 3, p. 340; Bigelow, *Florula Bostoniensis*, p. 68; Bigelow, *American Medical Botany* (Boston, 1817–1821), Vol. 1, pp. xv–xvi; Thomas P. Slaughter, *The Natures of John*

important to the scientific record, and the narrative provided a flexible format for blending these experiences.

This "search for sensuous contact," as historian Donald Worster puts it in his study of Thoreau, gave landscapes intrinsic value. Like poets and painters, naturalists became immersed in nature, composing an emotional and sensual perspective impossible to convey in a Linnaean catalog. William Bartram epitomized this technique in the rich sensual imagery he used to provide a multidimensional portrait of the southern wilderness.[111] He was, as he put it, "wholly engaged" in the natural landscape. "Any extensive study of his art cannot ignore his notation of gustatory, tactile, and olfactory sensations," a biographer wrote. "He notes the 'aromatic flavour' and the bitter taste of the palmetto royal tree . . . , the 'sweet and agreeable' taste of the live oak acorn."[112] Tactile sensations – the feel of the bark or the sting of the insect – were standard elements of the empirical method but, in the travel narrative, they became suggestive and fluid, making the journal of discovery a highly popular literary expression: a melding of science and literature.

The rambling naturalist observed nature on many levels – scientific, sensual, aesthetic, moral, and even theological. This open and receptive consciousness was the ultimate empirical method, but it also set the stage for a popular and sentimental appreciation of nature that would blossom into romantic discourse during the middle of the century. Like the Romantics who followed them into the forests and fields, naturalists found themselves immersed in nature, roused alternatively to fear, dread, scientific speculation, or religious celebration. The enthusiasm they wrote into their narratives was a distinctive mark of the early nineteenth century – a time when, as one historian put it, the rhapsodist was "never entirely separated from the scientist."[113]

---

and William Bartram (New York, 1996), p. 53; Henry Mühlenberg to Mannasseh Cutler, November 8, 1791, Manasseh Cutler Papers, APS.

[111] Donald Worster, *Nature's Economy: A History of Ecological Ideas* (New York, 1977), p. 78; Fagin, *William Bartram*, p. 76. See Bedell, *Anatomy of Nature*, pp. 17–18; Whitaker, "Culture of Curiosity," p. 84; Regis, *Describing Early America*, pp. 5, 11.

[112] Fagin, *William Bartram*, p. 104.

[113] Fagin, *William Bartram*, p. 102.

3

"A Despairing Curiosity"

Creating America's Scientific Academy

When Benjamin Silliman delivered his first lecture on geology at Yale College in 1804, his cabinet of minerals amounted to a half-bushel of unidentified rocks collected at random by former students. He taught during these early years without texts and without scientific consensus on even the most elemental explanations of earth history. With no one to guide him in geological principles, he gazed, as he put it, with a "despairing curiosity" on the unexplained and unclassified ridges and outcroppings of the Connecticut Valley. Silliman packed Yale's pitiful collection into a box and carried it off to Philadelphia, where he spread the rocks before Adam Seybert, a student of the eminent German geologist, Abraham Gottlob Werner. With some rudimentary lessons in mineralogy, Silliman traveled to Europe and consulted with other experts, then returned to Yale to begin laying a foundation for American science. He realized his goal in 1818 when he launched the *American Journal of Science*, the most successful scientific publication in the nation, and when he retired in 1856 his institution boasted the largest mineral collection in the country.[1]

Silliman's career spanned the most dynamic period of growth in the history of American science. In 1804, the American scientific academy was as rudimentary as Yale's cabinet. Aside from Thomas Jefferson, Benjamin

---

[1] *American Journal of Science* 1 (1818): p. 36; Benjamin Silliman, *Address Delivered Before the Association of American Geologists and Naturalists* (New Haven, 1842), p. 11; "James D. Dana's Address Upon Succeeding Silliman as Professor at Yale, February 18, 1856," Benjamin Silliman Manuscripts, Pennsylvania Historical Society (hereafter PHS); Dana in Daniel C. Gilman, *The Life of James Dwight Dana: Scientific Explorer, Mineralogist, Geologist, Zoologist, Professor in Yale University* (New York, 1899), pp. 160–2.

Franklin, Benjamin Rush, William Bartram, and a few others, the country boasted no internationally known scientific figures. A few scientific institutions existed, but their meetings and publications were sporadic and their collections, as Manasseh Cutler complained to an English colleague in 1799, were "kept merely for the purpose of getting money by showing them to common people, and consist principally of exotics."[2] America had one scientific journal, Samuel Mitchill's *Medical Repository*, and only a few literary magazines reviewed scientific literature. As DeWitt Clinton explained in 1815, America's broad distribution of wealth left no room for a leisured class to take up the unremunerated pursuit of truth, and its footloose, materialistic, and heterogeneous population offered no cultural validation for pure science. Before the Revolution, European scientific institutions like the Royal Society and the Swedish Academy had encouraged American scientific activity, but postwar diplomatic tensions strained these connections and cross-country exchanges were almost as difficult. American scientists were, as geologist Henry Darwin Rogers summarized, "scattered over a country of great extent and kept asunder by distance and the claims of professional duties." Mails were slow, and shipping specimens often required personal intervention all along the route. Those on the frontier labored in solitude, each "hewing his lonely path through the mighty wilderness" without the assumed understandings in procedure and discourse that came through face-to-face interaction with colleagues. Writing from Natchez, John Hart complained that he had "no person in this vicinity to sit with me in judgement upon the botany of this district, and almost everything I meet with is to me new." Like Silliman gazing up the Connecticut Valley, Hart despaired at the "innumerable plants which bear no names."[3]

---

[2] Manasseh Cutler to G. Paykull, February 14, 1799, William Parker Cutler and Julia Perkins Cutler, *Life, Journals, and Correspondence of Rev. Manasseh Cutler, LLD, by his Grandchildren* (Cincinnati, 1888), Vol. 2, pp. 299–300. See Correa de Serra to Sir James Edward Smith, November 18, 1813, James Edward Smith Correspondence, Vol. 3, p. 194, Linnaean Society of London (microfilm), American Philosophical Society (hereafter APS); John C. Greene, "Science and the Public in the Age of Jefferson," *Isis* 49 (1958): p. 15.

[3] Benjamin Smith Barton, *Fragments of the Natural History of Pennsylvania* (Philadelphia, 1799), p. viii; De Witt Clinton in *Port Folio*, 3d ser. 6 (August 1815): pp. 140, 145–7; Henry Darwin Rogers, *Address on the Recent Progress of Geological Research in the United States* (Philadelphia, 1844), p. 3; John A. Hart to Constantine Rafinesque, February 15, 1821, Constantine Rafinesque Papers, APS. See William Dunbar to Henry E. Mühlenberg, April 15, 1806, Henry E. Mühlenberg Manuscripts, PHS; W. W. Mather to Benjamin Silliman, January 30, 1836, Benjamin Silliman Papers, APS; Horace Hildreth to Samuel George Morton, June 29, 1837, Samuel George Morton Papers, APS; Brooke

Despite these difficult conditions, the pace of scientific development quickened in the first decades of the century. This resulted in part from advances in scientific equipment like telescopes, microscopes, chronometers, thermometers, navigational devices, and chemical extraction and distillation retorts, and in part from completion of the Linnaean catalog in the mid-1700s. Transatlantic trends in urbanization, global exploration, and wealth accumulation also encouraged more comprehensive scientific investigation, as did a fluid dialogue across disciplinary boundaries. However, events at home were equally as important. Westward migration and the 1802 Louisiana Purchase encouraged scientific exploration, and when the 1807 embargo and the War of 1812 depressed the transatlantic trade – once the engine of national growth – interest in the West intensified. Scientists became more nationalistic and less willing to export the fruits of their research, "little to our credit, and still less to our advantage," as Silliman put it. It was time, the *Medical Repository* opined, that Americans "turn[ed] their backs to the East, and direct[ed] their views to the inviting and productive regions of interior America."[4]

"Many Excellent Friends"

After the War of 1812, methods of internal communication improved, and American scientists, by choice or necessity, began developing their own networks of correspondence. As Martin Rudwick notes, they "lived in a world...[where] spontaneous and fluent letter writing was a routine accomplishment." Some exchanges were impersonal. Benjamin Barton sent out a notice to "every friend to Botany" seeking information on plants and published the replies in his various commentaries. In some cases, correspondents abstracted this scientific dialogue by simply exchanging numbered lists of species, to which the respondent

---

Hindle, *The Pursuit of Science in Revolutionary America, 1735–1789* (Chapel Hill, 1956), pp. 3–5, 59, 304; William Martin Smallwood in collaboration with Mabel Sarah Coon Smallwood, *Natural History and the American Mind* (New York, 1941), pp. 101, 251–2; Courtney Robert Hall, *A Scientist in the Early Republic: Samuel Latham Mitchill, 1764–1831* (New York, 1934), pp. 6, 67–8.

4 *Medical Repository*, 2d ser., 5 (1808): p. 42; *American Journal of Science* 39 (October 1840): pp. 344–6, 349. See George H. Daniels, *American Science in the Age of Jackson* (New York, 1968), pp. 7, 63–4, 66; Henry D. Shapiro, "Daniel Drake: The New Western Naturalist," *Bartonia* No. 54 (1988): p. 43; Joel R. Poinsett, *Discourse on the Objects and Importance of the National Institution for the Promotion of Science, Established at Washington, 1840* (Washington, 1841), pp. 7, 23, 29, 32, 37–9; Hall, *Scientist in the Early Republic*, p. 64; Samuel L. Mitchill, *A Lecture on Some Parts of the Natural History of New-Jersey*, p. 5, pamphlet, Vol. 5, No. 1160, APS.

commented *ad seriatim*. The lists contained technical descriptions, sometimes in Latin, and some included as many as two hundred items. Gerard
Troost sent a typical comment to J. (?) R. Buchanan: "No 48 – your label
says: '*Gryphite* in *argilaecous*'; . . . this can not be a *gryphea*. It is an interior cast of a shell which belongs perhaps to the *terebratula*, . . . ; 53. I am
not acquainted with this shell – I do not believe it an *ammonite*; the marks
of the internal des [ign?] . . . are not visible."[5] Sometimes this correspondence cemented close personal friendships. Henry Mühlenberg's scientific
request to Massaseh Cutler seemed almost incidental to a long and cordial
greeting: "If you happen to make any excursions on a fine winter day and
find some lichens or mosses, . . . please to lay some bye for your friend." In
the preface to their monumental *Flora of North America*, John Torrey and
Asa Gray acknowledged hundreds of correspondents, as did Thomas Say
and Louis Agassiz in their major works. John James Audubon's impressive inventory of American birds was possible, as he noted, only with the
help of "many excellent friends . . . in different portions of the country,
who have, at great trouble to themselves, . . . forwarded . . . notes upon the
habits of different species."[6] With few outlets for publication, American
science depended on these informal exchanges to disseminate information
and provide critical review. Henry Mühlenberg voiced the aspirations of
those who added their local expertise to these grand catalogs: "A beginning must be made," he wrote to Manasseh Cutler in 1791; "let each one
of our American Botanists do something, and soon the riches of America
will be known. Let [François André] Michaux describe South Carolina
and Georgia; [Samuel] Kramsch, North Carolina; [James] Greenway,
Virginia and Maryland; [Benjamin] Barton, Jersey, Delaware, and the
lower parts of Pennsylvania; [William] Bartram, [Humphrey] Marshall,
[Henry] Müthlenberg, their neighborhood; [Samuel] Mitchill, New York,
and you, with the northern Botanists, your states – How much could be
done!"[7]

5 Gerard Troost to J.? R. Buchanan, July 14, 1835, Miscellaneous Collection, APS. See
   Jacob Bigelow to Henry E. Mühlenberg, October 1, 1813, Mühlenberg Manuscripts,
   PHS; Charles William Capers to Thomas Say, ca. 1820, Thomas Say Papers, APS.
6 M. J. S. Rudwick, *The Great Devonian Controversy: The Shaping of Scientific Knowledge
   Among Gentlemanly Specialists* (Chicago, 1985), p. 36; James Anderson to Benjamin
   Smith Barton, August 3, 1804, Benjamin Smith Barton Papers, APS; Henry Mühlenberg
   to Manasseh Cutler, November 8, 1791, Manasseh Cutler Papers, APS; John James
   Audubon and John Bachman, *The Quadrupeds of North America*, Vol. 1 (New York,
   1849), p. vi.
7 John Torrey and Asa Gray, "Preface," *A Flora of North America: Containing Abridged
   Descriptions of All the Known Indigenous and Naturalized Plants Growing North of
   Mexico* (New York, 1969), Vol. 1; "Miscellaneous Notes on Conchology, etc.," Say

Scientific and philosophical societies formalized this exchange. Increase Mather founded a Boston Philosophical Society in 1683, patterned after the Royal Society of London, formed two decades earlier. Mather's organization proved ephemeral but, in the late colonial period, Philadelphia, with its cosmopolitan population, medical center, and Benjamin Franklin, rekindled this scientific interest. In 1743, Franklin, John Bartram, and several others formed the American Philosophical Society (APS), whose members met once a month to discuss questions of moral, political, and natural philosophy.[8] Among its goals was the discovery of "one or more entire skeletons of the Mamoth [sic], so called" and the publication of papers on all subjects under the broad rubric of natural history, including improvements in celestial navigation, orcharding, ship pumps, street lamps, and stoves. In 1784, Boston naturalists created the American Academy of Arts and Sciences with a mission similar to that of the APS, and in Philadelphia, the Academy of Natural Sciences was founded in 1812. Between 1815 and 1825, the number of scientific societies in America tripled, many of them publishing journals.[9]

West of the Appalachians, scientific institutions benefited from an intense booster mentality and a drive to duplicate the cultural achievements of the East. Struck by the low state of culture in his frontier

---

Papers, APS; Louis Agassiz, *Contributions to the Natural History of the United States* (Boston, 1857–62); Henry Mühlenberg to Manasseh Cutler, April 11, 1791, Cutler Papers, APS. See James D. Dana to John L. Le Conte, January 1, 1855, Le Conte Papers, APS; Henry Mühlenberg to Manasseh Cutler, November 12, 1792, Cutler and Cutler, *Life, Journals, and Correspondence of Rev. Manasseh Cutler*, Vol. 2, pp. 291–2.

[8] See Jeremy Belknap in Hindle, *Pursuit of Science in Revolutionary America*, p. 278; Ralph S. Bates, *Scientific Societies in the United States* (Cambridge, Massachusetts, 1945), pp. 1–4, 7–8; David Scofield Wilson, *In the Presence of Nature* (Amherst, 1978), pp. 6–7; Ralph S. Bates, *Scientific Societies in the United States*, pp. 5–6; Smallwood, *Natural History and the American Mind*, p. 132.

[9] American Philosophical Society, No. 106, Broadsides, APS. See "The American Philosophical Society, Held . . . May, 1796," Broadsides, APS; American Association for the Advancement of Science Circular, Broadsides, APS; Whitfield J. Bell, Jr., "The Cabinet of the American Philosophical Society" in Whitfield J. Bell Jr., et al., *A Cabinet of Curiosities: Five Episodes in the Evolution of American Museums* (Charlottesville, 1967), pp. 5, 8; Raymond Phineas Stearns, *Science in the British Colonies of America* (Urbana, 1970), p. 674; *Medical Repository* 2 (No. 2, 1798): p. 216; Whitfield Bell, "The Scientific Environment of Philadelphia, 1775–1790," *APS Proceedings* 92 (1948): p. 11; Hindle, *Pursuit of Science in Revolutionary America*, pp. 264, 271–2; Bates, *Scientific Societies*, pp. 10–11; American Academy of Arts & Sciences *Memoirs* 1 (1785), p. viii; Charlotte M. Porter, *The Eagle's Nest: Natural History and American Ideas, 1812–1842* (Tuscaloosa, 1986), pp. 30, 32; Simon Baatz, "Philadelphia Patronate: The Institutional Structure of Natural History in the New Republic, 1800–1833," *Journal of the Early Republic* 8 (Summer 1988): pp. 118–19, 121, 127.

city, Cincinnati's Daniel Drake became a western version of Benjamin Franklin, devoting his life to founding institutions of social welfare and learning. In 1813, he helped establish the Lancastrian Seminary and the District Medical Society; in 1819, he was involved in the Cincinnati Society for the Promotion of Agriculture, Manufactures, and Domestic Economy; and through the 1820s and 1830s, he was at least in part responsible for an incredible array of institutions including an insane asylum, a poorhouse, a bank, three medical colleges, an infirmary, a hospital, two lyceums, a library, several schools, a literary institute, the Western Museum, and the *Western Medical and Physical Journal*, which he edited. Gerard Troost, a founder with Drake of the Western Academy of Natural Science, pointed out that its members would have to be rigorous, "because if we greenhorns of the Far West commit some blunders, we will soon feel the parental rod of the eastern savants." These cultural anxieties were simply regional variations on a broader nationalistic sentiment. The "parental rod" of European science drove Americans in general to build an exacting foundation for their institutions.[10]

The scientific community matured quickly after the War of 1812. Philadelphia naturalists benefited from intellectual treasures like Benjamin Franklin's various legacies, William Bartram's garden, Charles Willson Peale's museum, the APS, the Library Company, the College of Physicians, the University of Pennsylvania, the Philadelphia Hospital, the Carpenter's Company, the Franklin Institute, and the Academy of Natural Sciences. Private cabinets and libraries belonging to Benjamin Barton, Thomas Say, Richard Harlan, John Godman, George Ord, Isaac Lea, and Isaac Hayes were more complete than many in Europe. When Swiss naturalist, Louis Agassiz, moved to the United States in 1846, he traveled first to Philadelphia, where he was awed by these "magnificent collections" and by the city's air of intellectual and religious tolerance. From the perspective of this one city, science seemed well positioned to represent nature before the American people.[11]

---

[10] Gerard Troost to J.? R. Buchanan, July 14, 1835, Miscellaneous Collection, APS. See Daniel Drake in Daniel Aaron, *Cincinnati: The Queen City of the West, 1918–1938* (Columbus, 1992), pp. 244–8; Charles D. Meigs, *A Biographical Notice of Daniel Drake, M.D., of Cincinnati* (Philadelphia, 1853), pp. 10, 14–16; Henry D. Shapiro, "Daniel Drake," pp. 40–3; Kastner, *Species of Eternity*, p. 216; Jeannette E. Graustein, *Thomas Nuttall: Naturalist Explorations in America, 1808–1841* (Cambridge, 1967), p. 106; *Port Folio*, 4th ser., 1 (January 1816): p. 26.

[11] Louis Agassiz to Rose Mayor Agassiz, December 1846, in Agassiz, *Louis Agassiz: His Life and Correspondence*, edited by Elizabeth Cary Agassiz (Boston, 1885), Vol. 2,

Museums, Gardens, and Other "Splendid Establishments"

Public museums and gardens were among the means of carrying out this mission. State museums were common in Europe in the late eighteenth century and private and quasi-public collections brought this legacy to America, beginning with the Charleston Library Society's public cabinet, founded in 1776, and Charles Willson Peale's Philadelphia Museum, founded in 1784. Peale, who studied in England under painter and architect, Benjamin West, moved to Philadelphia during the Revolution and rendered portraits of patriotic figures. In the 1780s, he began dissecting and illustrating specimens as curator for the APS and, in 1784, he acquired a collection belonging to the recently deceased Swiss scholar and painter, Pierre Eugéne Du Simitière, who had conducted tours of his collection hoping to transform it into a national museum. Peale added his own curiosities and opened a museum in his home in 1786; in 1794, he moved the collection to the APS's Philosophical Hall; in 1802, to the Pennsylvania State House; and in 1827, the year Peale died, to an arcade on Chestnut Street.[12]

Peale and his family pioneered the idea of nature as spectacle. The imagination, he thought, could conceive of nothing more interesting than a museum, and he bolstered this conviction with nationalistic and religious rhetoric.[13] His museum, he wrote in a broadside, was a "splendid establishment," arranged to present scientific specimens so as to delight and entertain the visitor. Animals stood in "lifelike attitudes" among earth, bush, and trees or against painted landscapes designed to draw visitors into the specimen's world. A marine room contained shells, corals, and fish, and in another corner, monkeys posed as though "employed in the occupations of men." Several eminent naturalists acted as curators or lecturers.[14]

pp. 417–20. See Graustein, *Thomas Nuttall*, p. 20; Bell, "Scientific Environment of Philadelphia."

[12] Mark V. Barrow, Jr., *A Passion for Birds: American Ornithology After Audubon* (Princeton, 1988), p. 9; Charles Willson Peale Lectures, APS, p. 13; Peale, *Introduction to a Course of Lectures on Natural History, Delivered in the University of Pennsylvania, Nov. 16, 1799* (Philadelphia, 1800), pp. 20–9, 30; Peale, "To the Citizens of the United States of America," Broadsides, APS; Bell, "Scientific Environment of Philadelphia"; Kastner, *Species of Eternity*, pp. 143–6, 149–50, 153.

[13] Peale, *Course of Lectures*, p. 35; Manasseh Cutler, "Diary of 1787," William Parker Cutler and Julia Perkins Cutler, *Life, Journals, and Correspondence of Rev. Manasseh Cutler, LL.D, by his Grandchildren* (Cincinnati, 1888), Vol. 1, pp. 259–62.

[14] Peale's Museum (1813), Broadsides, APS; Richard Rhodes, *John James Audubon: The Making of an American* (New York, 2004), p. 35; Charles Lucien Bonaparte to Isaac

Museums sometimes crossed the line between science and circus. Englishman Edward Hingston considered American museums mere places of amusement, "wherein there shall be a theatre, some wax figures, a giant and a dwarf or two, a jumble of pictures, and a few live snakes." Prince von Wied described them as collections of "stiff, awkward, wax figures; mathematical and other instruments, models, [and] bad paintings and engravings,...hung up without any order." Cincinnati's Western Museum failed to attract the public, he observed, until it redesigned the upper rooms as an "absurd representation of hell...in which a number of frightful skeletons are moving about, and among whom the devil acts a principal party." In 1829, English scientist, James Smithson, bequeathed his fortune to the United States to found a scientific institution in Washington. The bequest was locked in controversy for decades but, in 1842, Congress chartered the National Institute for the Promotion of Science and, finally, in 1846–7, the National Museum became a reality, with Princeton physicist Joseph Henry as its first secretary. Louis Agassiz's Museum of Comparative Zoology at Harvard gave America a second national repository of curiosities. Until then, several less somber institutions like Peale's excited the public imagination.[15]

Botanical gardens also brought nature before the American people. Of these, the Bartrams' garden in Philadelphia was clearly the most renowned.[16] Botanist Manasseh Cutler visited the garden while attending the Constitutional Convention in 1787, and he and William Bartram "ranged the several alleys," with Bartram identifying each plant by generic and specific name. The garden, Cutler wrote, "is finely situated, as it partakes of every kind of soil, has a fine stream of water, and an artificial pond, where he has a good collection of aquatic plants.... But every thing is very badly arranged, for they are neither placed ornamentally

Hayes, February 15, 1826, Hayes Papers, APS; Stroud, *Thomas Say*, p. 29; Charles Willson Peale, "Gentlemen, I Thank You," Broadsides, APS; Peale, *Course of Lectures*, pp. 34–5.

15 Edward Hingston in Louis Leonard Tucker, "'Ohio Show-Shop': The Western Museum of Cincinnati, 1820–1867," Bell, *Cabinet of Curiosities*, p. 74; Maximilian Alexander Philip, Prinz von Wied-Neuwied, *Travels in the Interior of North America*, H. Evans Lloyd (trans.), (London, 1843), pp. 8, 483. See *American Journal of Science* 1 (1818): pp. 203–5.

16 John Torrey to Amos Eaton, March 12, 1819, Torrey Papers, APS. See Ernest Earnest, *John and William Bartram: Botanists and Explorers, 1699–1777; 1739–1823* (Philadelphia, 1940), pp. 16, 20–1; *Port Folio*, 4th ser., 6 (August 1818): p. 151; Smallwood, *Natural History and the American Mind*, pp. 150–4; *North American Review*, n.s., 70 (January 1850): 213.

nor botanically, but seem to be jumbled together in heaps."[17] Although much has been made of the Bartrams' compulsion to impose order on nature, their garden was far less arranged than a taxonomical guide. Like museums, gardens emphasized variety and curiosity over scientific arrangement.

Along with museums and gardens, scientific journals helped convey observations to a broader public. At the beginning of the century, this medium was limited to irregular issues from the scientific societies and a few medical journals. America's first regularly issued scientific journal was Samuel Mitchill's *Medical Repository*. Founded in 1797, it ran until 1824, but it was eclipsed by Benjamin Silliman's *American Journal of Science* in 1818. Featuring articles by prominent naturalists William Maclure, Thomas Say, and Henry Mühlenberg in his inaugural issue, Silliman noted that American scientists were as active as any but their observations were not cumulative. This he would remedy by consolidating knowledge from across the country, promoting "the honour and prosperity of the nation." By the 1830s, America boasted five quarterly, eight monthly, and seven occasional scientific journals.[18]

University appointments brought together a more select scientific community, beginning the process of legitimizing natural history as an academic discipline. Harvard initiated a scientific curriculum in 1727 by appointing Isaac Greenwood as Hollis Professor of Mathematics and Natural Philosophy. A Harvard graduate, Greenwood studied in London and convinced London merchant Thomas Hollis to endow a chair at Harvard, and the trustees appointed Greenwood to fill it. Although successful as a teacher, Greenwood was discharged in 1738 for drunkenness and his place taken by astronomer John Winthrop and later the Reverend Samuel Williams. Williams resigned in 1788 under charges of forgery and

---

[17] Cutler, "Diary of 1787," pp. 272–3.

[18] *American Journal of Science* 1 (1818): pp. 2–3, 440. See Hans Huth, *Nature and the American: Three Centuries of Changing Attitudes* (Berkeley, 1957), pp. 26–7; John F. Fulton and Elizabeth H. Thomson, *Benjamin Silliman, 1779–1864: Pathfinder in American Science* (New York, 1947), pp. 7, 23, 28–9, 32, 88, 121, 123; *Newburyport Herald*, July 1829, "Clippings Relating to Appeal for Support of the *American Journal of Science,* 1829," Silliman Manuscripts, PHS; Hall, *Scientist in the Early Republic*, pp. 3, 5, 7–10, 23; Daniels, *American Science*, p. 13; Kastner, *Species of Eternity*, pp. 193–7; S. L. Mitchill, *Some of the Memorable Events and Occurrences in the Life of Samuel L. Mitchill of New-York, from the Year 1786–1828* (pamphlet, 1828?), APS; *American Journal of Science* 4 (No. 1, 1821): pp. 181, 195; *Journal of the Academy of Natural Sciences of Philadelphia* 1 (Part 1, May 1817): p. 1; *Port Folio*, 4th ser. 4 (December 1817): p. 485; For a listing of the scientific journals in circulation in 1832, see *Monthly American Journal of Geology and Natural Science* 1 (March 1832): pp. 399–400.

was replaced by Benjamin Waterhouse, a pioneering proponent of inoculations for smallpox and member of the Harvard Medical School faculty. Although controversial as a physician, Waterhouse attracted patronage from several wealthy Bostonians, who funded a Massachusetts Professorship of Natural History in 1805. For this chair, which came with funding for a botanical garden, the trustees nominated entomologist and biologist, William Dandridge Peck. Somewhat daunted by his position, Peck accepted mostly because he feared that an "obstinate refusal" would discourage the university's benefactors. Nevertheless, he established the garden on eight acres of land in Cambridge and died while holding the chair in 1822. Thomas Nuttall received the chair in 1825.[19]

Academic positions, journals, museums, libraries, and academies provided a diverse forum for natural history in America. Although these different venues would divide naturalists into amateur and academic camps by midcentury, in the early years, a fluid cultural and intellectual milieu kept communications open between naturalists of all stripes. The possibility of reaching a popular or specific audience lay before anyone inclined toward the natural sciences.

"Busy Triflers": Broadening the Appeal of American Science

As naturalists pursued their work in these various venues, they began to attract a broader readership, which many took to be the true mission of American science. In his *Contributions to the Natural History of the United States*, Louis Agassiz explained that in America, "so general is the desire for knowledge, that I expect to see my book read by operatives, by fishermen, by farmers, quite as extensively as by the student in our colleges or by the learned professions."[20] Although this may have been realistic when Agassiz's first volume appeared in 1857, the public was far less receptive in earlier years. Amos Binney of the Boston Society of Natural History recalled in 1845 that the early naturalist worked "without ... the approbation of the public mind, which, unenlightened as

[19] W. D. Peck to Henry E. Mühlenberg, April 17, 1812, Mühlenberg Manuscripts, PHS; Jacob Bigelow to Mühlenberg, November 10, 1813, ibid. See Herbert Leventhal, *In the Shadow of the Enlightenment: Occultism and Renaissance Science in Eighteenth-Century America* (New York, 1976), p. 18; Hindle, *Pursuit of Science in Revolutionary America*, pp. 311, 332; Nina Reid-Maroney, *Philadelphia's Enlightenment, 1740–1800: Kingdom of Christ, Empire of Reason* (Westport, 2001), p. 15; Smallwood, *Natural History and the American Mind*, pp. 328–9, 302, 331.

[20] Agassiz, *Contributions to the Natural History*, p. x.

FIGURE 3.1. Sensitive to public opinion, naturalists insisted on the practical value of their work. Even the most abstract or mundane discovery could yield benefits, Jacob Bigelow insisted; if the lowly *Datura* had medical applications, higher orders were surely worthy of careful scientific scrutiny. *Datura stramonium* (jimson weed or Jamestown weed), from Jacob Bigelow's *American Medical Botany* (1817–21). Courtesy of American Philosophical Society.

it was, . . . regarded them as busy triflers." Men of "mean and contracted minds," Thaddeus Harris added with perhaps a thought to his own field experience, "have made themselves merry at the expense of naturalists."[21]

---

[21] Amos Binney, *Remarks Made at the Annual Meeting of the Boston Society of Natural History, June 2, 1845* (Boston, 1845), p. 10; Thaddeus Mason Harris, *A Report on the Insects of Massachusetts, Injurious to Vegetation* (Cambridge, 1841), p. 19. See *North American Review*, n.s., 38 (January 1834): p. 33; Richard Ellsworth Call, *The Life and Writings of Rafinesque* (Louisville, 1895), p. 1; J. Martin Trippe, "A Journal of Observations in Mammalogy, Ornithology, Botany, and Other Branches of Natural History" (ms., 1869), pp. 21–2, APS.

Sensitive to this public perception, naturalists justified their work on practical terms. Even the most abstract discovery could yield benefits, Thomas Nuttall argued: "The labyrinthine avenues of knowledge,... often lead to useful results, which could not have been anticipated by their discoverers." Jacob Bigelow's *The Useful Arts, Considered in Connexion with the Applications of Science* scientifically described hundreds of plants and animals and their importance to manufacturing, food, medicine, or the arts. New discoveries, he remarked, would surely add to the list: "We are told that in China every plant is applied to some valuable purpose, and there is scarcely a weed that has not its determinate use." The earth, Constantine Rafinesque added, was clothed in a "vegetable wealth... far more important than all the mines of gold and precious stones."[22] Bigelow and Rafinesque were thinking mostly of *materia medica*, the medical use of plants. Botanists believed that all local diseases had local cures – that it was a "wise plan in Nature, to generally place an antidote where she has planted a poison," as Zadok Cramer wrote. Surrounded by evidence of this "superintending Providence," botanists saw their work in largely practical terms.[23]

Jules Marcou likewise promised that geologists would reveal "a mineral wealth almost without rival" in America – riches so vast and so widely distributed that no single person or group could monopolize them: "Thus it may be said, with truth, that the mineral kingdom itself contributes to the development of American democracy." Geologists showed farmers how to use their soils, where to find natural fertilizers, and how to drain off wetlands or springs. Entomologists instructed them in avoiding harmful insects. William Dandridge Peck's natural history of the slug worm (*Tubifex rivulorum*) showed that it preferred "different [orchard] trees in different places," and Thomas Say's natural history of the Hessian

[22] Thomas Nuttall, "Remarks and Inquiries Concerning the Birds of Massachusetts," *American Academy of Arts and Sciences Memoirs*, n.s., 1 (1833): p. 105; Jacob Bigelow, *The Useful Arts, Considered in Connexion with the Applications of Science* (Boston, 1840), Vol. 1, pp. 102–3; Bigelow, *American Medical Botany* (Boston, 1817–1821), Vol. 1, p. ii, Constantine Rafinesque, "First Lecture on Botany," Rafinesque Papers, APS; C. List, *Outlines of Botany; For the Use of Schools and Private Learners* (Philadelphia, 1846), pp. 148–9; Charles Daubeny, *Sketch of the Geology of North America, Being the Substance of a Memoir Read before the Ashmolean Society* (Oxford, 1839), p. 3; *Medical Repository* 2 (No. 4, 1799): p. 427; Hindle, *Pursuit of Science in Revolutionary America*, p. 193.

[23] Zadok Cramer, *The Navigator* (Pittsburgh: Cramer, Spear & Eichbaum, 1811), p. 22; Bigelow, *American Medical Botany*, p. 17; "Colden's Observations on the Bite of a Rattle Snake," Cadwallader Colden, *The Letters and Papers of Cadwallader Colden* (New York, 1917–1922), Vol. 3, pp. 67–8; *Medical Repository* 2 (No. 1, 1898): p. 73.

fly (*Mayetiola destructor*) suggested natural predators for this scourge of the wheat field. Science would protect the farmer, encourage the miner, strengthen the economy, and stiffen the national spirit; the time had arrived, Agassiz announced, when "scientific truth must...be woven into the common life of the world."[24]

While naturalists were gaining legitimacy at home, they defended their stature in international circles. "When we adventure into the field of science," De Witt Clinton complained in 1815, "the master-spirits who preside over transatlantic literature view us with a sneer of supercilious contempt, or with a smile of complacent superiority."[25] This changed as American scientists entered a long-standing debate over the relative size and vigor of New World plants and animals. All creatures, according to Buffon, had their "land of origin" and, where environmental conditions were most accommodating, they developed to perfection. When Old World quadrupeds migrated to the New World, perhaps driven by human predation, they grew smaller and weaker in the colder climate. America offered no counterparts to Africa's magnificent lions, elephants, rhinoceroses, and hippopotamuses, European naturalists pointed out, and even its indigenous humans were diminished in form and virility.[26] In his 1781–2 *Notes on the State of Virginia*, Thomas Jefferson included a brilliant defense of American animals based on empirical data and general observations that America's humid climate produced more foliage, which

[24] Jules Marcou, *Geology of North America, with Two Reports on the Prairies of Arkansas and Texas* (Zurich, 1858); Marcou, *A Geological Map of the United States, and the British Provinces of North America* (Boston, 1853), p. 77; William Dandridge Peck, *Natural History of the Slug Worm* (Boston, 1799), pp. 4, 6–7, 10; Thomas Say, "Some Account of the Insect Known by the Name of Hessian Fly, and of a Parasitic Insect that Feeds On It," Academy of Natural Sciences of Philadelphia *Journal* 1 (Part 1, July 1817): p. 45; Louis Agassiz, *Methods of Study in Natural History* (Boston, 1863), pp. 42–3.

[25] De Witt Clinton in *Port Folio* 6, 3d ser. (August 1815): p. 140. See Benjamin Smith Barton, "An Essay Toward a Natural History of the North American Indians," ca. 1788, Miscellaneous Collection, APS; Henry T. Tuckerman, *America and Her Commentators, with a Critical Sketch of Travel in the United States* (New York, 1864), pp. 256–7.

[26] Buffon in Roger, *Buffon*, p. 299; Peter Kalm, "Pehr Kalm's Observations on the Natural History and Climate of Pennsylvania: Excerpts from his Letter of October 14, 1748," Esther Louise (trans.), Larsen, *Agricultural History* 17 (July 1943): p. 173; Kalm, *Travels Into North America, Containing Its Natural History, and a Circumstantial Account of Its Plantations and Agriculture in General*, John R. Foster (trans.), (Warrington, 1770–1771), Vol. 2, pp. 190–1; Abbé Reynal in Gilbert Chinard, "Eighteenth-Century Theories on America as a Human Habitat," APS *Proceedings* 91 (February 1947): pp. 36–7; Antonello Gerbi, *The Dispute of the New World: The History of a Polemic, 1750–1900*, Jeremy Moyle (ed. and trans.), (Pittsburgh, 1955), pp. 45, 53, 55, 80.

in turn grew larger and more virile animals. Like Jefferson, Samuel Williams argued that the "energy and force of animated nature" depended on the richness of the land rather than its relative temperatures. If animals had migrated to the New World, it was undoubtedly "with a view to better accommodations." Benjamin Vaughan admitted that the American wolf, unlike the African lion, would retreat rather than challenge a human intruder, but he noted that the wolf's retreat "was not that of terror, for [the wolf] neither moved far nor in a straight line." When forced to stand, he "faced the dangers which surrounded him," and when his fate was decided by the hunters, "he not only shewed the vigor of his character by the promptness of the force of his leap, but by the anger expressed in his dying moments." The beast resisted "with the last remains of life."[27]

The debate over nature's virility reinforced the emphasis on first-hand observation in American natural history because Europeans speculated about American fauna largely in absentia. In their *Quadrupeds of North America*, Audubon and Bachman pointed out that field observations alone could "correct...the blunders,...the misrepresentations, and...the calamities which certain vain and superficial scribblers in Europe delight to propagate concerning America and its inhabitants." Alexander Wilson placed his crossbills (*Loxia leucoptera*) on a hemlock bough to show that the bill was designed to extract nuts from the cones, thereby dispelling Buffon's misconception that it was deformed. After describing an American woodpecker, he let loose a salvo against the French naturalist for assuming too much based on preserved specimens.

Let the reader turn to the faithful representation...given in the plate, and say whether his looks be 'sad and melancholy [as Buffon indicated]!' It is truly ridiculous and astonishing that such absurdities should escape the lips or pen of one so able to do justice to the respective merits of every species; but Buffon had too often a favorite theory to prop up, that led him insensibly astray; and so, forsooth, the whole family of Woodpeckers must look sad, sour, and be miserable, to satisfy the caprice of a whimsical philosopher, who takes it into his head that they are, and ought to be, so.[28]

---

27 Thomas Jefferson in Gerbi, *Dispute of the New World*, p. 256; Jefferson in Smallwood, *Natural History and the American Mind*, p. 127; Samuel Williams, *The Natural and Civil History of Vermont* 1 (Burlington, 1809), pp. 127, 129–31, 158–9; Benjamin Vaughan, December 22, 1807, Benjamin Vaughan Papers, APS. See Chinard, "Eighteenth-Century Theories," pp. 42–4.

28 John James Audubon and John Bachman, *The Quadrupeds of North America* (New York, 1851), Vol. 1, p. v; Alexander Wilson and Charles Lucian Bonaparte, *American Ornithology: or, the Natural History of the Birds of the United States* (Philadelphia, n.d.),

FIGURE 3.2. In defense of their own country, American scientists entered a long-standing debate over the relative size and vigor of New World plants and animals. European naturalists insisted that North America's colder climate diminished its fauna and flora. The natural history of the wolf reflected this debate: they were crafty, but never terrified, and when forced to stand, they faced death with truly regal courage. Debates like these emphasized the American naturalist's superior field methods and powers of firsthand observation. Titian Ramsay Peale, *Sketches, 1817–1875*. Courtesy of the American Philosophical Society.

European assessments of American natural history moderated when the outcome of the Revolution and the War of 1812 raised the country's stature in European eyes, and when explorers moved farther west, they brought back tales of ferocious alligators, huge bison, lordly grizzly bears, and mountains of dizzying height. Yet, during these sensitive years, Americans forged their dedication to field research and empirical methods in the fires of national pride. Their defensive endeavors projected a view that nature in America was more virile and more beautiful than in Europe.[29] This scientific declaration of independence was a necessary beginning for the American Romantic movement.

pp. 173–4; Ann Shelby Blum, *Picturing Nature: American Nineteenth-Century Zoological Illustration* (Princeton, 1993), p. 41. See *Monthly American Journal of Geology and Natural Science* 1 (April 1832): p. 462.

[29] Gerbi, *Dispute of the New World*, pp. 154, 157; Chinard, "Eighteenth-Century Theories," pp. 37–8.

At the beginning of the century, naturalists found their work challenged at home and abroad. They met this challenge by integrating science into the national interest. They found a receptive audience, and they responded by promising much to the American people. They would reveal the riches of the western landscape and complement the expansionary zeal for westward expansion. They would eschew European speculations and ground their theories in field experience. Most important, they would share the wonders they discovered with the American people, building a more precise and more reverential image of nature in the American mind.

The State Surveys

One indication that scientists were winning their battle for popular validation was a series of geological and natural history surveys commissioned by state governments beginning in the 1830s. As early as 1756, John Bartram proposed to Alexander Garden a scheme in which surveyors would bore into the earth at predetermined spots looking for marls, minerals, medicinal earths, coal, peat, salts, flints, metals, or mineral springs. "How exceeding useful and satisfactory will it be to curious philosophical inquirers to know the various terrestrial compositions that we daily walk over," he exclaimed. His proposal for a "curious subterranean map" had all the ingredients of the later state surveys: a faith in America's hidden natural abundance; the goad of scientific curiosity; the practical justification; and the belief that God could not possibly make a landscape without some useful purpose.[30]

In the decades after the American Revolution, Congress and the War Department sent several surveys west to locate these strategic resources, determine fort sites, map out routes of communication, and gather information about Native inhabitants. These included John Sibley's exploration of the Red River in 1803, the Lewis and Clark expedition in 1804, and Zebulon Pike's survey of the upper Mississippi and southern Colorado in 1805. In 1819, the War Department sent Major Stephen H. Long to the foothills of the Rocky Mountains as a test of the new Topographical Engineering Bureau created during the War of 1812. Long's

---

[30] John Bartram to Alexander Garden, March 14, 1756, in William Darlington, *Memorials of John Bartram and Humphry Marshall* (New York, 1967 [c. 1849]), pp. 392–3. See Julie R. Newell, "James Dwight Dana and the Emergence of Professional Geology in the United States," *American Journal of Science* 297 (No. 3, 1997): p. 274.

expedition was distinctive in having a complement of renowned naturalists and a riverboat designed especially to accommodate their work.[31] Following the Platte River to the Rocky Mountains, Long's party returned with specimens of more than sixty new or rare animals and insects. In the preface to Edwin James's 1823 account of the expedition, entomologist Thomas Say expressed hope that publishing these adventures would stimulate further exploration. "The time will arrive," he predicted, "when we shall no longer be indebted to the men of foreign countries for a knowledge of any of the products of our own soil."[32]

Based on these and other examples, states began financing their own geological and botanical surveys. In 1819, the Connecticut Academy of Arts and Sciences commissioned a state geological and mineralogical survey under Benjamin Silliman and, in 1823, North Carolina sponsored a similar survey under Denison Olmsted. Neither reported extensively on their findings but, in 1830, Massachusetts and the Boston Society of Natural History authorized Amherst College Professor Edward Hitchcock to lead a party of eminent naturalists on a survey of that state.[33] Hitchcock traveled in a wagon "fitted up *á la mode geographique*," recording his observations, collecting samples, and calling on local authorities in each district. His 692-page report, published in 1832–3, inspired a second survey in 1835, resulting in another report of 840 pages. Between 1825 and 1840, eighteen other states, two territories, and New Brunswick and Nova Scotia launched similar surveys. Together, these

---

[31] Richard N. L. Andrews, *Managing the Environment, Managing Ourselves: A History of American Environmental Policy* (New Haven, 1999), pp. 53, 75; Dorothy Anne Dondore, *The Prairie and the Making of Middle America: Four Centuries of Description* (Cedar Rapids, 1926), pp. 158–9; George P. Merrill, *The First One Hundred Years of American Geology* (New Haven, 1924), p. 65; Stephen H. Long, *The Northern Expeditions of Stephen H. Long: The Journals of 1817 and 1823 and Related Documents*, edited by Lucile M. Kane, June D. Holmquist, and Carolyn Gilman (Minneapolis, 1978), pp. 5, 11, 15; *North American Review*, n.s., 7 (April 1823): p. 242.

[32] Thomas Say in Stroud, *Thomas Say*, pp. 127–8. See James Ellsworth De Kay, *Anniversary Address on the Progress of Natural Sciences in the United States Delivered Before the Lyceum of Natural History of New York, February 1826* (New York, 1826), pp. 59–60.

[33] Edward Hitchcock, *First Anniversary Address Before the Association of American Geologists at Their Second Annual Meeting in Philadelphia, April 5, 1841* (New Haven, 1841), p. 8; Merrill, *First One Hundred Years of American Geology*, pp. 65, 126; C. T. Jackson, "Remarks on the Geology, Mineralogy, and Mines of Lake Superior," American Association for the Advancement of Science *Proceedings* (Boston, 1850): pp. 283, 286; *North American Review*, n.s., 56 (April 1843): pp. 435–6.

reports added enormous amounts of information to the natural history of America.[34]

Harvard geologist Charles T. Jackson's commission from Maine was typical. The legislature funded the survey hoping for an inventory of resources that could be "subjected to the cunning transforming hand of the artisan or manufacturer." Jackson began on the coast where the structure of the exposed strata could be clearly ascertained and moved inland by canoe through the major watersheds.[35] Like others, he roamed "somewhat at random," compiling notes in narrative form and including comments on the value and origins of these geological phenomena. As in Maine, New York's survey was conducted under the auspices of the state Board of Agriculture, and it was encouraged by Stephen van Rensselaer, De Witt Clinton, and Governor William H. Seward, all noted for their vigorous promotion of commerce and manufacturing. The multivolume report, completed by 1842, was the most thorough in the nation.[36] Like several other states, Maine and New York continued these surveys and, eventually, each created a permanent state geological office.

Their mandate was no less than mapping out the entire natural history of the state. Michigan commissioners told zoologist Abraham Sager "to investigate as far as practicable the mode of existence, the relative position, office, and influence in the sentient organic world of every animal native to our state, from the insect of ephemeral existence, ... to the quadruped of most varied and complicated structure and functions." He was to assess every creature's influence on the "happiness of man" and to discover the "means of rendering them directly subservient to our

[34] Edward Hitchcock, to ? (possibly governor of New York), June 21, 1836, Miscellaneous Collection, APS; Merrill, *First One Hundred Years of American Geology*, pp. 126–27, 143; George B. Emerson, *Reports on the Fishes, Reptiles, and Birds of Massachusetts* (Boston, 1839), pp. iv–v; *North American Review*, n.s., 56 (April 1843): pp. 436–7; Hitchcock, *Final Report on the Geology of Massachusetts* (Northampton, 1841), Vol. 1, p. 6; Hitchcock, *First Anniversary Address*, pp. 8–9; *American Journal of Science* 22 (1832): pp. 1–7.

[35] *Eighth Annual Report of the Secretary of the Maine Board of Agriculture, 1863* (Augusta, 1863), p. 54. See Wilson, *Lyell in America*, p. 56; Charles T. Jackson, *First Report on the Geology of the State of Maine* (Augusta, 1837), p. 11.

[36] Merrill, *First One Hundred Years of American Geology*, pp. 120, 190; Gerald M. Friedman, "Charles Lyell in New York State," in Derek J. Blundell and Andrew C. Scott, *Lyell: The Past Is the Key to the Present* (London, 1998), p. 71; Ebenezer Emmons, "Preface," in *Report of the Survey of the Second Geological District in Natural History of New-York, Part 4, Geology* (Albany, 1842–43), pp. 1, 3; James Ellsworth De Kay in Smallwood, *Natural History and the American Mind*, p. 164.

interests." As if this was not enough, he was also instructed to convey his findings so as to "disseminate a taste for the interesting and important study of zoology." Ignoring these terms, Sager simply codified his findings in a brief catalog at the end of the Michigan report; but, others took their charge more seriously, describing a full range of economic resources, adding instructions on their use, and providing philosophical commentary on their relation to the "happiness of man."[37] Jackson, for instance, found a beautiful white sand cove on an eastern Maine island, and because there was plenty of spruce nearby for furnaces, he suggested a glass-making factory. A second cove containing jasper inspired visions of a lapidary works, and elsewhere he discovered feldspar crystals, which suggested a porcelain factory. "I have had some of the mineral wrought into mineral teeth, by a distinguished dentist in Boston, . . . and he declares that it makes a most perfect porcelain, which is of a pure semitransparent appearance." Jackson imagined industries springing up all across the landscape, each on the location of a resource he discovered.[38]

These surveys concluded an important era in American scientific investigation. Expeditions to the western mountains and deserts and the Pacific islands, and those sponsored by the Smithsonian Institution around the world, continued this saga, but the era of eastern continental exploration was drawing to a close. The state studies were an important capstone to the era of continental investigation for several reasons. Their discoveries were mostly commonplace but, as the *Burlington Free Press* pointed out, one of their more valuable contributions was "finding what is *not* around, so we won't waste time digging and blasting." Ebenezer Emmons concluded that the Adirondacks offered poor prospects for farming, but they were "necessary accompaniments of the fertile plains." Without them, "all would be a barren waste."[39] In general, the surveyors found at least

---

[37] Douglass Houghton, *Second Annual Report of the State Geologist, of the State of Michigan, Made to the Legislature February 4, 1839* (Detroit, 1839), pp. 1–2; Emerson, *Reports on the Fishes, Reptiles, and Birds of Massachusetts*, p. vi; Denison Olmsted, *Report on the Geology of North-Carolina, Conducted Under the Direction of the Board of Agriculture* (Raleigh, 1824), Part 1, p. 3.

[38] Jackson, *First Report on the Geology of the State of Maine*, pp. 37–9, 43, 80–1, 91. See Charles T. Jackson, *Final Report on the Geology and Mineralogy of the State of New Hampshire* (Concord, 1844), p. 80; Naham Ward, *A Brief Sketch of the State of Ohio* (Glasgow, 1822), pp. 5, 8.

[39] *Burlington Free Press*, May 7, 1849; Edward Hitchcock, *Report on the Geology, Mineralogy, Botany, and Zoology of Massachusetts* (Amherst, 1833), pp. 68–71; Emmons, *Report of the Survey of the Second Geological District*, pp. 165–6. See Smallwood, *Natural History and the American Mind*, p. 214; Jackson, *Final Report on the Geology and Mineralogy*, p. 30.

some value in each of the landscapes they explored, confirming the notion that God made nothing in vain.

Scientifically, the reports provided a firmer foundation for the natural history of America. Teams from various states compared their findings to identify patterns running across the continent, resulting in a series of geological and biological composites that explained much more than the sum of the individual reports. Byrem Lawrence's 1842 *Geological Map of the Western States* provided a detailed summary of these findings, and in 1845, James Hall published North America's first continental-scale geological map using the same sources.[40] The state reports also forced geologists to harmonize their methodologies, nomenclature, and theories, and the ensuing discussion helped unify American natural history. Moreover, they raised the stature of American naturalists abroad. English geologist Sir Charles Lyell, who traveled through the United States in 1841 and 1842, incorporated a great deal of information from the surveys into his influential textbook on geology, legitimizing American science in the eyes of European readers. Finally, in light of their practical accomplishments, the surveys helped promote the natural sciences among farmers, landowners, and others interested in profiting from a better understanding of nature, bringing Agassiz's aspirations for a people's science to fruition.[41]

Natural History at the Crossroads

In 1845, Amos Binney announced to the Boston Society of Natural History that American science was now in the hands of American scientists. "We are no longer obliged to look to foreigners for information upon our natural history, but on the other hand, . . . foreign naturalists are coming among us to learn the results of our labors."[42] An important part of this process, the state surveys raised the stature of American natural history at home and abroad. At the same time, they facilitated the professionalization of the natural history, changing the way scientists thought about their work.

---

[40] Edward Hitchcock, *Outline of the Geology of the Globe, and of the United States in Particular* (Boston, 1853), pp. 71, 94.

[41] Charles Lyell, *Travels in North America, in the Years 1841–2; with Geological Observations on the United States, Canada, and Nova Scotia* (New York, 1845), Vol. 1, p. 76; Wilson, *Lyell in America*, p. 16; *American Journal of Science*, n.s., 42 (April 1842): pp. 51–2; Houghton, *Second Annual Report of the State Geologist*, p. 4.

[42] Amos Binney, *Remarks Made at the Annual Meeting of the Boston Society of Natural History, June 2, 1845* (Boston, 1845), p. 12.

In the two decades between the earliest surveys and the last, it is possible to trace a narrowing focus of interest among natural historians. The early reports rang with Olympian language. "Nature opens to us her illuminated page," Charles Jackson wrote, "and invites us to read her great and eternal laws, and by following her mandates, the elements become subservient to our will." A better understanding of nature would focus the country's economic ambitions, but it would also align its people with the grand scheme of creation. Lofty pronouncements like these, so characteristic of early nineteenth-century natural history, depended on a certain bold amateurism, a willingness to cross boundaries and see beyond specialties. Natural history's most expansive thinkers were those willing to combine theology and science, civil history and natural history, cosmology and entomology. Yet, even as American scientists were gaining the confidence and the public approbation to propose their grand theories, they were moving into professional niches that precluded the kind of freewheeling thought that inspired their observations on the basic laws of nature.[43]

The philosophical enthusiasm characteristic of the early surveys disappeared in the last reports. Exploring the glaciated landscapes of northern Michigan in 1846, William Burt and Bela Hubbard noted the curious erratic boulders that in earlier decades had triggered profound debates about the history of the earth, but they dismissed both boulders and theories as economically insignificant and left to the reader "the pleasure of drawing his own conclusions as to the causes which have produced these geological effects." The later surveys abandoned the traditional narrative to provide a straightforward inventory of minerals, marls, stones, clays, and strata, briefly explaining the location and economic implications of each. Even George Featherstonhaugh, who waxed philosophic in the first decades of the century, grew more sober. Geology was "altogether a science of observation," he admitted, "and the cautious spirit of the present times [gave] . . . no weight to any opinions which are not founded upon the practical examination of physical phenomena." Louis Agassiz, who never lost sight of this cosmic frame of reference, worried in 1847 that the state reports, despite their enormous contribution, would prove detrimental, "for the utilitarian tendency thus impressed on the work of American geologists will retard their progress."[44]

43 Charles T. Jackson, *Second Report on the Geology of the State of Maine* (Augusta, 1838), pp. vi–vii. See A. D. Bache, "Address," American Association for the Advancement of Science, *Proceedings* (Washington, 1852), p. xliii.

44 William A. Burt and Bela Hubbard, *Reports . . . on the Geography, Topography, and Geology of the . . . South Shore of Lake Superior* (Detroit, 1846), p. 20; Gerard Troost,

These changes reflected the development of new and more complex scientific techniques that enhanced the value of laboratory science and specialized expertise. Boston's Jacob Bigelow, who published a three-volume compendium of medicinal plants in 1817–21, was the first American botanist to systematically apply chemistry to *materia medica*, moving the science decisively out of the realm of folklore and into the laboratory. Bigelow's goal was to break down each plant into its irreducible properties and categorize these substances in terms of their medical effects. He dissolved his specimens in chemicals, then distilled the compounds with ether or sulfuric acid and analyzed the precipitate according to color, smell, taste, texture, and viscosity, applying it to his own body or to others either internally or externally to judge the relief from certain symptoms. Subjecting bloodroot to analysis, for instance, he reported that the alcohol "comes off from the root strongly impregnated with its colour and taste." The resulting solution was "rendered turbid by the addition of water" and, when dried, it left a "residuum partially, but not wholly soluble in water." Bigelow compared his chemical analyses with an older tradition of judging plants by sensible characteristics like shape, touch, feel, taste, smell, and color, and found a remarkable agreement in their medicinal qualities; but, as a pioneering organic chemist, he also paved the way for a generation of botanists completely divorced from the ancient theory of correspondences.[45]

Like chemical analysis, improvements in taxonomy encouraged the trend toward professionalization and specialization. The Linnaean system divided the vegetable kingdom into twenty-four classes based primarily on external sexual characteristics. Because his system employed fairly obvious features, it was easy to use, but as the number of known species multiplied, its idiosyncrasies became more burdensome. At the end of the eighteenth century, French naturalist Jacques Henri Bernardin de Saint-Pierre scrutinized the Linnaean descriptive nomenclature and brought the whole system into question.[46] Words, he thought, only inadequately

Third Geological Report to the Twenty-first General Assembly of the State of Tennessee (Nashville, 1835), pp. 3–4; David Dale Owen, *Report of the Geological Survey in Kentucky, Made During the Years 1854 and 1855* (Frankfort, 1856), p. 16; George Featherstonhaugh, *Geological Report of an Examination Made in 1834, of the Elevated Country Between the Missouri and Red Rivers . . .* (Washington, 1835), p. 6; Agassiz to Milne Edwards, May 31, 1847, in Agassiz, *Louis Agassiz*, Vol. 2, p. 437.

45 Bigelow, *American Medical Botany*, pp. ix–xi, 31, 51, 57–58, 76–7.
46 Smallwood, *Natural History and the American Mind*, pp. 348–9; Thomas Nuttall, *An Introduction to Systematic and Physiological Botany* (Cambridge, 1827), p. 27; Porter, *Eagle's Nest*, p. 76; Dupree, *Asa Gray*, p. 29; Agassiz, *Methods of Study in Natural History*, pp. 9–10; Jacques Henri Bernardin de Saint-Pierre, *Botanical Harmony Delineated;*

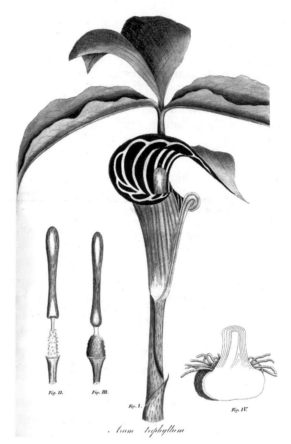

. *Arum triphyllum*

FIGURE 3.3. Jacob Bigelow, who published a three-volume compendium of medicinal plants in 1817–21, was the first American botanist to systematically apply chemical analysis to medicinal plants, moving the science out of the realm of folklore and into the laboratory. Bigelow's goal, breaking down each plant into its irreducible properties and categorizing these substances according to their medical effects, encouraged the trend toward professionalization and specialization in natural history. *Arum triphyllum* (Jack in the Pulpit), from Jacob Bigelow's *American Medical Botany* (1817–21). Courtesy of the American Philosophical Society.

expressed the infinite variety in nature. Form and color shifted almost imperceptibly from one species to the next, whereas language could only describe a few basic constructs.[47] Writing at about the same time, French

Or, *Applications of Some General Laws of Nature to Plants*, translated by Henry Hunter (Worcester, 1797), p. 9.

[47] Saint-Pierre, *Botanical Harmony Delineated*, pp. iv, 12–14, 16.

botanist, Antoine Laurent de Jussieu, developed a new botanical clas-sification in his 1789 *Genera plantarum*. De Jussieu's so-called natural system grouped species according to similarities in shape, internal struc-ture, functional organization, and even medicinal properties. Responding to St. Pierre's criticisms, he allowed for the fine gradations that defined the flood of new species arriving from all points of the world – gradations later explained by Darwinian evolution. Americans initially resisted De Jussieu's system. Benjamin Vaughan expressed the feelings of many in complaining about the "impertinence of some of our reformers in natu-ral history." If classification systems were "*tolerably* good," he thought, they should stand, "till they become *intolerable*; & then changes will be acceptable to every one." And, as long as the Linnaean system remained tolerably good, it lingered, partly because American naturalists were heav-ily invested in the system and partly because American science included many amateurs unskilled in the fine structural distinctions noted in the natural system.[48]

Among the earliest to adopt the natural system in America was Con-stantine Rafinesque, an independent-minded naturalist who claimed to discover new species almost on a weekly basis. "The natural orders . . . are deficient in arrangement, precision, names, synonymy & composition, their characters are vague, loose, incorrect, and unfit for study," he ful-minated. As early as 1818, he advised botanist John Torrey to abandon Linnaeus. Torrey stayed with the older system while he completed his sec-tion of the New York survey but, in 1831, he republished English botanist John Lindley's *Introduction to the Natural System*. By the mid-1830s, de Jussieu's system was well established in Europe and gaining adherents in America.[49]

The significance of the natural system, beyond its precision and flex-ibility, was its esoteric nature; it required complicated structural and functional comparisons usually beyond the capacity of the amateur.

[48] Benjamin Vaughan to Parker Cleaveland, May 20, 1819, Vaughan Papers, APS; Daniels, *American Science*, pp. 113–14; Rodgers, *John Torrey*, p. 81; *The Naturalist* 1 (March 1831): p. 67; *North American Review*, n.s., 38 (January 1834).

[49] Constantine Samuel Rafinesque, *The Good Book and Amenities of Nature; Or, Annals of Historical and Natural Sciences* (Philadelphia, 1840), p. 39. See Call, *Life and Writings of Rafinesque*, p. 103; *Monthly American Journal of Geology and Natural Science* 1 (February 1832): pp. 416–17, 419–20; Lewis C. Beck, *Botany of the Northern and Middle States . . . , Arranged According to the Natural System* (Albany, 1833), pp. v–vi; James E. De Kay, *Zoology of New-York, or the New-York Fauna* (Albany, 1842) p. 67; Rodgers, *John Torrey*, p. 81.

With characteristic disdain, George Featherstonhaugh explained both the
advantages and disadvantages of the older system.

Every young lady can count how many stamens there are on a plant, and refer
it to its class; but does she learn by this, what qualities the plant may possess, –
what other plants it is closely allied to, having similar qualities, – or what the
structure of the future fruit may be? No! She learns nothing of these; she admires,
and she talks Greek. When she takes in her hand the beautiful little forget-me-not
(*Myosotis palustris, L.*), she says, "This dear little flower belongs to *pentandra
monogyna*. What a romantic idea! Five husbands and one wife."

The simplicity of the Linnaean method appealed to the amateur naturalist
and the popular nature-writer, but when those in the academy found its
limitations no longer tolerable, they adopted a more precise classification,
widening the gap already apparent in the scientific community.[50]

The Eclipse of Field Work

Midcentury also marked the end of an era in which exploration and
fieldwork superseded academic research in American science. French naturalist Gorges Cuvier summarized the advantages and disadvantages in
each approach:

There is . . . much difference between the style and ideas of the field naturalist . . . and those of the sedentary naturalist. . . . The field naturalist passes through,
at greater or lesser speed, a great number of different areas, and is struck, one
after the other, by a great number of interesting objects and living things. He
observes them in their natural surroundings, in relationship to their environment,
and in the full vigour of life and activity. But he can only give a few instants of
time to each of them. . . . He is thus deprived of the possibility of . . . rigorously
describing its characteristics, and is often deprived even of books which would tell
him who had seen the same thing before him. Thus his observations are broken
and fleeting. . . . The sedentary naturalist, it is true, only knows living beings from
distant countries through reported information subject to greater or lesser degrees
of error, and through samples which have suffered greater or lesser degrees of
damage . . . Yet these drawbacks have also their corresponding compensations. If
the sedentary naturalist does not see nature in action, he can yet survey all her
productions spread before him. He can compare them with each other as often as
is necessary to reach reliable conclusions. He chooses and defines his own problems; he can examine them at his leisure. He can bring together the relevant facts
from anywhere he needs to. The traveller can only travel one road; it is only . . . in

[50] *Monthly American Journal of Geology and Natural Science* 1 (February 1832):
pp. 421–2. See Daniels, *American Science*, p. 38.

one's study . . . that one can roam freely throughout the universe, and for that, a different sort of courage is needed.[51]

These differences represented a growing rift in the American scientific community well represented in John James Audubon's response to criticism from Philadelphia sedentary naturalist George Ord. "The greatest portion of my life has been devotedly spent in the *active* investigation of Nature," Audubon pointed out.

For more than 20 years I have been in the *regular habit* of writing down every day all the incidents of which I have been an *eye-witness*, on the spot & without confiding to my memory, as many travellers have done and still do. . . .

To whom, then, . . . can I ascribe the birth of the animadversions expressed in the papers of Philadelphia! Is their author one [who] comes avowedly forward with a life spent in the woods, loaded with facts differing in every respect from mine . . . ? Or, is he one, who, writing at random and without any knowledge of his subject, merely wishes to push himself into notice by a blunt denial of my veracity?[52]

In the first half of the century, it was the field naturalist who took the moral high ground.

The qualities of Cuvier's field naturalist were most dramatically represented in the flamboyant wanderer, Constantine Rafinesque, who explored the West with little more than the clothes on his back and certainly without the library that, as Cuvier said, gave the sedentary naturalist a portal to roam the universe. Rafinesque was born near Constantinople in 1773. His father, a merchant, died in Philadelphia of yellow fever twenty years later, and Rafinesque moved with his mother to Italy, where he began his "herborisations" in 1795. He attended college in Switzerland, but his studies were cut short when the family's wealth dissipated during the French Revolution. In 1802, he moved to Philadelphia, studied briefly with Benjamin Rush, and set out for the West in 1804.[53]

---

[51] Cuvier in Dorinda Outram, "New Spaces in Natural History," N. Jardine, J. A. Secord, and E. C. Spary, *Cultures of Natural History* (Cambridge, 1996), pp. 259–61.

[52] Audubon in Francis Hobart Herrick, *Audubon the Naturalist: A History of His Life and Time* (New York, 1917), Vol. 2, pp. 68–71. See John James Aububon to Lucy Audubon, December 8, 1831, Audubon, *Letters of John James Audubon, 1826–1840*, Howard Corning (ed.) (Boston, 1930), Vol. 1, p. 164; *Monthly American Journal of Geology and Natural Science* 1 (November 1831): p. 221; ibid. (February 1832): pp. 412–13.

[53] Call, *Life and Writings of Rafinesque*, p. 38; Kastner, *Species of Eternity*, p. 252; Constantine Samuel Rafinesque, *A Life of Travels and Researches in North America and South Europe, or Outlines of the Life, Travels, and Researches of C. S. Rafinesque* (Philadelphia, 1836), pp. 1–15, 17.

FIGURE 3.4. Constantine Rafinesque was America's field naturalist par excellence. He grew up near Constantinople, moved to Italy, attended college in Switzerland, and in 1802 landed in Philadelphia, where he studied with Benjamin Rush before setting out for the West. Although more zealous than most, Rafinesque embodied the passions of the field naturalist: inexhaustible energy and curiosity, freewheeling judgment, and wildly eclectic interests. However, by midcentury, he had become, in the words of a biographer, an anachronism. Frontispiece, Richard Ellsworth Call, *The Life and Writings of Rafinesque* (1895). Courtesy of the American Philosophical Society.

In 1805, he returned to Sicily and acquired a small fortune by manufacturing medicines and whiskey but, on his return to America in 1815, his ship went down in a dense fog off Long Island. Left with only a small insurance settlement, he worked as a tutor in New York City and in 1818 left again for the West, traveling on foot "as every botanist ought."[54] In

---

[54] Rafinesque, *Life of Travels and Researches*, pp. 48, 53–6, 61, 316. See Constantine Rafinesque to Amos Eaton, March 15, 1818, Rafinesque Papers, APS; Call, *Life and Writings of Rafinesque*, pp. 16, 20.

1819, he lectured at Transylvania University in Lexington, but his eccentricities left him an easy target for student ridicule, and he took issue with the academy's emphasis on literature and the arts. "Metaphysics and idle vapid talk is the fashion in our University," he wrote to a friend. "I am thwarted in everything." During his stay, however, he collected some five thousand specimens, published an American ethnography, and contemplated a "history of the earth and mankind, chiefly in America." He returned to Philadelphia with his forty boxes of specimens and books and, in 1840, he died in his garret surrounded by his collections. Louis Agassiz summed up his life: "I am satisfied that Rafinesque was a better man than he appeared. His misfortune was his prurient desire for novelties, and his rashness in publishing them."[55]

As Agassiz suggested, Rafinesque's passion was discovery. More than most, he was a scientific opportunist, switching disciplines depending on which "curiosity of nature" appeared most intriguing at the moment. He discovered rare plants on the banks of the Potomac and undescript fishes in the Susquehanna and described with equal enthusiasm the soils, mollusks, and fossils farther west. On one western trip, he claimed to have found 15 new botanical genera, 180 new plants, 75 new animal genera, and 600 new animals, including nearly 70 fishes, 20 quadrupeds, 30 reptiles, 112 shells, and 250 new fossils. "My zeal increases every day instead of abating," he wrote to a friend, "and I hope to do great things yet.... While other superficial writers are busy in compiling, commenting, and illustrating, painting &c." It was indeed this unrestrained zeal that others distrusted. Being the field naturalist, he was, as Cuvier put it, deprived of the possibility of rigorously describing his specimens or learning who had seen them before, but Rafinesque seemed to flaunt this lack of rigor, and he seldom kept specimens for verification. Richard Harlan cautioned that his "insulated situation, and almost utter ignorance of the labours of other naturalists" caused "grievous errors in the record." By the law of averages, he was sometimes right; Asa Gray's definitive *Manual of Botany* credited him with thirteen genera, eight subgenera, and sixteen species. Still, "the task of sifting the comparatively few

55 Constantine Rafinesque to Zaccheus Collins, August 25, 1823; Charles Wilkins Short to Rafinesque, September 7, 1834, Rafinesque Papers, APS; Call, *Life and Writings of Rafinesque*, pp. 12, 34, 38, 49–50, 53, 55; 58–63; Rafinesque, *Life of Travels and Researches*, pp. 58, 61–3, 67, 73, 79; Louis Agassiz in David Starr Jordan, "Rafinesque," *Popular Science Monthly* 29 (June 1886): p. 219. See Elmer Drew Merrill, "Rafinesque's Publications from the Standpoint of World Botany," *APS Proceedings* 87 (No. 1, 1944), p. 110; Herrick, *Audubon the Naturalist*, Vol. 1, pp. 296–7.

perfectly sound grains from the chaff...is a thankless one," a later botanist wrote.[56]

At a time when American scientists were particularly sensitive about their credibility at home and abroad, Rafinesque's passionate but undisciplined fieldwork seemed dangerous indeed. One by one, editors and publication committees began refusing his work. John Torrey, although more charitable than most, cautioned against publishing Rafinesque's communications in Silliman's *American Journal of Science*: "The public is so much prejudiced against Mr. R. that whatever comes from his pen, let it be [bad?] or good, is treated with the greatest ridicule. It is very unfortunate for this laborious naturalist to have obtained such a character – a character which I am sure he does not deserve – But Mr. Silliman must consult his own interest & reputation." This ostracism was painful to Rafinesque. "I have been surprised to find that Prof Silliman has not published any of my essays in his late Journal. He has had 12 Memoirs of mine, some for 2 or 3 years! Is not this strange? Why am I used so?" Although more zealous than most, Rafinesque embodied the passions of the field naturalist: the inexhaustible energy and curiosity, the freewheeling judgment, and the wildly eclectic interest that drove American natural history in the age of continental exploration. However, by midcentury, he had become, in the words of a biographer, "an anachronism; a universal generalist in an era in which naturalists were progressing through greater attention to details."[57]

Benjamin Smith Barton's career highlights the more subdued passions of Cuvier's cabinet naturalist. Barton was born in Lancaster in 1766 and moved to Philadelphia in 1782, where he displayed an early talent for botanical illustration. He prepared for a medical career, studied in Scotland and Germany, and became a professor of natural history and botany at the College of Philadelphia.[58] As a young man, he traveled widely, but

[56] Constantine Rafinesque to Zaccheus Collins, October 18, 1817; Rafinesque to Collins, April 20, 1820; Rafinesque to Collins, July 21, 1817; Rafinesque Papers, APS; Richard Harlan, *Fauna Americana: Being a Description of the Mammiferoius Animals Inhabiting North America* (Philadelphia, 1825), p. vii; Merrill, "Rafinesque's Publications," p. 113.

[57] John Torrey to Amos Eaton, May 18, 1819, Torrey Papers, APS; Constantine Rafinesque to Zaccheus Collins, December 27, 1817; Rafinesque to Collins, June 25, 1820; Rafinesque, "Med. Repository, Raf."; Rafinesque, "Nova Genera plantarum vascularum Americanum, or New Genera of Vascular Plants from the United States," Rafinesque Papers, APS; Wayne Hanley, *Natural History in America: From Mark Catesby to Rachel Carson* (New York, 1977), p. 139; See Stroud, *Thomas Say*, pp. 52–3; Rafinesque, *Good Book and Amenities of Nature*, p. 38.

[58] Francis W. Pennell, "Benjamin Smith Barton as Naturalist," *APS Proceedings* 86 (September 1942), pp. 109–14; *Port Folio*, 4th ser., 1 (April 1816): pp. 273–87.

later he settled into his academic appointment and strayed little from that time on, beset with poor health and possibly hypochondria. He published his first paper, "Observations on Some Parts of Natural History," in 1787 and continued with *Collections for an Essay Toward a Materia Medica of the United States* in 1798. Naturalist Elliott Coues considered his *Fragments of the Natural History of Pennsylvania*, published in 1799, "one of the most notable special treatises on North American ornithology of the century." His *Elements of Botany*, America's first botanical textbook, appeared in 1803.[59]

Although prolific and at times brilliant in his experimental logic, Barton was mostly a compiler of information – a sedentary naturalist. "My various pursuits do not permit me to enter minutely into an investigation of the properties of the articles which I mention," he wrote in his *materia medica* in 1808. "My information concerning them has been derived from the experience of other persons." Despite the immense library and correspondence at his disposal, he remained insecure. He was, as Cuvier put it, distanced from the chaos of detail that characterized firsthand exposure to nature, but he seems to have benefited little from this detached perspective. Incapable of fieldwork and mistrustful of deductive systems, he took on many projects but completed few. His *Fragments*, as he wrote in a preface, was merely a "few facts...thrown together without any regard to order," of little use, he thought, except to "turn the attention of other persons, who possess more leisure and information than myself, to the subject."[60]

Barton, like most naturalists of his day, was eclectic. Yet, where another might wander across these disciplinary boundaries to achieve broader synthesis, he found his multiple perspectives overwhelming. In an early travel diary, he wrote that he found much of interest in the Oneida woods and could only hope that "this spot may be more carefully examined by some future botanist." This was characteristic; Barton passed through countless interesting places but denied himself the time to acquire a commanding knowledge of them. His writing was sporadic and diffuse,

---

[59] Benjamin Smith Barton, "Plants," pp. 25, 26, 36, 35, Barton Papers, Correspondence, PHS; *Port Folio*, 4th ser., 1 (April 1816): pp. 281–3; Francis Harper in Bartram, *Travels*, p. xxx; Pennell, "Benjamin Smith Barton," pp. 113–14.

[60] Benjamin Smith Barton, *Fragments*, p. 23. See *Medical Repository* 3 (No. 3, 1800): p. 184; Barton, *Collections for an Essay towards a Materia Medica of the United-States* (Philadelphia, 1804), p. vii; Barton, *Professor [William] Cullen's Treatise on the Materia Medica* (Philadelphia, 1812), Vol. 1, p. ix; *Port Folio*, 4th ser., 6 (July 1818): 47; Reid-Maroney, *Kingdom of Christ*, p. 45.

characteristic of those who maintained too many interests and entertained too many interruptions.[61] His career combined the disadvantages of the sedentary naturalist, who, in Cuvier's words, knew nature only through "samples which have suffered greater or lesser degrees of damage," and the field naturalist, who confronted "a great number of different areas, one after the other" that defied the ordering mind.

Thus, the most significant event in early botanical science took place not at the University of Pennsylvania but at Harvard University, where Asa Gray and John Torrey produced their magnificent *Flora of North America*. Although Rafinesque had advocated the natural system much earlier, even in correspondence with Torrey, it was Gray and Torrey, along with L. C. Beck, who introduced the new classification in America by literally rewriting American botany in the 1840s.[62]

While a professor of chemistry at West Point, Torrey published *A Compendium of the Flora of the Northern and Middle States* using the Linnaean system. In 1827, he moved to the New York College of Physicians and Surgeons (Columbia University), and as a cofounder and curator of the Lyceum of Natural History of New York, he began bringing together specimens from across North America. "Almost entirely by himself, in the space of a few years, [Torrey made] . . . New York a leading focal point for assemblages of North American botanical materials."[63] It was here that Torrey began experimenting with the natural system, gaining the support of Scottish botanist Asa Gray, who moved to the city from Utica in 1832.

Hoping to systematize American botany, Torrey and Gray broadcast a call for specimens across the country. With these and collections from the various western expeditions, they began publishing the known botanical species of North America in 1838, consummating the project Torrey began in the 1820s. In 1842, Gray joined the Harvard faculty, where botany had been foundering since Thomas Nuttall's departure in 1834, and at Harvard he transformed his laboratories into a national clearinghouse for American flora, achieving a dream that had begun with John Bartram and Henry Mühlenberg before the turn of the century. *Flora of*

[61] Barton, "Plants," pp. 11, 12, 15, 16; Benjamin Smith Barton, *Archaeologiae Americannae* (Philadelphia, 1814), p. vi; Elsa Guerdrum Allen, *The History of American Ornithology Before Audubon* (Philadelphia, 1951), p. 535.

[62] Kastner, *Species of Eternity*, pp. 284–5; Daniels, *American Science*, p. 114.

[63] John Torrey, *A Compendium of the Flora of the Northern and Middle States* (New York, 1826), pp. 24, 35, 36, 37, 38, 43, 218, 223; Rodgers, *John Torrey*, pp. 56, 80, 85; Kastner, *Species of Eternity*, p. 285.

North America, completed in 1843, established the natural system as the reigning form of classification in America.[64] Agassiz, also at Harvard, was accomplishing a similar project in American zoology, and Thomas Say, first in Philadelphia and then at New Harmony, Illinois, labored on his definitive *American Entomology* between 1817 and 1828. Richard Harlan's *Fauna Americana* was published in 1839 and Thomas Nuttall's supplemental *North American Sylva* in 1842. With this, an American natural history was largely in place.[65]

While natural history was shifting from the field to the academy, it was also separating into subdisciplines, each with its own discrete interests, standards, and methods. There were earlier specialists: William Dandridge Peck published almost exclusively on cankerworms and slug worms, André Michaux on trees, and Thomas Say on insects. In the middle of the century, this became the norm as specialized techniques, methods, and equipment widened the gap between disciplines. One of the dangers of specialization, as historian Hunter Dupree noted, is that it "relieves the scientist of the duty of asking big questions, of facing up to the philosophical implications of his work." With all of nature's production brought to their doorstep, academic naturalists began to narrow their vision and concentrate on investigative procedures, laboratory experiments, and empirically verified conclusions, seldom pausing to consider the philosophical or interdisciplinary implications of their work. The scientific community, Donald Worster writes, embraced the goal of detachment and objectivity: nature was to be analyzed, measured, and numbered rather than "studied through love or sympathy."[66] The holistic sensibility so characteristic of the first decades of the century was eclipsed, not to reappear until the rise of scientific ecology put nature's parts together again.

Benjamin Barton died in Philadelphia in 1815, well before the shift from fieldwork to the academy was underway, but even at this early period, he seemed to embody the difficulties of the classic naturalist at

---

[64] Asa Gray to W. J. Hooker, February 28, 1843, Jane Loring Gray (ed.), *Letters of Asa Gray* (London: Macmillan, 1893), Vol. 1, p. 299; Gray to Hooker, May 30, 1842, ibid., p. 289; Philip J. Pauly, *Biologists and the Promise of American Life: From Meriwether Lewis to Alfred Kinsey* (Princeton, 2000), pp. 17, 23–6, 28, 33, 32, 40; Rodgers, *John Torrey*, pp. 21–3, 91, 94–6, 100, 120, 135; Kastner, *Species of Eternity*, p. 289; Dupree, *Asa Gray*, 96.

[65] Porter, *Eagle's Nest*, p. 57.

[66] Dupree, *Asa Gray*, p. 135; Donald Worster, *Nature's Economy: A History of Ecological Ideas* (New York, 1977), p. 89–90. See Outram, "New Spaces in Natural History," pp. 249–50.

the dawn of the modern scientific age. Writing to Henry Mühlenberg, William Bartram noted Barton's inability to confine himself to any particular system or interest. Although his scientific manner was "neat & concise," he disadvantaged himself by tackling too many fields. "He is an ingenious, industrious young man," Bartram observed, but mastering even one field in the natural sciences required "time, experimental knowledge, great erudition, and even much traveling & researches." Perhaps, Bartram speculated, "he's not in a hurry." Bartram's observation spoke volumes about his friend's inability to publish more than "fragments" of natural history.[67] Barton was a man of the eighteenth century in his generalized curiosity, but the growing complexities in each of these fields left him paralyzed by his own perceived inadequacies, and he invariably published his work with a disclaimer. Characteristically, he confessed a "want of leisure" or good health that kept him from comprehending the larger picture of this scientifically untilled landscape. Whether he would continue, he added coyly, "will depend, in some measure, upon the reception given to the present work."[68]

There was something pathetic about Barton's plea for public support, but in an age when everything seemed interconnected, he found the problem of comprehending nature almost insurmountable. "Until there shall arise among us some happy genius, qualified by . . . talents, . . . leisure, and enthusiastic ardour, which is necessary to form the character a genuine naturalist," Barton pleaded, "every collection of facts, every individual fact, that will tend to illustrate the natural history of the United-States, *ought* to be received with candour, and intelligence."[69] Individual facts were easy to compile, but a much more fundamental problem loomed before the naturalist interested in connecting the parts to the whole. Synthesizing these facts into laws, as Cuvier said, required a different sort of courage, and this Barton did not possess.

Barton made his own excuses but, as with all naturalists of his generation, it was the irreducible complexity of the American wilderness that gave him pause. Like Benjamin Silliman standing before the Connecticut Valley in 1804, Barton stood at the edge of this magnificent geographical and intellectual frontier paralyzed by a "despairing curiosity." Silliman

---

[67] William Bartram to Henry E. Mühlenberg, November 29, 1792, Mühlenberg Manuscripts, PHS.
[68] Barton, *Fragments*, p. 24.
[69] Barton, *Fragments*, p. 24.

lacked the tools to understand the Connecticut Valley, and Barton, writing a few years later, lacked the confidence to use these tools to explore the grand scheme of nature. Later naturalists, standing back from the eclectic and chaotic work of exploration and discovery, learned to overcome these hesitancies by dissecting nature into manageable parts and developing special disciplinary tools for exploring these parts. Thus, the completion of an American natural history fell to the Grays, the Torreys, the Agassizs, and the Says, who relied on others to travel the solitary pathways into the wilderness while they – the sedentary naturalists – categorized and compiled the natural history of America. The eclectic philosophizing of the Humboldts and the Buffons was possible only so long as the naturalist turned a blind eye – as Barton did not – to the intimidating complexity of nature's grand system.[70] In the decades after Barton's death in 1815, the philosophy of natural history came of age and inspired a new and expansive interpretation of nature in America. Yet, even as it reached its heyday in the 1840s, scientists like Gray and Torrey were developing investigative protocols that would, in the second half of the century, undermine the academic credibility of this broad and imaginative approach. The philosophy of nature continued to inspire Americans, but in the second half of the century, the scientific study of nature became something altogether different.

The coalescence of empirical science and philosophical inquiry in the first half of the century left an important legacy. America's most inspiring twentieth-century naturalists – John Burroughs, John Muir, Aldo Leopold, Joseph Wood Krutch, Sally Carrighar, and certainly Rachel Carson – continued to view natural events and natural forms as part of a larger system operating across ecosystems and physiographic provinces – and even across academic disciplines. Although the Darwinian revolution gave this system coherence, it originated in the philosophical probings of America's earliest explorer-naturalists. And, because this system satisfied so well a deep-seated need to give meaning to nature, it has as much power today as it did in the nineteenth century. "It seems good," wilderness advocate Howard Zahniser wrote in a much more recent era, "to consider ourselves as members of a community of life that embraces the earth."[71] Zahniser's statement was an article of faith – an apparent good,

---

[70] Barton, *Professor Cullen's Treatise*, p. v.
[71] Howard Zahniser in Mark Harvey, *Wilderness Forever: Howard Zahniser and the Path to the Wilderness Act* (Seattle, 2005), p. 148.

not a scientific fact – but it summed up the generalized thinking about nature as these pre-Darwinians constructed it, with humans inescapably entwined in its web of connections. How this subtle understanding was formulated in the first half of the nineteenth century is the underlying story of American natural history.

PART TWO

THE NATURAL HISTORY OF AMERICA

4

Power and Purpose in the Geological Record

The Scientific Beginnings of American Romanticism

Lecturing before a lay audience in Paris, the eminent Franco-German naturalist, Baron Georges Cuvier, once likened the study of geology to the experiences of a traveler crossing a broad plain at the base of a towering range of mountains. On the plain, the wanderer observed a river meandering through a placid countryside of fields and villages: a landscape of assurance. The wanderer's mood changed as he climbed into the foothills, his eye drawn to the exposed strata that struck the eye as "so many proofs of the violent manner in which they have been elevated." Back on the plain, rock outcrops contained fossils, indicating a land made during the era of life on earth; the mountain rocks, far more ancient, were molded from the substance of primordia itself. Their broken forms brought to mind the "revolutions and catastrophes" that shaped this angular landscape. Wandering between the peaks and chasms of this rugged world, the traveler learned to see the land as a victim of gigantic, earth-rending forces, but where the traveler saw confusion and chaos, Cuvier, the careful student of earth history, saw system and evolution – perhaps even providence. These broken landscapes, he assured his audience, would reveal "a sequence...more or less the same" in all earthly productions.[1]

Cuvier's allegorical journey from settled plain to rugged peak – from civilization to wilderness – reflected a widely held belief that field

---

[1] Baron Georges Cuvier, *Essay on the Theory of the Earth*, Robert Kerr (trans.) (Edinburgh, 1815), pp. 7, 9, 15–16, 18–20. See Martin J. S. Rudwick, *Georges Cuvier, Fossil Bones, and Geological Catastrophes: New Translations and Interpretations of the Primary Texts* (Chicago, 1997), pp. 183, 186, 187, 188, 191.

observation in primitive places would reveal important truths about power and purpose in the geological record. The history written into the folded strata would disclose "an omnipotent creative force driving life to progressively higher stages with the passage of geological time," in the words of historian Stephen Mark, and to scientists like Cuvier, it was self-evident that these creative forces were best observed where their impress was most apparent to the naked eye. "It is not by walking in our cultivated fields . . . that the great effects of Nature's variations can be known," Comte de Buffon once wrote. "It is by going from the burning sands of the Torrid regions to the glaciers of the Poles, it is by descending from the summits of mountains to the bottom of the oceans, it is by comparing wastelands with wastelands that we will judge her better and admire her more."[2]

American naturalists agreed. Writing to Mark Catesby in 1740, John Bartram mused that in his travels, he chiefly searched out "ye most desolate craggy dismal places I can find where no mortal ever trode." Here, he observed the "transformations & transmutations" of the earth – the primal energies that "wound up" mountains and then dismantled them by "inclemency of weather." In nature's wildest recesses, he told Grovinius, the process of mountain-sculpting was made clear: The "dreadful precipices" were washed bare and undermined by "furious torrents & tumbled down into ye water courses." Henry Schoolcraft, standing at the brink of Niagara Falls and enveloped in its almost inconceivable energies, noted similarly that the scene of earth's "greatest convulsions" revealed unique insights about its past.[3] America was Cuvier's rugged steep and Buffon's vast extremes: a portal into the earth's misty past. The story naturalists like Bartram and Schoolcraft read into the American landscape was a beginning point for American natural history: nature was not static and timeless but rather dynamic and directed. Geology underscored the nation's strength and the spiritual value embedded in these uncultivated landscapes, setting the scene for a Romantic reinterpretation of nature at the middle of the century.

[2] Jacques Roger, *Buffon: A Life in Natural History* (Ithaca, 1997), p. 239; Stephen R. Mark, *Preserving the Living Past: John C. Merriam's Legacy in the State and National Parks* (Berkeley, 2005), p. 25.

[3] John Bartram to Mark Catesby, ca. March 1740, Edmund Berkeley and Dorothy Smith Berkeley, *The Correspondence of John Bartram, 1734–1777* (Gainesville, 1992), p. 152; Henry R. Schoolcraft, *Narrative Journal of Travels Through the Northwestern Regions of the United States* (Albany, 1821), p. 39. See Bartram to Charles Linne Barronet, ca. 1769, in Berkeley and Berkeley, *Correspondence of John Bartram*, p. 722; Bartram to John F. Gronovius, March 14, 1752, ibid., p. 339; Elisha Mitchell, *Elements of Geology, with an Outline of the Geology of North Carolina* (n.p., 1842), p. 13.

Creation Myths

Armed with new methods and theories, geologists approached the almost endless diversity of the American West hoping to find a window into the earth's beginnings. "Human reason, illuminated by God, has discovered the laws of planetary motion, and may yet . . . penetrate the laws of subterranean action," one wrote.[4] Europe – Cuvier's settled plain – had been explored, mined, and quarried for centuries, and its rock strata revealed few surprises. Testing the ideas emerging from this new discipline depended on expanding the scope of empirical observations, and there was no better place to do this than the peaks and chasms of America.

Late eighteenth-century geology challenged the literal sequence of creation laid out in Genesis, but it retained a number of theological assumptions. Naturalists chose among three possible interpretations of creation: the orthodox Christian view that the world was created in recent time and remained constant; a second view, popular among Enlightenment thinkers like Leibniz and the *philosophes*, that the world was changing, but only according to random causes; and a third view that posited a world of long duration trending toward a predetermined goal. The first offered little latitude for scientific debate, and the second recognized only chance occurrences; the third view appealed to the general optimism of the new nation and met the millennial expectations of the Second Great Awakening.[5] Most American geologists saw the earth moving toward perfection through the exercise of God's laws: a scientific articulation of manifest destiny.

Geologists imagined the earth, in its original and uncorrupted form, shaped like other heavenly bodies in even, concentric spheres, one stratum over the next. It was not clear whether the original elements were molten, liquid, or gas but, in whatever state, they eventually sifted into a primordial mud, with water rising to the top and earthy matter arranged beneath it in distinct layers according to specific gravity.[6] In time, these

---

[4] Anon., *An Essay on the Production & Circulation of Water, and an Explanation of the Phenomena of Volcanoes* (Troy, 1829), p. 15; M. J. S. Rudwick, *The Great Devonian Controversy: The Shaping of Scientific Knowledge among Gentlemanly Specialists* (Chicago, 1985), p. 3.

[5] Ernst Mayr, "The Idea of Teleology," *Journal of the History of Ideas* 53 (January–March 1992): p. 118.

[6] Roger, *Buffon*, p. 95; Edward Hitchcock, et al., *Report on the Geology of Vermont: Descriptive, Theoretical, Economical, and Scenographical* (Claremont, 1861), Vol. 1, p. 26; Rudwick, *Georges Cuvier*, p. 79; "Cebes," "Philosophical Disquisitions," *Niles Weekly Register* 1 (December 7, 1811): p. 248; Dennis R. Dean, "Benjamin Franklin and Earthquakes," *Annals of Science* 46 (No. 5, 1989): pp. 493–5.

layers were "deformed" by volcanoes, upheavals, comets, subsidences, floods, rain, changes in the earth's axis, or other profound natural forces, producing a diversified surface capable of hosting an almost endless profusion of life.[7]

The man who crafted this speculative history into a science was Abraham Gottlob Werner, professor of mineralogy at the School of Mines in Freiburg. Like many others, Werner envisioned the earth's materials forming out of the waters of a global ocean where they were held in solution. As the sea level dropped, strata were exposed and weathered into their present forms.[8] Werner's history was speculative, but his mineralogy was based on more inductive methods. Procedures for essaying minerals were available since the fifteenth century, but it was Werner who found a way to catalog them systematically. In his 1774 *External Characters of Minerals*, he set out a classification as universal as Linnaeus's system for plants, arranging his specimens according to external features – color, cohesion, unctuousness, weight, smell, taste, fracture, concretion, hardness, transparency, fungibility, flexibility, and sound. Later, he added chemical properties – earthy, saline, flammable, metallic, and magnetic – and, finally, he categorized them according to the context in which they were discovered.[9]

Werner's last mineralogical category, context, led to a field of endeavor that proved to be his most lasting contribution to geology. To determine context, he began classifying strata. The earliest he called *primitive*: rocks that could not be reduced further to constituent parts. Granite, gneiss, hornblende, mica, talcose, schist, and serpentine were the lowest and most ancient strata on earth, laid down before the beginning of life. The *transition* formations – argillite, sandstone, limestone, greywacke, trap, slate – were created later and contained fossils. The *secondary* and *tertiary* formations – floetz, sandstone, limestone, chalk, coal – contained progressively more modern fossils. Living in a region of Europe composed mainly of sedimentary rock, Werner imagined these strata as depositions from a universal ocean. His followers termed this the *neptunist school*.

---

[7] Mott T. Greene, *Geology in the Nineteenth Century: Changing Views of a Changing World* (Ithaca, 1982), p. 14; Roger, *Buffon*, p. 95; Hitchcock et al., *Report on the Geology of Vermont*, Vol. 1, p. 26; Rudwick, *Georges Cuvier*, p. 79; *Niles Weekly Register* 1 (December 7, 1811): pp. 248–9; Charles T. Jackson, *Final Report on the Geology and Mineralogy of the State of New Hampshire* (Concord, 1844), pp. 6–7, 31; Noah Webster, *An Address, Delivered Before the Hampshire, Franklin, and Hampden Agricultural Society* (Northampton, 1818), p. 3.

[8] David R. Oldroyd, *Thinking About the Earth: A History of Ideas in Geology* (Cambridge, 1996), pp. 99–100.

[9] Greene, *Geology in the Nineteenth Century*, p. 36; Allen G. Debus, *Man and Nature in the Renaissance* (Cambridge, 1978), p. 10; Oldroyd, *Thinking About the Earth*, p. 70.

Although his classifications were sometimes complicated, his conviction that rock strata and mineral deposits were predictable was a powerful influence on the emerging field of geology.[10] Werner's students fanned out across the globe seeking the universal laws of geological formation and, for at least a half-century, geologists employed his classifications as standard nomenclature.[11]

If Werner was the father of modern mineralogy, it was Georges Cuvier who began the modern debate on how these rock strata, laid down with such uniformity, became so intermixed. Having lived through the French Revolution, Cuvier was attracted to the idea of profound disruptions, and he used fossil evidence to confirm his belief that life itself had been altered by earth-rending geological events. Perhaps, he thought, a great comet once struck the earth, "overturning the order of things." Perhaps the ocean had been swept from its bed, rolling over the land and carrying everything before it; or perhaps the earth had changed its axis, upsetting the oceans and buckling the crust. Cuvier brought several disciplines to bear on the question of geological formation: comparative fossil anatomy, biology, paleontology, geology, comparative literature, and mythology, the latter two providing folk-memories of ancient floods, volcanoes, and earthquakes. As the core cooled, he reasoned, these convulsions moderated. Physics and providence dictated that the crust would become more stable once life appeared on the planet. Catastrophism resonated with biblical theory, appealing to those whose sense of geological time was foreshortened by theological assumptions, and the most catastrophic event imaginable, a flood of biblical proportions, explained a variety of confusing geological features, such as fossils buried beneath layers of sedimentary rock and boulders carried hundreds of miles to a new location.[12] The idea of catastrophe did not originate with Cuvier, but his stature among scientists gave it an *imprimatur* it had not had earlier.

[10] *American Quarterly Review* 13 (March 1830): p. 386; Louis Agassiz, *Geological Sketches* (Boston, 1866), pp. 12, 115–16; Charles Lyell, *Principles of Geology* (Boston, 1842), Vol. 1, pp. 82–3; Rudwick, *Georges Cuvier*, p. 5; *American Journal of Science* 21 (No. 1, 1832): p. 9; Greene, *Geology in the Nineteenth Century*, pp. 26, 32, 35, 46, 65; A. Hallam, *Great Geological Controversies* (New York, 1989), pp. 5, 23.

[11] Lyell, *Principles of Geology*, pp. 84. See Jackson, *Final Report... New Hampshire*, p. 10.

[12] Georges Baron Cuvier, *Essay on the Theory of the Earth... To Which Are Now Added, Observations on the Geology of North America* (New York, 1818), p. 410. See Robert Jameson, "Preface," in ibid., pp. viii; Rudwick, *Georges Cuvier*, pp. 3, 46, 80–2, 190; Hallam, *Great Geological Controversies*, p. 37; Martin J. S. Rudwick, "Lyell and the *Principles of Geology*," in Derek J. Blundell and Andrew C. Scott, *Lyell: The Past Is the Key to the Present* (London: Geological Society, 1998), pp. 4–5; 193; Anonymous, *A Short View of the Natural History of the Earth* (Boston, 1803), p. 74–5, 77.

Although catastrophism remained popular into the nineteenth century, some geologists preferred an explanation based on gradual influences. Foremost among these was Scottish chemist and gentleman-farmer, James Hutton. Shortly before his death in 1797, Hutton published his *Theory of the Earth, with Proofs and Illustrations*, in which he invoked the agency of observable geological processes, primarily erosion and volcanic uplift, operating over vastly grander time scales. As a farmer, Hutton knew that Scotland's rich soils were produced by a weathering of subsurface rocks, and he also understood that rains were washing these soils into the sea. New soils depended on a perpetual decay of rock strata; but, over a limitless expanse of time, these same forces would erode the earth into a level plain, ending the process of renewal. After corresponding with James Watt about steam engines, he envisioned the earth's interior as a great store of subterranean fuel, gradually and constantly bending and folding the crust and forcing molten rock to the surface. The reformulation of these irregular features – the core purpose of geological evolution – derived from this internal heat: a volcanic process. Although Hutton was not alone in visualizing heat and erosion as operant geological agencies, he, like Cuvier, gave this explanation standing by combining older speculations and modern empirical methods.[13]

The beauty of the gradualist vision was its uniformity, constituting a single sweeping explanation for events from primordia to the present – an endless cycle of mountain-building and mountain-leveling. Yet, the idea of catastrophe seemed inescapable to many who observed the massive and seemingly dramatic changes evident in the fossil and stratigraphic record.[14] At the turn of the century, vulcanists vied with neptunists, and gradualists with catastrophists, as evidence for each theory poured in from all corners of the globe. American naturalists incorporated elements of each into a vision of lineal geological evolution that began with primordia and ended with the settlement of the American West.

The Geological Foundations of America

As scientists set out to explore the peaks and chasms of America, their first task was to establish a broad geological matrix that later observers could

---

[13] Hallam, *Great Geological Controversies*, pp. 7–8, 10–11, 13; Oldroyd, *Thinking About the Earth*, pp. 92–3.

[14] Rudwick, *Georges Cuvier*, p. 43–4; Hallam, *Great Geological Controversies*, p. 30; Greene, *Geology in the Nineteenth Century*, pp. 47–8, 56, 61.

fill with meaning. Details, "carefully and steadily attended to," would fill the matrix and enable later theorists to draw grander conclusions.[15] American geology first took shape as early cartographers, interested mainly in military or commercial advantages, laid out the topography of the regions they explored. Later explorers were more general in their interests. German geographer, Johann David Schöpf, arrived in America as a surgeon to the Hessian troops during the Revolution, toured the eastern states after the war, and published an American topography in 1787 that distinguished the new nation as a broad coastal plain stretching from Maine to Florida and reaching back to a "fall line" marked off by transverse ledges that produced waterfalls in all the rivers running to the Atlantic.[16] Jedidiah Morse created a similar picture of America by compiling a growing body of local information into a national geography. More a compiler than a geographer, Morse sent out questionnaires to towns across the eastern seaboard asking about population, soils, boundaries, trade, religious denominations, and schools, among other things, and in 1796, published *The American Gazetteer*, the first comprehensive atlas of North America. Morse included seven large foldout maps that provided an elementary profile of American surficial geology.[17] His example was followed in dozens of somewhat formulaic local and state gazetteers, each beginning with a physical description of the land and an assessment of its potential for development. Robert Munro's *Description of the Genesee Country*, published in 1804, summarized the local geography as "generally hilly and broken" but with many fertile tracts along the valleys. He described each navigable river, each species of useful timber, and each soil pattern, usually in enthusiastic terms.[18]

This simple delineation was expanded by French philosopher Constantin François Chasseboeuf, Conte de Volney, who published *A View of the Soil and Climate of the United States of America* in Paris in 1803 and in Philadelphia in 1804. Volney moved to America during the Revolution

---

[15] Samuel Williams in American Academy of Arts and Sciences *Memoirs* 1 (1783): p. 234. See Thomas Nuttall in ibid., n.s., 1 (1833): p. 105.

[16] George P. Merrill, *The First One Hundred Years of American Geology* (New Haven, 1924), p. 4; Courtney Robert Hall, *A Scientist in the Early Republic: Samuel Latham Mitchill, 1764–1831* (New York, 1934), p. 68.

[17] Edward C. Carter II (ed.), *Surveying the Record: North American Scientific Exploration to 1930* (Philadelphia, 1999), pp. 30, 34; Amy DeRogatis, *Moral Geography: Maps, Missionaries, and the American Frontier* (New York, 2003), pp. 130–2.

[18] Robert Munro, *A Description of the Genesee Country* (New York, 1804), pp. 4–13. See Charles Varte, *Topographical Description of the Counties of Frederick, Berkeley, and Jefferson Situated in the State of Virginia* (Winchester, 1810).

but was forced to flee the country under threat from the Alien Act in 1798. While in America, he traveled as far west as the Wabash observing topography, geology, climate, and culture. His general impression of America was unflattering, reflecting his aristocratic background and his ill health during his travels, but his description of the country's physical characteristics was both astute and optimistic. The nation was bounded, he wrote, by the Atlantic Ocean, the Gulf, the western prairies, the St. Lawrence, and the Great Lakes – natural barriers immensely important to a European whose homeland was engulfed in war. The country was divided by a chain of high ridges running parallel to the sea. The rivers running west off this plateau were like the Nile in their periodical inundations, suggesting parallels between imperial Egypt and the emerging American civilization.[19]

Volney not only defined the basic topography of the United States, but he began piecing together a connection among climate, surficial geology, and vegetation to produce a general biogeography. He divided the eastern continent into a southern, middle, and northern forest. The former grew in a bed of gravel and sand and included pine, fir, larch, cypress, and other "resinous trees." The middle forest, blessed with deeper and richer soils, was composed of oak, beech, maple, walnut, sycamore, acacia, mulberry, plum, ash, birch, sassafras, and poplar, and in its western extremities, cherry, chestnut, papaw, and magnolia. The northern forest, a land of thin, granitic soils, grew pine, fir, larch, and cedar. If somewhat oversimplified, his classifications were bold and comprehensive, combining decades of local attempts to correlate climate, geology, and vegetation. Like Schöpf, Volney also divided the country by rock stratum and soil type: the marine sands and alluvial soils of the eastern seaboard; the mixed soils of the Piedmont; the granites of the Adirondacks; the sandstones of the Catskills, Alleghenies, and Blue Ridge; the limestones of the Mississippi and Shenandoah Valleys; the rich earths of the Gulf Coast and Cumberland Ridge; and the sandy rolling plains and natural meadows of the Northwest Territory.[20]

---

[19] Volney, *View of the Soil and Climate*, pp. 28–9; *Medical Repository*, 2d ser., 2 (1805): p. 173; Merrill, *First One Hundred Years of American Geology*, p. 27.

[20] *Medical Repository*, 2d ser., 2 (1805): pp. 171, 178–82; *North American Review*, n.s., 44 (April 1837): p. 336; Volney, *View of the Soil and Climate*, pp. 1, 12, 3–20, 29–32, 58–9. See *The Naturalist* 13 (November 1879): p. 759; James Mease, *Geological Account of the United States* (Philadelphia, 1807), pp. 6–7; Merrill, *First One Hundred Years of American Geology*, pp. 25–7; Nelson, "Toward a Reliable Geologic Map," p. 53.

He was also the first naturalist to provide an overview of America's climate. Globally, he understood that prevailing winds resulted from temperature differentials as the sun moved around the earth, causing heated air to rise along the equator and drawing in cooler air from the surrounding zones. The shift in air masses from the temperate to the torrid zone had its "collaterals," as Volney put it, in the prevailing northwest winds in America. The effect of this cold, dry wind was evident in tree bark in the forest and mortar in exposed walls. Volney envisioned the air mass above North America as "a kind of aerial ocean or lake," cradled in the continental basin between the Rocky Mountains and the Appalachians. The seasonal shift caused by the sun passing south of the equator – a "moment of revolutions and commotions" – pulled the warm Gulf Coast air southward, drawing cold air down from the north. With this basic understanding, he compiled the country's first climate map and raised questions that intrigued naturalists for decades.[21]

America's first trained geologist was William Maclure, whose *Observations on the Geology of the United States*, published in 1809, established rigorous empirical standards for the generation to follow. Maclure was born in Scotland in 1763 and, as a partner in a merchant house, he visited America in 1796. Back in England as a leisured gentleman in 1803, he traveled through Europe studying natural history and geology. He returned to the United States in 1807 and, being acquainted with Volney, continued his friend's geological explorations. He crossed the Alleghenies no less than fifty times "with his hammer in his hand and his wallet on his shoulder," visiting every state and territory in the Union. With few precedents before him, he commenced almost single-handedly the task of delineating the basic rock formations of America.

Maclure's method was to strike west from a designated point on the coast and conduct a transect, noting the geological features along the way. Beginning in Baltimore, for instance, he traveled west to Pittsburgh, noting the primitive bedrock formation across the first seventeen miles and, beyond that, the gravel soils and alluvial clays impregnated with hornblende and pyrites in the foothills. Moving on to Westminster, he discovered a primitive formation again with hornbeam, then mica and slate, "with beds and veins of quartz and now and then with beds of large grained granite in which they find the emerald Tourmaline &&&."

[21] Volney, *View of the Soil and Climate*, pp. 135, 158–9, 164–7, 179, 186; American Philosophical Society (hereafter APS), *Publications* 1 (1789): pp. 337–8; *American Journal of Science* 47 (October 1844): pp. 18–19.

Completing his journey to Pittsburgh, he summarized the transect according to three geographical provinces: tertiary and alluvial along the coast,
primitive in the Appalachians, and secondary west of the mountains.[22]

These features, he thought, would determine the basic contours of
American civilization. Guarded by mountains on the east and the Great
Lakes to the north, the interior seemed impregnable; as Volney pointed
out, westerners had only one great harbor to defend. United by its magnificent river system and secure against its enemies, the West was destined
to become the center of American civilization. The Atlantic Coast would
be vulnerable to ships of war, and this would involve its citizens in European conflicts, at enormous cost. Westerners would not bear these burdens with the "same feeling or interest," Maclure predicted, and nothing
could prevent disunion "but the utmost prudence and economy in the
federal rulers, by avoiding war and every cause of expense."[23]

Covering new ground and working far from the seats of learning in
Europe, American geologists remained aloof from the old battles over fire
and water; there was enough diversity in America, Maclure thought, to
verify both explanations. Naturalists remained eclectic, but they thought
deeply about the origins of the rocks and hills they inspected. The breadth
of the Adirondack Valleys relative to the rivers flowing through them
convinced John Bartram that they had been sculpted by great floods and
that the mountains were once much higher. "Winter rains beat against ye
naked rock," he observed, and dissolved the "natural cement" holding
them together. The landscape was "never at rest, but allway in a state of
contraction or expansion."[24] Lewis Evans, like his friend Bartram, tried to

[22] William Maclure, "Observations in Primative [sic] During a Journey to Pittsburgh and
Thence to Boston, New York in 1816," n.p., William Maclure Papers, APS; Edward
Hitchcock, *First Anniversary Address Before the Association of American Geologists*
(New Haven, 1841), p. 4; *American Journal of Science* 47 (October 1844): pp. 3–4;
William H. Seward, "Introduction," in James E. De Kay, *Zoology of New-York, or the
New-York Fauna* (Albany, 1842), p. 172.

[23] McClure in APS *Transactions*, n.s., 1 (1818): pp. 88–90. See *American Journal of Science*
1 (1818): pp. 213, 216.

[24] William Maclure in Academy of Natural Sciences of Philadelphia *Journal* 1 (Part 2,
1818): pp. 261, 263–4, 266–8, 270–1; Maclure in *American Journal of Science* 6 (No.
1, 1823): p. 98; John Bartram to Mark Catesby, November 14, 1751, in Berkeley and
Berkeley, *Correspondence of John Bartram*, pp. 334–5; Bartram to Catesby, ca. 1753,
in ibid., pp. 358–9; Bartram to Catesby, ca. March 1740, in ibid., p. 152; Bartram
in Peter Kalm, *Travels Into North America, Containing Its Natural History, and a
Circumstantial Account of Its Plantations and Agriculture in General*, John R. Foster
(trans.) (Warrington, 1753–1771), Vol. 1, p. 135. See *North American Review* 8 (March
1819): pp. 396–7; Edward Hitchcock in *American Journal of Science* 6 (No. 1, 1823):
p. 60.

imagine the processes that left fossil seashells high in the Appalachians. Perhaps, he thought, a huge sea once covered the western basin, held in check by the Appalachian ridge.[25] When the waters breached these ramparts, the western basin, "disburthened of such a load of waters," rose up, leaving the fossils high above the level of the sea. "There is no doubt but that many such accidents have happened in the world before it became settled in its present condition." Naturalists saw evidence of an evolving landscape and hoped to learn how and why these changes took place.[26]

The second and third decades of the century were important for American geology. Prior to Maclure's travels, surveys had been conducted chiefly by foreigners, like Schöpf and Volney, or by American naturalists chiefly interested in other subjects, like Bartram and Evans. Maclure provided a rough map of American geology and, in the next decade, others began filling in details. Benjamin Silliman explored the Connecticut Valley north from New Haven, and Edward Hitchcock later worked down the valley from Amherst. In 1816–18, Bowdoin College Professor Parker Cleaveland and Yale's Dwight Dana classified strata and minerals across the eastern states according to a Wernerian system; and Amos Eaton, Henry Schoolcraft, Horace Hayden, and T. Romeyn Beck began mapping the geology of the western states, providing detailed transverse views based on Maclure's pioneering method.[27]

It was the Appalachian chain that first thrust American geologists into the transatlantic debates about earth history, and it fell to two brothers, Henry D. Rogers and William B. Rogers, to parse the mystery of the folded strata that made up these mountains. The brothers saw the mountains as a series of strata laid out horizontally and then compressed by a gigantic and convulsive lateral thrust from east to west. Armed with maps based on their own painstaking fieldwork, they postulated that an

---

[25] Lewis Evans in Thomas A. Pownall, *Topographical Description of the Dominions of the United States of America* (Pittsburgh, 1949[c. 1776]), pp. 112–15.

[26] David Dale Owen, *Report of the Geological Survey in Kentucky, Made During the Years 1854 and 1855* (Frankfort, 1856), pp. 100–1; Pownall, *Topographical Description*, p. 116.

[27] Edward Hitchcock in *American Journal of Science and Arts* 7 (No. 1, 1824): p. 20; James Ellsworth De Kay, *Anniversary Address on the Progress of Natural Sciences in the United States* (New York, 1826), pp. 11, 18–20, 23–4; Gerald M. Friedman, "Charles Lyell in New York State," in Blundell and Scott, *Lyell*, p. 71; Hall, *Scientist in the Early Republic*, p. 75; *American Journal of Science* 1 (1818): p. 37; *North American Review* 12 (January 1821): p. 137; Jeremiah van Rensselaer, *Lectures on Geology; Being Outlines of the Science, Delivered in the New-York Athenaeum in the Year 1825* (New York, 1825), p. 5.

enormous earthquake, resonating through a great subterranean lava reservoir, warped the crust in undulatory waves, "producing the sinuousities of the major sections of the system." Their explanation, one of the boldest to emerge out of nineteenth-century American geology, was replaced after only a few years by another proposed by James Dwight Dana, who saw the Appalachians formed by a gradual contraction of the earth's crust due to a cooling of the core. The basin between the coasts was pulled between two subsiding ocean crusts, stretching the surface at the rims and causing an extrusion of magma.[28]

In 1842, Edward Hitchcock reported that progress in American geology seemed "more like a dream than the reality." The principal formations of the continent had been established, first by individuals and then by the state surveys, and the larger map was nearly complete. State governments were patronizing the sciences, public lectures on geology were drawing crowds, and new discoveries were matters of drawing-room conversation. Diffused through the popular press, these geological achievements helped crystallize a national identity by demonstrating, as the *Niles Weekly Register* put it, "the unexampled prosperity that will arise from our cultivating the advantages which nature has dispensed with so liberal a hand."[29] The evolutionary cant in these violent beginnings offered an appropriate metaphor for the newly forged republic.

Power and Violence in Primordial Nature

When American naturalists shifted from describing basic geological formations to explaining them, they compiled an amazing story of a land moving inexorably toward a destiny that included – indeed, culminated – in a new American civilization. This was the geologist's task, as Louis Agassiz explained: to discover the plan of creation "laid out in the course of time, and executed with the definite object of introducing man upon the

---

[28] Henry Darwin Rogers, *Address on the Recent Progress of Geological Research in the United States* (Philadelphia, 1844), p. 56. See Greene, *Geology in the Nineteenth Century*, pp. 122–7, 141; Leonard G. Wilson, *Lyell in America: Transatlantic Geology, 1841–1853* (Baltimore, 1998), p. 35; Oldroyd, *Thinking About the Earth*, p. 173; Julie R. Newell, "James Dwight Dana and the Emergence of Professional Geology in the United States," *American Journal of Science* 297 (No. 3, 1997): p. 278; Emma Rogers, *Life and Letters of William Barton Rogers* (Boston, 1896), pp. 210–11.

[29] Hitchcock, *First Anniversary Address*, p. 42; *Niles' Weekly Register*, Supplement, 9 (1816): pp. 145–9.

earth."[30] The search for meaning in the history of earth is an ancient one but, in America, geologists coupled their new powers of scientific investigation to an equally powerful thirst for a compelling national narrative. In the geological record, the new scientist could trace life back to its origins and see the evolutionary process still at work: river sediments hardening into rock, plants and animals becoming fossils, sand crystallizing on the shore, shells dissolving into chalk, plants decaying into vegetable soils, and salts metamorphosing into metals. These changes were bracketed by much more dramatic events that rent the surface and threw up the mountains, altering the earth's form in the geological blink of an eye. Contemplating the meaning of these alterations – the plan of creation laid out in the bedrock of America – provided observers with a new way of defining nationhood.[31]

National pride and available evidence disposed most early American geologists to favor catastrophe as the primary agent of geological change. Signs of geological violence were everywhere.[32] Huge boulders had been moved hundreds of miles by some unexplained effort of nature, and deep gouges in the bedrock, sometimes across the highest mountain-tops, suggested floods of unimaginable proportions. A vein of quartz and sandstone extending more than three hundred miles along the Hudson–Champlain highlands suggested "some mighty convulsion" by which two continental formations, one primitive and the other transitional, collided. In Pennsylvania, the Rogers brothers described a massive explosion that rocked the surface in primordial times and, in a "final paroxysmal movement," produced the wavelike Appalachian ridges. The explosion was followed by a "sudden sinking of the land" and a tidal wave from the open sea washing across the interior, dragging along organic debris to

[30] Louis Agassiz, *The Structure of Animal Life: Six Lectures Delivered at the Brooklyn Academy of Music in January and February 1862* (New York, 1866), p. 6.

[31] Thomas Ashe, *Travels in America, Performed in 1808, for the Purpose of Exploring the Rivers Alleghany, Monongahela, Ohio, and Mississippi* (Newburyport, 1808), pp. 54–6; Hitchcock, *Report on the Geology of Vermont*, Vol. 1, pp. 181–5; *Monthly American Journal of Geology and Natural Science* 1 (July 1831): p. 16; Thomas Say, "Miscellaneous Notes on Conchology, etc.," Thomas Say Papers, APS; Agassiz, *Geological Sketches*, p. 99; Jackson, *Final Report... New Hampshire*, p. 8; Roger, *Buffon*, pp. 97–100; W. Winterbotham, *An Historical, Geographical, Commercial, and Philosophical View of the American United States* (London, 1795), Vol. 1, p. 149.

[32] Agassiz, *Geological Sketches*, p. 98–9; Gilbert Chinard, "Eighteenth-Century Theories on America as a Human Habitat," *APS Proceedings* 91 (February 1947): p. 50; Cuvier, *Essay on the Theory of the Earth*, p. 369.

become Pennsylvania's coal deposits. As they inspected these ruins of nature, geologists filled their field journals with expressions of awe.[33]

Most naturalists rejected the biblical version of this directed geological sequence, but they clung to a belief that it reflected an order "imposed by an omnipotent, yet veiled, creative force." Each geological catastrophe served a larger design, laying a foundation, perhaps, for an equally important change in biology. "In conformity with the divine purpose," Noah Webster explained, huge geological pressures ground the surface strata into fine particles, producing a permeable and friable cover "easily pulverized by instruments of husbandry." The soils were made loose enough to admit plant roots but compact enough to hold up even the largest trees. Geological convulsions brought valuable minerals and ores to the surface and relieved pent-up pressures inside the earth, preventing even greater catastrophes. The earth's crust was fractured, bent, dislocated, folded, melted, and reconsolidated over the eons; yet, as Edward Hitchcock pointed out, these massive changes were aimed at achieving an equilibrium that left the earth a quiet and secure place for life: Cuvier's fertile plain.[34]

Water was the most obvious geological force operating on this scale, and it was, as Hitchcock put it, "at this point we . . . endeavor to decipher the hieroglyphics of nature." Volney and Maclure envisioned a "primeval ocean" that once covered the continent from the western Alleghenies to a series of isolated, cone-shaped "knobs" in Indiana. Maclure speculated that the West's relatively small populations of grazing quadrupeds, compared with the larger number of beavers, otters, muskrats, and aquatic birds, indicated the sea's recent retreat, and Hitchcock estimated from the size of the Mississippi Delta and the amount of silt washed out of the river yearly that the Mississippi emerged from under this sea 14,204 years earlier. Some saw this as a gradual process. The terraces along the Ohio and the other rivers of the inland basin indicated that the sea drained

---

[33] *American Journal of Science* 5 (1822): pp. 17–20; Rogers and Rogers in Merrill, *First One Hundred Years of American Geology*, p. 220. See Charles Daubeny, *Sketch of the Geology of North America, Being the Substance of a Memoir Read Before the Ashmolean Society* (Oxford, 1839), pp. 10, 11, 13; Lyell, *Travels in North America*, Vol. 1, p. 78; James Dwight Dana, *On American Geological History* (New Haven, 1856), p. 329.

[34] Mark, *Preserving the Living Past*, p. 157; Webster, *Address, Delivered Before the Hampshire, Franklin and Hampden Agricultural Society*, p. 3; Edward Hitchcock, *The Religion of Geology and Its Connected Sciences* (Glasgow, 1851), pp. 181–2. See Zadock Thompson, *Geography and Geology of Vermont* (Burlington, 1848), pp. 9, 49; Roger, *Buffon*, p. 102; Edward Hitchcock, *The Connection Between Geology and Natural Religion* (Edinburgh, 1835), pp. 3, 8–9.

away in several stages, and the basin's limestone strata appeared to have been deposited in calm water.[35]

Most, however, saw this subsidence in dramatic terms: The Appalachian chain had been "rent to its base" by some "great convulsion of nature" as the waters sluiced through the gap in a catastrophic flood. Volney found marine fossils, uprooted rock, and vast banks of sand, mud, and gravel in the Appalachian passes, the "principal breaches" through which the sea had drained away. Standing at the great gap near Harper's Ferry where the Shenandoah and Potomac joined in passing through the Blue Ridge Mountains, he noted the waters still weeping from the ragged cliffs.[36] On the southern seaboard, Edmund Ruffin found water-rolled stones that became progressively smaller as he approached the sea, having been deposited "in the order of the specific gravity." Perhaps a breach in the mountains sent a wall of water a thousand feet high across the Piedmont, sweeping off surface materials and depositing them in the lowlands near the ocean – a display of nature's power worthy of America's founding. Whether sudden or gradual, the retreat of the waters fulfilled the plan of creation. The falling waters left behind the incredibly deep soils of the Kentucky highlands – sometimes fifty feet – and exposed the ancient marshes and swamps at the base of the Appalachians, resulting in the vast coal deposits in western Pennsylvania.[37]

Water and Ice

These geological fantasies reflected the intense nationalism of the early republic and the pietistic sensitivities of the Second Great Awakening. Although few geologists subscribed to the Bible in a literal sense, the idea of a catastrophic flood spoke to the country's magnificent beginnings and

[35] Hitchcock, *Religion of Geology*, pp. 61–2; Volney, *View of the Soil and Climate*, pp. 72–3, 76–8; William Maclure in Academy of Natural Sciences of Philadelphia *Journal* 1 (Part 2, 1818): pp. 33–4; William W. Mather in *American Journal of Science* 49 (October 1845): p. 3; Maclure in ibid., 6 (No. 1, 1823): p. 102. See Horace H. Hayden, *Geological Essays* (Baltimore, 1820), p. 45; Dana, *On American Geological History*, p. 322; *Medical Repository*, 2d ser., 6 (1809): pp. 350–1; *North American Review*, n.s., 7 (July 1822): p. 230; *Monthly American Journal of Geology and Natural Science* 1 (July 1831): p. 18; Benjamin Silliman in *American Journal of Science* 19 (No. 1, 1831): pp. 6–7; S. P. Hildreth in ibid., 29 (1836): pp. 1–2; Owen, *Report of the Geological Survey in Kentucky*, p. 28.

[36] Hayden, *Geological Essays*, pp. 45–7, 63; Volney, *View of the Soil and Climate*, pp. 63–7; *Niles Weekly Register* 5, "Supplement" (1813): pp. 178–9.

[37] Edmund Ruffin, *Agricultural, Geological, and Descriptive Sketches of Lower North Carolina and the Similar Adjacent Lands* (Raleigh, 1861), pp. 25, 28–30, 33–4, 36–7.

its consonance with God's plan. Horace Hayden deemed the outwash debris he traced across the eastern landscape evidence of a global deluge, "decreed by the Almighty to accomplish the awful denunciations which he had pronounced against an impious race of men." Another geologist imagined the boulder-strewn landscape around Gloucester as the way the world appeared to Noah "as he came out of the ark."[38] Evidence for the deluge – so-called drift debris – came in several forms. The most suggestive were "horsebacks," or long, sinuous ridges of gravel, clay, and boulders located far from rivers and running in directions unrelated to general watershed features. In association with these were deep parallel scratches in the bedrock, boulders torn from their parent bedrock, and marine clays far inland from the coast. There was, as Henry Rogers put it, a "remarkable *general* parallelism" across all this evidence. Drift debris suggested forces moving generally from northeast to southwest unaffected by contours in the land; their association with clay and sand suggested water as one of the agents involved; they were found on Maine's Mount Katahdin at 5,200 feet but not atop Mount Washington at 6,200 feet; and they disappeared below forty degrees latitude. Finally, whatever created drift debris involved forces far more powerful than those operating in historical times.[39] While diluvial explanations were common across the Atlantic world, they were more persistent in America, given the abundance of evidence and the association with religion and American destiny.

There were several explanations for the rush of waters that created these debris. Early theories held that the earth's thin crust covered a fathomless abyss of water, or perhaps a series of enormous caverns, and the deluge resulted when the crust was torn open. Hayden proposed that the earth's axis shifted and the sun, passing over the poles, caused the "inconceivably rapid dissolution of those immense hemispheres of ice." Floods, he thought, poured down in great waves over Sweden and Norway, splashed up against the heights of Spitsbergen, turned westward to Newfoundland, and demolished the landforms of eastern America. "The awful denunciations of an offended God were fast fulfilling," he

---

[38] Hayden, *Geological Essays*, pp. 164–5; Edward Hitchcock, *Report on the Geology, Mineralogy, Botany, and Zoology of Massachusetts* (Amherst, 1833), pp. 148, 150. See Ebenezer Emmons, *Agriculture of New-York* (Albany, 1846), Vol. 1, p. 210; John Haywood, *The Natural and Aboriginal History of the Tennessee Up to the First Settlements Therein by the White People in the Year 1768* (Nashville, 1823), pp. 4–5.

[39] Rogers, *Address on the Recent Progress of Geological Research*, pp. 44–6; *American Journal of Science* 7 (No. 1, 1824): p. 42; Hitchcock, *Report on ... Massachusetts*, p. 151; Emmons, *Report of the Survey of the Second Geological District*, p. 15.

wrote, "by the sure and utter extermination of every beast of the field, and every creeping thing that creepeth upon the face of the earth." Others found this magnificently destructive vision attractive but attributed the melting of the poles to other causes.[40]

By the 1830s, another possibility had emerged. As early as 1802, British geologist John Playfair, known best as Hutton's advocate, conjectured that drift debris resulted from glaciation and, in 1821, Swiss engineer Ignaz Venetz similarly argued that his country's glaciers were once more extensive, accounting for the drift debris throughout central Europe. Jean de Charpentier, one of Switzerland's foremost scientists, adopted this theory, and Norwegian Jens Esmarch and Peter Dobson of Connecticut advanced similar ideas. The most forceful advocate, however, was Swiss naturalist, Jean Louis Rodolphe Agassiz, who had studied with Cuvier in Paris, then moved on to the College of Neufchatel in Switzerland. A noted ichthyologist, Agassiz joined the Harvard University faculty in 1848 as professor of geology and zoology, where his *Principles of Zoology* won him an international reputation.[41]

Agassiz initially connected drift debris with the biblical flood but, in 1836, he toured the Alps with de Charpentier and was impressed by the evidence pointing to glaciers. In 1837, he hypothesized an Ice Age to explain the vast reach of the glaciers. His *Études sur les glaciers*, published in 1840, described a period when "two vast caps of ice stretched from the Northern pole southward and from the Southern pole northward," scouring out the U-shaped valleys so typical of Switzerland and, indeed, the entire north temperate zone.[42] Agassiz's theory was widely accepted in Europe but not in America. His most ardent American critics – Charles Jackson, Benjamin Silliman, and Edward Hitchcock – objected that glaciers projected outward in radial fashion from mountains and

[40] Horace H. Hayden in *North American Review* 12 (January 1821): p. 139; Hayden, *Geological Essays*, pp. 59–60, 63–5. See Hayden in *American Journal of Science* 3 (1821): pp. 51, 53; Mitchell, *Elements of Geology*, p. 114; Hitchcock, *Report on...Massachusetts*, p. 141.

[41] *American Journal of Science* 46 (April 1844): pp. 169, 171; Elizabeth Cary Agassiz in Louis Agassiz, *Louis Agassiz: His Life and Correspondence*, Elizabeth Cary Agassiz (ed.), (Boston, 1885), Vol. 2, p. 457; Philip J. Pauly, *Biologists and the Promise of American Life: From Meriwether Lewis to Alfred Kinsey* (Princeton, 2000), pp. 33–8.

[42] Hitchcock, *First Anniversary Address*, p. 23. See Hallam, *Great Geological Controversies*, pp. 92–3; Merrill, *First One Hundred Years of American Geology*, p. 211; Agassiz, *Geological Sketches*, p. 212; Louis Agassiz, *Lake Superior: Its Physical Character, Vegetation, and Animals, Compared with Those of Other and Similar Regions* (Boston, 1850), pp. 397–8, 404.

moved along valleys, whereas drift debris ignored this topography. The debris found high in the White Mountains would have required a glacier several thousand feet thick, and that seemed at least as improbable as a global flood. Finally, the melting of these glaciers ran counter to the general notion that the earth was cooling.[43]

Edward Hitchcock, America's most important drift theorist, reflected the various religious and nationalistic pressures operating on American geologists as they wrestled with the problem of drift debris. Born in 1793 on a farm in Deerfield, Massachusetts, Hitchcock studied natural science while preparing for the ministry at Yale; as pastor of the Congregational Church in Conway, Massachusetts, he took up geological exploration to restore his health. In 1825, he was appointed professor of chemistry and natural history at the newly founded Amherst College and, in 1845, he became president of the college. He spent the rest of his life attempting to reconcile his theological and geological interests.[44] His earliest opinions on geology and theology stemmed from his Conway years, when he determined that the sacred texts he taught every Sunday provided a fitting guide for his scientific investigations. Gradually, he separated the geological flood from the biblical flood, although he continued to see the deluge as a providential act that mixed the strata; exposed valuable ores, minerals, and rocks; and pulverized the bedrock to make soils. He developed another perspective when British geologist, Charles Lyell, toured America on two occasions, in 1841 and 1853. At the time of his tours, Lyell was the world's most influential geologist, best known for his elaboration of Hutton's doctrine of gradualism. Although he acknowledged that geological movements occurred on a "far larger scale" during the earth's "hotter and more active infancy," he was convinced that geology could be brought into the Newtonian era only by analyzing events occurring in the present.[45]

---

[43] Jackson, *Final Report... New Hampshire*, pp. 24–5; Benjamin Silliman, "Consistency of Geology with Sacred History," supplement to Robert Bakewell, *An Introduction to Geology* (New Haven, 1833), pp. 435, 451, 462, 464; Hitchcock, *Report on the Geology of Vermont*, Vol. 1, p. 91; Merrill, *First One Hundred Years of American Geology*, pp. 121, 125–6, 206, 249; Robert H. Dott Jr., "Charles Lyell's Debt to North America: His Lectures and Travels from 1841 to 1853," in Blundell and Scott, *Lyell*, p. 61.

[44] Robert Horace Silliman, "Agassiz vs. Lyell: Authority in the Assessment of the Diluvium-Drift Problem by North American Geologists, with Particular Reference to Edward Hitchcock," *Earth Sciences History* 13 (No. 2, 1994): p. 182; Philip J. Lawrence, "Edward Hitchcock: The Christian Geologist," *APS Proceedings* 116 (No. 1, 1972): pp. 21, 23–4.

[45] Hitchcock, *Report on... Massachusetts*, pp. 142, 144–5, 164, 166; Hitchcock, *Religion of Geology*, pp. 155–66. See Lawrence, "Edward Hitchcock," p. 23; Merrill, *First*

To test his theories, Lyell toured North America inspecting the continent's abundant drift debris. In Nova Scotia, he discovered grooves in the sandstone ledges along a shore, made during the previous winter by huge blocks of ice laden with rocks. He imagined a period of intense cold during which ice islands perhaps hundreds of miles across grated along the bottom of the ocean with a force "sufficient . . . to move . . . the whole city of New-York before them!" In consultation with Hitchcock, he reasoned that New England had been submerged beneath an ancient sea while northern currents floated these ice islands southward. Running aground, they were forced along under their own momentum, polishing and furrowing the rocky bottom, and as they melted, they dropped their burdens of sand, gravel, and rock. Like Agassiz, Lyell was able to draw all drift phenomena under one theoretical umbrella – a "masterpiece of geomorphic synthesis when viewed in terms of knowledge then existing."[46]

Also like Agassiz, Lyell dismissed the diluvial theory, which would have dropped boulders in predictable patterns according to size and the violence of the currents. Icebergs would distribute their boulders in parallel lines but in random size. As a gradualist, he was uncomfortable with Agassiz's Ice Age because it called for global forces appreciably different from those existing in the human experience. By this time, Elie de Beaumont had broached the idea of global tectonic pressures moving continents over the ages. As continents changed position, climates would change accordingly and, on a continental if not a global scale, an Ice Age seemed possible. Yet, where Agassiz saw glaciers scouring the land, Lyell saw icebergs leaving their loads of rocks across the bottom of an ancient sea.[47]

Having reduced earth's history to a story of gradual erosive forces, Lyell reinvented geological time, extending this history back almost indefinitely to obviate the need for cataclysmic disjuncture. "We should be warranted in ascribing the erection of the great pyramid to superhuman power [only] if we were convinced that it was raised in one day," he

One Hundred Years of American Geology, p. 146; Greene, *Geology in the Nineteenth Century*, p. 25; Lyell, *Principles of Geology*, p. 94; Wilson, *Lyell in America*, p. 1, 274; Rudwick, *Lyell and the Principles of Geology*, pp. 5–7; Dott, "Charles Lyell's Debt to North America," p. 53.

46   Charles Lyell, *A Second Visit to the United States of North America* (New York, 1855), Vol. 1, pp. 33; Lyell, *Travels in North America*, Vol. 1, pp. 7–8, 55, 200; Dott, "Charles Lyell's Debt to North America," pp. 59–60, 65.

47   Greene, *Geology in the Nineteenth Century*, pp. 69–71; Charles Lyell, *Eight Lectures on Geology, Delivered at the Broadway Tabernacle in the City of New-York* (New York, 1842), p. 53–4; *American Journal of Science*, n.s., 42 (April 1842): p. 346.

explained. However, even in small increments, these changes required a certain balance if the earth was to sustain life uniformly across these vast ages. The mechanics of this balance Lyell did not make clear, but he saw it as part of the cosmic harmony that governed the world.[48] The proportion of dry land to sea would always be the same, as would the average and extreme altitudes and depths of the land and the seas. Here, Lyell abandoned inductive thinking, insisting, like Hutton, that an equilibrium between mountain-building and mountain-destroying was theoretically necessary. "Is it possible that this waste should have continued for . . . a great . . . number of years . . . unless their ruins have been repaired? Is it credible that the Author of Nature should have founded the world upon such laws?" The vast gulf of time over which these forces played made even a small disjuncture unthinkable. The theory of balance was common in scientific thinking, and probably necessary as geologists compared the titanic scale of these forces to the fragility of life on the planet; the alarming specter of ceaseless continental change required a calming vision of ultimate order.[49] Like Hitchcock, Lyell saw his icebergs operating according to providential design.

In 1845, Hitchcock inspected a train of loose boulders strewn in a direct line across a range of hills near Canaan, New York. The stones were angular, suggesting they had not been distributed by water, but icebergs provided an adequate explanation. Finding theoretical advantages in both water and ice, he adopted Lyell's "glacio-aqueous" compromise, thus preserving his conviction that the Northeast was once submerged and avoiding the fanciful notion that most of the northern hemisphere was enveloped in a blanket of ice.[50] Charles Jackson, another religious conservative, moved almost as effortlessly from the biblical deluge to the iceberg theory by incorporating the latter into his notion of providential history. Daniel Drake likewise explained the Ohio Valley's drift using icebergs, as did T. A. Conrad in his study of fossils in the basin west of the Appalachians.[51]

---

[48] Lyell, *Eight Lectures on Geology*, p. 9; Lyell, *Principles of Geology*, pp. 117–20.

[49] Lyell, *Principles of Geology*, pp. 66, 94, 176–7, 178. See James Rodger Fleming, "Charles Lyell and Climatic Change: Speculation and Certainty," in Derek J. Blundell and Andrew C. Scott, *Lyell: The Past Is the Key to the Present* (London, 1998), p. 164.

[50] Hitchcock, *First Anniversary Address*, p. 29; Hitchcock in *American Journal of Science* 46 (April 1844): pp. 169, 171. See Stanley Guralnick, "Geology and Religion Before Darwin: The Case of Edward Hitchcock, Theologian and Geologist," *Isis* 63 (No. 219, 1972), pp. 530, 535; Hitchcock in *Smithsonian Institution Contributions to Knowledge* 9 (1857), p. 2; Hitchcock in *American Journal of Science* 49 (October 1845): pp. 261–5.

[51] Edward Hitchcok, *Outline of the Geology of the Globe, and of the United States in Particular* (Boston, 1853), pp. 111–12; Jackson, *Final Report . . . New Hampshire*,

There were problems with the iceberg theory. Floating ice would not leave such uniform trails of scouring and debris, as Agassiz pointed out, and where icebergs ran aground, they would produce radial scouring. Ebenezer Emmons argued that ocean bottoms were typically composed of mud; icebergs would ground in this soft material without scratching the bedrock. Emmons preferred a composite theory, proposing first a wide, shallow river flowing through the Champlain, Hudson, and Mohawk Valleys to polish the pebbles, then a shallow sea to lay down a sedimentary deposit, then a flotilla of icebergs to distribute the region's erratic boulders, then a series of upheavals to raise these strata out of the sea, and, finally, a global flood to carry all this material southward. The hypothesis was complicated, he admitted, but it seemed necessary in order to account for all the phenomena he discovered in New York. The alternative was a series of catastrophes, but Emmons, like Lyell, preferred "to see things done in the most quiet way possible."[52]

In June 1848, Agassiz left Boston on the Western Railroad with a party of Harvard students and gentleman-scientists headed for Lake Superior. Camping on the north shore, Agassiz's party discovered that nearly every ledge and boulder was rounded and polished, showing that ice had once covered the entire country. The hills, rough and precipitous on the south slope, exhibited a "lee-side and a strike-side," like the hills of Norway and Sweden. This was the work of glaciers, not water. On his return, Agassiz sifted through the unstratified clays in the backyards of Brooklyn and found polished rocks similar to those on the windswept hills of the Lake Superior highlands. In neither place were there marine fossils to suggest ocean inundation. By this time, others had revealed that glaciers could move across flat terrain because their motive force was not gravity but rather pressure from the water in the ice. Agassiz's encounter with the Lake Superior shore rounded out a narrative that began decades earlier in Switzerland. Like Lyell, he explained the history of the earth without resorting to catastrophe, finding that a surprisingly subtle shift in climate could bring on the glaciers so essential to his system.[53]

Americans found the specter of glaciers moving up river valleys, over mountains, and across entire continents difficult to accept; but, as the dynamics of alpine glaciation became clear, Agassiz's explanation gained

p. 23; Drake in APS *Transactions*, n.s., 2 (1825): pp. 136–8; Merrill, *First One Hundred Years of American Geology*, p. 203.

[52] Agassiz, *Lake Superior*, pp. 10, 37, 405–6; Emmons, *Report of the Survey of the Second Geological District*, pp. 423–6.

[53] Agassiz, *Life and Correspondence*, Vol. 2, pp. 462–6; Agassiz, *Lake Superior*, pp. 103–5, 401–2, 408, 417; Lyell, *Eight Lectures on Geology*, p. 50.

credibility. In 1856, geologists explored the Humboldt glacier in Greenland, a sheet of ice some twelve hundred miles long that put Ice Age
glaciers in the realm of possibility. In the last edition of his *Elements
of Geology*, Hitchcock chose for the frontispiece an illustration of the
Greenland glacier. By 1863, even Lyell had accepted the glacier theory.
In America, the conversion was complete by 1870 – delayed, perhaps, by
the peculiar topography of the continent, the American fixation on erratic
boulders, the lingering effect of biblical explanations, and the impulse to
question European theory.[54]

The shift from catastrophic events to gradual processes was part of
a transatlantic scientific dialogue, but it was also a response to social
changes in America. As the western wilderness was subdued, geologists
saw its formation differently. The peaks and chasms of America, viewed
from the vantage point of the tilled field, seemed more likely to have been
brought into being gradually and gently. Pastoral America was a land
of "smooth transitions," as Angela Miller writes – from forest to farm,
from city to country, and from wilderness to civilization. There were
"no sudden ruptures, no hidden chasms." By midcentury, she continues,
"the operative metaphor, in landscape as in personality, was that of
integration – of a national market, of country with city, of locale or region
with nation."[55] However, in the first half of the century, nature seemed
raw and untamed in the western wilderness, and American science was
reined to the task of linking these primal energies to the strength of the
republic. Geologists looked to catastrophic events to explain America's
beginnings, and these awe-inspiring geological events gave nature a power
and majesty that helped shape American identity.

Dynamical Geology

As they peered into the well of deep time, geologists pondered the destiny of America. The track of civilization, as Lyell said, depended on
the "ancient state of things."[56] In his survey of Maine, Charles Jackson
considered the "various stages of improvement" that would unfold from
the natural conditions he inspected in the wilderness north of Bangor.

---

[54] Silliman, "Agassiz vs. Lyell," pp. 181, 184; Hitchcock, *First Anniversary Address*,
pp. 25–7; Oldroyd, *Thinking About the Earth*, pp. 147–51.

[55] Angela Miller, *The Empire of the Eye: Landscape Representation and American Cultural
Politics, 1825–1875* (Ithaca, 1993), p. 72.

[56] Lyell, *Principles of Geology*, p. 3. See Jackson, *First Report... Maine*, p. viii.

Abundant forests, fish, and game would nurture a society of primitive farmers content to live off the bounty of the land, he thought, but as these temptations disappeared, Maine's geological destiny would assert itself. Its numerous harbors, deep rivers, and abundant forests would stimulate shipbuilding and commerce, and its various stone and mineral deposits would encourage small industries all across the state. Rivers flowing over transverse ledges stepping down from the Appalachian plateau would power its mills and forges, and Maine would become a supplier of lumber, grain, cloth, iron castings, leather, shoes, saddlery, bricks, and household furniture. "Genius and taste" would "burst the confines of mere mechanical and mercantile employments," as literature and science blossomed and flourished.[57]

In his American edition of Robert Bakewell's *Introduction to Geology*, Benjamin Silliman appended his own essay on destiny and the American landscape, arguing once again that everything, from the shifting of the continents to the blossoming of the flower, revealed a meaningful trajectory. "The same beneficent laws" guided the evolution of the landscape in each age, and geologists showed how each age prepared the way for the next.[58] In a presidential address before the American Association for the Advancement of Science in 1855, Silliman's most prominent student, James Dwight Dana, elaborated this providential determinism in a system he labeled *dynamical geology*. Dana had been a major figure in American science for several decades when he presented his theory. Born in Utica in 1813, he studied under Silliman at Yale and then spent several months as a seafaring mathematics instructor to Navy midshipmen cruising the Mediterranean. He returned to work in Silliman's laboratory at Yale; then, in 1838, he accompanied Charles Wilkes on a government-sponsored scientific expedition to the South Pacific. He spent several years in Washington cataloging the materials he collected and in 1844 returned to Yale, married Silliman's daughter, assumed his mentor's chair, and, in conjunction with Silliman's son Edward, edited Silliman's journal. Dana's

---

[57] Charles T. Jackson, *Second Report on the Geology of the State of Maine* (Augusta, 1838), pp. xi–xii, xiv; Moses Greenleaf, *A Statistical View of the District of Maine* (Boston, 1816), pp. 37–8, 85, 109, 181–2, 217, 272–8, 284–6; Ezekiel Holmes, *Report of an Exploration and Survey of the Territory on the Aroostook River, During the Spring and Autumn of 1838* (Augusta, 1839), pp. 25–6.

[58] Silliman, "Consistency of Geology with Sacred History," pp. 390, 392, 394, 434. See Benjamin Silliman in John F. Fulton and Elizabeth H. Thomson, *Benjamin Silliman, 1779–1864: Pathfinder in American Science* (New York, 1947), p. 137; Silliman, *Lectures on Geology, Delivered Before the Wirt Institute, and Citizens of Pittsburgh* (Pittsburgh, 1843), pp. 33–4.

Manual of Geology became the standard textbook in the United States in the second half of the century.[59]

Like Lyell, Jackson, Agassiz, and Silliman, Dana saw earth history as a progressive unfolding of creation, and he wove this principle into a grand panorama of natural and human events. The primordial earth congealed out of a fiery ball in space; the land, seas, and mountains appeared; the continents expanded; the temperatures cooled; and life separated into kingdoms and tribes. During the Silurian Age – the age of mollusks, corals, and trilobites – the earth was too warm and the atmosphere too impure for more "exalted forms," but this was followed by the Carboniferous Age, when a lush growth of giant tropical plants cleansed the atmosphere. The world evolved, as Dana explained, "step by step,... until at last man stood up erect, fitted to subjugate the mightiest energies of nature." Physically, intellectually, and spiritually, they progressed in consonance with the cooling of the earth, suggesting a connection between climate and higher forms of humanity. Sweeping across the eons, Dana provided a cosmic framework for the natural history of America.[60]

By 1870, the great debates over earth history were over and gradualists like Dana had won the day, but the debates left an important philosophical residue, as Dana's dynamical geology demonstrated. The idea that powerful geological forces worked in harmony with God's plan for America extricated geology from its uncomfortable union with biblical truth but sustained the notion of providential guidance, giving Americans a modern inductive method that emphasized the divinity and sublimity of the natural landscape. Geology teaches, Ebenezer Emmons wrote, "that order has prevailed... through the lapse of ages, that there was a plan in the divine mind which has been working with a special reference to the good of our race." The debates brought to light frightening geological forces, but they held out the promise that these forces worked to

---

[59] Daniel C. Gilman, *The Life of James Dwight Dana: Scientific Explorer, Mineralogist, Geologist, Zoologist, Professor in Yale University* (New York, 1899), pp. 29, 32, 152; Greene, *Geology in the Nineteenth Century*, pp. 132–4; Newell, "James Dwight Dana," pp. 274–7.

[60] James D. Dana, *On American Geological History*, p. 331; Dana, *Manual of Geology* (Philadelphia: Theodore Bliss & Co., 1863), pp. 4–5, 573; Dana, *An Address Before the Alumni of Yale College, at the Comment Anniversary, August, 1856* (New Haven, 1856), p. 6; Dana, *Science and the Bible: A Review of "The Six Days of Creation" of Professor Tayler Lewis* (Andover, 1856), pp. 113, 119–21, 126–8; *American Quarterly Review* 13 (March 1830): p. 408; James Murphey, *Creation: Or the Bible and Geology Consistent: Together with the Moral Design of the Mosaic History* (New York, 1850), pp. 56, 58; 64–6.

consummate a benevolent and orderly plan. To the uninitiated wanderer, the peaks and chasms of America might seem chaotic but, as Cuvier suggested, they were part of a system designed to foster the rise of civilization: a landscape as hopeful as the record of its past was terrifying.[61]

To uncover the destiny written into the bedrock of the West, geologists linked science, divinity, and national pride. In so doing, they invested the peaks and chasms of America with enormous cultural importance. The gap at Harper's Ferry, the Natural Bridge in Virginia, the falls at Niagara, and, later, the Yellowstone Basin and the Grand Canyon became monuments to the creative energies and spiritual strength of the nation. There in the bedrock of the ages, Henry Rogers wrote, the scientist stood in the company of "great forces which sway events."[62] Imagining this transcendent link between past and future, geologists put the natural world at the center of American identity. No one contemplating a landscape so pregnant with meaning could ignore nature's place in the idea of America.

[61] Ebenezer Emmons, *American Geology* (New York, 1974 [c. 1855]), Vol. 1, p. 2; George W. Featherstonhaugh in *North American Review*, n.s., 31 (April 1831): p. 476; Featherstonhaugh in *Monthly American Journal of Geology and Natural Science* 1 (July 1831): p. 14; Andrew Denny Rodgers III, *John Torrey: A Story of North American Botany* (Princeton, 1942), p. 205; Lyell *Principles*, Vol. 3, p. 20; Hitchcock, *Religion of Geology*, p. 143; Jackson, *Second Report on the Geology of the State of Maine*, p. v.

[62] Rogers, *Address on the Recent Progress of Geological Research*, p. 57.

5

Integrated Landscapes

Mountains, Rivers, and Forests in the Balance of Nature

On a quiet morning in Summer 1836, Samuel P. Hildreth climbed to the top of a small promontory in the Muskingum Valley. The view was familiar to the 53-year-old naturalist who had thoroughly explored this upper Ohio region over the previous three decades while serving as a physician in Marietta. Born in Massachusetts, he arrived in Marietta in 1808, bringing with him a deep interest in natural history. By 1836, he was the valley's most renowned scholar, the local expert chosen to conduct a portion of the Ohio state survey when it was commissioned in 1838 and to guide Charles Lyell on a geological inspection of the Muskingum when the latter visited America a few years later.

Good naturalist that he was, Hildreth read deeply into the topography before him on his morning hike. As he wrote later in the *Journal of American Science*, the valley was divided into shallow ravines and low hills, "affording no spot much, if any, more elevated than the one on which the spectator stands." This nondescript terrain, however, entombed a phantom landscape with a history that Hildreth found much more interesting. Twenty or thirty feet beneath the surface lay a mysterious world of carbonized trees, marine clays, and water-worn pebbles deposited long before the present contours were laid down. In Hildreth's mind, this tranquil valley masked a geological world of ongoing change and fantastic forces – a spectral topography bending, rising, and subsiding like a wind-blown geological sea.[1]

---

[1] S. P. Hildreth in *American Journal of Science* 29 (1836): pp. 7–8. See Hildreth in *Medical Repository*, 2d ser., 5 (1808): p. 345; Leonard G. Wilson, *Lyell in America: Transatlantic Geology, 1841–1853* (Baltimore, 1998), pp. 95, 104.

Hildreth was not the first to discover the restless history beneath these tranquil landscapes. Broad, scoured-out valleys with little or no water flowing through them, gaps ripped through ridges of ancient crystalline rock, and huge blocks of stone strewn in confused heaps showed that immense forces were at work rearranging this landscape. In Philadelphia, construction workers discovered layers of black marsh mud and hickory trees, complete with branches and leaves, buried thirty feet below the surface. "How gratifying," a witness remarked, "thus to withdraw the curtain of time, and penetrate into the secrets of a remote antiquity."[2]

Nature was anything but constant. Rivers overflowed and ate away their banks; lakes expanded and contracted; rains brought down the mountains and filled the valleys with alluvium; bold coastal escarpments suggested the continent itself was on the move.[3] Impressed by the geologist's vision of purposeful change, naturalists inspected these natural forces with an eye to understanding how they improved the landscapes around them. Standing on a cobble beach during a storm, a contributor to the *American Journal of Science* sensed the effect of the waves against the rocks. "I could distinctly hear the motion of the larger and smaller rocks, brought inland and carried back...more than one hundred yards by every wave, and I could...feel the earth tremble under my feet from the quantity and great weight of some of them." Before him was the means by which the ocean prepared the land for cultivation. "Had it not been for this very benevolent process of grinding the granite...to powder,...and preparing the soil in that way, [America could not]...have been inhabited." In the high ridges along the Connecticut Valley, Edward Hitchcock

[2] Peter A. Browne in *Monthly American Journal of Geology and Natural Science* 1 (February 1832): p. 366. See David Christy, *Letters on Geology* (Rossville, 1848), pp. 2, 6, 52, 64; James Murphey, *Creation: Or the Bible and Geology Consistent: Together with the Moral Design of the Mosaic History* (New York, 1850), pp. 4–7, 17; Edward Hitchcock, *First Anniversary Address Before the Association of American Geologists* (New Haven, 1841), p. 42; Hitchcock, *The Religion of Geology and Its Connected Sciences* (Glasgow, 1851), pp. 171–2.

[3] *American Quarterly Review* 13 (March 1830): pp. 388–9. See Anonymous, *A Short View of the Natural History of the Earth* (Boston, 1803), pp. 4, 56–7; Charles Lyell, *Principles of Geology* (Boston, 1842), pp. 18–19; Samuel Williams, *The Natural and Civil History of Vermont* 1 (Burlington, 1809), pp. 46, 55, 61–2, 153–4, 156; Jeremy Belknap, *History of New-Hampshire* (Dover, 1812), Vol. 3, pp. 28, 51–2; Edward Hitchcock, et al., *Report on the Geology of Vermont: Descriptive, Theoretical, Economical, and Scenographical* (Claremont, 1861), Vol. 1, pp. 136–7; Jacob Bigelow, *Some Account of the White Mountains of New Hampshire* (Boston, 1816), p. 6; *Medical Repository* 1 (No. 3, 1898): pp. 310–11; Connecticut Academy of Arts and Sciences *Memoirs* 1 (Part 1, 1810): pp. 83–5; *American Journal of Science* 3 (1821): p. 55.

witnessed a similar process as he watched rainwater seep into fissures in the rock. There it would freeze, thaw, and freeze again, widening the fissures until an outcropping broke free and dropped to the valley floor. Exposed and angular, the rocks were quickly changed into gravel and then soil. Here again, the earth was evolving, not through catastrophic changes but through subtle nurturing forces working steadily toward a preordained end: an integrated landscape capable of supporting the greatest possible profusion of life. Where earlier geologists had been captivated by the idea of power and violence in the primordial landscape, a new generation found equal inspiration in watching the nation's destiny play out at their feet. Once freed to imagine change as an ongoing process rather than a cataclysmic event, they saw the landscape as a great stage upon which the plan of nature moved with a fixity that could only be divine.[4]

Still, the logic of evolution was not always evident. Skeptics could point to tracts of land across the earth either too hot or too cold, or too wet or too dry, to support the diversity of life one would expect of a nature given God's blessing. Mountains were too steep, rivers too capricious, and forests too thick to inspire confidence in God's perfect benevolence.[5] These lingering doubts touched off a widespread debate about how various natural forms and processes fit together into an integrated landscape. This was the dialogue that laid a basis for ecological understanding in America.

Dynamical Landscapes

Earthquakes posed an obvious challenge to the idea of perfectly integrated landscapes. In 1705, Increase Mather described the natural and divine history of a series of earthquakes in New England, finding reason to believe they produced a better world, both morally and physically.[6]

---

[4] "N" in *American Journal of Science* 9 (No. 1, 1825): pp. 29, 33–5; Edward Hitchcock in *American Journal of Science* 6 (No. 1, 1823): pp. 55–6; Benjamin Waterhouse, *The Botanist; Being the Botanical Part of a Course of Lectures on Natural History* (Boston, 1811), p. x, xii–x. See Horace H. Hayden, *Geological Essays; Or, Inquiry into Some of the Geological Phenomena to be Found in Various Parts of America, and Elsewhere* (Baltimore, 1820), pp. 8–9, 10; Williams, *Natural and Civil History of Vermont*, pp. 47–9, 151; *American Journal of Science* 6 (No. 1, 1823): pp. 55–6; *Monthly American Journal of Geology and Natural Science* 1 (July 1831): p. 13; ibid. (September 1831): pp. 108–9.

[5] Clarence Glacken, *Traces on the Rhodian Shore: Nature and Culture in Western Thought from Ancient Times to the End of the Eighteenth Century* (Berkeley, 1967), p. 69.

[6] Increase Mather, *A Discourse Concerning Earthquakes* (Boston, 1706), pp. 3, 5, 7–8, 10, 13. See Dennis R. Dean, "Benjamin Franklin and Earthquakes," *Annals of Science* 46

A half-century later, Harvard professor John Winthrop took up the question and, like Mather, described earthquakes first in apocalyptic terms, recounting tales of whole cities disappearing into the earth, mountains disintegrating, and people "shrieking or groaning in the agonies of death." After drawing attention to these terrifying effects, he compiled an index of severity based on how far bricks were thrown from the chimneys, calculated the geographic origins of the tremors, and recorded the meteorological conditions under which they occurred. With this information, he hypothesized a gigantic system of interlinked caverns winding through the earth, in which gasses ignited and exploded, minerals fermented, and subterranean rivers turned to steam and pressed outward. Although terrible to contemplate, these forces were both necessary and beneficial. Among other things, they kept the earth from compacting under its own weight and ensured a certain "openness and looseness" as a medium for plant life. They possibly fertilized the atmosphere in some manner, as thick vegetation near volcanos might suggest, or they facilitated the mechanical operations of the earth's interior. Like Mather, Winthrop saw them as mechanical processes that furthered both moral and natural ends.[7]

On December 16, 1811, the town of New Madrid in the Missouri Territory was rocked by a tremor strong enough to ring church bells in Charleston, South Carolina. Clearly, this heralded changes in the Mississippi Valley, all the more portentous because they occurred during a year of extraordinary natural phenomena: a spring flood that inundated the river valleys from Pittsburgh to New Orleans; a great "electric excitation in the air"; a magnificent comet blazing across the night sky; and an unusually brilliant aurora borealis. During this *annus mirabilis*, Benjamin Latrobe commented, a "spirit of change and a restlessness seemed to pervade the very inhabitants of the forest." Squirrels, "obeying some great and universal impulse, . . . left their reckless and gambolling life, and their ancient places of retreat in the north, and were seen pressing forward by tens of thousands in a deep and sober phalanx to the South."[8]

(No. 5, 1989): pp. 262–9, 276, 303–6, 483–90; Brooke Hindle, *The Pursuit of Science in Revolutionary America, 1735–1789* (Chapel Hill, 1956), p. 94; *Port Folio*, 2d ser., 7 (May 1812): pp. 422–3.

7 John Winthrop, *A Lecture on Earthquakes; Read in the Chapel of Harvard-College in Cambridge* (Boston, 1755). See Samuel Williams in American Academy of Arts and Sciences *Memoirs* 1 (Boston, 1783): p. 260.

8 Charles Joseph Latrobe, *The Rambler in North America* (London: R. B. Seeley and W. Burnside, 1835), Vol. 1, pp. 102–3. See Daniel Drake, *Natural and Statistical View, or Picture of Cincinnati and the Miami Country* (Cincinnati, 1815), pp. 239, 240–2, 248; Dorothy Anne Dondore, *The Prairie and the Making of Middle America: Four Centuries of Description* (Cedar Rapids, 1926), p. 182; *American Journal of Science* 31

Here again, the reports were apocalyptic. The earthquake began with the sound of dogs barking, cattle bellowing, and houses "bending and creaking." Then came a terrific roar accompanied by "violent explosions," and great chasms opened in the earth. The churchyard gave up its dead as it slipped into the Mississippi. "The gaping earth unfolded its secrets, and the bones of the gigantic Mastodon and Ichthyosaurus, hidden within its bosom for ages, were brought to the surface." The quake ignited a buried cache of carbonized wood, and jets of hot sand, mud, water, smoke, and charred wood vented out through the surface. A "subterraneous thunder" moved menacingly up the Mississippi over the next several months, and for years swamps gave off strange sounds, "as of some mighty cauldron bubbling in the bowels of the earth." [9] Again, naturalists scrutinized the earthquake for insights into nature's laws and nature's purpose. Isaac Lea thought it might have been caused by the ignition of wood or coal deposits; another noted that the whole region was a bed of quicksand, which shifted as the river changed course; and a third laid blame on the copious rains that followed a long drought. [10] Earthquakes, more than any other natural phenomena, suggested the mystery in the moving earth.

Stirrings like these challenged the idea of perfection in nature. In August 1826, a gigantic rock slide near Conway in the White Mountains buried the Willey family on their farm in the valley below, a tragedy made all the more poignant by the fact that the house the Willeys fled remained intact, with the slide passing on both sides. Visiting the site, Jeremy Belknap was struck by the volatility of this mountain landscape. Large boulders were detached from the valley walls, "some of them so distant from the base, that they could not have rolled thither but in some convulsion of the earth." Lyell attributed this dynamism to the

(January 1837): pp. 294–5; Anon., *An Account of the Earthquakes which Occurred in the United States, North America, on the 16th of December, 1811 ... 1812* (Philadelphia, 1812), pp. 12–13, 32.

9 M. Harvey to Benjamin Smith Barton, May 28, 1812, Benjamin Smith Barton Papers, American Philosophical Society (hereafter APS); Latrobe, *Rambler in North America*, Vol. 1, pp. 109–11; Anon., *Account of the Earthquakes*, pp. 32–3. See *Port Folio*, 2d ser., 7 (May 1812): pp. 421–2; Lyell in Wilson, *Lyell in America*, p. 253; *American Journal of Science* 3 (1821): pp. 20–1; ibid., 31 (January 1837): p. 296; Christy, *Letters on Geology*, pp. 24–5, 27.

10 Isaac Lea in *American Journal of Science* 9 (No. 2, 1825): pp. 212, 216; ibid., 3 (1821): pp. 20–1; ibid., 31 (January 1837): pp. 295–6; *Port Folio*, 2d ser., 7 (May 1812): pp. 421, 423–4, 428–9; Anon., *Account of the Earthquakes*, pp. 12, 35, 66–7; Hitchcock, *Connection Between Geology and Natural Religion*, pp. 2–3, 9; Hitchcock, *Religion of Geology*, pp. 276–7.

jointed rock structure and rapid decomposition from sharp changes in temperature. Henry and William Rogers found a pronounced horizontal fault in the cliffs above the Willey slide: The family's fate had been written into the "unstable equilibrium" of the rocks themselves. Like New Madrid, the Willey slide ruptured the illusion of solid ground and confirmed the fact that the earth was a place of ceaseless change.[11] Benjamin Dwight described a single rainstorm in the Hudson Valley that scoured out deep gullies, moved vast quantities of earth, toppled groves of trees, and changed the course of the streams.[12] Here, too, scientists looked for messages in the moving earth.

Ecologist Daniel Botkin records a conversation between Henry David Thoreau and an old farmer who claimed he had lost a "crittur" a few years earlier in a Cape Cod swamp. Since then, Thoreau said, the farmer had "lost the swamp" too, as it slipped under the restless cape sands. Concluding that Thoreau "began to understand that nature is dynamic," Botkin makes much of this epiphany: "The idea of the naturalness of change ran counter to the great, ancient myth of the balance of nature, which, before and during Thoreau's time, was the accepted explanation of how nature worked." In fact, Thoreau's contemporaries were quite familiar with changes like these. Edward Hitchcock, who talked at one point about the Cape "sliding from under his feet," compared his own observations of the Massachusetts coast with charts created by the British Admiralty in 1772 and noted that whole beaches and islands had appeared or disappeared in the course of a generation.[13] Naturalists hoped to interpret these changes according to the same laws geologists discovered in the evolution of the earth. They assumed an underlying harmony in the landscape features they inspected and worked to piece together the story of

[11] Belknap, *History of New-Hampshire*, pp. 27–8; Lyell, *Principles of Geology*, Vol. 1, p. 362; Charles Lyell, *A Second Visit to the United States of North America* (New York, 1855), Vol. 1, p. 61; Henry D. Rogers and William B. Rogers in *American Journal of Science*, n.s., 1 (May 1846): pp. 414–15. See *American Journal of Science* 34 (July 1838): pp. 76, 115; James Mease, *Geological Account of the United States* (Philadelphia, 1807), p. 58; Hitchcock, *Connection Between Geology and Natural Religion*, pp. 13–14; Eric Purchase, *Out of Nowhere: Disaster and Tourism in the White Mountains* (Baltimore, 1999).

[12] Benjamin W. Dwight in *American Journal of Science* 4 (No. 1, 1821): pp. 124–5, 128–9, 133–6, 138–39. See James Flint, *Letters from America*, Reuben Gold Thwaites (ed.), (Cleveland, 1904 [c. 1822]), p. 106.

[13] Daniel B. Botkin, *No Man's Garden: Thoreau and a New Vision for Civilization and Nature* (Washington, 2001), pp. 103–4, 107; Edward Hitchcock, *Report on the Geology, Mineralogy, Botany, and Zoology of Massachusetts* (Amherst, 1833), pp. 124–5, 128–30.

these dynamical landscapes. The world, William Bingley wrote, "is one connected train of causes and effects, in which all the parts, either nearly or remotely, have a necessary dependence on each other."[14] To explore this interconnectedness, they engaged in a series of teleological exercises. A form of inquiry into purposes and final ends dating back to Aristotle's times, teleology was freighted with classical associations, but it yielded a very modern understanding of ecological relations.

The Logic of Mountains

One purpose earthquakes served was to create mountains, but here the teleology of earthquakes became complicated. Some of the last places in eastern America to be explored, mountains posed difficult questions for the naturalist.[15] They were obviously less fertile – sometimes even barren – and they clearly made life difficult for those who lived on or near them. The vigor of life was diminished across these vast asymmetrical expanses, and naturalists struggled to account for this seeming disharmony. J. W. Bailey, the first naturalist to climb Maine's Mount Katahdin, described it as a "scene of wild confusion," with masses of granite "shivered by their fall from above" and scattered chaotically across the base. Lying exhausted near the summit, buffeted by rain and wind and raked by dark clouds scudding across the peak, he was at a loss to find meaning in this huge and barren mass of rock. Henry David Thoreau's much-discussed visit to Katahdin in 1846 ended similarly. Alone near the summit in the featureless gray light of a cloud bank, he felt diminished by Katahdin's "vast, Titanic" landscape.[16] Robert Sears's *New and Popular Pictorial Description of the United States* declared a large part of New Hampshire "rendered useless by lofty, wild, barren, and almost inaccessible mountains," and James Pierce found even the forests to be pointless above

---

[14] W. Bingley, *Animal Biography, or Popular Zoology* (London, 1813), Vol. 1, p. 3. See George H. Daniels, *American Science in the Age of Jackson* (New York, 1968), p. 144; Louis Agassiz, *An Introduction to the Study of Natural History* (New York, 1847), p. 5; Agrippa Nelson Bell, *A Knowledge of Living Things, with the Laws of Their Existence* (New York, 1860), pp. 6–7.

[15] Marjorie Hope Nicolson, *Mountain Gloom and Mountain Glory: The Development of the Aesthetics of the Infinite* (Ithaca, 1959), pp. 83, 85, 90, 149, 154; Major Robert Rogers, *A Concise Account of North America, Containing a Description of the Several British Colonies on that Continent* (London, 1765), pp. 47–8.

[16] J. W. Bailey, *American Journal of Science* 32 (July 1837): pp. 20, 28–30; Henry D. Thoreau, *The Maine Woods*, Joseph J. Moldenhauer (ed.), (Princeton, 1972), pp. 60–2, 63–5, 70. See *American Journal of Science* 34 (July 1838): pp. 120–1.

four thousand feet: mature birch, spruce, and balsam fir stood only three feet tall, their branches spreading horizontally to form an "entangled thicket" matted enough to walk over.[17] This obvious hostility to life was mystifying: Were mountains flaws in nature's otherwise perfect plan, or blemishes in the skin of an aging and cooling earth?

Explaining the role of mountains in a world of purposive landscapes was challenging. In his survey of Maine's rugged western tableland, naturalist Ezekiel Holmes wrote that it would "seem to have been a mistake of creative power in thus piling together so much rugged earth in a form and condition to make it entirely waste land." Yet, geology was a science of harmonies, not mistakes: "rough and misshapen as are the most of these enormous piles of crag and ledge, they have important and indispensable use in the great economy of animal as well as vegetable life." They generated the snows that protected the fields and meadows in winter; offered up their forests for building material and fuel; and provided homes for animals that yielded meat, furs, and skins. They drew water from the atmosphere, stored it in banks of ice and snow, and released it down perennial streams to nourish the valley below. Mountains were "elevated reservoirs, . . . destined by infinite wisdom to retain sufficient quantities of that element of indispensable necessity," Noah Webster wrote. Inequalities were essential to life; without them, the ground would be covered with stagnant pools and the air loaded with miasmas.[18] "Can we doubt, then, that it was the hand of benevolence that drove the ploughshare of ruin through the earth's crust, and ridged up its surface into a thousand fantastic forms?"[19]

Although mountains were clearly important as the sources of rivers and streams, no one fully understood how water found its way to these elevated places. The circulation of water from sea to mountaintop had fascinated naturalists since antiquity and, even into the nineteenth century, the process was considered in some senses mystical. Some imagined the earth's interior as a giant network of subterranean streams, running

---

[17] Robert Sears (ed.), *A New and Popular Pictorial Description of the United States* (New York, 1848), p. 34; James Pierce, *American Journal of Science* 8 (No. 2, 1824): pp. 172, 174–5. See Benjamin Silliman in ibid., 34 (July 1838): p. 79.

[18] Ezekiel Holmes, "General Reports upon the Natural History and Geology of Maine," *Sixth Annual Report of the Secretary of the Maine Board of Agriculture* (Augusta, 1861), pp. 105–6; Noah Webster, *Elements of Useful Knowledge* (Hartford, 1806), Vol. 1, pp. 17–19. See Christopher Christian Sturm, *Beauties of Nature Delineated*, Thaddeus M. Harris (comp.), (Charlestown, 1801), pp. 55–7, 59.

[19] Hitchcock, *Religion of Geology*, pp. 156–8.

FIGURE 5.1. Explaining the role of mountains in a world of purposive landscapes was challenging. Mountains, although they might seem to be blights on the land or barriers to travel, in fact served important ecological functions, not the least being a capacity for drawing water out of the atmosphere, storing it in banks of ice and snow or in thick mossy vegetation, and releasing it down perennial streams to nourish valley farms and forests. "Catterskill Falls," by W. H. Bartlett, from Nathaniel P. Willis, *American Scenery* (1840). Courtesy of the Special Collections Department, Fogler Library, University of Maine.

like arteries from the sea and drawn to the mountain slopes by "capillary attraction," like water climbing a dry rag. Geologist Mary Griffith theorized that mountain streams issued from a combination of causes. Rain and snow supplied some of the water but not enough to charge all the rivers that ran to the sea. Thus, she added subterranean reservoirs, reasoning that as waters seeped into the earth, centrifugal forces arrested their downward course and "hurried [them] back again, some in very different directions from what their original course indicated."[20] Most naturalists reasoned that water evaporated from the seas, and thick mountain forests raked this moisture from the passing clouds. Deep mosses on the forest floor absorbed water and measured it out in small, steady streams.[21] Whatever the mechanism, Benjamin Silliman thought, mountains were God's instruments for wringing water from the passing clouds and perpetuating nature's cycle of renewal and rebirth.[22]

Belknap saw mountains as renewing the soils as well. High on the mountain slopes, primitive lichens digested the barren rock and produced a sparse mineral earth. This, in turn, attracted ferns, grasses, and finally trees, which decayed into a more loamy soil. This "fine mould," Belknap concluded, washed to the lowlands and produced "corn and herbage in the most luxuriant plenty." Mountains shed millions of tons of alluvium each year, Charles Jackson added, "to contribute towards the completion" of God's work.[23] Mountains were necessary to the profusion of life in the valleys below – clearly, a centerpiece in the integrated landscape.

---

[20] Waterhouse, *Botanist*, p. 165; [Mary Griffith], *An Essay on the Art of Boring the Earth for the Obtainment of a Spontaneous Flow of Water* (New Brunswick, 1826), pp. 23–5, 32–4, 36; Williams, *Natural and Civil History of Vermont*, p. 31. See Nicolson, *Mountain Gloom and Mountain Glory*, p. 170.

[21] Williams, *Natural and Civil History of Vermont*, pp. 31–5, 36–9. See Manasseh Cutler to Jonathan Stokes, October 30, 1786, William Parker Cutler and Julia Perkins Cutler, *Life, Journals, and Correspondence of Rev. Manasseh Cutler, LL.D, by his Grandchildren* (Cincinnati, 1888), Vol. 2, p. 272.

[22] Waterhouse, *Botanist*, pp. 164, 167; Connecticut Academy of Arts and Sciences, *Memoirs* 1 (Part 3, 1813): p. 324; Benjamin Silliman, *Lectures on Geology, Delivered Before the Wirt Institute, and Citizens of Pittsburgh* (Pittsburgh, 1843), p. 34.

[23] Belknap, *History of New-Hampshire*, p. 42; Charles T. Jackson, *Final Report on the Geology and Mineralogy of the State of New Hampshire* (Concord, 1844), p. 243; Williams, *Natural and Civil History of Vermont*, p. 35; *American Journal of Science* 22 (1832): p. 213; ibid., 34 (July 1838): pp. 116–17. See William B. Rogers in Emma Rogers, with William T. Sedgwick, *Life and Letters of William Barton Rogers* (Boston, 1896), pp. 352–3; Varte, *Topographical Description*, pp. 30–1; Hitchcock et al., *Report on the Geology of Vermont*, p. 93; *APS Transactions* 2 (1786): pp. 42–9.

The Teleology of Rivers

These themes – purposive change and ecological interdependence – emerged in the scientific assessment of rivers as well. Like mountain-tops, America's grandest river, the Mississippi, was examined relatively late in the era of continental exploration, but the record of this hard-won accomplishment became an important expression of American identity. "National destiny and historical mission seemed to flow with its current," historian Finis Dunaway writes of the river. So like the Nile in its transportation advantages and its renewing annual floods, the Mississippi was clearly a river of purpose and destiny, and its headwaters assumed almost mystical significance. Inspired by classical illusions to the fountainheads of the Tiber, Po, and Rhine, naturalists approached the upper river expecting much in the way of natural curiosity and republican symbolism.[24]

The first Europeans known to see the Mississippi were Father Jacques Marquette and Louis Joliet, who entered the watershed from the Fox River out of Green Bay in 1673. In 1679, Robert de la Salle reached the Mississippi from the Illinois and continued south to the Gulf of Mexico. With him was Franciscan Father Louis Hennepin, who turned northward in a canoe and reached the Falls of St. Anthony, which he named. In 1766, Jonathan Carver led the first English expedition into the region and learned from his Indian guides that "the four most capital rivers on the Continent of North America, viz. the St. Lawrence, the Mississippi, the River Bourbon [Red], and the Oregon or the River of the West... have their sources in the same neighbourhood." From this fact, Carver speculated that he traveled toward the "highest lands in North America" – mountains sufficient to drive the waters of the heartland to the four corners of the continent. Winter's onset frustrated his efforts to reach this fabled tableland but, in August 1805, Zebulon Pike and a small military party headed upriver from St. Louis in a keel boat to trace the boundary between the United States and Canada. Pike pushed beyond the Falls of St. Anthony but, on the morning of August 16, he awoke to find two feet of snow on the ground. Proceeding northward, cold and hungry, under threat of Indian attack, and with snow falling and wood becoming

---

[24] Finis Dunaway, *Natural Visions: The Power of Images in American Environmental Reform* (Chicago, 2005), p. 61; L. Harper, *Preliminary Report on the Geology and Agriculture of the State of Mississippi* (Jackson, 1857), pp. 15–16; Thomas Hutchins, *An Historical Narrative and Topographical Description of Louisiana, and West-Florida* (Philadelphia, 1784), p. 27; *Universal Asylum and Columbian Magazine* 9 (July 1792): pp. 37–8; Mease, *Geological Account of the United States*, pp. 142–3.

scarcer, he stopped at a British trader's stockade on Leech Lake. A smaller party continued on foot thirty miles farther to Upper Red Cedar Lake, and this he declared the source of the Mississippi. Whatever elation he felt in reaching this point went unrecorded.[25]

Fifteen years later, Michigan Territorial Governor Lewis Cass and Henry Schoolcraft led an expedition to Lake Superior, up the St. Louis River, and down to Leech Lake. Reaching Red Cedar Lake, Schoolcraft renamed it after the Michigan governor but, like Pike's party, they grew short of supplies and headed back without reaching the headwaters.[26] In 1824, Italian naturalist Giacomo Beltrami accompanied Major Stephen Long's expedition up the Mississippi to the Red River. When Long headed north across the watershed separating the two rivers, Beltrami continued up the Mississippi to a small lake he named Julia, which he deemed the true source of the Red as well as the Mississippi Rivers. Standing astride the waters of these two great systems, Beltrami was anything but speechless. "Oh! What were the thoughts which passed through my mind at this most happy and brilliant moment of my life! The shades of Marco Polo, of Columbus, of Americus Vespucius, of the Cabots, of Verazani... appeared present, and joyfully assisting at this high and solemn ceremony." He alone, he wrote later, had "penetrated into the seclusion of this sanctuary, where the deity of the stream had concealed himself from mortal eyes." Beltrami's personal reflections were vivid but, like his predecessors, he saw nothing spectacular in this fabled locale. A place seemingly fitted for "nymphs and dryads" harbored nothing but mosquitoes and blackflies. Because Julia was the ultimate source of the Mississippi, it had no inlet and this perplexed him as well. Its waters, he thought, "must spring from... some... cavity of the bowels of the earth, and from there they flowed to the Gulf, the Arctic, the Atlantic,

[25] Jonathan Carver, *Three Years Travels Through the Interior Parts of North-America* (Philadelphia, 1796), p. 44; Zebulon Montgomery Pike, *An Account of a Voyage Up the Mississippi River, From St. Louis to Its Source* (Washington, 1807), pp. 3, 5–7, 18–25, 30, 37, 39–41; *Medical Repository*, 2d ser., 4 (1807): pp. 376–7. See Henry R. Schoolcraft, *Summary Narrative of an Exploratory Expedition to the Sources of the Mississippi River, in 1820* (Philadelphia, 1855), p. 17; Hutchins, *Historical Narrative and Topographical Description of Louisiana*, p. 26; John D. Gilmary Shea, *Discovery and Exploration of the Mississippi Valley* (New York, 1852), pp. 107, 111–13.

[26] Henry Rowe Schoolcraft, *Travels in the Central Portions of the Mississippi Valley* (New York, 1825), p. 8; Schoolcraft, *Schoolcraft's Expedition to Lake Itasca: The Discovery of the Source of the Mississippi*, Philip P. Mason (ed.) (East Lansing, 1958), pp. xi, 3, 4–5; *North American Review*, n.s., 7 (July 1822): pp. 224, 233; Charles Lanman, *A Summer in the Wilderness; Embracing a Canoe Voyage Up the Mississippi and Around Lake Superior* (New York, 1847), p. 85.

and the Pacific." Logic dictated that he stood upon the highest land in North America, but instead of towering mountains or gushing fountains, he found before him a small lake on a level plain. The river's nondescript beginnings seemed oddly unworthy of its momentous destiny.[27]

The fact that a foreigner had stumbled across the true source of the Mississippi seemed unsettling to American commentators, who criticized the Pike and Cass–Schoolcraft expeditions for stopping short of their goal. "How is it possible that [these] men . . . should turn back with their chief object unaccomplished?," the *North American Review* asked.

Persons sent to explore the sources of a river should follow it till they reach the point where they could hold all its water in the hollow of the hand. Objects of curiosity are not wanting in this quarter to occupy attention for days. A thorough search there would probably find out a spot as remarkable as the one on the Grison Alps, where a person may drink, without changing place, of water which flows into the Mediterranean, the Rhine, and the German ocean; and it would be still more wonderful to find a like point of approximation of the waters of the St. Lawrence, the Mississippi, the Red River of Hudson's Bay, and the River of the West.[28]

Expecting a fabulous region of immense mountains and abundant curiosities, commentators found it difficult to understand the American explorers' hesitancy.

It would be Schoolcraft who carried out this mission on the second of two return trips. In 1830, the War Department directed him westward from Sault Ste. Marie to treat with the Chippewa and Sioux; thus, ten years after his first expedition, he was once again headed up the Mississippi. Because a summer drought made the upper waters impassible, he concentrated on Indian affairs, but on a subsequent exploration in May 1832, he once again traveled up the St. Louis River, crossed the Savanna Summit to the Mississippi drainage, and proceeded downstream to the main river.[29] He reached Cass Lake and, with three Chippewa, eight *engages*, and four other explorers, proceeded northward against a

---

[27] Stephen Long in James Ellsworth De Kay, *Anniversary Address on the Progress of Natural Sciences in the United States* (New York, 1826), pp. 62–3; Giacomo Constantino Beltrami, *A Pilgrimage in Europe and America, Leading to the Discovery of the Sources of the Mississippi and Bloody River* (London, 1828), Vol. 1, pp. 309, 324–5, 405–14, 432, 544. See Schoolcraft, *Schoolcraft's Expedition to Lake Itasca*, p. xi.

[28] *North American Review*, n.s., 7 (July 1822): pp. 224, 241–2. See Alexander von Humboldt, *Views of Nature* (London, 1870), pp. 39–40.

[29] Henry Schoolcraft, *Schoolcraft's Expedition to Lake Itasca*, pp. xi, xii, xv; Schoolcraft, *Summary Narrative of an Exploratory Expedition*, pp. 223, 225.

brisk current. As the party wove its way through the confusing maze of rice marshes, swamps, and lakes, it became clear to Schoolcraft why "the absolute and most remote source of the Mississippi has so long remained a matter of doubt." The whole country seemed one flat surface, "where the sameness of the objects, the heat of the weather, and the excessively serpentine channel...conspired to render the way tedious," as did the "peculiar...virulence to the musquito."[30]

Along the way, they reached the stream that led Beltrami to Lake Julia. Passing with hardly a glance, Schoolcraft's guide, Oza Windib, chose another somewhat shallower fork and, to Schoolcraft's surprise, turned south into a remote region seldom visited even by Indian hunters. On July 13, the party marched across a thirteen-mile portage and on the last elevation, "the cheering sight of a transparent body of water burst upon our view" – the source of the Mississippi. Indians knew the lake as *Omushkos*, meaning elk, after its shape. Schoolcraft paddled out to a small island, hoisted a flag, and renamed the lake Itasca after the Latin phrase *veritas caput*, or true head.[31]

In 1836–40, French scientist and astronomer, Jean-Nicolas (Joseph) Nicollet, explored the land between the Mississippi and Missouri for the U.S. Topographical Bureau, pinpointing Itasca's location and following its largest feeder stream to a small lake at the base of some low hills, "from which the Mississippi flows with a breadth of a foot and a half and a depth of one foot." Several small streams issuing from the same hills flowed into the Red River. Like Schoolcraft and others before him, Nicollet found this nondescript headwaters region strangely unworthy of the mighty river. "I felt melancholy," he related. "The piercing, solitary cry of the northern diver [*Gavia immer*; common loon] – the precursor, according to the Indian tradition, of high winds and hurricanes – was the only evidence of living nature that presented itself." The "silence and solitude" were all but overwhelming.[32] Ten years later, Friedrich Ludwig

[30] Henry Schoolcraft, *Schoolcraft's Expedition to Lake Itasca*, pp. xii, xv, 5, 8, 12, 20, 25, 29, 30–1, 33–5; Schoolcraft, *Summary Narrative of an Exploratory Expedition*, pp. 111–15, 118, 123, 128–9, 227, 132. See G. W. Featherstonhaugh, *Monthly American Journal of Geology and Natural Science* 1 (July 1831): pp. 16–17.

[31] Henry Schoolcraft, *Summary Narrative of an Exploratory Expedition*, pp. 227, 232–3, 236–7, 240, 241–3; Schoolcraft, *Schoolcraft's Expedition to Lake Itasca*, pp. x, 35–7.

[32] Joseph Nicollet in Schoolcraft, *Schoolcraft's Expedition to Lake Itasca*, p. xxv; Nicollet in William J. A. Bradford, *Notes on the Northwest, or Valley of the Upper Mississippi* (New York, 1846), pp. 26–9.

Georg von Raumer once again recorded a disappointing conclusion to his headwaters quest: the "giant streams of North America, ... do not burst forth from lofty Alps [but] ... flow through tedious plains of the same aspect, and thus present but few images of beauty to the artist's eye."[33]

The search for the Mississippi headwaters proved how mundane even the mightiest of rivers could be in its origins but, more important, it suggested how tenaciously the aura of purpose and destiny could cling to these central landscape features. Like earthquakes and mountains, naturalists saw rivers as powerful unifying forces in the natural landscape, and their productive energies were an important source of American identity. Strewn along the banks of the Mississippi were the remnants of entire forests that had disappeared into its churning waters as the river rearranged the upper watershed. Each tree snagged along the bank stopped others, until a jam cut across the channel and sent the river off in a new direction. Snaking eastward or westward across the broad valley, it left behind a diversified landscape of thick, rich alluvium; bleaching timber; and stranded lagoons, lakes, and swamps. The rivers of the east likewise shifted from side to side in their more confined valleys.[34] During a violent storm in the White Mountains in 1775, the headwaters of the Merrimack found their way into the Saco, flowing eastward into Maine. After sweeping away mills, bridges, and farms, these errant waters burst the banks of the Saco and formed a new outlet to the sea, appropriately named the New River. Lyell discovered that Niagara Falls had moved forty or fifty yards up the Niagara River since first settlement. The river would someday disappear, he speculated, and with it perhaps Lake Erie. The rivers that emptied into the lower Great Lakes were moving steadily eastward as spits extended along the shore; and the islands in the Ohio River, composed of bare gravel in their upper end, loamy sand in the middle, and thick forests farthest downriver, were steadily moving upstream, in effect, migrating eastward against the current.[35]

---

[33] Friedrich Ludwig Georg von Raumer, *America and the American People*, William W. Turner (trans.) (New York, 1846), pp. 17–18. See Henry Rowe Schoolcraft to Benjamin Silliman, March 16, 1836, Benjamin Silliman Papers, APS.

[34] Nathaniel P. Willis, *American Scenery; Or, Land, Lake, and River: Illustrations of Transatlantic Nature*, drawings by W. H. Bartlett (London, 1840), Vol. 2, p. 28. See *American Journal of Science* 9 (No. 1, 1825): p. 28; Belknap, *History of New-Hampshire*, p. 51; Williams, *Natural and Civil History of Vermont*, p. 46; *American Journal of Science* 22 (1832): pp. 217–18.

[35] Zadok Cramer, *The Navigator* (Pittsburgh, 1811), pp. 157–8, 167; Hutchins, *Historical Narrative and Topographical Description of Louisiana*, p. 25; Harper, *Preliminary Report on ... Mississippi*, p. 257; Webster, *Elements of Useful Knowledge*, p. 46;

Here, too, naturalists searched for purpose in a shifting landscape. Rivers were undoubtedly useful: They carried mountain water for crops and mountain energy for mills and forges. Migratory fish made their way up these watercourses each spring with precise timing, appearing on the farmer's doorstep in perfect accord with the agricultural cycles of feast and famine. Rivers cooled the air, moistened the soil, and made the atmosphere more agreeable.[36] They conveyed tons of upland soils to the valleys, where forests and meadows grew under more propitious conditions. The Mississippi, in its meanders across the heartland, distributed and redistributed this valuable load of nutrients, enriching the whole region and leaving behind oxbows and swamps that provided lush habitat for animals and water life. Rivers filled lakes with sediments, forming shallows, bars, and deltas that attracted aquatic plants, reptiles, fish, and waterbirds. They transformed bays and inlets into marshes, meadows, and, in the course of time, farmlands.[37] Enriched each spring with a "healthy slime" from the mountains, river intervales contained the "strongest vegetative powers which Nature can give," Crèvecoeur thought.[38] Along the Connecticut, these soils were twenty feet deep, an almost inexhaustible source of fertility. Buried in these rich sediments were trees and brush still in a "high state of preservation," left behind

Bigelow, *Some Account of the White Mountains*, p. 6; William D. Williamson, *The History of the State of Maine from its First Discovery, A.D. 1602, to the Separation, A.D. 1820, Inclusive* (Hallowell, 1839), Vol. 1, p. 29; Charles Lyell, *Travels in North America, in the Years 1841–2; with Geological Observations on the United States, Canada, and Nova Scotia* (New York, 1845), Vol. 1, p. 45; Lyell, *Principles of Geology*, pp. 341–2, 346, 343–5; William Mather, *First Annual Report on the Geological Survey of the State of Ohio* (Columbus, 1838), pp. 15–18; Mather in *American Journal of Science* 34 (July 1838): pp. 349–50; Flint, *Letters from America*, pp. 159–60. See George Featherstonhaugh, *Geological Report of an Examination Made in 1834, of the Elevated Country Between the Missouri and Red Rivers* (Washington, 1835), pp. 82–4; *American Journal of Science* 3 (1821): p. 18; *Universal Asylum and Columbian Magazine* 9 (July 1792): p. 36.

36 Williams, *Natural and Civil History of Vermont*, pp. 40, 43, 147, 149–50, 150; Latrobe, *Rambler in North America*, Vol. 1, p. 54; Webster, *Elements of Useful Knowledge*, Vol. 1, p. 41; John Filson, *The Discovery, Settlement, and Present State of Kentuckie* (Wilmington, 1784), p. 39; J. Hector St. John de Crèvecoeur, *Letters from an American Farmer and Sketches of Eighteenth-Century America*, Albert E. Stone (ed.) (New York, 1986 [c. 1782]), p. 364; Holmes, "General Reports," p. 109; *American Journal of Science* 25 (No. 2, 1834): p. 219.

37 Cramer, *Navigator*, p. 159; Latrobe, *Rambler in North America*, Vol. 1, p. 54; McCauley, *Natural, Statistical, and Civil History of the State of New-York*, pp. 42–3; Lyell, *Principles of Geology*, pp. 353–4.

38 Crèvecoeur, *Letters from an American Farmer*, p. 365. See *American Journal of Science* 10 (February 1826): p. 3.

when the river changed its course to enrich some other section of the valley.[39]

The "made land" along the course of a river could reveal a number of curiosities. Well-diggers in Vermont discovered a bed of small frogs in a stump standing upright deep in the alluvial soils. Although to all appearance "perfectly stupified and dead," the frogs revivified when exposed to the sun. The naturalist recording the find supposed they had been dormant for a hundred years, judging from the age of the timber growing above the well pit. A correspondent to *Niles Weekly Register* cited Vermont road workers who blasted open a boulder and discovered a cavity "as large as a goose egg" encasing a frog. Placed in an enclosure, the frog revived and "struggl[ed] ... for deliverance." Noah Webster learned of frogs found in a torpid state about twenty-five feet below the surface near Vermont's Onion River, where they had apparently rested for ages. In his natural history of Vermont, Williams included an entire appendix devoted to buried frogs. "How vigorous and permanent must the principle of life be in this animal," he exclaimed. "Centuries may have passed since they began to live in such a situation; and had that situation continued, ... they would have lived for many centuries yet to come!"[40]

Rivers served most obviously to unify the nation. As early as 1708, John Clayton noted that Virginia's rivers interlinked with those flowing westward off the Appalachian Plateau and asked an Indian how closely the two systems flowed together. His informant "clapt the fingers of one hand 'twixt those of the other, crying, they meet thus.'"[41] In Clayton's day, this symbolized British vulnerability to French and Indian attack, but later explorers saw these interlinked watersheds in a more positive light. The seaboard and the West were separated by a series of "clashing interests," as a British writer put it, and many Americans believed that only a vigorous flow of commerce could unite them. Interlocked and interconnected, rivers "enable[d] the people inhabiting the whole country to keep up a constant intercourse with each other," Caleb Atwater

---

[39] Rodolphus Dickinson, *A Geographical and Statistical View of Massachusetts* (Greenfield, 1813), p. 8.

[40] American Academy of Arts and Sciences, *Memoirs* 2 (No. 1, 1793): pp. 62–4; *Niles Weekly Register* 1 (January 4, 1812): p. 326; *American Journal of Science* 25 (1834): pp. 42–4; McCauley, *Natural, Statistical, and Civil History of the State of New-York*, pp. 511–12; Webster, *Elements of Useful Knowledge*, Vol. 1, p. 51; Williams, *Natural and Civil History of Vermont*, pp. 153–4, 156.

[41] [John Clayton], *Miscellanea Curiosa: Containing a Collection of Some of the Principal Phenomena in Nature* (London, 1708), Vol. 3, pp. 295–6.

wrote; this would lead inevitably to "enterprise, to wealth, comfort, and happiness." Given these expectations, the headwaters of each navigable river – the links between one system and the next – were as mystical as the font of the Mississippi itself.[42]

Explorers ventured into these swampy tablelands and came away with plans for canals, dams, locks, and boat-warps that would bind one system to the next.[43] New York's upper Susquehanna and Delaware drained a territory rich in lead, sulfur, coal, and salt that could easily be connected with the St. Lawrence, and even greater possibilities lay within the reach of the Hudson, as the Erie Canal's promoters later pointed out.[44] Volney discovered that the swamps of Ohio, relics of an "ancient lake" that once covered the territory, drained both south and north during vernal floods. "We can pass in canoes from the Ohio to Lake Erie, as I myself witnessed in 1796." The headwaters of the Muskingum, flowing southward to the Ohio, came within a few miles of the Cuyahoga, draining north into Lake Erie; likewise, the Sciota intersected with the Sandusky, and the Great Miami with the Miami of the Lake.[45] During flood times, the Wisconsin River, a tributary of the Mississippi, flowed eastward back into Lake Michigan's Fox River, "so that a barge can at such times pass from one stream into another." The Illinois similarly interlinked with the Chicago. These and other discoveries inspired dreams of national unity and added to the teleology of the rivers. The whole continent, Edmund Dana wrote,

---

[42] Caleb Atwater, "Remarks Made on a Tour to Prairie du Chien," in *The Writings of Caleb Atwater* (Columbus, 1833), pp. 203–4. See William Edward Baxter, *America and the Americans* (London, 1855), p. 19; Horatio Seymour, *A Lecture on the Topography and History of New-York* (Utica, 1856), p. 8; McCauley, *Natural, Statistical, and Civil History of the State of New-York*, pp. 40, 129–31; "Dr. Tucker" in Anon., *An Historical Review of North America* (Dublin, 1789), Vol. 1, p. 76; Daniel Coxe, *A Description of the English Province of Carolina* (London, 1722), n.p.

[43] Moses Greenleaf, *A Statistical View of the District of Maine* (Boston, 1816), pp. 41, 46, 78, 81–4, 106, 119–29, 131; Ezekiel Holmes, *Report of an Exploration and Survey of the Territory on the Aroostook River* (Augusta, 1839), pp. 6–12, 15–24, 36, Part 2, p. 39.

[44] Blodget [or Carnac], *Facts and Arguments*, pp. 10–11; Henry T. Tuckerman, *America and Her Commentators, with a Critical Sketch of Travel in the United States* (New York, 1864), p. 408; Haines, *Considerations on the Great Western Canal*, pp. 11–12; *American Journal of Science* 8 (No. 2, 1824): 358; *Niles' Weekly Register* 9, "Supplement" (1816): p. 146; Seymour, *Lecture on the Topography and History of New-York*, pp. 7–9.

[45] Constantin Francois Chasseboeuf, comte de Volney, *A View of the Soil and Climate of the United States* (Philadelphia, 1804), pp. 74–5. See Jacob Ferris, *The States and Territories of the Great West* (New York, 1856), pp. 30, 32; *Niles' Weekly Register* 6 (August 20, 1814): p. 418.

"may be aptly resembled to a cluster of islands": rivers were the "high seas" of the western world.[46]

Preserved frogs, made land, unifying headwaters, and other signs of dynamic natural forces fueled endless discussion about the purposes of rivers. "Could we know the history of these intervales, how they were formed in the course of long ages, the record would be more interesting than anything we can say about its human inhabitants," a Vermont historian wrote. Rivers, mountains, and forests were linked together in a providential system that benefited all life, including the flood of settlers pouring into the trans-Appalachian West. Exploring this system of relations, naturalists began to envision the delicate ecological balances that framed the conservation argument at the end of the nineteenth century.[47]

The Teleology of Forests

Forests were equally as important as mountains and rivers to the balance of nature but, here again, their exact function was not immediately clear. The deep woods, with its high canopy and limited understory, seemed almost as sterile as the mountaintops. Belknap found them eerily silent because songbirds avoided such regions; others, accustomed to the more open landscapes of the East or Europe, described them as dreary and monotonous – a strange combination of abundance and wasteland. Despite their prodigious size and variety, trees in endless ranks generated mixed feelings among those who struggled to understand nature's grand tableau.[48]

It was clear that forests were products of the soil, and their distribution testified to the vigor and power of the landscape. Soils ranged from coarse to fine, from cold and wet to hot and dry, from calcareous and siliceous to saline, and from sterile gravel to rich loams, and each type hosted a

---

[46] George W. Featherstonhaugh, "On the Ancient Drainage of North America, and the Origin of the Cataract of Niagara," *Monthly American Journal of Geology and Natural Science* 1 (July 1831): p. 17; Featherstonhaugh, *A Canoe Voyage Up the Minnay Sotor* (London, 1847), pp. 191, 193; Edmund Dana, *Geographical Sketches on the Western Country* (Cincinnati, 1819), p. 7. See *American Journal of Science* 10 (No. 2, 1826): p. 306; Amos Stoddard, *Sketches, Historical and Descriptive, of Louisiana* (Philadelphia, 1812), pp. 367–8; *Niles' Weekly Register* 5, "Supplement" (1813): p. 176.

[47] Frederic P. Wells, *History of Newbury, Vermont, from the Discovery of the Coos Country to Present Time* (St. Johnsbury, 1902), p. 3.

[48] Belknap, *History of New-Hampshire*, p. 56; Volney, *View of the Soil and Climate of the United States*, pp. 6–7. See John Talbot, *History of North America* (Leeds, 1820), Vol. 1, pp. 183–4.

different species of trees. However, trees were not simply passive subjects of soil composition. Fallen trees, leaves, and needles were quickly reduced to rich, moist earth, adding to and sometimes changing the nature of the soils and reinforcing whatever characteristics encouraged tree growth in a particular region.[49] J. Correa de Serra found a stratum of ancient half-rotten wood and leaves beneath the topsoils in Kentucky – left behind, he thought, by the receding waters of a primeval flood. Exposed to the air, they dissolved into a "black, soft, [and] saponaceous" earth that would fertilize the land for ages to come. A product of geologic, climatic, and biological forces, soils and their forest species were subject to ceaseless change, an evolution that underscored the fact that in nature, each element existed "not only for itself, but [to] form . . . a portion of a great whole."[50]

Although naturalists understood the basic interaction between soils and trees, they faced some intriguing questions, among them the lack of forests west of the Wabash. Standing on the banks of the river in 1816, David Thomas pondered these seemingly barren landscapes. The forest, it seemed, simply ended in a "stately wood of honey locust, sugar maple, [and] blue and white ash," with no perceptible changes in soil or climate. Grazing animals might have consumed all the herbaceous growth, he thought, but no herd was vast enough to destroy an entire forest. There was evidence of recent fire along the borderlands, but not everywhere, and the forest edge seemed too abrupt to attribute the prairies to climate differences. Jane Haldimand Marcet thought that grass or trees maintained their advantage once they colonized an area. Grass smothered the seeds of the trees, while the deep shade of the forest prevented the seeds of the grass from sprouting. The more common assumption was that Indians maintained the prairies by burning them, although it seemed contrary that Indians would kill oak trees when they depended on acorns for food.[51] Virginia's Edmund Ruffin dismissed the theory that prairies

[49] Thomas Green Fessenden, *The Complete Farmer and Rural Economist* (Boston, 1835), p. 11; Henry O'Rielly, *Settlement in the West: Sketches of Rochester* (Rochester, 1838), p. 45; *North American Review*, n.s., 67 (July 1848): p. 180; Thomas A. Pownall, *Topographical Description of the Dominions of the United States of America* (Pittsburgh, 1949 [1776]), p. 24.

[50] Joseph Correa de Serra, APS *Transactions*, n.s., 1 (1818): pp. 178–9; Dana, *Geographical Sketches on the Western Country*, pp. 26, 29. See *American Journal of Science* 22 (1832): p. 218; Jackson, *Final Report on . . . New Hampshire*, p. 243.

[51] Thomas, *Travels Through the Western Country*, pp. 156–7; [Jane Haldimand] Marcet, *Conversations on Vegetable Physiology; Comprehending the Elements of Botany with Their Application to Agriculture* (New York, 1830), pp. 299–300. See Volney, *View of the Soil and Climate of the United States*, p. 7; *American Journal of Science* 1 (1818):

resulted from fires, considering how resilient forests were elsewhere, and countered with a simple proposition: lime-rich soils grew grass and lime-poor soils grew trees. Try as they might, farmers would never rid acid soils of their trees, and on calcareous soils, trees of any sort would be stunted at best. Farmers, he urged, should bend to the land's destiny and cultivate the prairies, leaving the more acidic lands as woodlots.[52]

Although Ruffin stressed the power of soils in determining the nature of the forest, some evidence suggested a more complex relation. The edge of the prairie, for instance, seemed to be in flux, whereas the soils were relatively stable; throughout the East, explorers found proof that forest composition was changing. Some forests were entirely composed of young growth; others were littered with rotting pine knots, with no living pine within miles. Local historian, John M. Weeks, noted that the first settlers in Salisbury, Vermont, found the decayed remains of sweet walnut (*Juglans nigra?*) but no living trees in the area. Black cherry, useful for household furniture, grew in "great abundance" in the original forest but, by the time Weeks wrote in 1860, it had disappeared and furniture-makers were using butternut. The town's first settlers wintered their hogs on beech mast, but a half-century later, beech too had almost disappeared. Some thought the forest was rebounding after centuries of Indian fires, while others pointed to introduced species as the cause.[53]

Forest regeneration was another mystery. John Godman, who spent several years in Michigan, noted that when the forest succumbed to fire, disease, or insect infestation, Norway pine was the first to return, its seeds sown by the wind. The young trees would "shoot up as closely and compactly as hemp" and continue in this crowded condition until their roots began to intertwine. Then, the best-rooted trees would overtop the rest, and gradually the forest would thin, leaving a few stately monarchs.[54] General William Henry Harrison explained this process with a bit more

pp. 116–24; ibid., 2 (1820): p. 33; Mease, *Geological Account of the United States*, p. 11; Benjamin Harding, *A Tour Through the Western Country* (New London, 1819), p. 9; Francois-André Michaux, *Travels to the West of the Allegheny Mountains, in the States of Ohio, Kentucky, and Tennessea [sic], . . . Undertaken in the Year 1802* (London, 1805), p. 168.

52 Edmund Ruffin, *Essays and Notes on Agriculture* (Richmond, 1855), pp. 213–20.

53 John M. Weeks, *History of Salisbury, Vermont* (Middlebury, 1860), pp. 71–3, 87–8, 106–7. See Volney, *View of the Soil and Climate of the United States*, p. 22; Lyell, *Travels in North America*, p. 48; *American Journal of Science* 25 (No. 2, 1834): p. 223.

54 Pownall, *Topographical Description*, p. 24; John D. Godman, *Rambles of a Naturalist* (Philadelphia, 1833), pp. 96–7.

flourish. Like the cycles of growth and decay that prescribed the history of civilization, reforestation was predictable, he thought.

> The first growth...is more homogeneous [than the original forest, and]...as thick as garden peas....The more thrifty individuals soon overtop the weaker of their own kind, which sicken and die....The young giants in possession, like another kind of aristocracy, absorb the whole means of subsistence, and leave the mass to perish at their feet. This state of things will not, however, always continue. If the process of nature is slow and circuitous, in...establishing the equality which she loves, and which is the great characteristic of her principles, it is sure and effectual. The preference of the soil for the first growth, ceases with its maturity. It admits of no succession, upon the principles of legitimacy. The long undisputed masters of the forest may be thinned by the lightning, the tempest, or by diseases peculiar to themselves; and whenever this is the case, one of the oft-rejected of another family, will find a great lesson in republican values!

The process, although fittingly American in its outcome, was as gradual as the growth and decay of civilizations themselves. Nature tended toward variety and magnificence, but its means were excruciatingly slow.[55]

Less understood was the fact that new forests were invariably different from the previous. "No sooner does the axe of the woodman, or the accidental burning of the forests, destroy one class of trees and brushwood – a class that may have apparently covered the soil for centuries – but another race, perfectly distinct, rises, as though by magic, from the disturbed...soil." Near the Kittatinny Mountains, Pownall found a tract of pine laid low by a windstorm and growing between the logs was a stand of hardwoods. That forests would vary so greatly on the same piece of ground seemed to defy the destiny written in their soils. Did soil chemistry change over time, favoring one tree first and then another? Did successive species possess such "powerful imbibing qualities" as to deprive all others of their sustenance in the soil? Why did nature "become so partial to the one and forgetful of the other of her productions?" According to Constantine Rafinesque, the "natural rotation of wild trees and plants" was among the great scientific inquiries of the age.[56]

---

[55] William Henry Harrison in Historical and Philosophical Society of Ohio, *Transactions* 1 (1839): pp. 248–9; Harrison in Lyell, *Travels in North America*, pp. 30–1; *American Journal of Science*, n.s., 4 (November 1847): pp. 161–4, 166.

[56] Latrobe, *Rambler in North America*, Vol. 1, p. 55; Pownall, *Topographical Description*, pp. 24, 102–3; Benjamin Lincoln to Manasseh Cutler, June 12, 1783, Cutler and Cutler, *Journals, and Correspondence of Rev. Manasseh Cutler*, Vol. 2, p. 219; Rafinesque in *Western Minerva, or American Annals of Knowledge and Literature* (n.p., n.d.), p. 63, APS.

As scientists developed a more sophisticated understanding of tree dynamics, they discovered that reforestation was not only cyclical but also evolutionary, perhaps providential. "A rotation of crops is as important in the forests as it is in cultivated fields," George Barrell Emerson surmised. The dispersion of seeds was a remarkable example of nature's planning. In some cases, seed casings exploded when they dried or when they were brushed; other seeds were borne aloft on wings or downy fleece; burrs attached them to animals, or fruity covering attracted birds that carried them to new locations. Mountain pines sent seeds aloft on high-altitude winds, and trees growing near lakes or streams enveloped their seeds in waterproof cases. The propagation of a single tree might be accidental, John Lee Comstock concluded, but, in the aggregate, this dissemination was marvelously planned and ordered.[57] Forest cycles, the transformation of death into life, melded into larger evolutionary processes by which landscapes became more diverse and more productive.

That forest succession moved toward a higher order of integration was apparent in the ambiance of the ancient forest. Walking among the huge sycamores, elms, walnuts, tulips, and beeches growing along the Ohio River was a religious experience, Philip Henry Gosse thought. The ground was clear of underbrush, and the trees, united at their tops, trailed their vines downward, suggesting verdure as old as time itself. The "perfect stillness and utter solitude" drew the devout spirit upward. It was, he concluded, "to this end [that] all... vegetative energy was directed." Benjamin Trumbull described Connecticut's original forest as a majestic and diverse stand of trees yielding a vast commissary of wild nuts, berries, and fruits.[58] Forest succession was as providential as the placement of mountains and the flow of the rivers.

Naval explorer, M. F. Maury, combined these teleological exercises into a sweeping view of natural elements on a continental scale – climate and seasons, clouds and mountains, rivers, soils, and forests. Prevailing westerly winds washed over the North American continent, he observed,

---

[57] George Barrell Emerson, *A Report on the Trees and Shrubs Growing Naturally in the Forests of Massachusetts* (Boston, 1846), p. 19; J. L. [John Lee] Comstock, *An Introduction to the Study of Botany* (New York, 1835), pp. 82–5; Benjamin Smith Barton in Jacques Henri Bernardin de Saint-Pierre, *Studies of Nature*, Henry Hunter (trans.) (Philadelphia, 1808), Vol. 2, p. 114n.

[58] Philip Henry Gosse, *Letters from Alabama (U.S.) Chiefly Relating to Natural History* (London, 1859), pp. 117–18; Benjamin Trumbull, *A Complete History of Connecticut, Civil and Ecclesiastical* 1 (New Haven, 1818), p. 38. See Morris Birkbeck, *Notes on a Journey in America, from the Coast of Virginia to the Territory of Illinois* (Philadelphia, 1817), pp. 82–3; Godman, *Rambles*, p. 95.

providing "immense volumes of water" to supply the rivers and nourish the forests that grew along their banks. The exact quantity of moisture in the atmosphere, determined by the arrangement of landforms relative to the sea, was proportioned to suit the "proper development of the vegetable and animal kingdoms." If the topography had been different, the calculus would be thrown off, and "whole families of plants would wither and die for the want of cloud and sunshine, dry and wet, in proper proportions; and, with the blight of plants, whole tribes of animals would also perish." Thinking hypothetically, Maury proved that the landscape had been perfectly designed to ensure the utmost profusion of life. "Here then we see the harmony in the winds, design in the mountains, order in the sea, arrangement in the dust. Here are signs of beauty and works of grandeur; and we may now fancy, that in this exquisite system of adaptations and compensations, we can almost behold . . . the [work of the] . . . Almighty hand." Mountains, rivers, and forests were indeed sources of wonder, but what most intrigued scientists like Maury was the way these elements fit together. "Nature is a whole, and all the departments thereof are intimately connected," Maury concluded. "If we attempt to study in one of them, we find ourselves tracing clues which lead us off insensibly into others."[59] Teleology – the basic question of why mountains, rivers, and forests existed – gave naturalists an essentially ecological understanding of nature.

Jehovah's Empire

Nature's purpose was the greatest proliferation of life possible: "orbs beyond orbs, without number, suns beyond suns, systems beyond systems, with their proper inhabitants of the great Jehovah's empire," as John Bartram summarized. "Everything that could be created was created," his friend Charles Willson Peale insisted, "every shrub, every leaf and tree are filled with living creatures, each as "perfect in their internal and external structure as man." God would be no less generous than to fill the universe with life and give each creature some "great and important work" to perform.[60]

[59] M. F. Maury, "On the Geological Agency of the Winds," *American Association for the Advancement of Science Proceedings* (Washington, 1852), pp. 277, 290–1, 293.

[60] Bartram to Alexander Garden, March 25, 1762, in William Darlington, *Memorials of John Bartram and Humphrey Marshall* (New York, 1967 [c. 1849]), p. 399; Peale Lectures; Humboldt, *Views of Nature*, pp. 210–11, 213. See Hugh Williamson in David Hosack, "A Biographical Memoir of Hugh Williamson," *New York Historical Society*

The search for connections in this blizzard of life began with an understanding that the three great kingdoms were interdependent: vegetables derived their nourishment from inorganic matter and made this material fit for animals, and each animal possessed some virtue that left it indispensable to the vegetable kingdom.[61] Harvard naturalist, Benjamin Waterhouse, traced the energies flowing through this integrated landscape. "When an organized body dies," he wrote,

> organic particles . . . circulate through the universe; pass into other beings, producing life and nourishment. . . . A quadruped receives the plant into its stomach for food; . . . and then the digesting apparatus animalizes the vegetable, and gradually converts it into the nature and substance of the creature. And when this animal dies, his constituent particles . . . are absorbed by the growing plant . . . and thus do animals and vegetables mutually nourish and support each other; so that what was yesterday grass, is to day part of a sheep, and tomorrow becomes part of a man."[62]

Nothing was created in vain, Hubbard Winslow explained: "All creatures are perfectly adapted to each other and to the world in which they are made to dwell." These connections, as historian Richard Grove wrote, introduced "a new ecological concept of relations between man and the natural world."[63]

The principle of interconnectedness was laid out systematically by French naturalist-theologian, Jacques Henri Bernardin de Saint-Pierre, whose 1784 *Studies of Nature* was translated and published in Philadelphia in 1808 by Benjamin Barton. A meditation on nature's harmonies, *Studies of Nature* was both religious and scientific. God fit each species perfectly to its environment, he showed. Flower petals were designed as "mirrors to reflect the heat of the sun upon the parts of fecundation, or as parasols, to shelter them from its violence." The corolla and petals were perpendicular, conical, spherical, elliptical, or parabolic,

---

Collections 3 (1821): p. 140; Julie R. Newell, "James Dwight Dana and the Emergence of Professional Geology in the United States," *American Journal of Science* 297 (No. 3, 1997): p. 277; Murphey, *Creation*, p. 18; Rogers, *Life and Letters of William Barton Rogers*, p. 353.

[61] Timothy Flint, *Lectures upon Natural History, Geology, Chemistry, the Application of Steam, and Interesting Discoveries in the Arts* (Boston, 1833), pp. 108–11; Bell, *Knowledge of Living Things*, p. 9. See Benjamin Vaughan, December 22, 1807, Benjamin Vaughan Papers, APS; *American Quarterly Review* 13 (March 1830): p. 407.

[62] Waterhouse, *Botanist*, pp. 41–2.

[63] Hubbard Winslow, *The Relation of Natural Science to Revealed Religion* (Boston, 1837), p. 10; Richard H. Grove, *Green Imperialism: Colonial Expansion, Tropical Island Edens, and the Origins of Environmentalism, 1600–1860* (New York, 1995), p. 11.

depending on the plant's relation to the sun, the earth, and the climate. Each color served in a specific way to "reverberate rays of the sun on the parts of fecundation." The leaves of mountain plants were hollowed into a furrow to conduct rain or mist to the branch, and from the branch to the root. Each color served a purpose: plants growing near water were bluish-green and those on higher ground blended with the "verdure of the meadows, and the azure of the Heavens." Each was unique, and their combined effect projected "delicious harmonies... productive of a still farther magic to the eye."[64]

Like Maury, Saint-Pierre wove these observations into a larger tapestry of ecological interdependencies. The "Author of Nature," he wrote, first adapted the "chains of mountains to the basins of the seas which were to supply them with vapours," then directed the course of the winds to deliver the moisture to the land. Each plant was placed according to its needs for water and sunshine. *Studies of Nature* was the ultimate expression of ecological purpose, tracing the adaptation of each plant and animal to its environment and, finally, the "wonderful subserviency" by which animals, plants, and minerals provided for the various needs of humankind. Along with Jean-Jacques Rousseau, Saint-Pierre was an important figure in drawing together theology and science in Europe, and his work was influential among Americans who sought meaning in the landscape features they explored.[65]

How the settler fit into this elegant system of ecological interdependencies was evident in the natural history of the beaver. In their studies, scientists invariably singled out this sagacious little creature for its social nature, its engineering achievements, and its humanlike characteristics. "Every thing is done by the blended united counsels and labours of the whole community," Samuel Williams believed. They so understood their natural surroundings that they never failed in their judgment: They located the perfect site for their project, judged the trees necessary for the dam, and cut them to lengths perfectly suited to build it. Whole communities – two or three hundred – worked together in perfect harmony,

[64] Saint-Pierre, *Botanical Harmony Delineated; Or, Applications of Some General Laws of Nature to Plants*, Henry Hunter (Worcester, 1797), pp. v–vi, 23–4, 26, 28, 31, 46–7, 54, 95–6, 104–5. See Benjamin Smith Barton, n.d., No. 237, Broadsides, APS; Frank N. Egerton, "Changing Concepts of the Balance of Nature," *Quarterly Review of Biology*, 48 (June 1973): p. 338.

[65] Saint-Pierre, *Botanical Harmony Delineated*, pp. vi, 43, 84–5, 110. See Alphonso Wood, *A Class-Book of Botany, Designed for Colleges, Academies, and Other Seminaries* (Troy, 1846), p. 3.

Williams had heard, all joining to "promote the common business and safety of the whole society." In this regard, they represented a perfect adaptation of species to its natural surroundings.[66]

Jeremy Belknap dismissed many of Williams's more extravagant claims but, like Williams, he saw beavers as a model for integrating humans into the natural landscape.

That Being by whom the universe is...wisely governed has a farther design in his little animal, who with unwearied labor builds a dam which stops the water...and makes it spread over a tract of land....By means of the waters...every thing which grew upon it is drowned....In course of time, the leaves, bark, rotten wood, and other manure, which is washed down by the rains from the adjacent high lands [is]...spread over this pond, and subside to the bottom, making it smooth and level. It is now that the hunter, ferreting the innocent beaver, is also made subservient to the great design of Providence, which is...opening the dam and destroying the beaver....Of consequence, the water is drained off and the whole tract, which before was the bottom of a pond, is covered with wild grass, which grows as high as a man's shoulders, and very thick. These meadows doubtless serve to feed great numbers of moose and deer, and are of still greater use to new settlers, who find a mowing field already cleared to their hands.[67]

Belknap fit the industrious beaver into the broader purposes of nature, showing how the colony improved the landscape according to nature's design, and then seamlessly wove into this scheme the settler whose work further improved and perfected the landscape.

Searching out nature's purposes, naturalists discovered the ecological harmonies that made sense of each landscape feature. From the towering mountains to the stately forests and the mighty rivers, and from the lowest form of life to the highest, everything moved in unison to achieve the greatest possible productivity and variety. Settlers were part of this system, and if they needed a lesson in how to adapt to the changing world around them, there was no better example than the industrious beaver, whose works, like everything else, complemented nature's plan. This was the premise on which the naturalist welcomed the flood of pioneers into the broad trans-Appalachian basin.

---

[66] Williams, *Natural and Civil History of Vermont*, pp. 113–15, 120–21.

[67] Belknap, *History of New-Hampshire*, pp. 115, 118–19.

6

"A Distant Intercourse"

Animal Character and Conservation

In a letter to Henry E. Mühlenberg written in 1792, William Bartram offered an opinion that animal character, like mountains, rivers, and forests, revealed the deeper purposes in nature. Each species, he thought, possessed particular attributes that conveyed "certain exclusive powers & privileges that another has not." Thus, each could "boast . . . their Creator's favors," and all these differences conjoined into a perfectly meshed system. Together, their behavior reflected "a kind of distant intercourse, or necessary dependence on each other," a mutuality that revealed "a sort of moral system" in nature. He believed that each animal displayed an essential ethical character, and recognizing this subtle course of conduct was important to understanding the relation among animals – and the relation between animals and humans.[1] As American scientists traced this distant intercourse through the systems of animated nature, they did indeed perceive a code of interdependencies that explained each animal's seemingly random conduct and, in the process of discovering this code, they formulated a practical and ethical argument for protecting and preserving creatures of almost every kind.

As they did with mountains, rivers, and forests, naturalists not only described animals but also speculated about why they existed. According to Enlightenment tradition, they saw this animate world in instrumental terms, as a collection of exploitable resources to be used for subsistence or exchange. Yet, as Bartram's letter suggested, this utilitarian perspective

---

[1] William Bartram to Henry E. Mühlenberg, November 29, 1792, Henry E. Mühlenberg Manuscripts, Pennsylvania Historical Society (hereafter PHS). See William Bartram, *The Travels of William Bartram*, Francis Harper (ed.) (New Haven, 1958), p. 37.

did not preclude assigning moral value to the animals. This assessment – the kernel of American wildlife conservation – had its basis in the way naturalists explained animal behavior.[2]

Pre-Darwinians like Bartram explained diversity among animals by assuming that God created each species, placed it in its appointed place, and gave it some unique task in the overall plan of existence. Nature was a giant puzzle with perfectly interlinked parts, and fitting the parts together was as important as discovering new species: The more perfectly it was understood, the more benevolent nature would seem. Turkey buzzards, Alexander Wilson wrote, might appear noxious and even loathsome but, in truth, they were gregarious and peaceable creatures performing a valuable service by ridding the world of carrion.[3] A better understanding of nature would reduce prejudice and demonstrate the importance of animals to humankind.

A "Soul to the Science of Anatomy"

Of all forms of early natural history, zoology was the least developed. In the second decade of the century, only America's most common creatures were listed and described, and their habits, migrations, and diets remained at least partially mythic. The first systematic zoology in America was Richard Harlan's *Fauna Americana*, published in 1825. John Godman's *American Natural History* focused largely on mammals and appeared in three volumes between 1826 and 1828; in 1849, John Bachman and John James Audubon produced *The Quadrupeds of North America*. These studies left huge gaps in the understanding of animal behavior.

The natural history of rattlesnakes highlights the mix of myth and science that shaped this understanding. Since colonial times, these New World creatures had fascinated naturalists. Crèvecoeur claimed that a person bitten by a snake would swell, change colors, and lapse into a mood of "madness and rage." The victim would "thrust out his tongue as the snakes do; ... hiss ... through his teeth, and then succumb ... in the space of two hours." Kalm heard that a certain species of snake

---

[2] Brian Morris, "Changing Conceptions of Nature," *Ecologist* 11 (May–June 1981): pp. 131–2.

[3] Alexander Wilson and Charles Lucian Bonaparte, *American Ornithology: Or, the Natural History of the Birds of the United States* (Philadelphia, n.d.), p. 12. See Louis Agassiz, *Contributions to the Natural History of the United States* (Boston, 1857), Vol. 1, p. 18; Benjamin Smith Barton, *Fragments of the Natural History of Pennsylvania* (Philadelphia, 1799), p. 22; *Medical Repository* 3 (No. 3, 1800): pp. 186–7.

could outrun a man, wrap itself around his feet, and trip him. "It then bites him several times in the leg, or whatever part it can get hold of, and goes off again." He provoked several hoping to witness this curious aggression, but they refused to cooperate. Rather than question his source, he questioned his experiment: "I know not for what reason they shunned me, unless they took me for an artful seducer." Many accepted the idea that snakes used a power of fascination to immobilize their victims, a belief inspired by Renaissance concepts of the eye as the mirror of the soul. Snakes caught their prey, William Byrd wrote, by "ogl[ing] the poor little animal, til by force of the charm he falls down stupify'd and senseless on the ground."[4]

This combination of observation, conjecture, and myth was typical of early zoology. More systematic than most, Benjamin Barton put a snake in a cage with birds and moles to test its powers of fascination. Finding no evidence to support the theory, he concluded that when birds built their nests low to the ground, they dove at snakes to protect their eggs or fledglings. The cries that other naturalists attributed to the snake's occult powers in fact "originated in an endeavour to protect their nest or young." Barton advanced the science of snakes from common custom to focused experiment, but he still depended on a certain amount of deduction. If nature gifted serpents with powers of fascination, their principal food, he thought, would be "those animals, viz. birds and squirrels, upon which this influence is generally observed to be exerted"; but, in fact, they mainly ate reptiles and rodents. And, if snakes could charm creatures down to the ground, why were some endowed with the ability to climb trees?[5]

While the snake's powers of fascination continued to draw comment, another question arose from time to time: What purpose did the rattlesnake's rattle serve? John Brickell, writing in 1737, assumed rattles existed to warn away interlopers, an opinion seconded by John Bigland in 1832. By use of the rattle, the snake was left in peace, and other creatures

---

[4] J. Hector St. John de Crèvecoeur, *Letters from an American Farmer and Sketches of Eighteenth-Century America*, Albert E. Stone (ed.) (New York, 1986 [c. 1782]) p. 181; Peter Kalm, *Travels into North America, Containing Its Natural History, and a Circumstantial Account of Its Plantations and Agriculture in General*, John R. Foster (trans.) (Warrington, 1753–1761), Vol. 1, pp. 318–19; ibid., Vol. 2, pp. 205–7; William Byrd, *History of the Dividing Line*, T. H. Wynne (ed.) (Richmond, 1866), Vol. 1, p. 87; Herbert Leventhal, *In the Shadow of the Enlightenment: Occultism and Renaissance Science in Eighteenth-Century America* (New York, 1976), pp. 137, 140–55, 163.
[5] Benjamin Smith Barton, *A Memoir Concerning the Fascinating Faculty Which Has Been Ascribed to the Rattle-Snake, and Other American Serpents* (Philadelphia, 1796), pp. 32–6, 57–9, 65.

were relieved of the "universal terror" that living in snake-infested woods might inspire. Rather than agents of horrific design, rattlesnakes, Bigland thought, were part of "the general system for the purpose of contributing to [nature's] perfection."[6] The rattlesnake was natural rather than supernatural but not entirely without its providential implications.

Rattlesnakes were only one puzzle in the teleology of animated nature; each creature's powers of predation, defense, and survival posed similar questions. Bats, like rattlesnakes, were repulsive, but they were created to serve nature and humankind and thus worthy of admiration. Their soft and silent velvet wings, their unabated vigor and huge appetite for insects, their delicate and unerring sense of direction, their large ears, and their sharp teeth were perfectly adapted to their role in the balance of nature.[7] The mosquito's teleology was less apparent. It seemed "a little mysterious," Benjamin Barton reflected while canoeing in western New York, that nature formed such myriads of these tormentors yet seemed at "a loss to invent an expedient to feed them." No doubt, he concluded, they were "intended in wisdom to induce man to cultivate the earth, which is a means of effectually dispersing them."[8] People associated the nocturnal cries of the owl with a "supernatural horror," Alexander Wilson noted, and he explained that the owl was simply a bird of prey designed to feed at night, its harsh voice nothing more than a function of the "width and capacity of its throat." Yet, why was the throat made so? It was intended, he deduced, "by heaven as an alarm and warning to the birds and animals on which it preys, to secure themselves from danger." The logic behind God's sporting nature was not subject to Wilson's speculation but, clearly, he saw something providential in the owl's distant intercourse.[9] Barton

---

[6] John Brickell, *The Natural History of North-Carolina, with an Account of the Trade, Manners, and Customs of the Christian and Indian Inhabitants* (Dublin, 1737), p. 142; John Bigland, *A Natural History of Birds, Fishes, Reptiles, and Insects* (Philadelphia, 1832), pp. 136, 138.

[7] John D. Godman, *American Natural History* (Philadelphia, 1826), Vol. 1, pp. 52–4, 95.

[8] Barton, Journals and Notebooks, 1785–1806, pp. 34–6, APS; Benjamin Barton, *A Discourse on Some of the Principal Desiderata in Natural History* (Philadelphia, 1807), pp. 34, 50. See Constantine Rafinesque, "First Lecture on Botany," Constantine Rafinesque Papers, American Philosophical Society (hereafter APS); Samuel Williams, *The Natural and Civil History of Vermont* 1 (Burlington, 1809), p. 158.

[9] Wilson and Bonaparte, *American Ornithology*, pp. 88, 95, 96; Alexander Wilson in *The Cabinet of Natural History and American Rural Sports, with Illustrations* (Barre, 1973), p. 73. See Charles Lucien Jules Laurent Bonaparte, *American Ornithology; Or, the Natural History of Birds Inhabiting the United States, Not Given by Wilson* (Philadelphia, 1825), pp. 68–9; William B. Ashworth, Jr., "Emblematic Natural History of the

and Wilson might have stretched the teleological point, but their search for purpose was common among scientists who struggled to enlarge the public understanding of nature's utility.

Scientists eschewed superstition but embraced providence. Finding mesmerizing powers in the snake's eye was superstitious, but finding higher purpose in the snake's rattle, the mosquito's bite, and the owl's hoot was scientific. The search for providence in nature was speculative, Benjamin Barton admitted, but it would bring scientists closer to understanding divinity. Although he never fully clarified the boundaries of this mode of analysis, he and others used it unabashedly in their search for meaning. The "final cause or intention of nature," he thought, "is a question which ought never to be neglected. It is a kind of soul to the science of anatomy." [10]

A "Wonderfull Order and Ballance"

The soul of anatomy, as Barton put it, joined animal behavior to the idea of balance in nature, a concept dating back to ancient Greece. As historian Frank Egerton noted, the balance of nature was a "background" idea, seldom argued explicitly, but amply illustrated by loose analogy and assertion. It was corollary to an appreciation for nature's astounding productivity: Each species kept another in check in the universal law of predation. [11] This formative ecological idea was clear in a calculation John Bartram made as early as 1737 in his observations on a vast army of caterpillars moving into eastern Pennsylvania. This instance of nature temporarily unbalanced had consequences for other species: "when they are in such swarms, they devour the whole woods before them, especially oaks of all kinds, leaving not a green leaf, that in June the woods appear like mid Winter." Bartram also recalled that twelve years earlier, a "great number of bears" appeared in the eastern settlements, a fact he attributed to a scarcity of acorns, their autumn food, farther west. He concluded that the caterpillar army was responsible for this scarcity and, reasoning further, remembered an earlier time when "incredible numbers

Renaissance," N. Jardine, J. A. Secord, and E. C. Spary, *Cultures of Natural History* (Cambridge, 1996), pp. 18–20, 21, 28.

[10] Benjamin Smith Barton, *Supplement to a Memoir Concerning the Fascinating Faculty Which Has Been Ascribed to the Rattle-Snake* (Philadelphia, 1800), p. 40. See Donald Worster, *Nature's Economy: A History of Ecological Ideas* (New York, 1977), p. 42.

[11] Frank N. Egerton, "Changing Concepts of the Balance of Nature," *Quarterly Review of Biology*, 48 (June 1973): pp. 322, 326.

of pigeons" descended on Philadelphia. Like the bears, they had been driven eastward by the caterpillars.

Having linked the appearance of the bears, the pigeons, and the cater-pillars, Bartram drew three conclusions about nature's dynamics. First, he remarked that Americans could expect the West to be a land of abundant productivity: "There must be very great forests and a fertil country . . . that can maintain & support so many millions of pigeons (besides other ani-mals)." Second, he marveled that creatures were endowed with powerful means of preservation in traveling great distances, then returning to their original homes. And, finally, he found in the relationship among bears, pigeons, and oaks evidence of a "wonderfull order and ballance that is maintain'd between ye vegetable and animal oeconomy" – a distant intercourse, as his son would put it, that under normal circumstances "the animal should not be too numerous to be supported by the veg-etable: nor the vegetable production be lost for want of gathering by the animal." Nature was superabundant, yet never overproductive. As for the caterpillars, Bartram was not worried that they would upset the equi-librium. "I have often with thankfulness observed, how good Providence has checked the devouring caterpillars, by a course of natural causes, and preserved a balance of his creatures," he wrote to Peter Collinson. "Each species has its natural check, – which arises from accidents we cannot forsee, or prevent."[12]

The balance of nature explained much about animal behavior, and naturalists were quick to show how this balance contributed to human welfare. Weasels occasionally killed chickens, but John Godman saw more good than harm in their behavior because the rodents they ate with even greater relish were so fecund that "nothing short of the destruction of the whole crop would ensue were it not that the weasel is contin-ually thinning their ranks." This was the true purpose of the weasel – not killing chickens. Its sleek body allowed access to the narrowest tun-nels, and it was ruthless in its destructive habits. "We have on several

---

[12] John Bartram to Peter Collinson, April 26, 1737, in Edmund Berkeley and Dorothy Smith Berkeley, *The Correspondence of John Bartram, 1734–1777* (Gainesville, 1992), pp. 44–5. See Collinson to Bartram, September 20 [1751?], in William Darlington, *Memorials of John Bartram and Humphrey Marshall* (New York, 1967 [1849]), p. 188; Collinson to Bartram, December 10, 14, 1737, in ibid., pp. 102–3; W. Bingley, *Animal Biography, or Popular Zoology* (London, 1813), pp. 8–9; Charles Christopher Reiche, *Fifteen Discourses on the Marvellous Works in Nature* (Philadelphia, 1791), pp. 110–11, 113; *Cabinet of Natural History*, p. 83; Godman, *American Natural History*, Vol. 1, p. 223.

occasions . . . witnessed the immense destruction which it occasioned in a single night," Bachman and Audubon wrote. "It enters every hole under stumps, logs, stone heaps, and fences, and evidences of its bloody deeds are seen in the mutilated remains of the mice scattered on the snow." Its "irresistible destiny" was the destruction of rodents.[13]

Discovering a creature's role in the balance of nature had important conservation implications, and scientists weighed these matters carefully. William Peabody's Massachusetts ornithology included a description of each bird's "services and depredations" so that farmers could "determine which it is the interest to protect, and which he has a right to destroy."[14] Crows, according to Wilson's ornithology, were the "least beloved of all our land birds, having neither melody of song, nor beauty of plumage, nor excellence of flesh, nor civility of manners, to recommend him." Although the worms, grubs, and caterpillars they ate consumed more produce than the crows did, Wilson was not inclined to be charitable: "To say to the man who has lost his crop of corn by these birds, that Crows are exceedingly useful for destroying vermin, would be as consolatory as to tell him who had just lost his house and furniture by the flames, that fires are excellent for destroying bugs." Godman likewise credited God's good intentions in creating crows but admitted that when cultivation upset the natural balance, they often became superabundant. "Whoever would devise a method of lessening their numbers suddenly, would certainly be doing a service to the community."[15] Wilson wrestled with a similar question involving purple grackles. He had seen *Quiscalus quiscula* descend "like a blackening, sweeping tempest" on a cornfield and strip the ears "as dexterously as if done by the hand of man," yet he cautioned that grackles were made for some reason, probably relating to their appetite for insects. It was important to "guard against their bad effects," but he opposed "the barbarous, and even impious, wish for their utter extermination." Charles Willson Peale insisted that "the links in the chain of interdependencies" should "all be maintained in those relative proportions necessary for the general good of the system." One species might

[13] Godman, *American Natural History*, Vol. 1, p. 195; John James Audubon and John Bachman, *The Quadrupeds of North America* (New York, 1851), Vol. 2, pp. 59–60.

[14] William B. O. Peabody, "A Report on the Ornithology of Massachusetts," in George B. Emerson, *Reports on the Fishes, Reptiles, and Birds of Massachusetts* (Boston, 1839), pp. 257, 259.

[15] Wilson and Bonaparte, *American Ornithology*, pp. 121–2, 124; John D. Godman, *Rambles of a Naturalist* (Philadelphia, 1833), pp. 104, 110. See Anon., *The Book of Nature, in Two Volumes* (Boston, 1826), p. 4.

predominate for a time, but "counter checks" were in place to restore the balance. Thus, he revealed the naturalist's faith "that an unseen hand holds the reins, now permitting one to prevail and now another, . . . and saying to each, 'Hither shalt thou come and no further.'"[16]

In most cases, these exercises proved the importance of protecting species. Shrew moles ate grubs, slugs, and insects in huge quantities, and thus might be excused for minor mischief among vegetable roots. Each red-winged blackbird devoured about fifty grubs a day, Peabody calculated, and a pair of sparrows, 3,360 caterpillars each week. The busy little sapsucker that perforated apple trees as though by "successive discharges of buck-shot" was actually grooming the trees; close inspection revealed that the branches remained "broad, luxuriant, and loaded with fruit."[17] The red-headed woodpecker (*Dryocopus pileatus*) could leave "cart-loads" of bark and chips at the base of a tree but, again, the forest as a whole benefited. Using language that stressed the importance of the woodpecker's work, Wilson pointed out that diseased trees were the woodpecker's favorites: "There the deadly crawling enemy have formed a lodgment, between the bark and tender wood, to drink up the very vital part of the tree." Until some more effective means of destroying insects was devised, he concluded, "I would humbly suggest the propriety of protecting, and receiving with proper feelings of gratitude, the services of this and the whole tribe of Woodpeckers, letting the odium of guilt fall to its proper owners."[18]

Assessing the balance of nature, scientists found value for each species beyond its obvious economic use. Careful observations, Barton promised, would reveal "which are our friends, and which are our enemies; which deserve to be cherished and preserved, and which it will be our interest to banish or destroy." The argument was not simply sentimental; nor was it aimed at saving all of nature. Rather, it asked for justice and due consideration in the treatment of birds and animals, if not for the creature's sake, then for the operation it performed on behalf of nature and humankind.[19]

[16] Barton, *Journals and Notebooks*, p. 67; Wilson and Bonaparte, *American Ornithology*, pp. 157–8; Peale Lectures.

[17] Godman, *American Natural History*, Vol. 1, p. 95; Peabody, "A Report on the Ornithology of Massachusetts," p. 278; Wilson and Bonaparte, *American Ornithology*, pp. 185–6; Charles Willson Peale, Lectures, APS.

[18] Barton, *Fragments of the Natural History*, p. 22; Wilson and Bonaparte, *American Ornithology*, p. 163–4, 170–1, 176.

[19] Barton, *Fragments of the Natural History*, p. 24.

The Perfect Web of Nature

Balance and purpose were the bases for what historian John Gatta called a "pre-Darwinian but effectively ecological recognition of...adaptive interaction." The harmonious interaction of such a vast array of plants and animals implied divine governance and this, in turn, that every creature was "stamped with the characters of the infinite perfection," as William Bingley explained. Scientifically, the term *perfect* suggested a mature stage in the life cycle of a plant or insect: a flower in full bloom or an insect in its adult stage. Philosophically, it indicated a species adapted flawlessly to a unique constellation of natural circumstances, each performing a special task in this broader scheme. A petrel skimming a threatening wave suggested to Timothy Flint that "even the storms have their inhabitants." The bird fulfilled its purpose "beyond the possibility of improvement."[20]

Species perfection led to questions about species formation. The most acceptable theory involved special creation, a concept dating to Aristotle's time. In each new age, God created animals perfectly adapted to the world they inhabited, and each age included species more perfect than those preceding it. This implied absolute and ordained distinctions between species and a hierarchically arranged Great Chain of Being. "Revelation teaches that there is no such thing as *equivocal* production or generation," Hubbard Winslow lectured. This reassuring concept ordered the universe and fixed humanity at the apex of creation. The entire plan, Agassiz thought, had been "laid out in the course of time, and executed with the definite object of introducing man upon the earth." Nevertheless, scientists questioned the notion of absolute hierarchy as they discovered subtle similarities among species and began placing fossils in chronological order. By the 1820s, most considered the Great Chain of Being a "philosophical reverie," as zoologist James DeKay put it.[21]

---

[20] John Gatta, *Making Nature Sacred: Literature, Religion, and Environment in America from the Puritans to the Present* (New York, 2004), p. 51; Bingley, *Animal Biography*, p. 3; Timothy Flint, *Lectures upon Natural History, Geology, Chemistry, the Application of Steam, and Interesting Discoveries in the Arts* (Boston, 1833), p. 101; Peale Lectures, APS.

[21] Hubbard Winslow, *The Relation of Natural Science to Revealed Religion: An Address Delivered Before the Boston Natural History Society* (Boston, 1837), p. 8; *Columbian Magazine* in Leventhal, *Shadow of the Enlightenment*, p. 236; Louis Agassiz, *The Structure of Animal Life* (New York, 1866), pp. 3, 6, 90; James Ellsworth De Kay, *Anniversary Address on the Progress of Natural Sciences in the United States* (New York, 1826), p. 69.

The idea of species fixity, like the Great Chain of Being, had roots in classical literature but here, too, naturalists interested in the progressive realization of purpose in nature were beginning to think of species as a more fluid concept. According to Lamarck, species changed, becoming more perfectly adapted, through gradual transmutation. Erasmus Darwin found evidence for this in the improvement of domesticated dogs, horses, and rabbits, and even Linnaeus assumed that in the beginning, God created no more than sixty plants, all others being formed through changes in their "solitary or sexual reproductions." Each mating pair reproduced in a manner similar to themselves but "with frequent additional improvements," resulting in a more perfect world.[22] In 1832, Constantine Rafinesque explained differences in species as a matter of "gradual deviations of shapes, forms, and organs ... in the lapse of time," and Charleston's John Bachman saw plants and animals adapting to new environments as they spread across the continent.[23] Benjamin Barton and Louis Agassiz, however, maintained that classifications were fixed and God-given, and the fact that different species could not mate proved the point. According to historian Hunter Dupree, species fixity "was not only deeply ingrained in the thinking of Christians, but was the best guess that the scientists of the day could make from their own data."[24] Agassiz inspected hundreds of fossils reputed to be transitional and invariably found them "marked [by] ... differences," and he raised fundamental questions his evolutionist colleagues could not answer: If species changed

---

[22] Egerton, "Changing Concepts of the Balance of Nature," p. 335; Barbara Novak, *Nature and Culture: American Landscape and Painting, 1825–1875* (New York, 1980), p. 53; Erasmus Darwin, *The Temple of Nature; Or, The Origin of Society: A Poem, with Philosophical Notes* (Baltimore, 1804), pp. 44–5.

[23] Rafinesque in E. D. Merrill, "Introduction," Rafinesque, "A Life of Travels and Researches in North America and South Europe," *Chronica Botanica* 8 (No. 2, 1944 [c. 1836]): p. 294; John Bachman, *An Examination of Professor Agassiz's Sketch of the Natural Provinces of the Animal World and Their Relation to the Different Types of Man* (Charleston, 1855), pp. 6–9. See John William Draper, *A Treatise on the Forces Which Produce the Organization of Plants* (New York, 1844), pp. 2–6; Patricia Tyson Stroud, *Thomas Say: New World Naturalist* (Philadelphia, 1992), p. 46; Barton, *Discourse on Some of the Principal Desiderata*, p. 20; Bigland, *Natural History of Birds, Fishes, Reptiles, and Insects*, p. 139.

[24] Louis Agassiz, *Methods of Study in Natural History* (Boston, 1863), p. 73; Barton in Godman, *American Natural History*, Vol. 1, p. 19; A. Hunter Dupree, *Asa Gray: 1810–1888* (Cambridge, 1959), pp. 54, 139. See Philip Henry Gosse, *Letters From Alabama (U.S.) Chiefly Relating to Natural History* (London, 1859), p. 29; William Martin Smallwood in collaboration with Mabel Sarah Coon Smallwood, *Natural History and the American Mind* (New York, 1941), p. 229; John Anderson, *The Course of Creation* (Cincinnati, 1851), pp. 293–4.

perpetually, how could they be perfect? And, if species came and went, was the balance of nature as fragile as most naturalists thought?[25]

In 1845, an anonymously written book titled *Vestiges of the Natural History of Creation*, originally published in England in 1844, appeared in an American edition, animating the debate over mutability and perfection. The book's author, Robert Chambers, argued that species were not individually created by God; each evolved through a progressive and dynamically interrelated process Chambers called a "universal gestation of nature," in which each stage of organic development was progressively more complex. Dinosaurs were adapted to low, muddy coastal marshes; marsupials appeared when the surface was flat and largely without variety; mammals evolved when the land could support their various forms; and humans rose through various races to the Caucasian.[26]

Although Chambers's theory was not totally unprecedented, its appearance in a single popular edition shocked the scientific community. A few American naturalists, notably Henry Darwin Rogers, championed *Vestiges*, but most, like their European colleagues, found it far too outspoken as an explanation for species differentiation. Agassiz declared it scientifically and theologically unsound, and Asa Gray devoted the first of his popular Lowell lectures to "showing that the objectionable conclusions [in *Vestiges*] rest upon gratuitous and unwarranted inferences." In particular, they rejected the idea that organic and inorganic processes obeyed the same laws, and that these laws alone could account for a sweeping progression from the lowest forms of creation to the highest – and to humankind. American naturalists preferred a more interactive relation between God and nature. Creatures "not only *had* a Creator, but *have* a Governor," according to Gray.[27]

[25] Louis Agassiz, *An Introduction to the Study of Natural History* (New York, 1847), pp. 8–9; Agassiz to A. Sedgwick, June 1845, in Agassiz, *Louis Agassiz: His Life and Correspondence*, Elizabeth Cary Agassiz (ed.), (Boston, 1885), Vol. 1, pp. 390–2; ibid., Vol. 2, p. 540. See Robert Horace Silliman, "Agassiz vs. Lyell: Authority in the Assessment of the Diluvium-Drift Problem by North American Geologists, with Particular Reference to Edward Hitchcock," *Earth Sciences History* 13 (No. 2, 1994), p. 181.

[26] Robert Chambers, *Vestiges of the Natural History of Creation and Other Evolutionary Writings*, James A. Secord (ed.) (Chicago, 1994), pp. xiv, 76, 80, 149–50. See Louis Agassiz in Dupree, *Asa Gray*, p. 227; Silliman, "Agassiz vs. Lyell," p. 181.

[27] *North American Review*, n.s., 60 (April 1845): pp. 426–7, 433; Anderson, *Course of Creation*, pp. 294, 296; Asa Gray to John Torrey, February 12, 1845, in Jane Loring Gray (ed.), *Letters of Asa Gray* (London, 1893), Vol. 1, p. 328; Gray in Dupree, *Asa Gray*, p. 146. See Stanley Guralnick, "Geology and Religion Before Darwin: The Case of Edward Hitchcock, Theologian and Geologist, *Isis* 63 (No. 219, 1972): pp. 533–4, 539; Hugh Miller, *The Foot-Prints of the Creator: Or, the Asterolepis of Stromness . . . with*

Despite the charges of secularism, Chambers kept divinity at the center of his system. God need not interfere "on every occasion when a new shell-fish or reptile was to be ushered into existence," but the overall plan was no less divine. By focusing on the laws rather than the First Cause, Chambers freed natural history from the idea of special providence without denying the perfect and providential relation between species. Transmutation resulted in the "most harmonious relation to the things of the outward world, thus clearly proving that *design* presided in the creation of the whole." The hierarchical Great Chain gave way to "an array of interlinked and carefully ordered entities": a perfectly crafted web of ecological relations.[28]

Thus, the system laid out by Chambers, despite its iconoclastic overtones, gained currency in American science. As Boston naturalist, W. J. Burnett, summarized in 1852, each creation passed through "divers metamorphoses to suit the wants of the globe, renewing itself without the necessity of a special creation at the beginning of each period." Divine intervention went the way of the Great Chain of Being, but the idea of perfect balance remained, giving spiritual overtones to the new focus on adaptation and connectedness. Exploring the tightly knit system of relations among animals provided an ecological justification for protecting their species because each was an expression of God's handiwork. Philosophically, the argument for animal conservation was in place by the middle of the nineteenth century.[29]

The Essence of Animal Behavior

Along with the practical and theological implications of this distant intercourse, naturalists debated its ethical dimensions. The ethical framework for animal behavior reflected a common tendency to describe animals in human terms, a practice fueled by popular interest in American fauna. Anthropomorphizing served a variety of scientific and literary purposes. It conveyed in shorthand an animal's essential behavior patterns:

---

a *Memoir of the Author* by Louis Agassiz (Boston, 1959), p. xi; Philip J. Lawrence, "Edward Hitchcock: The Christian Geologist," *APS Proceedings* 116 (No. 1, 1972): pp. 28, 32.

[28] Chambers, *Vestiges*, pp. 152–4, 203, 324.

[29] W. J. Burnett, "Relations of Embryology and Spermatology to Animal Classification," American Association for the Advancement of Science *Proceedings* (Washington, 1852), p. 333; see James Murphey, *Creation: Or the Bible and Geology Consistent: Together with the Moral Design of the Mosaic History* (New York, 1850), p. 47.

"timid" deer, "wary" elk, "surly" bears, "crafty" foxes, "ravenous" wolves, "devouring" panthers, "insidious" wildcats, or "haughty" buffalo. It revealed a number of character traits worthy of emulation, such as courage, family devotion, ingenuity, cheerfulness, and maternal love. It offered a means of understanding the inner essence of the animal – the "soul to the science of anatomy," in Barton's terms. And, finally, it conveyed an ethical judgment about animals.[30] The *Cabinet of Natural History*, a zoological volume based on the Philadelphia Museum displays, concluded its discussion of the rough-billed pelican (*Pelecanidae erythrorhynchus*) with a note on its personality: "These birds are said to be torpid and inactive to the last degree, so that nothing can exceed their indolence but their gluttony, and the powerful stimulus of hunger is necessary to excite them to exertion." A cougar was not only ferocious but also cruel, taking "delight...in carnage," and a raccoon combined "the capricious mischievousness of the monkey, [with]...a blood-thirsty and vindictive spirit peculiarly his own."[31]

Anthropomorphic did not necessarily mean simplistic. A hawk could be grave and noble; the *Cabinet* showed its red-tailed with bill in profile and wings in full sweep, demonstrating its imperiousness; but, it was also duplicitous, waiting on their barnyard depredations "until the farmer is absent from his home."[32] Benjamin Franklin's well-known denigration of the eagle on the occasion of its elevation as a national symbol shows how perplexing the essence of each creature could be. His description of the bird's "bad moral character" was only partly tongue-in-cheek:

He does not get his living honestly; you may have seen him perched on some dead trees, where, too lazy to fish for himself, he watches the labour of the Fishing Hawk [*Pandion haliaetus*]; and when that diligent bird has at length taken a fish, and is bearing it to his nest for the support of his mate and young ones, the Bald Eagle pursues him, and takes it from him.... Like those among men who live by sharping and robbing, he is generally poor, and often very lousy. Besides, he is a rank coward; the little Kingbird, not bigger than a Sparrow, attacks him boldly, and drives him out of the district. He is, therefore, by no means a proper emblem for the brave and honest cincinnati of America, who have driven all the *Kingbirds* from our country.... In truth the Turkey is, in comparison, a much more respectable bird, and withal a true original native of America. Eagles have been found in all countries, but the Turkey was peculiar to ours. He is, besides,

---

[30] Humphrey Marshall, *The History of Kentucky* (Frankfort, 1812), pp. 6–7.
[31] *Cabinet of Natural History*, pp. 13, 24, 71, 85; Samuel Williams, *Natural and Civil History of Vermont*, pp. 101–3.
[32] *Cabinet of Natural History*, pp. 13, 39, 49.

Lepus palustris.

from S.ᵗ Carolina (dried sk

FIGURE 6.1. Naturalists debated the ethical dimensions of animal behavior and indulged a common tendency to describe animals in human terms. Anthropomorphizing conveyed in shorthand an animal's essential behavior patterns – timid, wary, surly, crafty, ravenous, insidious, or haughty. It revealed character traits worth emulating, such as courage, family devotion, ingenuity, cheerfulness, or maternal love, and it offered a means of understanding the essence of the animal – the "soul to the science of anatomy," in Benjamin Smith Barton's words. Titian Ramsay Peale, *Sketches, 1817–1875*. Courtesy of the American Philosophical Society.

(though a little vain and silly, 'tis true, but not the worse emblem for that), a bird of courage, and would not hesitate to attack a grenadier of the British guards, who should presume to invade his farmyard with a red coat on.[33]

Lucien Bonaparte characterized the eagle as a "distinguished" emblem for the country, but his assessment was ambivalent. They were "fierce, contemplative, daring, and tyrannical," yet no bird was more solicitous of its young; they carried so many fish to the nest that "the putrid smell . . . may be distinguished at the distance of several hundred yards." Another naturalist pointed out that they could be "most easily discovered on evenings by their loud snoring while asleep on high oak trees."[34] These complex

[33] Benjamin Franklin in Bonaparte, *American Ornithology*, p. 95.
[34] Bonaparte, *American Ornithology*, pp. 34–5, 38–9; Wilson and Bonaparte, *American Ornithology*, p. 36; *The Naturalist* 1 (December 1831): pp. 360–1.

representations were based on a conviction that each creature harbored an inner essence, and this was part of the animal's natural history.

This anthropomorphic assessment was clear in Audubon's *Birds of America*. Early ornithologists displayed birds in relief against a spare background in order to accent their identifying taxonomical characteristics. Beginning with Catesby, they experimented with richer background illustrations and a more narrative context; the effect, a review of Alexander Wilson's *Ornithology* opined, "was to fill the reader with "amiable feelings for an interesting class of beings." Narrative illustration became a defining feature of Audubon's work; his birds, as he put it, were engaged in their "natural avocations, in all sorts of attitudes," some pursuing prey through the air and others searching among the foliage, each in its "allotted element." Both Wilson and Audubon – the former in his "little characteristic stories" and the latter in his illustrations – developed this narrative technique to reach beyond a select circle of scientists. For the "closet naturalist," Audubon included in each drawing at least one subject representing the "necessary characteristics" of the standard taxonomy. Otherwise, he devoted his art to capturing the bird's spirit – its essential personality. He carefully observed the specimen's behavior, then shot it and arranged the bird in its most characteristic pose. The positions, he admitted, might "in some instances appear *outre*" but only if the observer was unacquainted with the species in the wild.[35] Each bird expressed a characteristic bearing; his peewees and flycatchers were pensive, sitting "uprightly, now and then glanc[ing] . . . their eyes upward or sideways to watch the approach of their insect prey." His house wren was mischievous: "What can be more amusing, cheerful, and ridiculous, at the same time, than the family picture of plate 83," a reviewer recalled, "where the nest is in an old hat, stuck on a twig, the male beginning his song on the edge of the hat, and the anxious mother arriving with a fine fat spider, which one of the pets is squeezing himself through a hole to

[35] *Port Folio* 8, 2d ser. (July 1812): pp. 7–8; John James Audubon, *My Style of Drawing Birds* (Ardsley, 1979), pp. 17–18; Audubon, "Method of Drawing Birds," in Audubon, *The Complete Audubon* (Kent, 1978–1979), Vol. 4, pp. 21–3; Audubon, "Birds of America, Prospectus" (1827), Broadsides, APS; Audubon, "Drawings Made During a Residence of Upwards of Twenty-Five Years in the United States and Its Territories," Broadsides, APS; Francis Hobart Herrick, *Audubon the Naturalist: A History of His Life and Time* (New York, 1917), Vol. 1, pp. 183–4, 359–60. See Charles Willson Peale, *Introduction to a Course of Lectures on Natural History, Delivered in the University of Pennsylvania, Nov. 16, 1799* (Philadelphia, 1800), pp. 11–12; Audubon in *Monthly American Journal of Geology and Natural Science* 1 (April 1832): pp. 462–3.

get at." His birds sometimes looked directly at the viewer, "creating the startling impression of coming upon the bird and making eye contact." Each conveyed a personality true to its own species.[36]

If anthropomorphizing created a stronger moral bond with animals, so too did the practice of domesticating specimens. This, according to historian John R. Knott, reflected "a blurring of distinctions between wild and domestic that may seem surprising to modern readers." Alexander Wilson kept crows, hawks, owls, opossums, squirrels, snakes, and lizards, and John Godman, who shared his home with several animals, noted from experience that "nothing can possibly exceed the domesticated raccoon in restless and mischievous curiosity." Audubon's beaver gnawed through a door and escaped, and his bobcat, chained in the yard, lured poultry into its reach by leaving bits of food at the door of its house.[37] This intimate although, at times, inconvenient contact changed the relation between observer and observed. Alexander Wilson's "boys" brought him a mouse, which he intended to mount in the claws of a stuffed owl. "The pantings of its little heart showed it to be in the most extreme agonies of fear," he related. It "looked in my face with such an eye of supplicating terror, as [to] perfectly overcome me. I immediately untied it, and restored it to life and liberty." He carried a Carolina parakeet in his pocket on one collecting journey, liberating the bird in the evening and returning it to his pocket for the journey on the following day. Domesticated beavers and snowshoe hares showed affection when caressed and could be taught a variety of tricks. Peale described the "soft cooing notes" voiced by a swan when its former owner returned to the museum. Such signs of affection in animals, he thought, were "sufficient to shew our obligations to treat them [in turn] with kindness."[38]

Botanists were similarly intimate with their subjects. Threeleaf goldthread *(Coptis trifolia)* was a "friendly little plant" growing in the perpetual shade of a sphagnum swamp. "The coldest situations seem to favour its growth," Jacob Bigelow wrote, conveying an obvious admiration for this elegant recluse. Here and elsewhere, he described plant habits

---

[36] *Monthly American Journal of Geology and Natural Science* 1 (April 1832): p. 464; Ann Shelby Blum, *Picturing Nature: American Nineteenth-Century Zoological Illustration* (Princeton, 1993), p. 106; Herrick, *Audubon the Naturalist*, Vol. 1, pp. 359–60.

[37] John R. Knott, *Imagining Wild America* (Ann Arbor, 2002), p. 40; Godman, *American Natural History*, Vol. 1, pp. 168–9; Audubon and Bachman, *Quadrupeds*, Vol. 1, pp. 14, 355. See *Cabinet of Natural History*, p. 58; Anon., *Book of Nature*, p. 43; Alexander Wilson, *American Ornithology* (Philadelphia, 1878), Vol. 1, p. xxix.

[38] Wilson, *American Ornithology*, p. xxix; Wilson and Bonaparte, *American Ornithology*, p. 113, 171; Peale Lectures; Anon., *Book of Nature*, p. 60; *Cabinet of Natural History*, p. 47; *Port Folio*, 2d ser., 8 (July 1812): pp. 7–8.

in active rather than passive voice, as though they carved out their own destinies. According to art historian Barbara Novak, American botanical illustrators were particularly sensitive to the essential qualities of their plants – "the characteristic bend of a leaf, the vector of a stem, the inclination of a petal." Like ornithologists, they achieved this sensitive rendering through close observation in the field, but they were also attentive to the characteristic spirit in all living things: "The growing flower contains in small all the vulnerability of the organic world, which we ourselves share." Botanists, ornithologists, and other naturalists sought out the essence that defined each species – its inner quality – and conveyed this romanticized image in their journals and catalogs.[39]

"The Spark of Divinity": Reason and Emotion in Animals

These anthropomorphic representations gave Americans a more sentimental and romantic image of nature, but they also triggered a more philosophical debate about reason and instinct in animals. If animals acted solely on the instinct, it seemed clear that there was an unbridgeable gap between humans and other species; but, if they acted according to reason, humans and animals had much in common. European naturalists Comte de Buffon and Georges Cuvier considered animals mechanistic, acting out of blind allegiance to the task at hand, like a somnambulist performing "without being conscious of it."[40] Others denied reason in animals because this challenged the idea of divine guidance. A children's devotional instruction written in 1790 pointed out that each bird in a particular species built its nest at exactly the same distance from the ground, in the same style, and with the same materials. Imagine, the writer asked, thousands of workmen building homes in exactly the same fashion: Would "all these workmen [come] . . . together by chance? . . . Would you not rather believe, that some great architect, after having drawn the lines, and contrived the plans, had summoned the workmen, laid down the plans before their eyes, and hired them to work?"[41]

---

[39] Jacob Bigelow, *American Medical Botany* (Boston, 1817–1821), Vol. 1, p. 60; Barbara Novak, "Introduction," in Ella M. Foshay, *Reflections of Nature: Flowers in American Art* (New York, 1984), pp. xv–xvi.

[40] Buffon in William Smellie, *The Philosophy of Natural History* (Edinburgh, 1790), p. 422; *North American Review*, n.s., 63 (July 1846): p. 104.

[41] Charles Christopher Reiche, *Universal Asylum and Columbian Magazine* 5 (November 1790): pp. 335–6. See Bingley, *Animal Biography*, p. 11; Flint, *Lectures upon Natural History*, p. 75; *North American Review*, n.s., 63 (July 1846): p. 118; Draper, *Treatise on the Forces*, p. 5; Charles Buck, *On the Beauties, Harmonies, and Sublimities of Nature* (New York, 1841), pp. 53–4.

Others, supported by a variety of classical, medieval, African, and Native American traditions, saw animals as reasoning creatures. British naturalist, William Smellie, conceded that no animal was endowed with all the powers of the human mind, but each participated in some fashion in rational behavior, displaying a capacity for imagination, imitation, curiosity, cunning, ingenuity, devotion, respect, or gratitude. "They build in various styles; they dig; they wage war; . . . they modulate their voices so as to communicate their wants, their sentiments, their pleasures and pains, their apprehensions of danger, and their prospects of future good."[42] Alexander Wilson placed a jay in a cage with a woodpecker, and the latter delivered "such a drubbing" that he removed the jay and put it in a cage with an oriole. This time, the jay applied the art of diplomacy: He picked up a few chestnut crumbs and in a "humble and peaceable way" offered them to the oriole. "All this ceremonious jealousy vanished before evening, and they now roost together, feed, and play together, in perfect harmony and good humor." Complex problem-solving inspired admiration. Migrating birds seemed to grasp the nuances of weather and season better than humans, William Bartram thought: Did they understand the "metaphysicks, astronomy, or philosophy" of nature's rhythms? "Why not," he declared. "I say, they are ingenious little philosophers, and my esteemed associates."[43]

Although animal sagacity might be contested, almost all naturalists interpreted animal behavior in emotional terms. Some animals were savage or desperately voracious and thus unlike humans, but most expressed familiar feelings: "No doubt the fly enjoys the idle buzzing of its own wings, the bee the hum which accompanies its thrifty flight, and the loud chirrup of the locust is probably as much an expression of ease and pleasure, as the full gush of song from the breast of his neighbor, the merry wren."[44]

[42] Smellie, *Philosophy of Natural History*, p. 157. See Allen G. Debus, *Man and Nature in the Renaissance* (Cambridge, 1978), p. 35; Flint, *Lectures upon Natural History*, p. 31; Priscilla Wakefield, *Instinct Displayed, in a Collection of Well-Authenticated Facts, Exemplifying the Extraordinary Sagacity of Various Species of the Animal Creation* (Boston, 1816), p. v.

[43] Wilson and Bonaparte, *American Ornithology*, pp. 136–7; Anon., *Rural Rambles; Or, Some Chapter on Flowers, Birds, and Insects, By a Lady* (Philadelphia, 1854), pp. 73–4; William Bartram to Benjamin Smith Barton, December 25, 1792, Benjamin Smith Barton Papers, APS. See Bartram, *Travels*, p. lv; Bartram in Ernest Earnest, *John and William Bartram: Botanists and Explorers, 1699–1777; 1739–1823* (Philadelphia, 1940), p. 144.

[44] Susan Fenimore Cooper, *Rural Hours* (New York, 1850), p. 250. See Peale Lectures, APS; Godman, *American Natural History*, Vol. 1, pp. 122, 303.

Raccoons expressed "the greatest delight on meeting after having been separated for a short time, by various movements, and by hugging and rolling one another about on the ground." A male bird offering a feather to his mate became effusive when she accepted it: "He poured forth such a gush of gladsome sound! It seemed as if pride and affection had swelled his heart till it was almost too big for his little bosom." Timothy Flint described these bonds as a universal communion – a "grouping of harmonies, affinities, sensations, affections," in which love inspired all living things, imparting "life to all that lives."[45] The widely shared conclusion that animals were capable of love and affection gave natural history one of its most endearing popular features.

The clearest case for animal emotion was maternal love – the "spark of the divinity," according to Barton, that bound each creature to its fellow beings. Erasmus Darwin thought the attachment of mother to offspring was simply an acquired characteristic, derived from parents by imitation or from a feeling of relief in mammals from nursing. Most American naturalists saw maternal love as innate and therefore a moral bond. Zoologist Richard Harlan related the story of a boy who removed two baby Pennsylvania red bats from a nest. The mother "flutter[ed] . . . round the thoughtless urchin in whose grasp was centered all her hopes," and eventually she settled on the boy's chest, "preferring captivity to freedom, with loss of progeny."[46] The *Cabinet of Curiosities* described a similar sacrifice performed by female birds in luring predators away from their young:

Sometimes, when an enemy approaches, . . . the mother [quail] will . . . throw herself in the path, fluttering along, and beating the ground with her wings, as if sorely wounded. . . . This well-known manoeuvre, which nine times in ten is successful, is honourable to the feelings and judgment of the bird, but a severe satire on man. The affectionate mother, as if sensible of the avaricious cruelty of his nature, tempts him with a larger prize, to save her more helpless offspring; and pays him, as avarice and cruelty ought always to be paid, with mortification and disappointment.[47]

---

[45] *Cabinet of Natural History*, pp. 35, 85; Anon., *Rural Rambles*, pp. 168–9; Flint, *Lectures upon Natural History*, p. 33.

[46] Barton, *Memoir Concerning the Fascinating Faculty*, p. 60; Darwin, *Temple of Nature*, p. 47; Anon., *Life in the Insect World: Or, Conversations upon Insects, Between an Aunt and Her Nieces* (Philadelphia, 1844), pp. 155, 160–1; Richard Harlan, *Fauna Americana: Being a Description of the Mammiferoius Animals Inhabiting North America* (Philadelphia, 1825), pp. 23–4.

[47] *Cabinet of Natural History*, p. 17.

Witnesses to these emotional displays could hardly avoid an ethical judgment: "Can we view these pleasing traits of affection . . . and not esteem them?"[48]

Peale, like several others, chose a lowly spider to make the case for parental love. Preparing a den for the young was equivalent to digging "in a few days out of hard clay or sand, with no other tools than . . . nails and teeth, five or six caverns twenty feet deep and four or five wide," but motherly devotion transformed this insect travail into a willing sacrifice. He wrote, "The kind Author of their being has associated the performance of an especial duty with feelings evidently of the most pleasurable description." William Bartram likewise described a bee digging a den in the seasoned pine of his window frame: "I am sure he'll find his teeth in such a condition to never to afford him any more pleasures. . . . tho' not before leaving seed for another generation with sense to enjoy the same toil when his sire is no more." More than any other form of behavior, maternal sacrifice demonstrated the ethical underpinnings of Bartram's distant intercourse.[49]

Some considered plants rational as well. John Bartram reasoned that "when we nearly examine ye various motions of plants & flowers, in thair evening contraction & morning expantion thay seem to be operated upon by something superior to . . . heat & cold or shade & sunshine." If not reason, he suggested, "it must be some action next degree inferior to it for which we want a proper epithet, or ye immediate finger of god to whome be all glory & praise." The younger Bartram confessed that he was "equally a Friend to, & admirer of the Vegetable Order of Nature" because plants were "undoubtedly animated, organical, active Beings." Rafinesque, too, considered plants sensate: "They . . . direct themselves toward the light. . . . They choose the climates, places, & soils which agree with their constitutions, . . . & they elaborate . . . the juices & liquors which maintain them in health & strength." Flowers shed pollen on the approach of the stigma.[50] The beauty of their petals reflected their joy,

---

[48] Peale Lectures, APS. See Anon., *Book of Nature*, p. 60.

[49] Peale Lectures, APS; William Bartram to Isaac Bartram, 1764 (?), Miscellaneous Collection, APS. See Smellie, *Philosophy of Natural History*, p. 274.

[50] John Bartram to Alexander Garden, March 25, 1762, Berkeley and Berkeley, *Correspondence of John Bartram*, p. 552; William Bartram in Earnest, *John and William Bartram*, pp. 134–5; Constantine Rafinesque, "First Lecture on Botany," Rafinesque Papers, APS; *Port Folio*, 3d ser., 6 (May 1815): p. 429; ibid. (January 1815): pp. 19–20 (September 1815): pp. 237–8; Flint, *Lectures upon Natural History*, pp. 77–8, 122; Smellie, *Philosophy of Natural History*, pp. 5–9; *Monthly American Journal of Geology and Natural Science* 1 (September 1831): pp. 109–11. See William Bartram in Foshay, *Reflections of*

pride, exultation, and love, Timothy Flint explained: Why else would they appear in places where no human eye could witness them?

> I have seen the splendid *nymphaea nelumbo* [water lily] spreading a cup of prodigious size and of the purest and most brilliant white on the surface of the pestilential lakes, in the dark and inundated forests of the Arkansas. Poisonous insects swarmed about them in countless millions. The huge moccasin snake basked upon their broad leaves, and the unwieldy alligator pursued its sports in the deep waters beneath them. Who . . . take[s] pleasure in beholding the splendid wonders of those dreary fens? If these glorious flowers have sensibility from their unions, rear their families, and feel their solitary joys unwitnessed by man, cannot we discover new reasons for placing flowers in the desert?

Were plants, like animals, worthy of moral consideration? Flint thought so: "Should the stately and noble trees of our country thus cry out against every rude Vandal who cut them down without necessity, what an appalling shout would issue from our groves!"[51]

In several works written in the mid-eighteenth century, Swiss philosopher Jean-Jacques Rousseau argued that ethical considerations should extend beyond the human race. Animals, he felt, were sentient and therefore worthy of pity, and if human compassion had not been suppressed by civilized society, people would feel a kinship with other creatures. In America, the Bartrams were known for their belief that both plants and animals were sentient, and this conviction informed their ethical approach to nature. Early in his travels, Bartram killed any snake that crossed his path but, as he grew older, he would simply "tease" them to observe their reactions; as his son William put it, "we are no murderers."[52]

Like his father, the younger Bartram considered snakes, like humans, morally complex. When agitated, they presented a horrible visage: "His beautiful particoloured skin becomes speckled and rough by dilation, his head and neck are flattened, his cheeks swollen and his lips constricted, discovering his mortal fangs; his eyes red as burning coals, and his brandishing forked tongue of the colour of the hottest flame, continually menaces death and destruction." Yet, their behavior was not altogether malevolent. Bartram once passed a coiled snake unknowingly

Nature, p. 29; Thomas P. Slaughter, *The Natures of John and William Bartram* (New York: Alfred A. Knopf, 1996), p. 64.

[51] Flint, *Lectures upon Natural History*, pp. 43, 47.

[52] Steve Vanderheiden, "Rousseau, Cronon, and the Wilderness Idea," *Environmental Ethics* 24 (Summer 2002): pp. 173–4; John Bartram to Mark Catesby, August 8, 1763, Berkeley and Berkeley, *Correspondence of John Bartram*, p. 606; John Bartram, letter, n.d., Vol. 1, file 102, Bartram Family Papers, PHS.

several times during the night while carrying water to his camp. "However incredible it may appear, the generous, I may say magnanimous creature lay as still and motionless as if inanimate." Clearly, the snake could have chosen to attack, but it declined, and Bartram pondered its mood and message. As a youth, he, like his father, had routinely killed snakes, but this creature's forbearance altered his thinking: "I promised myself that I would never again be accessary to the death of a rattle snake, which promise I have invariably kept to." The serpent had made a moral choice regarding Bartram's life, and the naturalist could do no less.[53] In this flash of communion with another creature, Bartram laid out the emerging premise of romantic zoology. Humans, like animals, were engaged in a distant intercourse – a web of morality that connected all of nature.

The lesson Bartram drew from this encounter was well represented in his *Travels*, the most notable incident being his description of a guide shooting a mother bear alongside her cub.

Not seemingly the least moved at the report of our piece, [the cub] approached the dead body, smelled, and pawed it, and appearing in agony, fell to weeping and looking upwards, then towards us, and cried out like a child. Whilst our boat approached very near, the hunter was loading his rifle in order to shoot the survivor.... The continual cries of this afflicted child, bereft of its parent, affected me very sensibly, I was moved with compassion, and charging myself as if accessary to what now appeared to be a cruel murder, and endeavoured to prevail on the hunter to save its life, but to no effect! For by habit he had become insensible to compassion towards the brute creation, [and] being now within a few yards of the harmless devoted victim, he fired, and laid it dead, upon the body of the dam.[54]

Bartram conjectured that a person more sensitive to the emotional bond between mother and cub would have avoided this act of cruelty: there would be no "slaughter of the bears."[55]

In what might have been the draft of a letter dating from around 1774, Bartram outlined his beliefs on animal nature, a matter of "little moment to mankind in general at this time, yet to me of much importance." Linnaeus divided the world into three kingdoms and placed humans at the head of the highest of these divisions. Bartram challenged this grand system, particularly the "bland assumption" that humans stood at the

53 Bartram, *Travels*, pp. 167, 170. See Noah Webster, *History of Animals* (New Haven, 1812), p. 224.
54 Bartram, *Travels*, p. lvii. See Earnest, *John and William Bartram*, p. 143.
55 Bartram, *Travels*, p. lvii.

pinnacle of creation. "I will agree that it is impossible that any animal...can weave a piece of brocade, make a compleat ship, a watch or clock, mariners compass, iron or steel, a sewing needle...[but] it is equally impossible for man to make a spiders web, a honeycomb with wax & honey after the manner of the *Apis mellifica* [honeybee]." Humans exceeded other animals in the comprehensiveness of their rational powers, but animals, he thought, possessed a higher moral integrity. They conducted no national wars and engaged in no manner of "madness, brutality, wretchedness, and depravity of nature." When predators were not obliged by hunger to kill, their behavior indicated a moral sensibility. They might be "Heaven instructed," as some insisted, but in Bartram's judgment, this was simply reason by another name: an emanation from "the Immortal Soul of Nature."[56] Bartram saw this divine fellowship as a moral web rather than a hierarchy of being. Intelligence allowed humans to "subjugate & even tyrannize over every other animal," but this dominion gave them no claim to superiority. "I cannot believe, I cannot be so impious, nay my Soul revolts, is destroyed by such conjectures as to desire or imagine, that Man who is guilty of more mischief & wickedness than all the other Animals together in this World, should be exclusively endowed with knowledge of the Creator & capable of imposing his love gratitude & homage to the Great Author of Being." In Bartram's web of nature, animals provided a moral guide for human behavior because they acted on simple passions like love, maternal affection, sacrifice, courageousness, and fortitude.[57]

Bartram never published his thoughts on the moral web of nature, but the implications of his pan-rationalism informed his general approach to natural history. "Within the circle of my acquaintance I am known to be an advocate or vindicator of the benevolent and peaceable disposition of animal creation," he wrote in his *Travels*. In this, he was somewhat unique: His philosophy was inspired by his own upbringing and temperament, his Quaker sense of humility, his love of natural beauty, and his

---

[56] William Bartram, untitled paper, Vol. 1, file 81, Bartram Family Papers, PHS (emphasis removed). See Bartram to Benjamin Smith Barton, December 25, 1792, Barton Papers APS; Bartram, letter, n.d., Vol. 1, file 102, Bartram Family Papers, PHS; Earnest, *John and William Bartram*, pp. 144–5; Bartram in N. Bryllion Fagin, *William Bartram: Interpreter of the American Landscape* (Baltimore, 1933), p. 42; Kerry S. Walters, "The 'Peaceable Disposition' of Animals: William Bartram on the Moral Sensibility of Brute Creation," *Pennsylvania History* 56 (No. 3, 1989), pp. 169–71.

[57] William Bartram, untitled paper, Vol. 1, file 81, Bartram Family Papers, PHS; Bartram, letter, n.d., Vol. 1, folder 83, Bartram Family Papers, PHS.

somewhat reclusive preference for nature over civilization. His moral sensibilities, historian Kerry Walters wrote, "are frequently written off even today as the sentimentalities of a naive romantic," but this is inappropriate: Bartram's compassion rested on a lifetime of empirical observation and careful philosophical reasoning within the logical framework of his time, and his ethical vision, also apparent in the "Peaceable Kingdom" landscape paintings by fellow Quaker Philadelphian Edward Hicks, influenced other naturalists.[58] Charles Willson Peale elaborated on Bartram's curious ethical reversal: Do animals, he asked, levy war against their kind? "Does the Lyon destroy the Lyon? – does the Hawk prey upon Hawk? . . . No! So foul an infamy is found alone on man!" The analogy, according to Walters, "gave rise to an environmental vision of universal harmony between humans and nature in which divinely inspired love and compassion would overcome intolerance, species-chauvinism, and utilitarian abuse of land."[59]

Although few American scientists followed Bartram this far in his exploration of animal sagacity, the argument that animals should be treated with respect for practical, religious, or ecological reasons echoed through the scientific community. John Lee Comstock, author of youth books on natural history, hoped to "impress on the mind of the child, that brutes, though they cannot speak and reason, are not therefore mere machines, but that they are subjects of pain, of pleasure, and of attachments like ourselves."[60] Another naturalist lectured young readers on their treatment of birds and fishes: "Though they cannot cry, and make a pitiful noise when they are hurt, [they] have feeling as well as you, and like you, were made by the Great Creator of Heaven and Earth, for some good purpose." Rebecca Eaton wrote her *Geography of Pennsylvania* to encourage "feelings of benevolence" toward God's creatures, who "ought . . . to [be] consider[ed] as brethren."[61] After inspecting a mother opossum, Benjamin Barton related that there was "one particular fact with respect to this animal, which I have myself witnessed, and

---

[58] Bartram, *Travels*, p. 168. See Walters, "'Peaceable Disposition' of Animals," pp. 158–9, 163–4, 168, 171–2.

[59] Peale, *Introduction to a Course of Lectures*, p. 9; Walters, "'Peaceable Disposition' of Animals," p. 164.

[60] J. L. [John Lee] Comstock, *Natural History of Quadrupeds* (Hartford, 1829), pp. ii–iii.

[61] Anon., *Life in the Insect World*, pp. 33–4, 241; Comstock, *Natural History of Quadrupeds*, p. 78; Rebecca Eaton, *A Geography of Pennsylvania for the Use of Schools, and Private Families* (Philadelphia, 1835), p. 2; J. F. Cropsey in Novak, *Nature and Culture*, p. 5.

FIGURE 6.2. The argument that animals should be treated with respect for practical, religious, or ecological reasons echoed through the scientific literature. After inspecting a mother opossum, Benjamin Smith Barton related that he was "sometimes almost deterred" when opening the mother's marsupium by her distressed and supplicating manner: She seemed to be shedding tears. The debate over animal passions linked science and romanticism in proclaiming the dignity and sensibility of all living creatures. Anonymous, "Quadrupeds," *The Book of Nature* (1826), detail of the original. Courtesy of the Library Company of Philadelphia.

which sometimes almost deterred me from prosecuting my inquiries into [its] . . . history. . . . I have seen the mother, when her marsupium has been opened (and tenderly opened) to bring into view the contained embryons, manifest her distress by a kind of supplicating manner – and evidently shed tears!"[62]

The debate over animal sagacity linked empirical rationalism to the emerging romantic appreciation for the dignity and sensibility of all living creatures. Historian Elsa Guerdrum Allen notes a shift in natural history in the early nineteenth century from "objective knowledge" to a "deeper more contemplative interest." This contemplative inquiry raised ethical questions: Were humans and animals linked in the same moral web? If animals showed such compassion among themselves, were they not worthy of human concern? Bartram's distant intercourse echoed in the moral

[62] Benjamin Smith Barton, *Additional Facts, Observations, and Conjectures Relative to the Generation of the Opossum of North-America* (Philadelphia, 1813), p. 20.

tone of other zoological treatises, bearing witness to the observation made by Hans Huth nearly a half-century ago that as scientists delved more deeply into the dynamics and purposes of life on earth, their "dogmatic limitations" gave way to "an entirely new relationship... between man and nature." Although this understanding was shared among a relatively small group of scientific writers, it laid the foundation for a romantic perception of nature in the decades to follow, and for the conservation movement that emerged at the end of the century.[63]

Extinction and the Logic of Nature

In his detailed natural history of the opossum, Benjamin Barton noted that the creature was edible and even marketable but, indeed, no delicacy. Although there was little reason to hunt this harmless woodland creature, he felt certain it would become wholly extinct as the settlement frontier pushed westward, and he predicted a similar fate for other creatures whose languid habits rendered them vulnerable to human killing instincts. "Future naturalists will only know these animals by their histories and pictures, which may be preserved, as we now know the *elephas mastodontus*, the *megatheria*, and other lost animals, by their bones."[64]

Extinction was a matter of endless scientific debate. Here, indeed, were "vast organized bodies, many of them... endowed with an immense portion of intelligence, which the God of Nature had created; and after suffering them to grow and exist through ages,... has, at length entirely removed from the earth; not merely as individuals, but as species." There was something awesome in the subject, Barton thought, because it raised fundamental questions about divine planning and perfection in nature. If species were interdependent, how could God condone extinction? Was not the harmony of nature disturbed by the total destruction of "what many have deemed necessary integral parts of a common whole"? Did new species appear, according to design, to replace them? Extinction was undoubtedly part of God's plan, but its logic was by no means apparent.[65]

---

[63] Elsa Guerdrum Allen, *The History of American Ornithology Before Audubon* (Philadelphia, 1951), p. 543; Hans Huth, *Nature and the American: Three Centuries of Changing Attitudes* (Berkeley, 1957), p. 23.

[64] Barton, *Conjectures Relative to the Generation of the Opossum*, pp. 18–19.

[65] Benjamin Smith Barton, *Archaeologiae Americannae Telluris Collectanea et Specimina, Or Collections with Specimens, for a Series of Memoirs on Certain Extinct Animals and Vegetables of North-America* (Philadelphia, 1814), pp. 32–3.

And, if extinction in the geological past was difficult to explain, no less so was the human role in the destruction of an entire species.

Not everyone saw extinction as evil. In Massachusetts, Ebenezer Emmons observed, moose had disappeared more than thirty years earlier, and to this his reaction was mixed:

> In some respects, it is desirable that so fine an animal should be saved from entire extirpation, though it is quite doubtful whether it could be made profitable to man in the present state of society. If it could be suffered to exist in those parts of the country which are so sterile and cold that they cannot be cultivated with much profit, it is all that could be expected or wished for. Its meat is certainly delicious.... However, ... so far as game and hunting are concerned, the sooner our wild animals are extinct the better, for they serve to support a few individuals just on the borders of a savage state, whose labors in the family of man are more injurious than beneficial. It is not, therefore, so much to be regretted that our larger animals of the chase have disappeared. What comforts their fur and their skins have provided, can be abundantly supplied by animals already domesticated, at far less expense, both of time and money, and are not subject to that drawback, the deterioration of morals.[66]

Perhaps, some thought, the balance of nature could be restored by incorporating wild animals into the systems of husbandry that displaced them. Jared Kirtland recommended domestic deer, elk, and buffalo to replace those lost to extinction in Ohio. A buffalo, he thought, could be "taught to yield its neck to the yoke as well as the Ox." Farmers found wild turkeys, ducks, geese, prairie hens, pheasant, quail, and partridge useful in the barnyard, and several fish varieties had been cultivated behind the milldams that destroyed their indigenous cousins. Beaver, otter, and muskrat could be farmed or even kept as house pets. Introductions were as easy as extinctions.[67]

Audubon, who witnessed the destruction of nature on a grand scale as he traveled across the frontier, was similarly ambivalent. The self-proclaimed "American Woodsman" took great pride in his hunting prowess and, like other ornithologists, he shot birds in astounding numbers in order to perfect his drawings. He once shot twenty-five brown pelicans to revise one drawing of the adult male bird. "I really believe I would have shot one hundred of these reverend sirs, had not a mistake taken place in the reloading of my gun." Given the scope of his *Birds*

---

[66] Ebenezer Emmons, *A Report on the Quadrupeds of Massachusetts* (Cambridge, 1840), pp. 75–7.

[67] Jared P. Kirtland, "Report," in William Williams Mather, *First Annual Report on the Geological Survey of the State of Ohio* (Columbus, 1838), pp. 67–8.

Engineer Cantonement Mo.
1820

FIGURE 6.3. Naturalists took a heavy toll in the birds and animals they killed
for scientific study. Audubon, like other ornithologists, shot birds in astounding
numbers in order to perfect his drawings. Yet, he and others weighed the ethical
arguments for protecting certain species and encouraged wildlife preservation
for sentimental, practical, and ecological reasons. Titian Ramsay Peale, *Sketches,
1817–1875*. Courtesy of the American Philosophical Society.

of America, this suggests a truly exhausting demand, and Audubon also
supplied birds to museums and other collectors. Unlike the Bartrams,
he clearly relished the hunt.[68] Yet, as biographer Francis Herrick pointed
out, all ornithologists hunted extensively before the excesses of the feather
trade were known widely; in his time, these scientific kills would not have
seemed extraordinary. And, despite his own excesses, Audubon was critical of those who wasted game. "More than once, out of compassion for
individual birds that he chanced to be studying,... he would not permit
them to be shot even when needed for his collections."[69]

Audubon was concerned for species preservation, if not for individual birds or mammals. In part, this reflects his attempt to romanticize
his bird and animal descriptions, biographer John Knott observes, but in
some cases it was more than sentimentalism.[70] Bison, he and Bachman

[68] John James Audubon in *Monthly American Journal of Geology and Natural Science* 1
(February 1832): pp. 408–9; Audubon, *Complete Audubon*, Vol. 4, p. 24.

[69] Herrick, *Audubon the Naturalist*, Vol. 2, p. 17; ibid., Vol. 1, p. 239.

[70] Audubon, *Complete Audubon*, Vol. 4, pp. 22–3; Knott, *Imagining Wild America*,
pp. 41, 43.

wrote in *Quadrupeds of North America*, were "decidedly the most important of all our contemporary American quadrupeds," a link between the mastodon and the less magnificent modern ungulates, and their loss would be a "terrible destruction of life," made doubly so by the frivolity of the hunt. Having been driven to the "arid and nearly impassable deserts of the western table lands," they would, "like the Great Auk," eventually disappear. Having linked the buffalo to the auk and the mammoth, the authors reminded readers that losses like these were irreversible: "And here we may be allowed to express our deep, though unavailing regret, that the world now contains only few and imperfect remains of the lost races, of which we have our sole knowledge through the researches and profound deductions of geologists."[71]

Against a backdrop of growing appreciation for nature's interrelatedness, American scientists wavered between sanctioning the manipulation – even eradication – of animals and concern for their preservation. Surveying the countryside around Philadelphia in 1763, John Bartram noted that "all our small creeks used to abound with trouts, but I have not seen one catched these three or four years... nor one wild goose, a very few ducks, and but three or four small flocks of turkeys." The woods of western New York, once abounding in game, were now "still as death," William Strickland wrote as early as 1794.[72] Beaver drew the greatest concern among naturalists, given their humanlike social and engineering behavior; Barton admitted that he had "sometimes been so extravagant as to wish that the laws of my country were extended, in their influence, to the protection of this sagacious quadruped." Likewise, Crèvecoeur mourned the passing of the beaver – "the philosophers of the animals; the gentlest, the most humble, the most harmless." During one massacre he watched, the victims "shed tears, and I wept also; nor am I ashamed to confess it." The most anthropomorphized of all North American animals, the beaver best expressed the connection between affinity with wildlife and concern for its preservation.[73]

[71] Audubon and Bachman, *Quadrupeds*, Vol. 2, pp. 35–6; Audubon in Herrick, *Audubon the Naturalist*, Vol. 2, pp. 255–6.

[72] John Bartram to Peter Collinson, January 6, 1763, Darlington, *Memorials of John Bartram and Humphrey Marshall*, p. 245; William Strickland, *Journal of a Tour in the United States of America, 1794–1795* (New York, 1971), pp. 146–7; *North American Review*, n.s., 41 (October 1835): p. 427.

[73] Benjamin Smith Barton, "On the Animals of North America," pp. 1, 11, Barton Papers, APS; Godman, *American Natural History*, Vol. 2, pp. 34, 34–5; Crèvecoeur, *Letters from an American Farmer*, p. 301. See John Andrew Graham, *A Descriptive Sketch of*

Given the complex and delicate intercourse they discovered among animals, naturalists found the settler's callous destruction alarming. John Palmer watched hunters destroy whole forests by driving game with fire, leaving behind a dreary legacy of barren tree trunks and wasted animals. William Byrd recounted the devastating scene:

It is really a pitiful sight to see the extreme distress the poor deer are in, when they find themselves surrounded with this circle of fire; they weep and groan like a human creature, yet can't move the compassion of those hard-hearted people, who are about to murder them. This unmerciful sport is called fire hunting, and is much practic'd by the Indians and Frontier Inhabitants, who sometimes, in the eagerness of their diversion, are punish't for their cruelty, and are hurt by one another when they shoot across at the deer which are in the middle.[74]

Kentucky's deserted salt licks told a similar story. Buffalo once arrived in unending trains, tens of thousands in a herd. One settler recalled killing six or seven hundred for the skins, and when he returned two years later, he repeated the process, leaving the "mangled and putrid bodies" on the ground. Thomas Ashe, who listened to this tale, found it appalling: "In consequence of such proceedings, not one buffaloe is at this time to be found east of the Mississippi; except a few domesticated by the curious, or carried through the country as a public shew."[75]

Amid the ecological carnage of the pioneering moment, naturalists found their scientific principles of balance and harmony severely challenged. Elk, moose, and beaver were all but extinct east of the Appalachians, and deer, muskrat, and caribou were becoming rare.[76] Ohio's Daniel Drake declared in 1818 that the larger quadrupeds had become "so rare as to be unknown to all but our oldest emigrants." Samuel Hildreth remembered earlier days when the woods were full of buffalo, deer, bear,

the Present State of Vermont, One of the United States of America (London, 1797), p. 88; Godman, *American Natural History*, Vol. 2, pp. 22–3, 25, 35.

74 John Palmer, *Journal of Travels in the United States of North America, and in Lower Canada, Performed in the Year 1817* (London, 1818), p. 44; Byrd, *History of the Dividing Line*, p. 170.

75 Thomas Ashe, *Travels in America, Performed in 1806, For the Purpose of Exploring the Rivers Allegheny, Monongahela, Ohio, and Mississippi* (Newburyport, 1808), pp. 48, 134.

76 Palmer, *Journal of Travels in the United States*, p. 115; Benjamin Smith Barton, "On the Animals of North America," p. 4, Barton Papers, APS; Emmons, *Quadrupeds of Massachusetts*, p. 79; Timothy Dwight, *Travels in New England and New York*, Barbara Miller Solomon and Patricia M. King (eds.) (Cambridge, 1969), pp. 33, 125; John Brickell, *The Natural History of North-Carolina, with an Account of the Trade, Manners, and Customs of the Christian and Indian Inhabitants* (Dublin, 1737), pp. 107–8.

and wolf, and although he passed no judgment on those who destroyed them, his natural histories included a wistful lament: Where the hunter once lived in plenty on the spoils of the chase, it would be difficult to find "a single victim for his rifle." Even the fish had deserted his beloved Muskingum.[77] "Nothing but the establishment of laws," Barton concluded, "will prevent many of our animals from being almost entirely extirpated, in a few years, through the whole of that extensive tract of territory within the limits of the United States." Thomas Green Fessenden pointed to an "alarming increase of worms and insects in making ravages upon our fruit-trees" as birds disappeared from the woods and fields.[78] This "thoughtless cruelty," Charles Willson Peale insisted, would "scarcely be known" if naturalists could impress upon the public the fact that "the same god 'who gives lustre to an insects wing' ordains with it a right to life and happiness as well as ourselves."[79]

Peale's thoughts on theology and killing highlighted an argument against species destruction taking shape in the first decades of the nineteenth century. If, indeed, all nature was a reflection of God's benevolence, then thoughtless destruction was a form of desecration. There was a certain irony in this point of view, as Audubon's avid bird-collecting made evident. Barbara Novak points out that the beauty of the flower "equally demands to be left alone in situ and invites amputation," and more than one naturalist found it necessary to kill the living creature to preserve the archetype.[80] However, in harboring this contradiction, naturalists learned to condemn at least the unnecessary destruction of birds and animals. Acutely aware of nature's distant intercourse – the delicate and divine web that connected species to species – they began to express their reservations, although with ambivalence, about the settlement process that seemed so central to the destiny of the nation. Nature was designed

---

[77] Daniel Drake, et al., in *American Journal of Science* 1 (1818): pp. 204–5; Samuel Deane, *The New-England Farmer* (Worcester, MA, 1790), p. 5; *Monthly American Journal of Geology and Natural Science* 1 (October 1831): pp. 186–8; Samuel P. Hildreth, *Contributions to the Early History of the North-West* (Cincinnati, 1864), pp. 18–19; Flint, *Lectures upon Natural History*, p. 33.

[78] Benjamin Smith Barton, "On the Animals of North America," p. 10, Barton Papers, APS; Thomas Green Fessenden, *The Complete Farmer and Rural Economist* (Boston, 1835), p. 307–9.

[79] Bonaparte, *American Ornithology*, p. 80; Bigland, *Natural History of Birds, Fishes, Reptiles, and Insects*, p. 128; Charles Willson Peale, "Lecture No. 2, 'Natural History and the Museum,'" Peale Lectures, APS. See Godman, *American Natural History*, Vol. 2, pp. 34, 307.

[80] William Bartram in Fagin, *William Bartram*, p. 48; Barbara Novak, "Introduction," Foshay, *Reflections of Nature*, p. xvii.

by providence as the abode of humankind, and the settler was compelled to improve this untilled garden and control or eliminate its recalcitrant forms. Yet, the willful destruction of entire species seemed strangely at odds with the naturalists' understanding of this destiny. Although they offered no answers, they raised questions, and thus fueled a debate that would echo through the rest of the century.

PART THREE

IMPROVERS, ROMANTICS, AND THE SCIENCE OF CONSERVATION

7

From Forest to Fruitful Field

Settlement and Improvement in the Western Wilderness

On September 21, 1796, Yale College President Timothy Dwight set out on a journey of discovery along the northeastern coast of America. A man of wide-ranging intellectual pursuits, Dwight was the grandson of Jonathan Edwards and, like his famous relative, he was a respected man of religion and letters. Entering Yale College at age 13, he received a master's degree at age 20. He was a chaplain in the Continental Army, a member of the Connecticut legislature, a farmer, a preacher, and, in 1795, president of Yale College, where he taught philosophy, theology, literature, and oratory and published poems, satires, religious tracts, and hymns. Seeking respite from his college duties, he decided to travel during his summers and kept his observations in a journal. Although not trained as a naturalist, he was a careful observer with a keen interest in natural process. "He looked at nature . . . with the eye of a poet, a philosopher, and a Christian," an early biographer wrote. "He loved . . . to mark the laws that regulate the various works of God, from the minutest insect to the starry heavens." Dwight also loved to mark the laws of civil progress in the places he visited; but, in a society changing so rapidly, this was a challenge. The countryside, he wrote, "must, if truly exhibited, be described in a manner resembling that in which a painter would depict a cloud. The form and colors of the moment must be seized, or the picture will be erroneous."[1]

---

[1] Timothy Dwight, *Travels in New England and New York*, Barbara Miller Solomon and Patricia M. King (eds.) (Cambridge, 1969), pp. 6, 8, 9; Henry T. Tuckerman, *America and Her Commentators, with a Critical Sketch of Travel in the United States* (New York, 1864), p. 391; *Port Folio*, 4th ser., 4 (November 1817): p. 361.

This evanescence was especially pronounced in the so-called uncultivated districts. The term, used to describe the pioneering fringe west of the established settlements, was itself pregnant with meaning, suggesting a state of becoming – a place of expectations. Although difficult to describe, these were the districts that fascinated Dwight. "The conversion of a wilderness into a desirable residence for man," he wrote, "is an object which no intelligent spectator can behold without... strong... interest.... A forest, changed with a short period into fruitful fields... can hardly fail to delight." This, indeed, was the new republic's crowning achievement, encompassing new forms of government, arts, education, sciences, and religion, all freshly forged in the crucible of wild nature. Dwight's interest in America's progress was shared by spectators across the Atlantic World and, thus, the pioneering moment, fleeting though it was, became infused with moral drama. Converting the wilderness was a duty, a mission to "cut down the trees, and open... the fields to the enlivening influence of the air and the sun."[2]

To most observers, the settlement process seemed deceptively simple. Emigrants purchased one or two hundred acres from the government or from land companies and, with assistance from neighbors, constructed a hut of notched logs. They plastered the cracks in the walls with clay, moss, or straw, and covered the roof with bark or split boards. A drystone chimney directed smoke from the fire through a hole in the roof, and another hole served as a window. With shelter provided, the family began pushing back the forest by some combination of chopping, girdling, and burning. With a brush harrow, they turned the ash-strewn soil and, among the charred stumps or dying trees, planted a crop of corn, buckwheat, or wheat. Soon, Basil Hall wrote, a civilization emerged "in the shape of a smoky log-hut, ten feet by twelve, filled with dirty-faced children, squatted round a hardy looking female [and]... a tired woodsman seated at his door, reading with suitable glee... the *Democratical Journal* of New York."[3] This was not exactly Dwight's fruitful field but, over time, the stumps decayed, the fences improved, the weeds diminished, and the proprietor became a Whig.[4]

---

[2] Dwight, *Travels in New England and New York*, p. ix. See ibid., pp. x, 1, 6, 7, 130; Tench Coxe, *A View of the United States of America* (Philadelphia, 1794), p. 1.

[3] Basil Hall, *Travels in North America, in the Years 1827 and 1828* (Philadelphia, 1829), Vol. 1, p. 75; Jeremy Belknap, *History of New-Hampshire* (Dover, 1812), Vol. 3, pp. 195–6; I. Finch, *Travels in the United States of America and Canada* (London, 1833), p. 319.

[4] Samuel Williams, *The Natural and Civil History of Vermont* (Burlington, 1809), Vol. 1, p. 8.

With ax and hoe, the pioneer family could only do so much to expand the agrarian republic but, given the numbers of emigrants, the effect was dramatic. The older sections of America seemed to be breaking up and moving westward, Englishman Morris Birkbeck thought. During his journey over the Appalachians in 1819, Thomas Nuttall wrote, "All day I have been brushing past waggons heavily loaded with merchandise, each drawn by five and six horses." The road he traveled appeared like "the cavalcade of a continued fair." Gazing west from the ridges of the Alleghenies, Giacomo Beltrami pondered this flood of migrants, free of want and "as prolific as the soil." In a few years, "the spot which only swarmed with insects, swarms with children, the log-house becomes a hamlet, a village, a town, the capital of a province," and the frontier moved another hundred miles to the west. Compressing a thousand years of development on a European scale into a single generation, this was clearly a transformation unlike any in the history of Western civilization.[5]

Like many observant travelers, Dwight stamped this process with a sense of inevitability by describing the rise of civilization as a progression of stages, beginning with the primitive hunters and trappers who laid the groundwork for succeeding waves of better-off farmers and townsfolk. Like the blossoming flower or the metamorphosing insect, the primitive clearing was destined to become a settled republican society.[6] In Dwight's estimation, New Englanders were particularly disposed to realize this destiny. New England sent forth "the only people on this continent who originally understood, and have ever since maintained, the inseparable connection between liberty and good order, . . . who . . . knew that genuine freedom is found only beneath the undisturbed dominion of equitable laws." Dwight's faith in the New Englander is understandable, given his deep roots in Puritan divinity, but it also conveyed an ambiguous message about the rest of this human tide sweeping westward across the Appalachians. It was clear that the settler would change the wilderness but, for better or worse, the wilderness would change the settler as well.

---

5 Thomas Nuttall, *Journal of Travels into the Arkansa [sic] Territory, During the Year 1819* (Philadelphia, 1821), p. 14; Morris Birkbeck, *Notes on a Journey in America, from the Coast of Virginia to the Territory of Illinois* (Philadelphia, 1817), pp. 38–40, 34; Giacomo Constantino Beltrami, *A Pilgrimage in Europe and America* (London, 1828), pp. 95–6.

6 Dwight, *Travels in New England and New York*, pp. xxxiii–xxxiv, 218; Joseph Churchman, *Rudiments of Natural Knowledge, Presented to the Youth of the United States, and to Enquiring Foreigners* (Philadelphia, 1833), p. 250. See Angela Miller, *The Empire of the Eye: Landscape Representation and American Cultural Politics, 1825–1875* (Ithaca, 1993), p. 82; Andrew R. L. Cayton, *The Frontier Republic: Ideology and Politics in the Ohio Country, 1780–1825* (Kent, 1986), p. 15.

Did the pioneer possess the strength of character to maintain the "inseparable connection between liberty and good order"? In an era fascinated
by causal links between civilization and nature, there were ample grounds
for concern.[7]

Like Dwight, America's naturalists celebrated the westward movement. A coming-together of evolutionary naturalism and manifest destiny, the change from forest to fruitful field would complete the logic of
the integrated landscape. Yet, like Dwight, they displayed a subtle uncertainty about the pioneering family in its new wilderness home. These misgivings brought the first systematic expressions of conservation thought
in America.

Settlement and Civilization

In 1856, Jacob Ferris published a sweeping history of the American frontier titled *The States and Territories of the Great West*, in which he
chronicled the advance of the pioneer into the trans-Appalachian frontier. He, too, celebrated this national pageant but, again, his feelings were
mixed. Pioneers would certainly subdue the wilderness, but what sort of
civilization would they create out of the coarse fabric of primal nature?
Would this land of free spirits bend to the obligations and constraints of
an untested government? He regarded the West, as he said, with "min-
gled emotions of curiosity and dread" – not yet altogether clear, even
as late as 1856, about how this dance of settlement and savagery would
end.[8]

The western wilderness, Ferris began, might be compared to a vast
ocean: Both were beyond the reach of civilizing institutions and both
were lawless and perilous places. Both had their busy ports, where the
moral and amoral landscapes met, and, in both cases, these ports swarmed
with people uprooted and on the move. On the northern frontier, Albany
and Pittsburgh competed for the role of entrepôt to the West, and each
was, accordingly, a place of ambiguities, wildly inconsistent in its cultural achievements and its displays of base instinct. Passing beyond these
portals was an adventure indeed.[9] Just as life at sea became coarse and
spiritually destitute, so the western traveler entered the oceanic forest at
considerable moral risk.

---

[7] Dwight, *Travels in New England and New York*, p. 123.
[8] Jacob Ferris, *The States and Territories of the Great West* (New York, 1856), p. 13.
[9] Ferris, *States and Territories of the Great West*, p. 100.

Ferris opened his history by following a fictional family westward across the Appalachians and down into the broad Ohio Valley. As they approached the mountains, fields became the exception, and the dark forest closed in. "Savage sights and savage sounds" accentuated their estrangement from civilization, and huge trees "lifted on high their umbrageous tops, and shut out the heavens." Displaying the steady resolve familiar in later celebrations of the West, the family continued, "day after day, amid scenes of solitary grandeur . . . with no other guides than the sun and stars." The deeper they plunged into the woods, the more sullen nature became. Branches that "danced to the music of the winds" at the beginning of the journey "writhe[d] . . . and shriek[ed]" in the storm-tossed western landscape. Gone was the sense of wonder at God's creation. "The woods of a country . . . [being], uniform, . . . after a while, began to blunt the senses and weigh down upon the spirits," Ferris explained; "the most attractive scenery, if perpetually before the eyes, will lose its power to please." Taking from nature their dress, their log houses, their furniture, and their food, settlers assumed a character as monotonous as the land itself. "How they cracked jokes over their victuals, seated around on the carpet of leaves, and laughed, and shouted, and poked fun at each other. Altogether, it was a delightful picnic. But picnics, three times a day for a month or two, will become odious."[10]

Despite their epic resolve, Ferris's pioneers were morally vulnerable. Perhaps they would advance along the path to civilization or, perhaps, Ferris's account suggested, they might just as easily take on the character of the land around them. "A great deal of the literature in the early United States was vested in this process of making one's home in a wilderness," historian Thomas Hallock writes, "and the narratives often take unexpected – on the surface, contradictory – turns as they grapple with the paradoxes of expansion."[11]

Hoping to understand the relationship between nature and society, observers scrutinized the pioneer. From the stony soils of New England came a hardy, calculating, and frugal migrant, and from the South a more impetuous and adventuresome counterpart, whereas Europe sent a diverse crowd of peasants and yeomen chasing exaggerated rumors of

---

[10] Ferris, *States and Territories of the Great West*, pp. 20, 21, 25–7, 142.

[11] Ferris, *States and Territories of the Great West*, p. 25; Thomas Hallock, *From the Fallen Tree: Frontier Narratives, Environmental Politics, and the Roots of a National Pastoral, 1749–1826* (Chapel Hill, 2003), pp. 4, 6; Cayton, *Frontier Republic*, pp. x, 8. See Gregory H. Nobles, "Breaking into the Backcountry: New Approaches to the Early American Frontier," *William and Mary Quarterly* 46 (October 1989), pp. 644–5.

land and liberty. The typical settler seemed "bold, hardy, manly, hos-
pitable, generous, and kind-hearted" and, yet, at the same time, "violent
and vindictive in temper, reckless, improvident, often intemperate, and
almost always without local attachment." Anthony Trollope concluded
that "one never meets an uncivil or unruly man, but the women of the
lower ranks are not courteous"; Joseph Whipple insisted that backwoods
women were "generally much more polished" than the men.[12] Class
distinctions offered no guide whatsoever. "Men who are appointed Captains, or Majors, and may have been present at trainings for a short
time, are called Captains or Majors ever afterwards.... The persons who
take charge of keel-boats are also Captains.... All are gentlemen. The
wife is, of course, Mrs.; the daughter and maidservant are indiscriminately saluted Miss, or Madam." The pioneer represented not so much
a regional or national character or a social class but rather a "collection of isolated independent individuals."[13] Beltrami considered them
"as laborious as the Swiss; as frugal and economical as the Tyrolese...;
as cunning and industrious as the Genoese; as droll as the Gascons; as
cold and proud as the English; and as selfish and avaricious as those men
of all nations who banish themselves from their country to make money."
David Thomas, an American who deplored the characterizations made
by "roving foreigners," added a precaution: Those who judged the new
nation ought not forget "that the track of a traveller is but a line drawn
through a country."[14]

The motives behind this pioneering impulse were equally as mysterious.
Some observers stressed freedom from taxes, poverty, and greedy lords
or priests as a reason for migrating, whereas others saw westward migration as an elaborate hoax perpetrated by land speculators and real-estate
barkers. A down-to-earth Vermont farmer told Francois-André Michaux
that he "had seen published [reports] upon the extraordinary salubrity
and fertility of the banks of the river Yazous," and so he left behind
Vermont's long, cold winters and headed for the land of opportunity.
Here, in the great meeting ground of Puritan and planter, of German,

[12] Edmund Dana, *Geographical Sketches on the Western Country* (Cincinnati, 1819),
pp. iv, 6–7; Anon., *The Americans at Home; or, Byeways, Backwoods, and Prairies*
(London, 1854), pp. vii–viii; Anthony Trollope, *North America* (New York, 1862), p. 30;
Joseph Whipple, *A Geographical View of the District of Maine* (Bangor, 1816), p. 42.

[13] James Flint, *Letters from America*, Reuben Gold Thwaites (ed.) (Cleveland, 1904),
p. 169; Anon., *Americans at Home*, p. vii.

[14] Beltrami, *Pilgrimage in Europe and America*, p. 97; David Thomas, *Travels Through
the Western Country in the Summer of 1816* (Auburn, 1819), p. 42.

Briton, and Gaul, the question remained: Would the West nurture the finest characteristics in each or accent the more degenerate?[15] The human history of America, unlike its natural history, dissolved into a confusing mélange of seemingly inconsistent variables.

"The Touch of a Feather": Nature Influences the Settler

Nature's influence on the western settler was a topic of general concern. The Ohio Valley was crucial to the young nation, strategically, financially, and ideologically, and the many instances of frontier restiveness in the years between the Shays' Rebellion in 1787 and the Aaron Burr conspiracy in 1806–7 suggested its allegiance could not be taken for granted.[16] Even Jefferson, who believed in the civilizing effect of cultivating the land, remained guarded. "If only the frontiersmen could be retained 'til their governments become settled and wise, they will remain with us always," he predicted. Manasseh Cutler, a director of the powerful Ohio Company, expressed similar fears: "What troubles may we not apprehend, if the Spaniards on their right, and Great Britain on their left, instead of throwing stumbling-blocks in their way, as they now do, should hold out lures for their trade and alliance?" Westerners, he thought, "stand, as it were, upon a pivot. The touch of a feather would turn them any way."[17]

These fears were exacerbated by the westerner's belligerently democratic mentality. Travelers noted an aggravating disregard for social distinction in the frontiersman's habit of interrogating strangers of any class.

---

[15] Thomas Hulme in William Cobbett, *A Year's Residence in the United States of America* (New York, 1816), Vol. 3, pp. 312–14; Thomas Ashe, *Travels in America, Performed in 1808, for the Purpose of Exploring the Rivers Alleghany, Monongahela, Ohio, and Mississippi* (Newburyport, 1808), pp. 32–3; Dorothy Anne Dondore, *The Prairie and the Making of Middle America: Four Centuries of Description* (Cedar Rapids, 1926), p. 169; Francois-André Michaux, *Travels to the West of the Allegheny Mountains, in the States of Ohio, Kentucky, and Tennessea [sic],... Undertaken in the Year 1802* (London, 1805), pp. 65, 74; Flint, *Letters from America*, pp. 76, 181; Constantin Francois Chasseboeuf, comte de Volney, *A View of the Soil and Climate of the United States* (Philadelphia, 1804), pp. 326–8; John W. Monette, *History of the Discovery and Settlement of the Valley of the Mississippi... Until the Year 1846* (New York, 1846), Vol. 2, pp. 20–1.

[16] Cayton, *Frontier Republic*, pp. 2, 7, 11–13, 16, 20, 91–2.

[17] Thomas Jefferson in Cayton, *Frontier Republic*, p. 23; Manasseh Cutler, "Journal," ca. 1784, in William Parker Cutler, and Julia Perkins Cutler, *Life, Journals, and Correspondence of Rev. Manasseh Cutler, LL.D, by his Grandchildren* (Cincinnati, 1888), Vol. 1, pp. 134–5.

They were never satisfied, Charles Augustus Murray complained, "till they had found out who I was, where I came from, why I came, and where I was going to, how long I meant to stay, and, in addition to these particulars, how much my umbrella cost, and what was the price of my hat." In his *American Tourist's Pocket Companion*, George Temple advised readers to return the local's stare "with good interest, minutely examining the starer from head to foot. To their inquiries hatch up any cock-and-bull story you may think of.... This will be... at least of some amusement to you." The near universal comment on these inquisitions suggests something more than simple annoyance; the assumption of equality was deeply troubling to those who saw deferential behavior as essential to the orderly development of western society.[18]

A confusing and often troubling amalgam of characteristics clouded the future of the West, and the one great constant in this equation was the land: Observers looked to the dynamic of nature and people to cipher this capricious mingling of regions, races, and nationalities. Yet, here, too, their conclusions were contradictory. The West indeed stood upon a pivot, and observers turned to the science of nature to anticipate its future.[19]

Natural history offered several generalizations about the transition from forest to field. The first was obvious: America spread an incredibly generous repast before the advancing settler; but, just as clearly, this was a mixed blessing. Marietta naturalist Samuel P. Hildreth related the story of a backwoodsman who attracted a flock of wild turkeys to his hog pen by feeding them: "The owner of the cabin, standing in the door,... every day shot one or two of the unsuspecting birds." Next, he trained a female deer to visit the farm every day in autumn, bringing a male companion. "Without leaving his cabin, he had killed fourteen deer... by the innocent aid of his little pet." The prospect of nature bringing food to the door seemed idyllic – almost Edenic – but it also led observers to ponder the

---

[18] Michaux, *Travels to the West of the Allegheny Mountains*, pp. 37, 39–41; Charles Augustus Murray, *Travels in North America During the Years 1834, 1835, & 1836* (London, 1839), p. 190; George Temple, *The American Tourist's Pocket Companion* (New York, 1812), pp. 17–18. See Nuttall, *Journal of Travels into the Arkansa*, p. 29; Flint, *Letters from America*, p. 168; Nobles, "Breaking into the Backcountry," pp. 644–5.

[19] See Gilbert Chinard, "Eighteenth-Century Theories on America as a Human Habitat," American Philosophical Society (hereafter APS) *Proceedings* 91 (February 1947): p. 28; *North American Review*, n.s., 53 (October 1841): p. 321; Amy DeRogatis, *Moral Geography: Maps, Missionaries, and the American Frontier* (New York, 2003), pp. 1, 56; Timothy Flint, *The History and Geography of the Mississippi Valley* (Cincinnati, 1832), pp. 136–7.

moral effects of effortless living. Alexander Wilson was shocked by the primitive farms along the Ohio River. Inhabitants talked with pride of their rich soils and abundant land, but their houses were "worse than pig-sties; their clothes an assemblage of rags; their faces yellow, and lank with disease; and their persons covered with filth." Perhaps, he thought, the land was too kind: "The corn is thrown into the ground in the spring, and the pigs turned into the woods, where they multiply like rabbits. The labor of the squatter is now over till autumn, and he spends the winter in eating pork, cabbage, and hoe-cakes." Erstwhile farmers were lured into the woods, at first using the gun only when necessary but increasingly drawn to the excitement of the chase: "The labours of the field are neglected, and habits unfavourable to industry acquired." Abundance dulled the impulse to transform nature, leaving the frontier family in perpetually primitive conditions.[20]

The amount of land available to the settler also caused concern. It encouraged homesteaders to leave home and community and move far beyond the constraints of civilized society. Naturalist John William Draper stressed the bracing effects of this wanderlust – the conquest of the continent, the dynamic mix of national and regional characteristics, the challenge of new circumstances – but he also saw drawbacks: the "love of the homestead, so characteristic of the settled populations of Europe, can scarcely be said to exist among us."[21] The Ohio River, with its westward flow and powerful influence on the imagination, encouraged this restlessness, Timothy Flint added. "No wonder that the severe and unremitting labours of agriculture, performed directly in the view of such scenes, should become tasteless and irksome. No wonder that the young along the banks of the great streams, should detest the labours of the field, and embrace every opportunity... to escape." The valley's entire population would be overturned in a single generation, another added: "Where then, will be the traditions of Ohio?"[22] Draper and Flint

---

[20] S. P. Hildreth in *American Journal of Science* 29 (1836): pp. 85–6; Alexander Wilson, *American Ornithology* (Philadelphia, 1878), Vol. 1, pp. lxxvii; Edward Augustus Kendall, *Travels Through the Northern Parts of the United States, in the Year 1807 and 1808* (New York, 1809), Vol. 3, pp. 70–1, 73–746; Priscilla Wakefield, *Excursions in North America* (London, 1810), p. 191.

[21] Benjamin Rush, *Essays, Literary, Moral, and Philosophical* (Philadelphia, 1806), p. 223; John William Draper, *Thoughts on the Future Civil Policy of America* (New York, 1865), pp. 54, 82–3, 84–6, 90–1, 160–1. See Andrew Ellicott, *The Journal of Andrew Ellicott* (Philadelphia, 1803), p. v.

[22] Timothy Flint, *Recollections of the Last Ten Years* (Boston, 1826), pp. 16, 76; *North American Review*, n.s., 53 (October 1841): p. 322. See Thomas, *Travels Through the*

saw the greater good in national expansion, but their fears were no less palpable.

Like the land and the flowing rivers, the deep woods seemed to lure settlers beyond the bounds of civilization. At war with nature and exhilarated by the prospect of new beginnings, they roamed from chopping to chopping, Basil Hall complained, seeking gratification in the destruction of the woods. Hall told of a New Englander who uprooted himself, moved to western New York, cleared a farm, built a large brick house, and in time amassed a large family and a comfortable fortune. Although he enjoyed the means for a "quiet, hearty, green old age," nothing was farther from his thoughts.

He missed the ardent excitement of his past life, and sighed to be once again in the heart of the thicket, . . . so he made over his farm to his children, and carrying with him only his axe and his wife, a few dollars, a team of oxen, and a wagon and horses, set off for the territory of Michigan, the lord knows how far off in the North-West. There he is now chopping down wood, and labouring in a sort of wild happiness from morning till night, to bring new lands into cultivation; which, in the course of time, if he live, he will dispose of to newer settlers, and again decamp to the westward.[23]

Tyrone Power saw the same mad glint in the settler's eye and marveled at the "apparent indifference, if not positive pleasure, [with which] . . . people of this country quit their ancient homes, and wander forth in search of new ones." This grim fascination with wilderness had its positive side – a certain primal energy and experimental character – but shallow roots boded poorly for the civilization rising west of the Appalachians. The "epithet of elegant," Birkbeck noted, "implies . . . usefulness in America, but has nothing to do with taste."[24]

In addition to the social lethargy and rootlessness resulting from abundant land and resources, observers expressed concern about the influence of the wilderness environment. Fascinated by the idea of environmental determinism, philosophers and naturalists paid close attention to the air people breathed, the food they ate, and the climate in which they lived. Intimate contact with nature was clearly a civilization-shaping influence.

Western Country, p. 83; Henry Ashworth, *A Tour in the United States, Cuba, and Canada* (London, 1861), p. 119.

[23] Hall, *Travels in North America*, Vol. 1, pp. 79–81.

[24] Tyrone Power, *Impressions of America During the Years 1833, 1834, and 1835* (London, 1836), Vol. 1, pp. 332–3; Birkbeck, *Notes on a Journey in America*, p. 152. See William Dalton, *Travels in the United States of America, and Part of Upper Canada* (Appleby, 1821), p. 226; Monette, *History . . . of the Mississippi*, Vol. 2, pp. 21–2.

FIGURE 7.1. Compelled by the idea of environmental determinism, naturalists thought carefully about the relation between settlers and the land they hoped to subdue. That nature spread such a generous repast before the advancing settler was as much a curse as a blessing. Abundance dulled the impulse to transform the land, it promoted lethargy, and it left the frontier family in perpetually primitive conditions. Naturalists paid similar attention to the air people breathed, the food they ate, and the climate they inhabited. Titian Ramsay Peale, *Sketches, 1817–1875.* Courtesy of the American Philosophical Society.

Naturalists pointed to America's original inhabitants, who succumbed to the "freedom of the woods," as Daniel Drake put it, and remained, to the European eye, indifferent to any form of improvement. Having failed to transform the land, they were doomed to extinction, "like the great elephant of his native woods – the mastodon – [that] has preceded him."[25] The conflation of Native American and pioneer culture, evident in numerous descriptions of the West, produced a deep anxiety. Crèvecoeur fantasized about moving his family from New York to the Ohio Valley. "Half a dozen of acres...will yield us a great abundance of all we want.... Thus shall we metamorphose ourselves...into a...simpler people." However, thinking of the Indians who cohabited this wilderness,

[25] Daniel Drake, *Discourse on the History, Character, and Prospects of the West* (Gainesville, 1955 [1834]), p. 21; John W. Draper, *The Influence of Physical Agents on Life* (New York, 1850), p. 10; Peter Kalm, *Travels Into North America, Containing Its Natural History, and a Circumstantial Account of Its Plantations and Agriculture in General,* John R. Foster (ed.), (Warrington, 1753–1771), Vol. 2, p. 193; Birkbeck, *Notes on a Journey in America,* p. 143.

his misgivings mounted. Like Indians, his family would be at war with nature.

The deer often come to eat their grain, the wolves to destroy their sheep, the bears to kill their hogs, the foxes to catch their poultry.... They watch these animals, they kill some; and thus by defending their property, they soon become professed hunters.... [and] once hunters, farewell to the plough. The chase renders them ferocious, gloomy, and unsocial; a hunter wants no neighbour, he rather hates them because he dreads the competition.... Carelessness in fencing often exposes what little they sow to destruction... To make up the deficiency, they go oftener to the woods. That new mode of life brings along with it a new set of manners, which... being grafted on the old stock produce a strange sort of lawless prolificacy, the impressions of which are indelible.... They grow up a mongrel breed, half civilized, half savage.[26]

The rigorous demands of forest-clearing seemed evidence of hard work but, in fact, there was something in the "prodigious power of vegetation" that left the settlers "languid and cadaverous." Birkbeck claimed he could predict the pallor of the local settlers from the "depth of their immersion" in the woods. Gloomy forests provided too little oxygen and, without this, settlers grew tall and pale, stretching skyward "like vegetables that grow in a vault, pining for light."[27]

Scientists embraced the Enlightenment notion of progress from the state of nature, but their ruminations on western settlement – easy living, heedless mobility, environmental influences – betrayed an underlying uncertainty. Forest and swamp offered too many retreats for the miscreant, who needed only to steal a skiff or a horse and disappear into the night. "Jails are constructed of thin brick walls or of logs, fit only to detain the prisoner while he is satisfied with the treatment he receives."[28] Cut loose from the bonds of family and civil society, and freed from the press of honest labor and class distinction, this heterogeneous western population was at enormous moral risk. The West, at the touch of a feather, could progress toward civilization or degenerate into a continental "rogues' jubilee."[29]

---

[26] J. Hector St. John de Crèvecoeur, *Letters from an American Farmer and Sketches of Eighteenth-Century America*, Albert E. Stone (ed.) (New York, 1986 [c. 1782]), pp. 76–7, 221–2, 225–6, 359. See Benjamin Silliman, *Remarks Made on a Short Tour Between Hartford and Quebec in the Autumn of 1819* (New Haven, 1824), pp. 18–19.

[27] Crèvecoeur, *Letters from an American Farmer*, pp. 71–3, 78; Flint, *Recollections of the Last Ten Years*, pp. 28–9, 43; Birkbeck, *Notes on a Journey in America*, pp. 139–40.

[28] Flint, *Letters from America*, pp. 113, 167.

[29] Gouveneur Morris, *Notes on the United States of America* (Philadelphia, 1806), pp. 21–2; Ferris, *States and Territories of the Great West*, p. 14.

The Settler Influences Nature

If naturalists were interested in the way the land shaped the settler, they were equally interested in the way the settler shaped the land, although here, they were initially more optimistic. The logic of evolution seemed to suggest that cultivation would improve the earth, just as centuries of cultivation improved the land in Europe. Fish and game would disappear but so too would frontier indolence, and farmers would replace these wild creatures with cattle, pigs, poultry.[30] Some birds would be eliminated, but robins, sparrows, finches, woodpeckers, swallows, bobolinks, kingbirds, waxwings, and others adapted to open lands would replace them. Primitive soils forced plants into tall, coarse stalks; cultivation "tamed" the earth and fitted it for agriculture. Turning up the ground dissolved the original vegetable matter and mixed these organic nutrients with underlying minerals scoured up by the plow. To this, the farmer would add lime, chalk, marl, shells, soot, ashes, and dung. As imported plants adapted to the climate, the land would become even more productive.[31] Changes like these were part of a unified, forward-sweeping panorama of evolution.

The single most important proof of this improvement was climate change. Being environmental determinists, scientists were closely concerned about the natural history of America's climate. Florida's summers, for instance, produced "such abundant perspiration that water, as soon as drank, penetrates the open pores, so that the human skin seems to be comparable to a wet spunge [sic] when squeezed." Such conditions could dampen the body's "harmonious concordance," producing "weaknesses, lassitudes, and finally dangerous and fatal disorders." Concerns like these fueled interest in climate as did the desire to predict a region's agricultural prospects.[32] Hoping to identify seasonal patterns and their influences, Benjamin Barton talked with Native Americans and old pioneers

---

[30] Williams, *Natural and Civil History of Vermont*, pp. 79–80; Hugh Williamson in APS *Publications* 1 (1789), p. 343; William Newnham Blane, *An Excursion Through the United States and Canada During the Years 1822–23* (London, 1824), p. 87.

[31] Amos Eaton, *Geological and Agricultural Survey of Rensselaer County, in the State of New York* (Albany, 1822), p. 23; Thomas, *Travels Through the Western Country*, p. 59; Greenleaf, *Statistical View of the District of Maine*, p. 87; *American Journal of Science*, n.s., 4 (November 1847): pp. 161–4, 166; Ashe, *Travels in America*, p. 221; Dana, *Geographical Sketches*, pp. 27–8; APS *Publications* 1 (1789), pp. 342–3.

[32] Bernard Romans, *A Concise Natural History of East and West Florida* (New York, 1775), pp. 14–15; John Drayton, *A View of South Carolina, as Respects Her Natural and Civil Concerns* (Charleston, 1802), pp. 20–1; James Glen, *A Description of South Carolina* (London, 1761), p. 11.

and recommended a "careful examination of the annual circles of some of our largest trees." This he compared to the onset of diseases across various regions. Stephen W. Williams's *Calendrarium Florae* included, as he put it, "any thing which has a tendency to elicit facts with regard to the climate of a country," among them trees blossoming, birds nesting, sap rising, frogs singing, buds appearing, leaves disappearing, and asparagus becoming "fit for the table."[33]

These variables did indeed yield predictions about weather. With an eye to their effect on agriculture, Jeremy Belknap described New Hampshire's seasons. Mid-September evenings were chilly enough for a small fire and, by October, a constant fire was necessary. Autumnal rains in November brought a month of variable weather, with the ground "frequently frozen and thawed." Cattle were housed from the beginning of November and, in the depths of winter, barn fowl roosted on the backs of the cattle to keep their feet from freezing. January brought a thaw and February saw the "deepest snows and coldest weather." March was "blustering and cold," but the sun was high enough to melt the snow at noon. The fields were clear in April and, within a few weeks, the grass was "sufficiently grown for cattle to live abroad." July was "clear and hot" and prone to violent southeast storms.[34]

Naturalists searched for laws in these seasonal rhythms. Samuel Forry thought them to be, in reality, a system of "vast cycles, which will enable us to predict, no doubt, with some degree of certainty, the condition of future seasons."[35] Expectations like these were inspired by an observation made by Alexander von Humboldt that if the earth's surface was of unvarying color, density, and smoothness, all isothermal lines would be parallel to the equator.[36] Hugh Williamson thought the ocean, being of uniform substance and surface, might act as a basis for understanding

[33] Benjamin Smith Barton, *A Discourse on Some of the Principal Desiderata in Natural History* (Philadelphia, 1807), pp. 62–4; Stephen W. Williams in *American Journal of Science* 1 (1818): p. 359. See *American Journal of Science* 1 (1818): pp. 77–9; Manasseh Cutler to Samuel Williams, June 20, 1780, in Cutler and Cutler, *Journals, and Correspondence of Rev. Manasseh Cutler*, Vol. 1, p. 81; *Monthly American Journal of Geology and Natural Science* 1 (July 1831): pp. 21–2; *American Journal of Science* 3 (1821): pp. 273–5.

[34] Belknap, *History of New-Hampshire*, p. 18.

[35] Samuel Forry in *American Journal of Science* 47 (October 1844): p. 230; Forry, *The Climate of the United States and Its Endemic Influences* (New York, 1842), p. 29.

[36] Alexander Humboldt, *Cosmos: A Sketch of a Physical Description of the Universe* (New York, 1870), Vol. 1, p. 313, 318; Louis Agassiz, *Address Delivered on the Centennial Anniversary of the Birth of Alexander von Humboldt* (Boston, 1869), pp. 12–13, 23–4, 28. See Williams, *Natural and Civil History of Vermont*, pp. 53–5, 57–8.

why weather differed from place to place, and Timothy Flint saw the Great Plains in the same way. Moving from south to north across this endlessly flat surface, he noted a uniform decline in temperature and a corresponding change in vegetation. Others remained skeptical. Discovering a temperature mean in a country that experienced "20, 30, or 40 degrees of [temperature] variation in the twenty-four hours" was futile, Volney thought. Even on the high seas, "mariners generally agree that all is caprice and confusion."[37]

Challenged by these debates, naturalists searched for a way of understanding the conditions that influenced climate. Volney proposed first measuring latitude and altitude, and then elaborating this basic matrix according to the particularities of the region: its proximity to water, the height, angle, and axis of its mountains, its prevailing winds, and its state of cultivation. To explain Pennsylvania's climate, geographer Joseph Scott began with the latitude and added, progressively, the Great Lakes to the north, the "uncultivated country" to the northwest, the level and partially cultivated country to the southeast, the Atlantic Ocean to the east, and the Allegheny Mountains, the region's great weather machine, in the center. The result was a pattern of great variety, Scott concluded, characterized by "sudden transitions, from one extreme to another."[38] Using a questionnaire sent to colleagues across North America, Boston botanist Jacob Bigelow mapped the blossoming of peach trees in each region. The data showed a two-month variation from March 4 in South Carolina to May 12 in Montreal. By the 1850s, Smithsonian director Joseph Henry and meteorologist James Pollard Espy were collecting daily weather data from locations across the country and, with the spread of the telegraph, Henry had operators begin their mornings by sending Washington a report on local conditions. Thus, scientists tracked storms and, as Forry hoped, were able to make elementary predictions about the weather.[39]

Although naturalists understood that latitude was not the only variable in determining climate, differences between Europe and America in the same parallel were so dramatic as to require an explanation. Maine,

---

[37] Hugh Williamson in APS *Publications* 1 (1789), p. 339; Flint, *History and Geography of the Mississippi Valley*, p. 31; Volney, *View of the Soil and Climate of the United States*, pp. 111–12, 203.

[38] Volney, *View of the Soil and Climate of the United States*, pp. 102, 127; Joseph Scott, *A Geographical Description of Pennsylvania* (Philadelphia, 1806), pp. 17–18.

[39] Jacob Bigelow in *American Journal of Science* 1 (1818): p. 77; Bigelow in American Academy of Arts and Sciences *Memoirs* 4 (No. 1, 1818): pp. 77–78. See William B. Meyer, *Americans and Their Weather* (New York, 2000), p. 56.

for instance, should have enjoyed a climate comparable to the Mediterranean, being in the same latitude. These differences triggered a great deal of speculation. In 1769, John Bartram explained to Linnaeus that because America had no mountains protecting it from the Arctic winds, the "condensed Northern air rusheth upon us & is extreme cold," and in 1793, Samuel Hale, Edward A. Holyoke, and Matthew Wilson published articles offering other explanations. Jeremy Belknap speculated that the snows lingering in New England's White Mountains imparted "a keenness to the winds which blow over them," and William Maclure pointed to the "constant supply of caloric" from the Gulf Stream warming Europe. In 1822, Robert Hare showed that the Gulf Stream remained six to seven degrees higher than the surrounding water. Humboldt explained further that Europe's prevailing westerly winds carried this warm sea air across the land, whereas North America's westerlies crossed a continental land mass, with no such moderating effect in the East.[40]

There were many explanations for America's colder climate, but the most popular involved the relative state of cultivation on the two continents. Classical and biblical references to weather seemed to indicate that Europe had once been colder, and most naturalists attributed this to the thick forests that covered the continent in ancient times. Caesar's troops had marched through snow six feet deep near Rome and, in King David's time, the weather in Palestine included frost, snow, and hail. Based on this insight, most Americans thought the country's climate would moderate as its forests were cleared away. As early as 1708, John Clayton's contacts told him that thirty or forty years earlier, "when the country was not so open," the climate had been more severe. Peter Kalm

---

[40] John Bartram to Charles Linne, ca. 1769, in Edmund Berkeley and Dorothy Smith Berkeley, *The Correspondence of John Bartram, 1734–1777* (Gainesville, 1992), p. 722; Samuel Hale in American Academy of Arts and Sciences *Memoirs* 2 (No. 1, 1793): pp. 61–3; Edward A. Holyoke in ibid., 2 (No. 1, 1793): pp. 65–92; Matthew Wilson in *APS Transactions* 3 (1793): pp. 326–8; Jeremy Belknap in *APS Transactions* 2 (1786): pp. 42–9; Charles Lyell, *Principles of Geology* (Boston, 1842), Vol. 1, pp. 165–6; Robert Hare in *American Journal of Science* 5 (No. 2, 1822): pp. 352–4. See James Rodger Fleming, "Charles Lyell and Climatic Change: Speculation and Certainty," in Derek J. Blundell and Andrew C. Scott, *Lyell: The Past Is the Key to the Present* (London, 1998), p. 22; American Academy of Arts and Sciences *Memoirs* 1 (Boston; 1783): p. 3; Zadock Thompson, *History of Vermont, Natural, Civil, and Statistical* (Burlington, 1842), pp. 21–2; *North American Review*, n.s., 28 (April 1829): p. 273; James Mease, *Geological Account of the United States* (Philadelphia, 1807), pp. 82–3; Forry, *Climate of the United States*, p. 90; Charles Daubeny, *Sketch of the Geology of North America, Being the Substance of a Memoir Read Before the Ashmolean Society* (Oxford, 1839), p. 35; APS *Transactions*, n.s., 1 (1818): p. 22.

discovered a similar opinion among old Swedes in the Delaware Valley, and Volney noted a widespread conviction that the frontier was growing warmer and dryer "in proportion as the land has been cleared." Soon, he thought, the "tender vine, which would now be destroyed by our winter's frost,... shall supply the North-American with every species of wine."[41] Land-clearing made the weather warmer and the soil drier, according to Samuel Williams; and, as the water table fell, swamps disappeared and roads became more passable.[42] In his explorations of northern Maine, Moses Greenleaf discovered a wilderness valley cleared of trees by fire. Here, he discovered,

the snow disappears earlier in the spring, and does not permanently cover the earth so early in the autumn, as in the contiguous forests. The leaves appear on the trees, and the surface exhibits the lively green of spring, from one to three weeks earlier than is seen within thirty miles to the south of it. The temperature in the summer is sensibly warmer, particularly during the night. The wild fruits also ripen earlier, and the whole appearance of the tract indicates the favorable change produced in the climate by the extensive destruction of the original forest.

Extricated from its oppressive forest cover, the burned-over tract had become an oasis of springtime in the wintry Maine landscape. "We can see no very good reason to doubt, that in some future day, when all our immense forests are cleared,... Maine,... will then, under the genial influence of the sun, yield to her inhabitants 'all the rich luxuries of the vegetable kingdom.'"[43]

---

[41] [John Clayton], *Miscellanea Curiosa: Containing a Collection of Some of the Principal Phaenomena in Nature* (London, 1708), p. 290; Kalm, *Travels into North America*, Vol. 2, pp. 127–8; Volney, *View of the Soil and Climate of the United States*, pp. 215–16. See Richard H. Grove, *Green Imperialism: Colonial Expansion, Tropical Island Edens, and the Origins of Environmentalism, 1600–1860* (New York, 1995), p. 67; John Mitchell and Arthur Young, *American Husbandry: Containing an Account of the Soil, Climate, Production of the British Colonies in North-America and the West-Indies* (London, 1775), Vol. 1, p. 46.

[42] Williams, *Natural and Civil History of Vermont*, pp. 70, 73, 75–8. See American Academy of Arts and Sciences *Memoirs* 1 (Boston, 1783): pp. 9, 17; Rodolphus Dickinson, *A Geographical and Statistical View of Massachusetts* (Greenfield, 1813), pp. 14, 15, 18–20; *American Journal of Science* 11 (No. 2, 1826): pp. 228–9; Anon., *Historical Review of North America*, p. 165; James Rodger Fleming, *Meteorology in America, 1800–1770* (Baltimore, 1990), pp. 2–3.

[43] Moses Greenleaf, *A Survey of the State of Maine in Reference to Its Geographical Features, Statistics, and Political Economy* (Augusta, 1970 [c. 1829]), pp. 87, 89–90, 106–7; Greenleaf, *Statistical View of the District of Maine*, pp. 21–3, 87; Greenleaf in *North American Review* 3 (September 1816): pp. 275–6. See Whipple, *Geographical View of the District of Maine*, pp. 6–7.

America's most optimistic student of climate was Hugh Williamson, a Pennsylvania native who studied medicine in Edinburgh, London, and Utrecht, and taught at the College of Philadelphia and New York's College of Physicians and Surgeons.[44] A surgeon for the Continental Army and delegate at the Constitutional Convention, Williamson was intensely nationalistic, and his climate predictions mirrored his optimistic assessment of America. Deforestation, he thought, would eventually equalize climate conditions in America and Europe, and as America grew warmer, its larger land base and richer resources would provide enormous advantages in natural and civil productions. "The cold, blustering, and drying winds from the west and northwest are evidently decreasing," he wrote confidently, "and . . . the more mild, moderate, and moist currents from the east are become [sic] prevalent." To prove his contention, he cited Virgil's observation that cattle were sheltered in winter in early Rome and wine froze in the casks in a land where the climate was "now like Georgia." Certainly, Italy was widely cultivated in this earlier age but, as he pointed out, central Europe was still a wilderness: "From these uncultivated deserts, piercing North-Winds used to descend in torrents on the shivering Italian, though his own little commonwealth were finely cultivated." Edward Holyoke added similar classical and biblical references and concluded that "no change [is] . . . so remarkable as that of cutting down and clearing the earth's surface of those woods and thick forests."[45]

Naturalists had several explanations for this phenomenon. Forests, they observed, kept the soils cold and wet and this, in turn, cooled the atmosphere. Deserts were hot because they had no trees. Samuel Williams buried two thermometers in the earth, one in an open field and another in a forest. The cleared ground, he discovered, was 10 to 12 degrees warmer to a depth of one foot, and this surface acted like a giant radiator, heating the air above it. Jefferson, among others, attributed climate change to the inward incursion of sea breezes, drawn landward by updrafts from the cleared lands. In the space of a generation, Rodolphus Dickinson added, easterly winds had extended forty to sixty miles farther inland, "exactly in proportion as the land is divested of wood." Changing sea winds also brought steadier rains and carried ships across the Atlantic faster than in

44 New York Historical Society *Collections* 3 (1821): pp. 135–8, 163, 168; *Port Folio* 4th ser., 12 (December 1821): pp. 402–5; Hugh Williamson in APS *Publications* 1 (1789), pp. 336–7.
45 *Medical Repository*, 3d. ser., 3 (1812): pp. 160–1. See American Academy of Arts and Sciences, *Memoirs* 2 (No. 1, 1793): pp. 70–1; Volney, *View of the Soil and Climate of the United States*, pp. 219–20.

earlier times. When the forests were gone, William Currie summarized, "how glorious, how enviable, will be the lot of the Americans." Naturalists were not unanimous in this theory, but the weight of opinion in the early decades of the century, influenced by the optimistic and expansionist mood of the early republic, accepted the transition from forest to fruitful field as a double blessing, leaving the land more productive and the climate more appealing.[46]

The Hygienic Landscape

Naturalists also found the connection between forest-clearing and disease a cause for optimism. Here, Hugh Williamson wrote, "every friend to humanity must rejoice . . . in the . . . advantages we may gain in point of health, from the cultivation of this country."[47] To Europeans, frontier America seemed beset by afflictions like colds, coughs, catarrhs, fevers, and agues. Virtually every foreign traveler commented on the virulence of these diseases, and virtually everyone suggested possible causes. Kalm thought watermelons, peaches, and other juicy fruit dangerous, along with water containing bugs. Other possibilities included air quality, extravagant living, sudden weather changes, "odoriferous plants," putrid water, fogs, sweet meats, ardent spirits, tea, coffee, or chocolate.[48] Volney blamed American foodways:

At breakfast they deluge the stomach with a pint of hot water, slightly impregnated with tea . . . and they swallow, almost without mastication, hot bread, half baked, soaked in melted butter, with the grossest cheese, and salt or hung beef, pickled pork or fish, all which can with difficulty be dissolved. At dinner they devour boiled pastes, called, absurdly, puddings, garnished with the most luscious sauces. Their turnips and other vegetables are floated in lard or butter. Their pastry is nothing but a greasy paste, imperfectly baked. To digest these various substances, they take tea, *immediately after dinner*, so strong that it is bitter to the taste, as well as utterly destructive of the nervous system. Supper presently follows, with salt meat and shell fish in its train. Thus passes the whole day, in heaping one

---

[46] Samuel Williams in Volney, *View of the Soil and Climate of the United States*, p. 216; Dickinson, *Geographical and Statistical View*, pp. 14–15, 20; Thomas Jefferson in Fleming, "Charles Lyell and Climatic Change," p. 29; William Currie, *An Historical Account of the Climates and Diseases of the United States of America* (Philadelphia, 1792), pp. 82, 85–9; APS *Publications* 1 (1789): p. 344.

[47] Hugh Williamson in APS *Publications* 1 (1789), p. 344.

[48] Kalm, *Travels into North America*, Vol. 1, pp. 241–3, 361–3, 366–71; ibid., Vol. 2, pp. 254–5; Volney, *View of the Soil and Climate of the United States*, pp. 223–4, 226, 229, 230.

indigestive mass upon another. To brace the exhausted stomach, wine, rum, gin, malt spirits, or beer are used with dreadful prodigality.[49]

William Blane arrived in New York City during a yellow fever epidemic and found several neighborhoods shuttered and deserted and strewn with lime. Streets, he reported, were unpaved and filthy, privies unwalled, and yards covered with stagnant water or heaped with garbage. Hogs were set loose to devour the offal thrown in the gutter, and the churchyards were "so crowded that the corpses were buried three deep."[50] Poor diet and sanitation in these gateway cities drew attention to the deplorable state of health in America and to the environmental causes of this malaise.

Moving westward through an unknown country renowned for its agues and fevers, travelers remained acutely sensitive to the hygienic properties of the landscape. In Ohio, Thomas Ashe found himself thrashing through "a wilderness so thick, deep, and dark, and impenetrable that the light, much less the air of heaven, was nearly denied access." Driven nearly mad by mosquitoes, he pronounced the western atmosphere "so mephitic and offensive, as to give me vomitings and headaches."[51] During the humid season in Charlestown, one besieged visitor noted that "water may be seen pouring down looking-glasses and whatever is painted: candles burn dimly, the flames appearing as if surrounded with *Halos*; marshy grounds, ditches, sinks, and shallow standing waters emit an offensive smell; and all things are rendered so damp within doors where no fires are kept, that on entering a house a musty disagreeable smell is perceived, like that of the chambers of those who are sweating in fevers." Neither wind nor sunlight penetrated the southern woods; decay thickened the air and gave it a "mephitic quality"; and warm, moist south winds swept in a sultry atmosphere laden with the effluvia of the numerous southern swamps.[52] Considerations like these helped determine the flows and eddies of immigration across the West. Travelers, explorers, and prospective settlers carefully noted the hygienic qualities of the land they traversed: soils, bedrock composition, vegetation, proximity of swamps. Promotional tracts often included comparative mortality rates.[53]

---

[49] Volney, *View of the Soil and Climate of the United States*, p. 257.

[50] Blane, *Excursion Through the United States and Canada*, pp. 9, 12. See Dalton, *Travels in the United States of America, and Part of Upper Canada*, p. 5.

[51] Ashe, *Travels in America*, pp. 50, 180. See Henry Bradshaw Fearon, *Sketches of America* (London, 1818), p. 221; Volney, *View of the Soil and Climate of the United States*, p. 224.

[52] Currie, *Historical Account of the Climates and Diseases*, pp. 349, 351, 360.

[53] See Thaddeus Mason Harris, *The Journal of a Tour into the Territory Northwest of the Mountains* (Boston, 1805), pp. 109–10; *Medical Repository* 1 (No. 3, 1898): 526; ibid., 2 (No. 1, 1898): p. 39; *American Journal of Science* 10 (No. 2, 1826): pp. 306,

Hoping to compile these observations into a single systematic treatise, William Currie, a fellow at the College of Physicians of Philadelphia, published a four-hundred-page tome in 1792 on disease and environment based on extensive correspondence with physicians in the western states. Convinced that diseases were predictable natural events, he arranged them into a matrix according to the social and environmental conditions under which they flourished. Men of means were subject to apoplexy, palsy, epilepsy, dyspepsia, jaundice, gout, asthma, hypochondria, and dropsy; fashionable women were inclined to headaches, stomach ailments, spasms, asthma, hysteria, dyspepsia, and melancholia; and workingmen, to hemorrhoids, edema, itch, and gravel. More important than class were natural circumstances, such as the presence of standing water or the particular atmosphere brought by prevailing winds.[54] Moving systematically region by region, season by season, and disease by disease, he isolated the environmental components of the hygienic landscape. Benjamin Rush, Noah Webster, and Daniel Drake also wrote studies of environment and disease, taking into consideration all possible sources, including the mix of gravel and muck in the streams, the seasonal floods in the larger rivers, the amount of moisture in the soils, the circulation of the air, the proximity of swamps, the advent of extreme weather, the amount of underbrush in the forest, and any remarkable celestial or geological events.[55]

Among these variables, climate was critical. High temperatures promoted atmospheric vapors and "the multiplication of minute but visible animals." Summer droughts lowered reservoirs and exposed decomposing organic matter, and the South's "ardent sun" encouraged rapid plant growth and subsequent vegetative decay. Heat also caused perspiration, which affected the internal organs and predisposed Southerners to fever.[56]

311, 316; Edmund Ruffin, *Essays and Notes on Agriculture* (Richmond, 1855), p. 314; Bradbury, *Travels in the Interior*, p. 311; Dana, *Geographical Sketches*, p. 33.

[54] Currie, *Historical Account of the Climates and Diseases*, pp. 2, 95–8, 105.

[55] Brooke Hindle, *The Pursuit of Science in Revolutionary America, 1735–1789* (Chapel Hill, 1956), pp. 300–1; Forry, *Climate of the United States*, pp. 16–17, 20; Fleming, *Meteorology in America*, pp. 6–7. See Manasseh Cutler to Edward Wigglesworth, February 14, 1783, in Cutler and Cutler, *Journals and Correspondence of Rev. Manasseh Cutler*, Vol. 2, pp. 212–13; Charles D. Meigs, *A Biographical Notice of Daniel Drake, M.D., of Cincinnati* (Philadelphia, 1853), p. 20.

[56] Daniel Drake, *Systematic Treatise, Historical, Etiological, and Practical, on the Principal Diseases of the Interior Valley of North America* (Cincinnati, 1850), pp. 715–16; Benjamin Smith Barton, "Journals," in Barton, *Journals and Notebooks, 1785–1806*, APS; Dana, *Geographical Sketches*, p. 31–2; Dwight, *Travels in New England and New York*, pp. 47, 58; Currie, *Historical Account of the Climates and Diseases*, p. 2; Ellicott, *Journal*, p. 225.

Humid air, Volney thought, drew vital "igneous" and "electric" fluids out of the body, slowing the circulation of blood and other fluids. Atmosphere was another important component of the hygienic landscape. A composite of gasses, spores, seeds, and other emanations from the earth and the forest, the air was almost as full of life as the landscape it washed across. It had various tangible and intangible properties such as moisture, weight, density, chemical composition, caloric, and electricity – a "rich manure" of ingredients capable of influencing plants, animals, and humans. Western winds were "serene and clear," bringing "thin and pure" air, but northwest winds were "sharp and piercing," and those from the South, "hot and unwholsom [sic]," encouraging "tempestuous" constitutions. Winds off a plateau or mountain were "gloomy, chilly, [and] oppressive," producing "torpor and head-ache." Opinion varied on specific causes or symptoms, but everyone agreed that atmosphere was an important ingredient in regional health.[57]

Vegetation determined much of this atmospheric environment and thus contributed to the naturalists' inventory of unhealthy conditions. Organic materials were in a constant state of decomposition, and this putrescence was borne into the atmosphere by swamp fogs and other "dismal glooms," corrupting the air and spreading fevers. Thick forests also blocked the wind, preventing the dissipation of these miasmas, and kept the sunlight from reaching the ground to purify the soil. Benjamin Vaughan cautioned against traveling to the "leeward of a moras" or lingering near "stinking water."[58] Although the miasmas were invisible, the plants that caused them were clearly evident, giving physicians a vector they could identify.

Swamps brought all these variables together. A correspondent writing to Benjamin Barton described the Onondaga low country as a physician's

---

[57] John Brickell, *The Natural History of North-Carolina, With an Account of the Trade, Manners, and Customs of the Christian and Indian Inhabitants* (Dublin, 1737), pp. 24–6; Daniel Drake, *Natural and Statistical View, or Picture of Cincinnati and the Miami Country* (Cincinnati, 1815), pp. 100–1, 110; Volney, *View of the Soil and Climate of the United States*, pp. 126, 133, 135–8, 198–200; Dana, *Geographical Sketches*, p. 34. See Fleming, "Charles Lyell and Climatic Change," p. 13.

[58] William Byrd, *History of the Dividing Line*, T. H. Wynne (ed.) (Richmond, 1866), Vol. 1, p. 44; Drayton, *View of South Carolina*, pp. 16–17; J. F. D. Smyth, *A Tour in the United States of America* (London, 1784), Vol. 1, p. 148; Currie, *Historical Account of the Climates and Diseases*, pp. 328–9, 331; Benjamin Vaughan, "Hints Drawn Up for the Use of a Gentleman on the Point of Making a Tour Through the West India Islands," Vaughan Papers, APS; Hugh Williamson, *The History of North Carolina* (Philadelphia, 1812), p. 205.

nightmare: ponds and marshes swarmed with "bats, gnats, flies, and muschetoes," and the thick swamp mud was laden with corrupted organic matter, producing a "black mould of considerable depth [that] . . . when trod up has the appearance of lamp black and hogs fat mixed together." The vegetation was thick and prolific, and the Onondaga's "unsteady" summer temperatures rotted this organic matter rapidly. Rains left the land "cloudy and misty" and just before sunset, a dense, ground-hugging vapor emerged from the swamps and forests and spread through the lowlands.[59]

The best defense against this threat was felling the trees, breaking up the soil, and draining the swamps. These improvements would also reveal latent benefits in these unwholesome places. Low, wet lands contained valuable organic materials washed down from adjacent hills. Drained and exposed to air and sun, they were incredibly fertile but transforming them was not easy; swamp muck clung to the shovel or plow like wet mortar and, even when drained, the ground was uneven and encumbered by roots, turf, and tufts of sod. Still, the results affirmed the belief that human modifications fit the broader scheme of evolution. Hugh Williamson pointed out that landscapes naturally evolved toward a drier state, as forest growth and decay elevated the ground relative to nearby rivers and lakes. "The natural operations of time would reduce those extensive and numerous swamps, . . . but this event must be greatly accelerated by the progress of cultivation."[60] Felling forests and draining swamps was as natural as nature itself.

Searching for the environmental antecedents of America's frontier fevers, improvers like Williamson helped shape popular attitudes toward nature. The land was clearly an object for improvement, a consideration borne out in the medical history of the Onondaga country: When farmers removed the forests, drained the meadows, macadamized the roads, and sweetened the soils, the fevers abated. "It is a very trite, but true and important remark, that in proportion as the country becomes opened,

---

[59] John H. Frisbie to Benjamin Smith Barton, November 4, 1803, Benjamin Smith Barton Papers, APS. See *First Supplement to the Philadelphia Medical and Physical Journal,* Part 1 (Philadelphia, 1806): pp. 6, 8; *American Journal of Science* 11 (No. 2, 1826): pp. 225–6.

[60] Williamson, *History of North Carolina,* pp. 180–2, 185. See *Farmer's Monthly Visitor* 5 (October 31, 1843): p. 154; Ruffin, *Essays and Notes on Agriculture,* p. 315; Fleming, "Charles Lyell and Climatic Change," p. 30; Noah Webster, *An Address, Delivered Before the Hampshire, Franklin and Hampden Agricultural Society* (Northampton, 1818), pp. 16–17; *Massachusetts Agricultural Journal* 4 (June 1816): pp. 162–3.

cultivated, and peopled, in proportion as the redundance and rankness of natural vegetation is replaced by that of cultivation, the country becomes more healthy." Converting the "mephitic Pool into the verdant Lawn" improved the hygienic landscape.[61]

Improvers and Doubters

Even in the early decades of the century, there were some who questioned the idea of environmental melioration. These reservations were based partly on scientific logic and partly on a growing sense of unease with the settlement process. Scarred land, boulder piles, blackened forests, acres of stumps or deadened trees, and smoke-darkened skies challenged the idea that cultivation completed nature's purpose.[62] Writing in 1784, at the beginning of the age of expansion, William Strickland voiced a vigorous dissent from the idea that settlers improved nature. The backwoodsman, he wrote,

has an utter abhorrence for the works of the creation that exist on the place where he unfortunately settles himself.... First... he drives away or destroys the more humanized savage, the rightful proprietor of the soil; in the next place he thoughtlessly and rapaciously exterminates all living animals that can afford profit or maintenance to man; he then extirpates the woods that cloath and ornament the country, and that to any one but himself would be of the greatest value; and finally he exhausts and wears out the soil, and with the devastation he has thus committed usually meets with his own ruin; for by this time he is reduced to his

---

[61] Henry O'Rielly, *Settlement in the West: Sketches of Rochester* (Rochester, 1838), pp. 98–102; Drake, *Systematic Treatise*, pp. 403–5; Flint, *History and Geography of the Mississippi Valley*, pp. 39–40; Nathaniel Greene M. Senter, *A Lecture on the Beauty, Principles, & Importance of Agriculture* (Bangor, 1818), pp. 8–9. See Samuel Hildreth to Samuel Morton, November 22, 1834; Hildreth to Morton, February 23, 1835, Samuel George Morton Papers, APS; *American Journal of Science* 11 (No. 2, 1826): p. 225; *Philadelphia Medical and Physical Journal*, Part 2, Vol. 1, Section 1 (1804): p. 77; Bradbury, *Travels in the Interior*, pp. 310–11; John Regan, *The Emigrant's Guide to the Western States of America, or Backwoods and Prairies* (Edinburgh, 1852), p. iv.

[62] Michaux, *Travels to the West of the Allegheny Mountains*, p. 26; W. Faux, *Memorable Days in America*, Reuben Gold Thwaites (ed.) (Cleveland, 1904), pp. 168–9. See *North American Review*, n.s., 66 (January 1848): p. 194; Timothy Flint, *Lectures upon Natural History, Geology, Chemistry, the Application of Steam, and Interesting Discoveries in the Arts* (Boston, 1833), pp. 249–50; Blane, *Excursion Through the United States and Canada*, pp. 125–6; Henry Tudor, *Narrative of a Tour in North America* (London, 1834), pp. 411–12; John Palmer, *Journal of Travels in the United States of North America, and in Lower Canada, Performed in the Year 1817* (London, 1818), p. 44; Mitchell and Young, *American Husbandry*, Vol. 1, pp. 168–9; Thomas Twining, *Travels in America 100 Years Ago, Being Notes and Reminiscences* (New York, 1893), p. 75; William Edward Baxter, *America and the Americans* (London, 1855), p. 21.

original poverty; and it is then left to him only to sally forth and seek on the frontiers, a new country which he may again devour.

Strickland was no romantic; as a frontier surveyor, he saw the necessity of forest-clearing, but he felt no little remorse that it was done so heedlessly. The towns of western New York had been cut from the woods "without taste, judgement, or foresight"; nothing was spared, and the waste was even more tragic given the wood shortages developing in the downriver cities.[63]

Benjamin Vaughan, who owned a vast tract of land on the Kennebec frontier, saw this waste as a consequence of restricted access to markets. Writing also in the 1790s, he noted that wood was "too abundant and labor too deare in a new country to admit of [any] other... coarse [sic] of operations for clearing lands." Settlers left no trees standing because shallow roots made them vulnerable to wind-throw and drought, and the "want of lateral branches, arising from their having stood close to other trees," made them useless for shade. Strangers would judge this improvidence harshly, Vaughan wrote, but there was no recourse. "The Kennebecker... would be pleased to turn his timber to account, yet where no purchaser offers, this consideration cannot stop him." The waste would continue as long as land was cheap, labor dear, and markets remote.[64]

Later travelers shared little of Vaughan's understanding of frontier economics. They found the bleak farms laid out on the ruins of nature unsightly. The clearings were studded with scorched tree stems, and the wooded backdrop marred by a "black sort of gigantic wall formed on the abrupt edge of the forest." The American, Basil Hall thought, could "hardly conceive the horror with which a foreigner beholds such numbers of magnificent trees standing round him with their throats cut, the very Banquos of the murdered forest!"[65]

Other settler practices were equally as shocking. Andrew Burnaby's distaste for fire-hunting was obvious: animals were "blinded and suffocated by the smoke, and scorched by the fire," only to be shot point-blank as they forced their way through the flames.[66] The fires ruined the

---

[63] William Strickland, *Journal of a Tour in the United States of America, 1794–1795* (New York, 1971), pp. 138–9, 145–7.

[64] Benjamin Vaughan, "An Account of the Method of Preparing Woodlands for Cultivation, Used in the Vicinity of the River Kennebec in the District of Maine," January 24, 1798, Vaughan Papers, APS.

[65] Hall, *Travels in North America*, Vol. 1, pp. 71.

[66] Andrew Burnaby, *Travel Through the Middle Settlements in North-America, in the Years 1759 and 1760, with Observations upon the State of the Colonies* (London, 1775), p. 153.

forest, drove away the larger animals, and destroyed the small game and birds, leaving "only the most dreary and irrecoverable barrenness in their place," botanist Thaddeus Harris wrote. Traveling near Laurel Hill, he remarked that his party "seemed to have ridden all day in a chimney, and to sleep all night in an oven." Smoke drifting eastward across the mountains seemed an omen of the civil and natural changes underway in the West.[67]

Images of the violent death of nature were inseparable from the travelers' misgivings about frontier society. Zigzag fences, fields strewn with prostrate trunks, and log huts without windows or furniture mirrored the moral state that many feared was implicit in the pioneering process.[68] Like the primordial events that prepared the West for the advance of civilization, the wave of forest destruction sweeping across the continent was awe-inspiring; but, where primordial floods and upheavals conformed to the logic of evolutionary development, the settler's use of nature seemed base and wanton. Philosophically, naturalists applauded the pastoral landscape emerging from the untilled garden because it augured a more salubrious climate, a more hygienic landscape, and a more productive nature. Yet, their actual encounters with the ravaged land clouded this vision of improvement. The specter of savagery lingered in the ruined landscapes left behind as pioneers pulled up stakes and moved farther west.

The Stages of Civilization

The relation between wilderness and civilization was on Timothy Dwight's mind as he traveled a path along the Ammonoosuc River into New Hampshire's White Mountains. Beyond the lowland villages, he wrote in his *Travels*, the "overshadowing forest trees" closed in, and the furious rush of water in the stream intruded on his serenity. The path was "strewn with sharp and misshapen rocks," showing the "marks of frequent and fearful inundations." Close-ranked trees and contorted rocks brought to mind the implacable natural forces that shaped the world of the first settlers.

---

[67] Harris, *Journal of a Tour into the Territory*, pp. 22–3. See Duke de la Rochefoucault Liancourt, *Travels Through the United States of North America, the Country of the Iroquois, and Upper Canada, in the Years 1795, 1796, and 1797* (London, 1799), Vol. 2, p. 231; Maximilian Alexander Philip, Prinz von Wied, *Travels in the Interior of North America*, H. Evans Lloyd (trans.) (London, 1843), p. 22; *North American Review*, n.s., 35 (October 1832): pp. 414–15.

[68] Hall, *Travels in North America*, Vol. 1, p. 71.

Dwight emerged from this threatening landscape into the beauty of Crawford Meadow, deep in the heart of the White Mountains. With the sun breaking through a bank of clouds, he lingered to enjoy the prospect of fruitful fields stretching back from a humble home: a landscape of assurance wrought from the raw natural energies of the mountain forest. "A broad and level lawn now spread before me, covered with the rich green which the herbage here receives in the short but rapid summer; and the solitary dwelling of the hardy mountaineer appeared, with a few cattle straying here and there." The meadows were "shut out from the world by a wall of immense mountains," but, from a distance, these peaks seemed less angular and less threatening. Just as distance smoothed the rough contours of the mountains, time had weathered the raw edges of this little settler society. Nature was a powerful influence on the frontier, but it was not irresistible. Western travelers encountered similar scenes that reinforced their faith in progress. A scattering of neat frame houses and plumb outbuildings suggested the pastoral harmonies that time would lend to the frontier process.[69]

Like Dwight following the Ammonoosuc, naturalists traced the path from savagery to civilization in the stages of frontier growth, linking the pioneer to the evolution of the natural landscape. First to arrive would be a class of migrants with visceral pioneering instincts: men and women who mirrored the casual violence of the forested landscape before them. Only these hearty souls could carry through the fatiguing and graceless work of clearing the forest; thus, the border country was a "place of retreat for rude and even abandoned characters." Very quickly, Benjamin Rush explained, society caught up with the pioneer. "Formerly his cattle ranged at large, but now his neighbours call upon him to confine them with in fences, to prevent their trespassing upon their fields of grain. Formerly, he fed his family with wild animals, but these, which fly from the face of man, now cease to afford him any easy subsistence." Repelled by the arrival of laws and religion, the woodsman-farmer once again headed west, leaving a small clearing to the next arrival. These new pioneers farmed in an equally primitive manner and once again deserted the exhausted land. Next to arrive was a group with capital and resolve; they built sawmills and brickworks, fenced in their fields, and planted a variety of crops. Wrestling the land into a primitive model of the East, they worked manure into the soil, improved the orchard, enlarged the barn,

---

[69] Dwight, *Travels in New England and New York*, pp. 145–50. See Dalton, *Travels in the United States of America, and Part of Upper Canada*, pp. 82–3.

and added outbuildings. This "last comer" completed the transition from forest to fruitful field.[70]

Some saw this agrarian republic passing further into an "insolent aristocracy," but most found reason to hope that the latent energies in the natural landscape would ensure a stable republican civilization. Natural abundance would invoke generosity more than sloth; mobility would encourage innovation rather than rootlessness; and the forest environment would impart its vigor and constancy to the new inhabitants. The results of this progression were most evident in the rural Northeast, insulated as it was from the uncertainties of urban or slave society and more stable and orderly than the West. The "carrier of national identity," as historian Angela Miller puts it, this was the region that inspired a genre of American literature and landscape painting that emphasized the harmony of nature and society. Here, the traveler was assured that the wilderness would yield an agrarian republic.[71]

Like most nineteenth-century travelers and explorers, Timothy Dwight described the scenery of the Northeast in didactic terms. Landscapes without improvement were threatening: in the West, wilderness seemed to engulf each pathetic little clearing and waited at the border of each field, "fermenting, germinating, and sprouting" – a constant reminder that those standing on the pivot of civilization and savagery must remain resolute.[72] Landscapes without nature – farms without trees – were similarly failed landscapes, victims of crass commercial impulses. By contrast, Timothy Dwight's beloved Connecticut River intervales were perfect examples of the evolutionary change from forest to field. Natural meadows extended back from the river, sculpted "like terraced gardens" into pastures, orchards, and fields. Each hosted a compact village where close residential association promoted industry and morality – each community "a single congregation."[73] The intervales were "naturally beautiful," Nathaniel Willis added, their borders carved by smooth, even swings

---

[70] Benjamin Rush, *Essays, Literary, Moral, and Philosophical*, pp. 213, 215, 217–19, 222. See Birkbeck, *Notes on a Journey in America*, pp. 104, 107, 136; Michaux, *Travels to the West of the Allegheny Mountains*, pp. 111, 114; Bradbury, *Travels in the Interior*, p. 280; Flint, *Letters from America*, pp. 233–6.

[71] Miller, *Empire of the Eye*, p. 16. See Hall, *Travels in North America*, pp. 264–5.

[72] Johann Georg Kohl, *Travels in Canada, and Through the States of New York and Pennsylvania* (London, 1861), Vol. 1, p. 245. See Latrobe, *Rambler in North America*, Vol. 1, pp. 52–3.

[73] Dwight, *Travels in New England and New York*, pp. 219, 244, 259, 262; Miller, *Empire of the Eye*, pp. 61–2, 80–1. See Dickinson, *Geographical and Statistical View*, pp. 6–7; Sears, p. 120.

of the river and their edges fringed with magnificent elms. "As they are seldom enclosed . . . , there is a look . . . of . . . wildness about them." Farmers welcomed the relics of primeval nature in their fields; wild shrubs and flowers, rock outcroppings, sentinel trees, and grass-bordered streams reminded the observer how far civilization had come and how much it retained of its natural energies. Small streams cascaded down from the wooded foothills and nourished the fields, and cathedral-like woods stood outside each village, the understory cleared to the browse line by pasturing livestock. Beyond this pastoral scene, the softened forms of forest-cloaked mountains beckoned. Nature was subdued and reintegrated into the improved landscape.[74]

The Connecticut Valley expressed the American genius for blending nature and culture. "The signs of long and steady cultivation may be remarked on the face of the landscape," Charles Latrobe rhapsodized, "which contrasts agreeably with that air of rawness and newness which is imprinted upon the works of man in other portions of the continent."[75] It was time and patience, then, that stood between the raw western clearing and the Arcadian republic. Time would determine the psychic battle with savagery and confirm the logic of evolution in the West.

The Northeast defined the destiny of the West. Yet, on the long and uncertain path between savagery and civilization, naturalists glimpsed a scene of unimaginable destruction that clouded their faith in the meliorating influences of human modification. The idea of improvement made sense as long as the true ends of evolutionary naturalism remained in view. However, at midcentury, the agrarian landscapes of the Northeast, so delicately sculpted in the crucible of time and resolute character, began to show signs of decay. When these exemplars of the agrarian republic began to lose their moral bearing, the Enlightenment faith in the inevitability of improvement gave way as well.

[74] Nathaniel P. Willis, *American Scenery; Or, Land, Lake, and River: Illustrations of Transatlantic Nature*, drawings by W. H. Bartlett (London, 1840), Vol. 2, p. 28. See Thornton, *Diary of a Tour*, pp. 21–2; Hall, *Travels in North America*, Vol. 1, p. 266.

[75] Charles Joseph Latrobe, *The Rambler in North America* (London, 1835), Vol. 1, pp. 42–3.

8

The Naturalist's Mirror

Popular Science and the Roots of Romanticism

In a short book titled *The Northern Lakes: A Summer Residence for Invalids of the South*, Cincinnati naturalist Daniel Drake romanticized the natural history of a small island lying in the waters of northern Lake Huron. He conducted the reader along a winding path through pine-scented hills and meadows to a small cobble beach below Mackinac Island's famed Arch Rock, where at twilight on a summer evening, a crisp steady breeze drove in across the cool waters. "Wave after wave will break at his feet, over the white pebbles, and return as limpid as it came. Up the Straits he will see the evening star hanging on the ruffled surface, and the loose sails of the lagging schooner flapping in the fitful land breeze, while the milky-way...will dimly appear on the waters before him." For two decades, Drake had been collecting data for his ponderous *Systematic Treatise, Historical, Etiological, and Practical, on the Principal Diseases of the Interior Valley of North America*, and in this shorter volume, published in 1842, he addressed the same relation between health and environment.[1] Yet, here, he was speaking to a different audience with a different message about nature and human well-being. Who were these readers, and why was Drake so interested in conveying to them his own sentimental interpretation of natural history?

Daniel Drake had always worked at the borders of popular and academic science. Like Charles Willson Peale's Philadelphia Museum, his

---

[1] Daniel Drake, *The Northern Lakes: A Summer Residence for Invalids of the South* (Cincinnati, 1840); Drake in James Alwin van Fleet, *Old and New Mackinac* (Grand Rapids, 1880), p. 160. See Charles D. Meigs, *A Biographical Notice of Daniel Drake, M.D., of Cincinnati* (Philadelphia, 1853), p. 28.

Western Museum was founded on the popular appeal of natural curiosities and, like Peale, he wrote his science for the ordinary citizen. His *Northern Lakes*, a study of the recuperative potential of the upper Great Lakes region, put this impressive understanding of nature and health before a popular audience. Drake's view of the Mackinac region was part of a new approach to natural history emerging in the middle decades of the century in tandem with the Romantic movement, as Americans adopted a new appreciation for beauty and design in the natural landscape. Never entirely removed from popular cultural trends, American naturalists responded to this growing interest and gave it scientific cache. The American Romantic movement owes much to this development.

Science, Subjectivity, and the Sublime

American ornithology, Alexander Wilson once complained, appeared in the general literature "like the hazy and rough medium of wretched window-glass . . . [so] strangely distorted that one scarcely knows his most intimate neighbors." In his own work, he promised to strip away the "supernatural portents" that clouded this image and present only the "authentic particulars" of each bird – a "faithful mirror" of his own careful observations. However, as Wilson well knew, the essence of the bird was more than the sum of its authentic particulars.[2] His own text, in fact, mirrored an imaginative blend of perspectives that included scientific observation, folk wisdom, theological deduction, and appeal to emotion. Naturalists like Wilson painted nature with many brushes and, so doing, they quickened and enriched the Romantic imagination.

The American Romantic tradition began, in most accounts, with the famous 1836 essay "Nature," in which Ralph Waldo Emerson presented his subject as a commodity and a mirror of divinity. The former was a given in America during the 1830s; it reduced nature to its component authentic particulars and integrated these features into the economic landscape. The latter – nature's spirituality – was a relatively new idea. "Every earnest glance we give to the realities around us," Emerson wrote, "proceeds from a holy impulse, and is really songs of praise." Holding up his own faithful mirror, he found proof of this transcendence in the unifying spirit that flowed through each of nature's particulars, a force

---

[2] Alexander Wilson and Charles Lucian Bonaparte, *American Ornithology: Or, the Natural History of the Birds of the United States* (Philadelphia, n.d.), p. 174.

that "knows neither palm nor oak, but only vegetable life, which sprouts
into forests, and festoons the globe with a garland of grass and vines."
This was the connection that integrated Emerson's spiritual landscape,
just as ecological connection united the landscapes of natural history.[3]
Wilson and Emerson represent two allegiances, one to empirical observation and the other to divine contemplation, but their message was the
same: Understanding nature was an exercise in imagination as much as an
observation about authentic particulars. Subjective appreciation bridged
the gap between Enlightenment science and literary romanticism.

Romanticism emerged in Great Britain and Germany in the late eighteenth century, its approach to nature best represented by Sir Edmond
Burke's *Philosophical Inquiry into the Origins of the Sublime and the
Beautiful*, in which the Irish statesman and philosopher discussed the passions aroused through contemplating magnificent landscapes. In the sublime, Burke thought, "the mind is so entirely filled with its object, that it
cannot entertain any other, nor by consequence reason on that object
which employs it." Attracted to the idea of intensely emotional experience, European Romantics abandoned the austere, mechanical view of
nature described by Newton, Bacon, and Descartes and found inspiration
in a more imaginative and emotional reaction to the world around them –
in particular, to the mysterious ancient ruins that dotted the European
countryside and the primitive natural landscapes in more remote areas
of the world. Romanticism validated the subjective assessment of nature
that made up so much of the scientific record, whereas science kindled the
popular interest in nature upon which the Romantic writer depended. The
two approaches were mutually reinforcing, and both were necessary to
the conservation message that crystallized at the end of the century. This
fusion of perspectives – the emotional response to nature – gave American
landscapes transcendent meaning and positioned nature at the center of
American identity.[4] Science and Romanticism laid the groundwork for
modern conservation thinking.

---

[3] Ralph Waldo Emerson, *The Method of Nature: An Oration, Delivered Before the Society
of Adelphui, in Waterville College, in Maine, August 11, 1841* (Boston, 1841), pp. 9, 11.
[4] Edmund Burke, "Of the Passion Called the Sublime," in Burke, *On the Sublime and
the Beautiful* (Cambridge, 1904–14), p. 51. See Barbara Novak, *Nature and Culture:
American Landscape and Painting, 1825–1875* (New York, 1980), pp. 3–4; Stephen
R. Mark, *Preserving the Living Past: John C. Merriam's Legacy in the State and National
Parks* (Berkeley, 2005), p. 168; Finis Dunaway, *Natural Visions: The Power of Images
in American Environmental Reform* (Chicago, 2005), p. xvii.

Late eighteenth-century Romantics traveled to America expecting its wilderness to unleash "earnest and solemn thoughts," in Humboldt's words. In 1791, French author François René, Vicomte de Chateaubriand, recorded his intoxicated mood as he stepped beyond the pale of civilization on the Niagara frontier: "I went from tree to tree, to the right and the left indiscriminately, saying to myself – Here are no more roads to follow, no more towns, no more close houses, no more presidents, republics, or kings." He stood at the threshold of nature's own world, the landscape before him unscripted and undefiled:

Who can describe the feelings that are experienced on entering these forests, coeval with the world, and which alone afford an idea of the creation, such as it issued from the hands of the Almighty. The light falling from above, through a veil of foliage, diffuses through the recesses of the wood a changing and moveable chiaro-scuro, which gives to objects a fantastic grandeur.... In vain I seek an outlet in these wilds, ... but I arrive only at an open spot formed by some fallen pines. The forest soon becomes darker again; the eye discerns nothing but the trunks of oaks and walnut-trees, succeeding each other, and appearing to stand closer and closer according to their distance: the idea of infinity presents itself to my mind.[5]

Chateaubriand's exposure to the American wilderness was fleeting and, in some cases, invented rather than experienced, but his florid descriptions became a model of sorts for later scientific explorers. Touring the states in 1833–4, Edward Abdy of Cambridge fused the scientific and the sublime as he stood before the great Natural Bridge that Jefferson had immortalized in his *Notes on Virginia*. It was here, Abdy thought, that the waters of the inland sea had forced their way through the mountains in their rush to the Atlantic, and he pondered the scene from a point of view steeped in catastrophism and religious Romanticism:

The mind of the spectator is overwhelmed in admiration and astonishment at the contemplation of that mysterious force that could thus rend the enormous mass of rock, and leave the stupendous work unfinished. He trembles, lest its completion should be instantly effected. When the first emotion has subsided, the imagination is carried back to that unknown era, when the globe was shaken to its foundation.... The flight of time, – the duration of the world, – the insignificance

[5] Alexander Humboldt, *Cosmos: A Sketch of a Physical Description of the Universe* (New York, 1870), Vol. 1, p. 25; Francois Auguste Rene, Vicomte de Chateaubriand, *Travels in America and Italy* (London, 1828), Vol. 1, pp. 111, 148–9. See Thomas R. Cox, "Americans and Their Forests: Romanticism, Progress, and Science in the Late Nineteenth Century," *Journal of Forest History* 29 (October 1985): p. 157.

NATURAL BRIDGE. VIRGINIA.

FIGURE 8.1. Geological science complemented the art of romantic observation. At Virginia's Natural Bridge, made famous by Thomas Jefferson's moving description, the waters of a great inland sea once forced their way through the mountains in their rush to the Atlantic. This exercise in geological imagination was laden with religious overtones and romantic illusions. Nature in America was sublime, evocative of the grandest passions imaginable. "Natural Bridge, Virginia," by W. H. Bartlett, from Nathaniel P. Willis, *American Scenery* (1840). Courtesy of the Special Collections Department, Fogler Library, University of Maine.

of man, – the omnipotence of the Creator, – all that can humble and ennoble, – pass in rapid succession through the mind, and leaves a remembrance that will quit it but with life.[6]

In the decades that followed, science-inspired emotions like these found their way into the landscape paintings of the Hudson River School, the poetry of William Cullen Bryant, and the historical novels of Washington Irving and James Fenimore Cooper, forming a literary and artistic movement that profoundly shaped the way Americans regarded their scenic heritage.[7]

American naturalists had always recorded emotional responses in their journals, but mid-nineteenth-century cultural and social circumstances gave this category of understanding greater popular currency. The romantic veneration of nature followed, as Bruce Greenfield notes, a period of epic national expansion that combined a ruthless mining of nature with extermination or removal of its original inhabitants. As the American economy found footing, the logic of this militaristic sweep across the continent seemed less self-evident, and the primeval quality of the remaining natural landscape assumed a nostalgic cast. Americans continued to view economic resources as the most valuable feature of the western wilderness and the pioneering process as the medium for realizing this value, but the social tensions generated by urbanization and industrialization encouraged a more subtle – and more conflicted – understanding of the untilled garden. More distanced from the wilderness and sensitive to the tensions between republican values and commercial motives, artists, writers, and scientists reconstructed the rural and the wild as the true American landscape.[8]

---

[6] Edward Strutt Abdy, *Journal of a Residence and Tour in the United States of North America, from April, 1833, to October, 1834* (London, 1835), pp. 295–6. See Maximilian Alexander Philip, Prinz von Wied, *Travels in the Interior of North America*, H. Evans Lloyd (ed.), (London, 1843), pp. 39–40; John Moring, *Early American Naturalists: Exploring the American West, 1804–1900* (New York, 2002), p. 93; Charles Varte, *Topographical Description of the Counties of Frederick, Berkeley, and Jefferson Situated in the State of Virginia* (Winchester, 1810), pp. 27–8; Joseph Churchman, *Rudiments of Natural Knowledge, Presented to the Youth of the United States, and to Enquiring Foreigners, by a Citizen of Pennsylvania* (Philadelphia, 1833), p. 279.

[7] Mark V. Barrow, Jr., *A Passion for Birds: American Ornithology After Audubon* (Princeton, 1988), p. 11; Cox, "Americans and Their Forests," p. 156; Hans Huth, *Nature and the American: Three Centuries of Changing Attitudes* (Berkeley, 1957), p. 32.

[8] Bruce Greenfield, *Narrating Discovery: The Romantic Explorer in American Literature, 1790–1855* (New York, 1992), p. 2. See Duncan Faherty, "The Borders of Civilization: Susan Fenimore Cooper's View of American Development," in *Susan Fenimore Cooper: New Essays on Rural Hours and Other Essays*, Rochelle Johnson and Daniel

"Mysterious Converse with the Soul of Nature"

Like Daniel Drake on Mackinac Island, scientific writers transformed their field experiences into a narration of discovery. Scientist and reader would venture forth, "now plunging into the deep cavern, . . . now mounting the lofty ridge and drinking in the glories of the vast landscape." Along the way, the naturalist guided the reader in the proper reaction to nature. "A noble tree, an exquisite flower, or the song of a bird" should "bring the tear to the eye, and soften the heart," Alabama naturalist, T. A. Conrad, instructed.[9] Thomas Nuttall prefaced his detailed and technical ornithological catalog by offering a sentimental and seductive invitation to his readers. Birds, he wrote,

play around us like fairy spirits, elude approach in an element which defies our pursuit, soar out of sight in the yielding sky, journey over our heads in marshaled ranks, dart like meteors in the sunshine of summer, or, seeking the solitary recesses of the forest and the waters, they glide before us like beings of fancy. They diversity the still landscape with the most lively motion and beautiful association; they come and go with the change of the season, and as their actions are directed by an uncontrollable instinct of provident nature, they may be considered as concomitant with the beauty of the surrounding scene. . . . How volatile, how playfully capricious, how musical and happy, are these roving sylphs of nature, to whom the air, the earth, and the waters are almost alike habitable.[10]

Louis Agassiz detoured on his scientific tour of Lake Superior to a dry, sandy, windswept tableland wooded in scrub pine. Beyond the trees, he could see wide openings covered by withered grass where ancient fires had traced their paths across the country. This, he presumed, was "the general character of the interior." No mere untilled garden, this was nature's own

---

Patterson (eds.) (Athens, 2001), p. 112; Richard M. Magee, "An Artist, or a Merchant's Clerk: Susan Fenimore Cooper's *Elinor Wyllys* and Landscape," in ibid., p. 104; Sally McMurray, "Evolution of a Landscape: From Farm to Forest in the Adirondack Region, 1857–1894," *New York History* 80 (April 1999): p. 117; Benjamin Waterhouse, *The Botanist; Being the Botanical Part of a Course of Lectures on Natural History* (Boston, 1811), p. viii; Angela Miller, *The Empire of the Eye: Landscape Representation and American Cultural Politics, 1825–1875* (Ithaca, 1993), pp. 12, 21.

9 Edward Hitchcock, *First Anniversary Address Before the Association of American Geologists* (New Haven, 1841), p. 45; T. A. Conrad in *Advocate of Science and Annals of Natural History* 1 (No. 1, 1834): p. 27. See Charles Willson Peale, *Introduction to a Course of Lectures on Natural History, Delivered in the University of Pennsylvania, Nov. 16, 1799* (Philadelphia, 1800), p. 12; Dillingham, *Discourse on the Advantages of the Study of Natural Sciences*, p. 5; *North American Review*, n.s., 56 (January 1843): p. 192.

10 Thomas Nuttall, *Manual of the Ornithology of the United States and of Canada* (Cambridge, 1832), p. 1.

realm: deathly still, ragged, unmastered, and clearly made for purposes other than farming or logging.[11] Aware of the romantic associations European writers attached to landscapes like these, American naturalists added their own nuances, creating a unique blend of unflavored scientific description and richly sublime sentiment that would become a hallmark of American natural history.

Audubon's *Birds of America* exemplified this blend of technical detail and inviting personal narrative. His birds swayed on the twigs of a birch or maple or fed their young with "gaudy or green insects," as the reader "imagined himself in the forest."[12] Audubon's brown pelican description was a textual complement to this narrative rendering:

But see, the tide is advancing; the billows chase each other towards the shores; the mullets, joyful and keen, leap along the surface, as they fill the bays with their multitudes. The slumbers of the Pelicans are over; the drowsy birds shake their heads, stretch open their mandibles and pouch by way of yawning, expand their ample wings, and simultaneously soar away. Look at them as they fly over the bay; listen to the sound of the splash they make as they drive their open bills, like a pock-net, in the sea, to scoop up their prey; mark how they follow that shoal of porpoises, and snatch up the frightened fishes that strive to escape from them.[13]

This approach was not simply sentimental. Biographer Richard Rhodes points to the unveiled violence in some of Audubon's drawings: "the golden eagle's talon piercing the northern hare's eye, or, elsewhere, the bleeding American hare urinating in pain and terror in the grip of a female red-tailed hawk itself under attack from a swooping, larcenous male, are images fully as harrowing as Goya's nightmare acquaints." Still, his vibrant illustrations are as poetic as they are scientific, offering, as John R. Knott says, "a vision of the American wilderness as a place of Edenic abundance and sublime spectacle."[14]

Drawing the reader into the narrative of discovery, naturalists redefined the American response to nature. Catharine H. Waterman's description of a white birch was scientifically accurate but also crafted to inform

[11] Louis Agassiz, *Lake Superior: Its Physical Character, Vegetation, and Animals, Compared with Those of Other and Similar Regions* (Boston, 1850), p. 84.

[12] *Monthly American Journal of Geology and Natural Science* 1 (September 1831): p. 137; *Edinburgh Magazine* in ibid., 1 (April 1832): p. 462.

[13] Thomas Nuttall, *An Introduction to Systematic and Physiological Botany* (Cambridge, 1827), pp. 11–12; John R. Knott, *Imagining Wild America* (Ann Arbor, 2002), p. 26; John James Audubon, *The Complete Audubon* (Kent, 1978–1979), Vol. 4, p. 34.

[14] Anon., *Rural Rambles; Or, Some Chapter on Flowers, Birds, and Insects, By a Lady* (Philadelphia, 1854), pp. 66–7; Richard Rhodes, *John James Audubon: The Making of an American* (New York, 2004), p. 378; Knott, *Imagining Wild America*, pp. 10–11.

the reader's emotional response. "In every season, and under all circumstances, it is a lovely object," she advised:

nothing can exceed the tender hue of its vernal leaves, as they wave to and fro in the sunshine. In summer, perhaps, it loses something of its beauty, as its bright tints then subside into a more sober green. Still, it preserves its gracefulness of aspect. In autumn it almost more than regains what it lost in summer; whilst winter, which deprives most other vegetable productions of their charms, by displaying more fully the slight silvery stem and delicate ramifications of the birch, seems but to invest it with new attractions.[15]

In his *Introduction to Systematic and Physiological Botany*, Thomas Nuttall narrated his dissections as though the reader were standing beside him. The technique established intimacy and conveyed the excitement of discovery. In similarly inviting terms, Constantine Rafinesque described nature, presumably to an audience of male students, as "a beautiful and modest woman, concealed under many veils, some of which she throws aside occasionally, or allows them to be removed by those who deserve such a high favor. It is thus that they are enabled to acquire an idea of her features, and take a glimpse at her beauty."[16] The piping of the chipping squirrel (*Sciurus [Tamias] lysteri*), Bachman and Audubon wrote, would "recall . . . the mature mind to days of boyhood, . . . when hours and days were spent in almost fruitless exertion to make it prisoner."[17] Peale's broadside for the Philadelphia Museum's mammoth re-created the epic saga of primeval America.

Long before the pale men, with thunder and fire at their command, rushed . . . to ruin this garden of nature . . . a race of animals were in being, huge as the frowning Precipice, cruel as the bloody Panther, swift as the descending Eagle, and terrible as the Angel of Night. The pines crashed beneath their feet; and the lake shrunk when they slaked their thirst . . . Forests were laid waste at a meal, the groans of expiring animals were every where heard; and whole Villages, inhabited by men, were destroyed in a moment.[18]

---

[15] William Barton Rogers, *Address Before the Lyceum of Natural History of Williams College, August 14, 1855* (Boston, 1855), p. 7; Catharine H. Waterman, *Flora's Lexicon: An Interpretation of the Language and Sentiment of Flowers* (Philadelphia, 1840), p. 42. See N. Bryllion Fagin, *William Bartram: Interpreter of the American Landscape* (Baltimore, 1933), p. 106.

[16] Nuttall, *Introduction to Systematic and Physiological Botany*, pp. v–vi, 219; Constantine Rafinesque, "Lecture on Knowledge," Rafinesque Papers, APS.

[17] John James Audubon and John Bachman, *The Viviparous Quadrupeds of North America* (New York, 1851–1854), Vol. 1, p. 67. See Anon., *The Cabinet of Natural History and American Rural Sports, with Illustrations* (Barre, 1973), p. 39.

[18] "Skeleton of the Mammoth Is Now to Be Seen At the Museum," 1801, Broadsides, APS.

American naturalists used a variety of popular affections to limn the American landscape, appealing to myth, curiosity, nostalgia, emotion, beauty, and spirituality. In tandem with Europe's great Romantics – Jean-Jacques Rousseau, Sir Walter Scott, Robert Southey, Samuel Taylor Coleridge, William Wordsworth, Friedrich Schlegel – they explored the emotional connection to nature. In the words of English nature writer, William Howitt, they were "holding mysterious converse with the soul of nature."[19]

Naturalists like Drake, especially those independent of academic affiliations, shared a commitment to writing in an "intelligent and popular style," as the Connecticut Academy of Natural Sciences put it. Swiss-born geologist, Louis Agassiz, laid plans for a grand synthesis of American natural history soon after arriving in America and in his prospectus, he appealed to both citizen and scientist. The volumes, he announced, would be "written in America, and...for Americans."[20] Amos Eaton, William Maclure, Thomas Say, Constantine Rafinesque, and Charles Willson Peale were equally enthusiastic about reaching out to the public; nearly every scientist at some level expressed a belief that nature, rightly described, would offer a "perpetual feast," as one put it, for the reading public. Robert Murdie's *Popular Guide to the Observation of Nature* likened his study to a universal symphony performed for the benefit of humankind: "Wherefore sings the breeze in the forests, why whispers the zephyr among the reeds,... as if the earth were one musical instrument of innumerable strings, if... not to tempt us forth in order to learn?"[21]

---

[19] William Howitt, *The Book of the Seasons; Or, The Calendar of Nature* (Philadelphia, 1831), pp. xvii–xviii.

[20] *Advocate of Science and Annals of Natural History* 1 (No. 1, 1834): p. 14; Louis Agassiz, *Methods of Study in Natural History* (Boston, 1863), pp. 42–3; Elizabeth Cary Agassiz in Louis Agassiz, *Louis Agassiz: His Life and Correspondence*, Elizabeth Cary (ed.) (Boston, 1885), Vol. 2, pp. 533, 535. See *American Quarterly Review* 13 (March 1830): p. 406; Charles Buck, *On the Beauties, Harmonies, and Sublimities of Nature; With Notes, Commentaries, and Illustrations* (New York, 1841), p. 248; Patricia Tyson Stroud, *Thomas Say: New World Naturalist* (Philadelphia, 1992), p. 24; *Port Folio* 8, 2d ser. (July 1812): pp. 7–8; J. L. [John Lee] Comstock, *The Young Botanist: Being a Treatise on the Science, Prepared for the Use of Persons Just Commencing the Study of Plants* (New York, 1836), pp. 47–8; Peale, *Introduction to a Course of Lectures*, pp. 11–12; John Lindley, *Introduction to the Natural System of Botany* (New York, 1831), pp. lxiii, lxiv; *North American Review*, n.s., 41 (October 1835): pp. 406–8; Whitfield Bell, "The Scientific Environment of Philadelphia, 1775–1790," *APS Proceedings* 92 (1948): pp. 6–7; George H. Daniels, *American Science in the Age of Jackson* (New York, 1968), p. 36.

[21] Alphonso Wood, *Leaves and Flowers; Or, Object Lessons in Botany, With a Flora, Prepared for Beginners in Academies and Public Schools* (New York, 1875 [c. 1860]),

In a time of transition in both science and letters, naturalists helped forge a popular interest in nature.

Scientists pursued this public mission because they saw a connection to the country's moral fiber. Natural history was a sensual pleasure, but it was inspiring rather than hedonistic and thus a higher form of recreation. It sharpened the intellect, cultivated local and national pride, and provided a "powerful antidote to the degrading influence of factious politics and unfeeling cupidity." Youth should be instructed in natural history, a *North American Review* editor argued, "not because it may lead to something useful, but because . . . its mere pursuit is improving to the mind and heart."[22] Understanding nature was a devotional exercise as well, although this claim required some delicate compromises. Early Christianity was laced with superstitions about nature, and the scientific challenge to these ideas touched on sensitive themes. As James Murphey pointed out in his *Creation: Or the Bible and Geology Consistent*, lay readers understood the empirical method only vaguely, and they remained suspicious. Clement Moore's 1804 *Observations upon Certain Passages in Mr. Jefferson's Notes on Virginia, Which Appear to Have a Tendency to Subvert Religion, and Establish a False Philosophy* offered a potent example of the fate awaiting those who premised their science purely on material considerations. It was clear, a scholar wrote, that science was "in more or less serious collision with received interpretations of Scripture."[23] Nevertheless, science had much to gain from the religious

p. 5; Robert Mudie, *A Popular Guide to the Observation of Nature* (New York, 1833), pp. 67–8. See Anon., *The Book of Nature* (Boston, 1826), Vol. 1, pp. 3–4.

[22] *Port Folio* 6, 3d ser. (August 1815): pp. 147–8; Wilson and Bonaparte, *American Ornithology*, p. 1; *American Quarterly Review* 13 (March 1830): pp. 365, 406; *North American Review*, n.s., 50 (April 1840): p. 404; ibid., 41 (October 1835): pp. 409, 417–18; Academy of Natural Sciences of Philadelphia, *Journal* 1 (Part 1, May, 1817): p. 2; *Connecticut Courant* (Hartford), July 14, 1829, "Clippings Relating to Appeal for Support of the *American Journal of Science* 1829, Benjamin Silliman Manuscripts, Pennsylvania Historical Society (hereafter PHS); "Preamble," Patterson [New Jersey] Philosophical Society, Constitution, June 19, 1827, Broadsides, APS; Churchman, *Rudiments of Natural Knowledge*, p. xvi; Daniels, *American Science*, p. 49.

[23] James Murphey, *Creation: Or the Bible and Geology Consistent: Together with the Moral Design of the Mosaic History* (New York, 1850), p. v; Clement Moore, *Observations Upon Certain Passages in Mr. Jefferson's Notes on Virginia, Which Appear to Have a Tendency to Subvert Religion, and Establish a False Philosophy* (New York, 1804), pp. 7, 8, 9, 11–12; Shields, *Natural and Revealed Science*, pp. v, 1. See Benjamin Silliman, "Consistency of Geology with Sacred History," supplement to Robert Bakewell, *An Introduction to Geology* (New Haven, 1833), p. 391; Louis Agassiz, *The Structure of Animal Life* (New York, 1866), p. 91; *American Journal of Science* 39 (October 1840): p. 347; *North American Review*, n.s., 31 (April 1831): p. 472; Nina Reid-Maroney, *Philadelphia's Enlightenment, 1740–1800: Kingdom of Christ, Empire*

FIGURE 8.2. Naturalists, particularly those with a strong religious bent, saw divinity in every natural form. This belief infused scientific description with spiritual meaning and reinforced the ecological idea that each plant and animal played a role in God's plan for the universe. Titian Ramsay Peale, *Sketches, 1817–1875*. Courtesy of the American Philosophical Society.

enthusiasm of the early nineteenth century. By tracing "the finger of God" in each scientific discovery, naturalists warded off the two darkest shadows hanging over their discipline: the public perception that they were dilettantes, and the equally dangerous perception that they were godless. Despite the "distrustful eyes" fixed upon it, James D. Dana insisted, American science was both useful and reverential.[24]

This pietistic theme – divinity revealed in natural form – infused the scientific description of landscapes with spiritual meaning and reinforced the ecological idea that each plant and animal was part of God's plan

of Reason (Westport, 2001), pp. 1, 3; Raymond Phineas Stearns, *Science in the British Colonies of America* (Urbana, 1970), p. 513; John G. West, Jr., *The Politics of Revelation and Reason: Religion and Civic Life in the New Nation* (Lawrence, 1996), pp. 6, 16; Jon Butler, "Magic, Astrology, and the Early American Religious Heritage, 1600–1760," *American Historical Review* 84 (No. 2, 1979): pp. 318, 325, 334–5.

[24] Reid-Maroney, *Philadelphia's Enlightenment*, pp. 1, 3; James D. Dana, *An Address Before the Alumni of Yale College, at the Comment Anniversary, August, 1856* (New Haven, 1856), pp. 4–5. See Huth, *Nature and the American*, pp. 10–11; *Monthly American Journal of Geology and Natural Science* 1 (July 1831): p. 7; Amos Binney, *Remarks Made at the Annual Meeting of the Boston Society of Natural History* (Boston, 1845), pp. 8–9.

for the universe. "The more thoroughly we study and the more closely we observe nature in all its parts, the more shall we learn to admire and adore that being who holds our own eternal destiny in his hands," William Dillingham wrote. Agassiz, whose father and grandfather were ministers, considered taxonomy only a point of departure for exploring this divine plan. "We must understand the connection between the various parts of Creation, and, rising higher still, direct our contemplations to the Author of all, who has formed the whole and subjected it to all those modifications extending through long ages."[25]

An American Sublime

Given these devotional biases, naturalists helped create a romantic sublime for America. The essentials of romantic landscape appreciation – gloom, fear, awe, powerlessness, piety – had been part of the language of discovery since colonial times, but religious symbolism gave the explorers' emotional reaction an elevated tone. Naturalist-historian James McCauley described West Canada Creek in New York in terms worthy of the sublime: "You tremble with reverential awe when you consider that one false step might precipitate you into the resistless torrent below, and in an instant consign you to a watery grave – you see what a feeble creature man is, and are forcibly impressed with ideas of the wisdom and power of that Mighty Being, who commanded the earth to emerge from the deep and the waters to flow."[26] Traveling through a land of unusual beauty and grandeur, naturalists used rich devotional language as one among several elements of their analysis. God, according to Rhode Island minister-naturalist, John Bristed, had "scattered the great works of his creation" with "a bold and magnificent profusion" in this quarter of the globe.[27]

This religiously inspired scientific assessment was important to the American scenic tradition. European landscapes had been freighted with centuries of literary, historical, and artistic interpretation, so that European travelers understood perfectly which features were worthy of

---

[25] Dillingham, *Discourse on the Advantages of the Study of Natural Sciences*, p. 6; Louis Agassiz, *An Introduction to the Study of Natural History* (New York, 1847), p. 5.

[26] James McCauley, *The Natural, Statistical and Civil History of the State of New-York* (Albany, 1829), Vol. 1, p. 201. See Novak, *Nature and Culture*, p. 34; Pamela Regis, *Describing Early America: Bartram, Jefferson, Crevecoeur, and the Influence of Natural History* (Philadelphia, 1992), p. 64.

[27] John Bristed, *The Resources of the United States of America* (New York, 1818), p. 12. See Bedell, *Anatomy of Nature*, p. 4.

admiration and which were not. America was largely empty of these affec-
tive references; western rivers and mountains were visually grand, James
Hall noted, but they were "nameless to the poet and historian." Nothing was "romantic or incredible."[28] Naturalists translated the European
Romantic tradition into an American idiom. Harvard geologist Charles
Jackson described Maine's rugged eastern coast as a series of "dark overhanging battlements, raised high in air, amid the surf, bidding defiance
to the storm." As his reference to ancient castles suggests, the European
practice of venerating cultural ruins was on his mind, but Jackson and
others applied this inspiration to America's natural landscapes as they
explored new rules of perspective appropriate to the young nation. In
Europe, one writer remarked,

the soul and centre of attraction in every picture is some ruin of the *past*. The
wandering artist avoids every thing that is modern, and selects his point of view so
as to bring prominently into his sketch, the castle, or the cathedral, which history
or antiquity has hallowed.... [In America] the objects and habits of reflection
in both traveller and artist undergo...a direct revolution. He who journeys
here...must feed his imagination on the *future*....His mind, as he tracks the
broad rivers of his own country, is perpetually reaching forward.[29]

Being newly discovered, American landscapes were "naturally...cheer-
ful," whereas those in Europe – mountains, moors, and deserts – had an
"old, worn-out exhausted appearance." Thus, nature in America evoked
thoughts of the future: "Instead of inquiring into its antiquity, he sits over
the fire with his paper and pencil, and calculates what the population will
be in ten years."[30]

Nature was new but also magnificently ancient. Giant boulders scraped
hundreds of miles across the bedrock, deep gorges carved through the
Appalachian ridges, and sedimentary formations thousands of feet thick
suggested a glorious epic played out across the great gulf of time – a

[28] James Hall, *Sketches of History, Life, and Manners in the West* (Philadelphia, 1835),
Vol. 1, pp. 14–15; Charles T. Jackson, *First Report on the Geology of the State of Maine*
(Augusta, 1837), p. 30. See Captain Basil Hall, *Travels in North America, in the Years
1827 and 1828* (Philadelphia, 1829), Vol. 1, pp. 111–12.

[29] N. P. Willis, *American Scenery; Or, Land, Lake, and River: Illustrations of Transatlantic
Nature*, drawings by W. H. Bartlett (London, 1840), Vol. 1, p. 1.

[30] [Susan Fenimore] Cooper, "A Dissolving View," in Nathaniel Willis, *The Home Book
of the Picturesque: American Scenery, Art, and Literature* (New York, 1852), pp. 81–3,
88–90; Willis, *American Scenery*, p. 2. See J. Hector St. John de Crèvecoeur, *Letters
from an American Farmer and Sketches of Eighteenth-Century America*, Albert E. Stone
(ed.), (New York, 1986 [c. 1782]), p. 42; William Edward Baxter, *America and the
Americans* (London, 1855), p. 6; Edward W. Watkin, *A Trip to the United States and
Canada, in a Series of Letters* (London, 1852), p. xii; Parrish, "Women's Nature,"
p. 205.

story "so interesting that the most splendid fictions of the human imagination sink into insignificance when compared with it." Edward Hitchcock divided his geological surveys of Massachusetts and Vermont into three parts: an "economical geology" describing the useful minerals and rocks he discovered; a "scientific geology" outlining the principles that explained those features; and a "scenographical geology" containing descriptions of "the most remarkable natural scenery of the State, accompanied by drawings of the most interesting spots." Into the latter, he encoded the geological epics necessary for a Romantic view of New England: the angular granite peaks of the White Mountains were ancient and sublime, while the Merrimack Valley's rounded sedimentary formations were newer and more picturesque.[31] "If we ... are destitute of the antiquity of human institutions," a scientific reviewer wrote in 1818, "we should never forget that we possess the antiquity of nature."[32]

This cultural mapping carried a certain ambiguity. George Featherstonhaugh wrestled with the relative weight of nature and cultivation as he stood on a hilltop above a settlement recently carved from the wilderness. From his remote vantage, the clearing seemed charming indeed, and he too found his thoughts "perpetually reaching forward" to a vision of orderly fields, orchards, and meadows. He valued these stump-clogged pastures over the equally charming natural landscape but found it prudent "to lend to such scenes the advantage of distance" rather than accept them as beautiful in themselves. Charles Jackson achieved the same effect by careful framing. On Maine's upper St. John River, he encountered a "most magnificent waterfall" where mist and spray produced a "gorgeous iris ... floating in the air, waving its rich colors over the white foam and forming a beautiful contrast with the sombre rocks [of] ... the abyss." A local lumberman had recently erected a mill beside the falls, and Jackson described the improvement with a great deal of ambivalence: "Although it is sometimes agreeable to see the useful combined with the beautiful, I do not suppose that lovers of the picturesque will imagine the beauty of

---

[31] Edward Hitchcock, *Report on the Geology, Mineralogy, Botany, and Zoology of Massachusetts* (Amherst, 1833), p. 92; Hitchcock et al., *Report on the Geology of Vermont: Descriptive, Theoretical, Economical, and Scenographical* (Claremont, 1861), Vol. 2, pp. 874, 875, 878–9.

[32] Jackson, *First Report on the Geology of the State of Maine*, p. viii; *North American Review* 6 (March 1818): p. 345. See Charles Daubeny, *Journal of a Tour Through the United States, and in Canada, Made During the Years 1837–38* (Oxford, 1843), p. 16; Varte, *Topographical Description*, pp. 27–9; *American Quarterly Review* 13 (March 1830): p. 472; John D. Godman, *American Natural History* (Philadelphia, 1826), Vol. 1, p. 43.

the Falls enhanced by the erection of saw mills by its side." Nevertheless, he concluded, "if they prove advantageous to the public, we must yield in matters of taste, to the demands of commerce," and there was, he added, "nothing repulsive in the appearance of these works, and they may be shut out of the view, if found to detract from its interest."[33] Naturalists offered a forward-looking perspective on nature but found the loss of ancient and pristine landscapes a difficult compromise.[34]

Although they failed to resolve the contradiction between the pastoral and the sublime, naturalists did map out a new vision of nature that made room for the past and the future, the domestic and the wild, the subtle and the sublime. From this mix of opposites, they crafted an American identity that drew deeply from the energies they discovered in the rocks, rivers, and forests of the west. This they bequeathed to the American Romantics and to the conservationists and preservationists who followed them.

Softening the Sublime

As Featherstonhaugh and Jackson made clear, American identity depended on a subtle tension between unsullied nature and the tilled garden. As historian Finis Dunaway puts it, America was "a place altered by human labor but still tied to natural cycles and governed by forces beyond human control." This blend of natural forces and human will was apparent in the essays of Susan Fenimore Cooper, who drew the reader back from the wilderness fringe – the sublime – to the neighborhood environment – the pastoral.[35] The daughter of James Fenimore Cooper, she composed her best-known book, *Rural Hours*, in 1850 as a celebration of her own western New York setting, which had been cleared from the forests within the memory of some still living in the area. For Cooper, as for many American naturalists and Romantics, the rural Northeast was the ideal pastorale, the West being too raw and the South too tainted by slavery to represent the rise of the American Republic.[36]

---

[33] George William Featherstonhaugh, *A Canoe Voyage Up the Minnay Sotor* (London, 1847), pp. 17–18; Jackson, *First Report on the Geology of the State of Maine*, pp. 15–16, 70–1.

[34] W. Winterbotham, *An Historical, Geographical, Commercial, and Philosophical View of the American United States* (London, 1795), Vol. 2, p. 4. See Regis, *Describing Early America*, p. 61; Novak, *Nature and Culture*, p. 35.

[35] Dunaway, *Natural Visions*, p. 205.

[36] Rochelle Johnson and Daniel Patterson (eds.), *Susan Fenimore Cooper: New Essays on Rural Hours and Other Essays* (Athens, 2001), p. xiv; Lucy Maddox, "Susan Fenimore Cooper's Rustic Primer," in ibid., pp. 85–6, 94.

Cooper was no wilderness explorer, but she understood the importance of nature in the American sense of place and, as with many sedentary naturalists, she relished her fieldwork in the familiar neighborhood. "Our own highland lake can lay no claim to grandeur; it has no broad expanse, and the mountains about cannot boast of any great height, yet there is a harmony in the different parts of the picture which gives it much merit, and which must always excite a lively feeling of pleasure." Like other naturalists, she stressed the satisfactions of a close bond with nature in its most familiar forms: a half-tamed nature in a half-tilled landscape. "Many birds like a village life," she noted. "They seem to think man is a very good-natured animal, building chimneys and roofs, planting groves, and digging gardens for their especial benefit; only, they wonder not a little, that showing as he does a respectable portion of instinct, he should yet allow those horrid creatures – boys and cats – to run at large in his domain."[37] Cooper wove these village improvements into her vision of the integrated landscape.

Two years after publication of *Rural Hours*, Nathaniel P. Willis produced a volume of essays on American landscapes as an experiment, he explained, "to ascertain how far the taste of our people may warrant the production of home-manufactured presentation-books, and how far we can successfully compete with those from abroad." More than an experiment, his *Home Book of the Picturesque* heralded Romanticism's coming of age and laid out the rules for interpreting the American landscape. Like Cooper, he valued the integrated landscape more than nature or culture on its own. In emphasizing this, Willis borrowed heavily from the naturalist tradition, showing how America drew its energies from a dynamic natural foundation and linking these energies to the future of the republic.[38] America was a work in progress. Its primeval forest was monotonous, and its freshly occupied frontier, stark and unappealing: "The appearance of girdled trees, of drowned woods, burnt or fallen stumps, rough enclosures, and stony land, are blemishes which an unaccustomed eye can with difficulty overcome." However, for those with vision, the scene was pregnant with possibilities: "It requires the prospective glance of an American to see the form of nature, which is now in dishabille, restored to her neat drapery, glowing with vegetation, and decked with flowers." In a country so fresh and so untilled, the observer

[37] Susan Fenimore Cooper, *Rural Hours* (New York, 1850), p. 63.
[38] Willis, *American Scenery*, Vol. 1, pp. 1, iii, 7; Sue Rainey, *Creating Picturesque America: Monument to the Natural and Cultural Landscape* (Nashville, 1994), p. 4.

could "finish the portrait to his fancy, and make a flowery Temple of a prostrate wilderness."[39]

In an essay included in Willis's volume, James Fenimore Cooper expounded similarly on nature and the pastoral. Europe excelled in the sublime, with its venerable cultural monuments and soaring peaks. The Appalachians lacked the grandeur of the Alps, but their unique blend of forest cover and arable soils was compelling: The "agricultural and the savage unite to produce landscapes of extraordinary beauty and grace." As civilization advanced into these umbrageous ridges, America would boast "a line of mountain scenery extending from Maine to Georgia . . . that will scarcely have a parallel in any other quarter of the world." Nature would complement society, giving the scene an "air of freshness . . . seldom, if ever, met with in Europe."[40] In a companion essay, Susan Cooper acknowledged this unique alliance of primitive energies and village improvements. "A broad extent of forest is no doubt necessary to the magnificent spectacle, but there should also be broken woods, scattered groves, and isolated trees; and it strikes me that the quiet fields of man, and his cheerful dwellings, should also have a place in the gay picture."[41]

The authors in Willis's volume were responding to a set of social anxieties emerging in the Northeast at midcentury. The country was new and its trajectory not yet clear. To many Americans, the future was a matter of great concern. Other democratic civilizations had succumbed to corruption and greed, and this lack of certainty produced, in the words of historian Angela Miller, a "thinly disguised social hysteria, channeled into evangelical crusades and pulpit jeremiads against wealth." In 1834–6, landscape artist Thomas Cole unveiled his *Course of Empire*, a masterpiece of interpretative landscape art that depicted a generic civilization – possibly America – in stages of growth and decay ranging from the savage and Arcadian to the jaded empire and its apocalyptic end. The work, exhibited shortly before the devastating depression of 1837, highlighted the contingent nature of the pastoral ideal and drew attention to corrupting influences like political aggrandizement, commercial greed, and thoughtless self-indulgence.[42]

---

[39] Willis, *American Scenery*, Vol. 2, p. 26.

[40] James Fenimore Cooper, "American and European Scenery Compared," in Willis, *Home Book of the Picturesque*, pp. 52, 54, 60–1, 67–9.

[41] Cooper, "Dissolving View," p. 83.

[42] Miller, *Empire of the Eye*, pp. 23–4, 36–8, 61; Novak, *Nature and Culture*, p. 10.

It was in this context that the Coopers composed their thoughts on nature's socializing and invigorating potential: America could avoid the perils of jaded society by grounding its identity in nature. Forests abounded in ruins that brought to mind the continuities in nature's ongoing process: "Old trees, dead and dying, are left standing for years, until at length they are shivered and broken by the winds, or they crumble slowly away to a shapeless stump." These cycles of death and rebirth lent constancy and texture to the landscape. "The arbutus is now open everywhere in the woods and groves," Susan Cooper wrote in her natural history of the seasons. "How pleasant it is to meet the same flowers year after year! If the blossoms were liable to change – if they were to become capricious and irregular – they might excite more surprise, more curiosity, but we would love them less." To appreciate this regularity was to be elevated above society's "fickle change." This fixity of purpose – seasonal cycles and quiet resolve – provided lessons for a people swayed by the "fancies of each passing generation." Maywings (*Trillium lanceolatum?*), the heralds of springtime, knew "nothing of vanity," she wrote. Their "unconscious, spontaneous beauty" was emblematic of America's "innate grace" and simplicity.[43]

The scenic harmony Cooper discovered in the integrated landscape implied a subtle conservation lesson. America was at its worse when the settler endeavored to "rise above his true part of laborer and husbandman, when he assumes the character of creator, and piles you up hills, pumps you up a river, scatters stones, or sprinkles cascades," and it was at its best when he accepted nature's guidance. The astute observer would know "where there is something amiss in the scene" – where improvement transgressed good judgment, as when "a country is stripped of its wood to fill the pockets or feed the fires of one generation." Like other naturalists, Cooper viewed human improvements as part of the scheme of nature, until, as she put it, the improver transgressed the harmonies of the integrated landscape.[44]

Women and Nature

Between 1827 and 1832, Constantine Rafinesque published ninety-six short illustrated popular periodical articles using a literary form

---

43 Cooper, *Rural Hours*, pp. 48–9, 87, 206–7. See Faherty, "Borders of Civilization," p. 109; Magee, "Artist, or a Merchant's Clerk," pp. 101–3; Miller, *Empire of the Eye*, p. 14.
44 Cooper, "Dissolving View," p. 82.

developed in Europe that rendered botanical taxonomy as a "language of flowers." He presented each blossom as a "moral emblem," adding lyrically written anatomical descriptions, lists of medical and ornamental uses, descriptions of habitat and "botanical companions," folk legends, and instructions on how the reader should respond emotionally. Rafinesque's ties with academia were loose at best, leaving him at liberty to explore this sentimental presentation of botany. By midcentury, few other men of science were so inclined but female naturalists, for the most part barred from participating in professional and academic activities, used this romantic genre freely. Although Rafinesque introduced the floral calendar to America, women naturalists were its primary agents. At a time when many male naturalists were drawing disciplinary boundaries around their work, women extended the tradition of broadening the study of nature and appealing to a popular audience.[45] Emphasizing nature's religious, aesthetic, and moral significance, they helped forge a conservation ethic for America.

Women contributed a great deal to the American scientific tradition, although their accomplishments are poorly documented.[46] Among several colonial female naturalists, Jane Colden stands out. She was born in 1724 and when she was four, her father, pioneering Linnaean botanist Cadwallader Colden, moved his family to a country estate in the Hudson Highlands. As he later put it, this deprived his children "of all those amusements in which young people take delight" and, in order to relieve their ennui, he put them to work studying nature. His daughter "Jenny," he remembered, demonstrated a particular aptitude for botanical illustration and classification: "she eagerly swallow'd the bait & you cannot imagine with what pleasure she has passed many an hour which otherwise might have been very dull & heavy." Colden's mother, who valued education for her daughters, instructed Jane in gardening and illustrating, and her father provided access to his considerable library and introduced her to Linnaeus's binomial system, believing that "the ladies are at least as well fitted for this study as the men by their natural curiosity & the accuracy & quickness of their Sensations." At a time when most botanies were written in Latin, Colden helped his daughter with translations and

---

[45] Beverly Seaton, "Rafinesque's Sentimental Botany: 'The School of Flora,'" *Bartonia* (No. 54, 1988), pp. 43, 98, 102–4.

[46] See William Martin Smallwood in collaboration with Mabel Sarah Coon Smallwood, *Natural History and the American Mind* (New York, 1941), p. 105; Emanuel D. Rudolph, "Almira Hart Lincoln Phelps (1793–1884) and the Spread of Botany in Nineteenth-Century America," *American Journal of Botany* 71 (No. 8, 1984), p. 1164.

hoped to see the day when vernacular texts would render this information less "tiresome & disagreeable."[47]

Colden herself learned to translate Linnaeus and freed his writing of technical jargon by "using two or three words in place of one." With introductions from her father, she sent her specimens, descriptions, and drawings to Europe's best scientists and, by 1755, she had completed a local botany of around four hundred plants. To aid her in identification and illustration, she developed a technique for making leaf impressions using printer's ink and a rolling press; the results caught the eye of several European naturalists, including Linnaeus and Gronovius.[48] Peter Kalm, Alexander Garden, and the Bartrams helped spread Colden's reputation through the colonies.[49] Her father, as he grew older, shifted the burden of his correspondence to his daughter, who won considerable acclaim as the only woman of the time to master the Linnaean system. Colden died in childbirth in 1766.[50]

Although Colden was an important representative of women's accomplishments in botany, it would be dangerous to read uniquely feminine characteristics into her taxonomy. Like her male colleagues, she gathered much of her information from conversations with "country people" – settlers and Indians – and, thus, her listings included practical lore as well as scientific taxonomy. Her style of description was simple but precise:

[47] Cadwallader Colden to John Fothergill, October 18, 1757, in Cadwallader Colden, *The Letters and Papers of Cadwallader Colden* (New York, 1917–1922), Vol. 5, p. 203; Colden to John Frederic Gronovius, October 1, 1755, in ibid., pp. 29–30; Colden to John Fothergill, October 18, 1757, in ibid., p. 203; Thomas Hallock, *From the Fallen Tree: Frontier Narratives, Environmental Politics, and the Roots of a National Pastoral, 1749–1826* (Chapel Hill, 2003), pp. 138–9.

[48] Sally Gregory Kohlstedt, Michael M. Sokal, Bruce V. Lewenstein, *The Establishment of Science in America: 150 Years of the American Association for the Advancement of Science* (New Brunswick, 1999), p. 10; Cadwallader Colden to John Frederic Gronovius, October 1, 1755, Colden, *Letters and Papers of Cadwallader Colden*, Vol. 5, pp. 30–1; Colden to John Fothergill, October 18, 1757, in ibid., p. 30.

[49] Frederick Brendel, "Historical Sketch of the Science of Botany in North America from 1635 to 1840," *The Naturalist* 13 (November 1879), p. 757; Elizabeth C. Call, "The Gentlewoman, Jane Colden, and Her Manuscript on New York Native Plants," in Jane Colden, *Botanic Manuscript of Jane Colden, 1724–1766* (New York, 1963), pp. 17–18.

[50] William Darlington, *Memorials of John Bartram and Humphrey Marshall* (New York, 1967), pp. 19–21; Cadwallader Colden in Stearns, *Science in the British Colonies*, pp. 566–7; H. W. Rickett, "Jane Colden as Botanist, in Contemporary Opinion," in Colden, *Botanic Manuscript*, pp. 22–4; John Bartram, "A Journey to the Katskill Mountains, with Billy, 1753," in Darlington, *Memorials of John Bartram and Humphrey Marshall*, p. 202; Call, "Gentlewoman, Jane Colden," p. 21; Susan Scott Parrish, "Women's Nature: Curiosity, Pastoral, and the New Science in British America," *Early American Literature* 37 (No. 2, 2002): pp. 20–7.

her *Pedicularis tuberosa* (yellow lousewort or snapdragon), "call'd by the Country People Betony," developed flowers that "grow upon the top of the Stem in a short S'pike, set thick without foot stalks; at the bottom of each flower Cap grows a small Leaf, scallop'd or jugged on the edge like the Feathers of the Leaves on the Stem." She carefully described each plant's context – wetland, meadow, upland, swamp, or "about the roots of old trees" – and like her father, at times she would "beg Leave to differ" with Linnaeus. As with her male counterparts, she was particularly interested in medicinal plants, sending her "country" remedies to physician-correspondents for confirmation. The medicinal use of silk grass (*Asclepias tuberosa*) she learned from a Canada Indian but verified by corresponding with doctors in New England and Maryland. Pike (or poke) weed (*Phytolacca decandra*) was useful in cancers, but botanists found it difficult to propagate. In the wilds, she found it growing "in the Dung of birds," and she advised her European colleagues to plant the seeds accordingly.[51]

Colden's prospects, if not her accomplishments, were somewhat unique, as women rarely enjoyed such a nurturing atmosphere. Although they were generally encouraged as consumers of scientific information, women were seldom expected to produce it in the way Colden did.[52] Some specialized in botanical medicine or worked as scientific illustrators. Lucy Say prepared and colored thousands of engravings for her husband's *Conchology*, and Orra White Hitchcock, an accomplished scholar in her own right, accompanied her husband on scientific expeditions and drew fossils and geological scenes for his books and reports. Maria Martin, a trained botanist, illustrator, and associate of John James Audubon, painted flowers, plants, and insects for *Birds of America*.[53] Most, however, approached nature in the manner pioneered by Rafinesque. As a moral discipline, science was compatible with women's traditional domestic responsibilities. It offered valuable lessons on maternal virtues

---

[51] Colden, *Botanic Manuscript*, pp. 21, 46, 53, 80, 83. See Call, "Gentlewoman, Jane Colden," p. 21.

[52] Ann B. Shteir, *Cultivating Women, Cultivating Science: Flora's Daughters and Botany in England 1760–1860* (Baltimore, 1996), pp. 2, 37. See Anon., *Rural Rambles*, pp. 37–8; William Darlington, *A Lecture on the Study of Botany, Read Before the Ladies' Botanical Society at Wilmington, Delaware, March 2, 1844* (Wilmington, 1844), p. 4; Peale, *Course of Lectures on Natural History*, p. 14; Parrish, "Women's Nature," p. 200.

[53] Shteir, *Cultivating Women*, p. 37; Stroud, *Thomas Say*, pp. 238–9; *North American Review*, n.s., 42 (April 1836): p. 433; Lois Barber Arnold, *Four Lives in Science: Women's Education in the Nineteenth Century* (New York, 1984), pp. 14, 32–3.

such as sensitivity, benevolence, and cooperation, and women scientists passed these on to mothers and children. It was in this spirit that Timothy Flint dedicated his *Lectures upon Natural History* to female seminary students.[54]

Most women scientists were drawn to natural history through gardening. So long as it did not involve digging in the earth, applying manure, or preparing compost, gardening was considered an appropriate occupation for middle- and upper-class women and, like gardening, botany cultivated a sense of delicacy and proportion, fostered regard for the welfare of plants, and involved no killing or dissecting.[55] Rafinesque condescendingly wrote from the University of Transylvania that his classes were "patronized by the ladies, and [I] must endeavour to please them by telling them pretty things, rather than by displaying too much learning," but others were more genuine, providing specimens, advice, and technical information for women who wrote popular natural histories. John Finch of Boston urged women to explore the world beyond the garden, where richer soils and wilder plants offered "pleasing and useful information when addressed in the language of science."[56]

William Smellie, the great English popularizer, worried that women would find the Linnaean sexual system offensive. Linnaeus, he cautioned, "pushed analogy ... beyond all decent limits." The calix, according to Linnaeus, "represents the marriage *bed*; the corolla the *curtains*; the filaments the *spermatic vessels*; the antherae the *testes*; the pollen the *male semen*; the stigma the extremity of the *female organ*; the stylus the *vagina*; the germen the *ovarium*; the pericarpium the *impregnated ovarum*; and the seeds the *eggs*." Some women were, indeed, circumspect in approaching these classifications. One, for instance, carefully rephrased Linnaeus's sexual symbology: "The pistil nourishing the young fruit in its bosom

54 Timothy Flint, *Lectures upon Natural History, Geology, Chemistry, the Application of Steam, and Interesting Discoveries in the Arts* (Boston, 1833), p. viii. See Arnold, *Four Lives in Science*, p. 7; Almira Hart Lincoln Phelps, *Botany for Beginners: An Introduction to Mrs. Lincoln's Lectures on Botany* (Hartford, 1833), pp. iii–v, 13–14, 29.

55 Almira H. Lincoln [Phelps], *Familiar Lectures on Botany* (Hartford, 1829), pp. 13–14. See Darlington, *Lecture on the Study of Botany*, p. 5; Laura Johnson, *Botanical Teacher for North America* (Albany, 1834), p. 15; Priscilla Wakefield, *An Introduction to Botany, in a Series of Familiar Letters with Illustrative Engravings* (Philadelphia, 1818), p. iii; Phelps, *Botany for Beginners*, pp. 16–17.

56 Constantine Rafinesque to Zaccheus Collins, December 1, 1819, Rafinesque Papers, APS; John Finch (1830), Broadsides, APS. See Darlington, *Lecture on the Study of Botany*, p. 3; Wakefield, *Introduction to Botany*, pp. iv–v; Anon., *Rural Rambles*, p. 37; Almira Phelps in Rudolph, "Almira Hart Lincoln Phelps," p. 1163; Phelps, "Preface," n.p., *Familiar Lectures on Botany*.

is considered as the mother, and bears a Greek name, *gynia*, signifying wife; while the stamen, which supplies her with food for her young family, is termed *andria*, the husband."[57] Yet, in general, women's taxonomies suggest a high level of comfort with sexual references and with scientific or technical language in general. Acknowledging this, Peale insisted that women were in no sense a "weaker vessel" intellectually; those who devoted their lives to science gave "every demonstration of the intensity and depth of their intellectual powers."[58]

Peale was referring specifically to several notable European female naturalists, including Linnaeus's own daughter, who paved the way for women in America. Maria Sybilla Merian, born in Frankfort in 1647, learned illustration from eminent Dutch painters among her mother's acquaintances and published two volumes on the plants, reptiles, and insects of Surinam. Her glistening serpents and hairy spiders were drawn, as a commentator put it, with "horrible precision." Elizabeth Blackwell's aptitude for botanical illustration made her the Atlantic world's best known female natural scientist. A physician as well as an artist, she published *A Curious Herbal, Containing 500 Cuts of the Most Useful Plants Which Are Now Used in the Practice of Physic* in 1737 to free her husband from debtor's prison.[59] Priscilla Wakefield's 1796 *Introduction to Botany*, the first general botany written by a British woman, was composed as a correspondence between two teenage sisters, a technique that brought nature into the home and eased the reader into the more arcane aspects of the science. Citing examples like these, Benjamin Waterhouse urged American women to take their pencils and brushes out into the woods and fields. "Time ... devoted to the charming art of copying nature and acquiring some knowledge of her works," he wrote, would "embellish our system of female education."[60]

If Jane Colden was America's most accomplished female botanist, Almira Phelps was the discipline's most important popularizer and, in this regard, she fulfilled a role more typical among early scientific women. Born in Connecticut in 1793, Phelps displayed a passion for nature study

---

[57] Anon., *The Young Lady's Book: A Manual of Elegant Recreations, Exercises, and Pursuits* (Boston, 1831), p. 35.

[58] William Smellie, *The Philosophy of Natural History* (Edinburgh, 1790), p. 248; Darlington, *Lecture on the Study of Botany*, pp. 7–9; Peale Lectures, APS. See Stearns, *Science in the British Colonies*, p. 532; Waterhouse, *Botanist*, pp. 208–9.

[59] Waterhouse, *Botanist*, p. 211; Shteir, *Cultivating Women*, pp. 40, 51.

[60] Waterhouse, *Botanist*, pp. 213, 215; Shteir, *Cultivating Women*, pp. 62, 83; Hallock, *From the Fallen Tree*, pp. 143–4.

and education early on. Her sister, Emma Willard, directed the nation's first female college-level curriculum at Troy Female Seminary in New York, while Phelps supervised a female academy in Pittsfield, Massachusetts. When her husband died in 1823, Phelps returned to school to study Latin, Greek, and natural history. She taught at the Troy Female Seminary from 1823 to 1831, and her scientific interests flourished in the institution's vernacular-based instruction. While teaching in New York, Vermont, Pennsylvania, and Maryland, Phelps wrote a series of popular books on botany, chemistry, geology, and natural philosophy. Her *Familiar Lectures* went through at least thirty-nine printings between 1829 and 1869 as one of America's most successful textbooks. Phelps retired in 1856 to Baltimore, where she became the third woman elected to the American Academy of Arts and Sciences.[61] "With respect to botanical facts, I have no claim to any discoveries," she told her readers. Rather, she innovated by providing scientific perspective on domestic arts, beauty, delicacy, and moral refinement. Properly instructed, she felt, a woman became "fitted for the companion of enlightened man; without education, she is but his toy or his slave."[62]

Phelps's approach was sentimental but not evasive. In confronting the issue of sexual reproduction, she directed the reader's attention to the "moisture upon the pollen" and explained that "the stigma was... imbued with a liquid substance, and... the anther, when ripe, opens its lids or valves, and throws out the pollen." The pistil, she continued, "falls upon the stigma; swelled with the moisture which it there finds, each little sack of the pollen explodes, and the oily substance which it contains is absorbed by the stigma, and passes through minute pores into the germ." Having delved into the intimate sex life of a plant, she turned the reader's attention to the divine purposes of procreation and, here, her scientific romanticism became apparent. "Nature does not form a beautiful flower and then leave it to perish without any provision for a future plant," she wrote. The flower was beautiful as well as sexually functional, but mostly it was a "link in the chain of vegetable existence between the old and new

---

[61] Arnold, *Four Lives in Science*, pp. 38, 50, 54; Sarah Josepha Hale, *Woman's Record; Or, Sketches of All Distinguished Women* (New York, 1853), p. 771; Rudolph, "Almira Hart Lincoln Phelps," pp. 1161–2; clipping insert, Phelps, *Familiar Lectures on Botany*, Library Company, Philadelphia.

[62] Phelps, *Familiar Lectures on Botany*, pp. x, 1, 12–13; Almira Phelps in Rudolph, "Almira Hart Lincoln Phelps," p. 1165. See Arnold, *Four Lives in Science*, pp. 58–9; Parrish, "Women's Nature," p. 204.

plant, ensuring that 'Seed time and harvest shall continue unto the end of the world."[63] Although more technical than most popular botanists, Phelps bridged the gap between science and sentimentality, offering an intimate appreciation of nature that blended technical details and arcane processes into a compelling vision of harmonious design.

Phelps's intent was to convey this detailed record to a broad popular audience. Sarah Josepha Buell Hale wrote with the same goal but with less scientific precision. Born in 1788 in Newport, New Hampshire, Hale was educated in the classics and, when widowed in 1822, she supported herself and her five children by writing poetry and novels and, from 1828 to 1836, editing *Ladies' Magazine*. In 1837, she became editor of *Godey's Lady's Book* and continued in this position while publishing her own volumes until 1877. Among many other things, she wrote *Flora's Interpreter: Or the American Book of Flowers and Sentiments*, in which she combined flower descriptions with poetry hoping to stimulate interest in botany and, at the same time, "promote a better acquaintance with the beauties of our own literature." Like Phelps, whom she admired, Hale saw natural history as a rational system and, thus for women, a liberating pastime.[64]

Hale encouraged women to venture into the woods and fields; those inured to the beauty of the garden would find inspiration in the uncommon flower in its natural home. To promote a better understanding of these wild flowers, she included generic and specific names, described their habitat, and noted particulars that made them suitable for the garden. Compared to Phelps's taxonomy, her science was sparse: "Althea, Frutex. *Hibiscus, Syriacus*; Class 16. Order 13 (Syrian Mallow) a shrub 4 to 6 feet high. Native of the East. Flowers white and rose color." Clearly, she was more interested in the moral lessons these specimens conveyed and, as with many popular scientific writers, male and female, these lessons included love of country: "It is not without pride...that I have found so many fair specimens of the kind flourishing in a land that has been stigmatized as producing nothing but corn and cotton." Hale offered poetry selections appropriate to each flower, and her poems, like her flowers, were invariably American. "The mountain pine, neglected and exposed to fierce winds and raging tempests, took strong root and

---

[63] Phelps, *Familiar Lectures on Botany*, pp. 82, 89; Phelps, *Botany for Beginners*, p. 118.
[64] Sarah Josepha Buell Hale, *Flora's Interpreter; Or the American Book of Flowers and Sentiments* (Boston, 1832), p. iii.

grew into a lofty tree, delighting the eye by its strength and beauty," she wrote, alluding to her own country's tempestuous beginnings.[65]

Hale's emphasis on the beauty and symbolism of form was standard in women's botanies. Lucy Hooper's *Lady's Book of Flowers and Poetry* celebrated the "harmony of...colors" among her plants, and Elizabeth Washington Gamble Wirt's *Flora's Dictionary* began with poems dedicated to each flower, then carefully described the plant's structure, emphasizing the mutually beneficial relations among the parts and the proportioned relations among petal, stamen, filament, and anther.[66] Flower anatomy provided moral lessons about beauty, harmony, and cooperation.

Visions of perfection, balance, and purpose underlay all scientific description, but botanies written by women were distinctive in the degree to which they wove these virtues into their work. The "language of flowers" charmed the reader and glorified nature's forms. "Its corolla was full-blown, its petals were of the brightest carnation, sweetly blended with the purest lily. The stamens and pistils were perfect, having filaments and elegant styles; its anthers and stigmas were finely organized, and richly powdered with golden pollen, pendant upon a rose-bush verdant with life; it was redolent of love!"[67] Although their approach to nature appreciation was not unique, their literary fluorescence was timely, as midcentury scientists were beginning their retreat to the academy. Women naturalists elevated beauty as botany's highest standard and, in so doing, introduced nature study to the public as a romantic discourse.

The Lessons of Natural History

Popular science changed the way Americans looked at the natural world. At the beginning of the century, as historian Mark Barrow points out, most Americans viewed the natural landscape as a wasteland or a storehouse of commercial resources. Midcentury science broadened this perspective. Translating natural history into popular narrative, naturalists gave Americans reason to imagine nature as a gift of divine providence: Fireflies enlivened the evening walk; flowers poured out their delicious fragrances; crickets sang their evening song – all to render the earth more

---

[65] Hale, *Flora's Interpreter*, pp. iii, iv; Hale, *Woman's Record*, pp. 772–3.
[66] *The Lady's Book of Flowers and Poetry*, Lucy Hooper (ed.) (New York, 1846), p. 8; Elizabeth Washington Gamble Wirt, *Flora's Dictionary* (Baltimore, 1855), pp. 5–7, 11.
[67] Amy Matilda Cassey Album, LCP.

blissful.[68] Writing from his island respite in northern Michigan, Daniel Drake helped pioneer this new point of view, and his example drew from a tradition of emotive description embedded in the American natural history. Drake came away from his island ramble neither a romantic nor a conservationist in the traditional sense. Yet, as a practical scientist with an appreciation for the recuperative benefits of an integrated landscape, he gained an entirely different perspective on the value of nature in America. This perspective was an important part of the American conservation tradition.

[68] Barrow, *A Passion for Birds*, p. 11; Anon., *Life in the Insect World: Or, Conversations upon Insects, between an Aunt and Her Nieces* (Philadelphia, 1844), pp. 235–6.

9

Challenging the Idea of Improvement

In fall 1823, geologist S. Edwards Dwight hiked with a few friends to the headwaters of the Barton River, a tributary to Vermont's Lake Memphremagog, tracing the path of a great flood that ravaged the valley some thirteen years earlier. After a considerable distance, the party reached the bed of Long Lake, which had been emptied of its waters in the summer of 1810 by a torrent that passed down the Barton River and through the towns below. After a lapse of thirteen years, the desolation – a furrowed gully six to seven hundred feet wide and twenty to forty feet deep – was clearly visible from the tableland. In a correspondence to the *American Journal of Science*, Dwight pieced together the details of the incident that drained the lake and caused such devastation below. The article was not unusual; geologists were intensely interested in sudden and violent occurrences that had reshaped the landscape in living memory because these events offered clues to the larger forces that made up the history and natural history of the earth. What was different about this instance was its causes: The catastrophe was completely artificial. As he guided his reader through the ruined landscape, he related the story behind the flood.

On June 6, 1810, around a hundred individuals from Glover, Barton, and a few adjacent towns assembled with shovels and pickaxes and marched up the Barton River, intending to cut a channel from Long Lake, which drained southward into another river system, into Mud Lake, which drained northward to Barton. Thus, they hoped to increase the storage capacity of the Barton River system. As the workmen opened their channel across the sandy bench between the lakes, water began flowing through the upper end; but, to their surprise, it failed to reach the lower end of the cut. Instead, it dropped through a layer of hardpan and quickly furrowed out a tunnel into Mud Lake. Impelled by the pressure of the lake above, the water tore through the opening, leaving a deep gully where the trench had been. In a few minutes, an expanse of water a mile and a half long disappeared into the lower lake, bearing with it trees, earth, and rocks. Gathering momentum, the wave moved with "irresistible impetuosity" across the lake, leaving a crevasse some thirty feet deep at the outlet and continuing down the Barton River. The flood swept away houses, trees, and barns and shook the earth "like a mighty earthquake." It destroyed the mill the excavators had hoped to benefit and, below the town, it entered a level country, fanned out, and scoured the earth down to bedrock. Left dry, Long Lake became a meadow of sedges and brush, while Mud Lake remained thirty feet lower than its original surface. Not surprisingly, the proprietor of the Barton mill sued his erstwhile benefactors; surprisingly, he was awarded only a hundred dollars in damages.

As Dwight put it, the trial confirmed an opinion "extensively entertained in this country respecting the changes which various parts of its surface have in former periods undergone." Natural landscapes were in flux: Lake levels rose and fell, rivers changed their courses, banks eroded and filled, whole forests disappeared and grew back. The sudden shift in waters from Long Lake to Mud Lake and down the Barton River was, in the eyes of these Vermonters, nothing extraordinary. "We now *know the fact* . . . that lakes may be suddenly and finally emptied, and their beds changed to fertile valleys," Dwight summarized. What the workmen accomplished, nature would have effected in due time, and thus it was a "favourable circumstance that Long Lake was drained while the country on Barton River was [still] a wilderness." By encouraging nature in its play across this restless mountain landscape, the workmen, in Dwight's estimation – and in the estimation of the court – had rendered an "essential service . . . to the community." There were, he pointed out, other water bodies that could be "discharged with even less labour."[1]

The events at Barton River reflect an attitude toward nature that prevailed through much of the early nineteenth century. Americans considered forest-clearing, river-damming, and other landscape alterations

---

[1] S. Edwards Dwight in *American Journal of Science* 11 (No. 1, 1826): pp. 45–9, 51–2. See Benjamin Silliman, *Lectures on Geology, Delivered Before the Wirt Institute, and Citizens of Pittsburgh* (Pittsburgh, 1843), p. 42.

"improvements," not unlike the incessant changes that occurred in nature as landscapes became more productive or integrated. Like the Barton River flood, improvements could be destructive, but they were part of an evolutionary process as old as the hills themselves.[2] Given the search for purpose in natural events, it is not surprising that commentators saw human improvements as a capstone to geological and biological evolution. Natural change was not capricious; neither were human modifications.

Yet, even while the people of Barton were pondering the causes and effects of the recent flood, naturalists and other Americans were beginning to rethink the idea of improving nature. These reservations culminated in the writings of Vermonter George Perkins Marsh, who delivered a widely published speech before the Rutland County Agricultural Society in 1847 on forest destruction and its ecological consequences. Seven years later, in 1864, he completed his monumental *Man and Nature*, which supported his earlier arguments with voluminous observations from around the world and across two thousand years of human history. Unlike the Barton judge, Marsh distinguished human disturbances from natural balances. His purpose in writing *Man and Nature* was to indicate "the evils resulting from too extensive clearing and cultivation, and other so-called improvements," and his erudite warnings marked a change in thinking about forests and the progress of America.

Although Marsh was clearly a pioneer in conservation thinking, his audience was well prepared for the message. In a matter of months after the 1847 Rutland address, warnings about forest destruction were ringing through the northeastern agricultural press. In 1848, Vermonter F. Holbrook recalled the little streams and brooks that were "familiar friends in boyhood." Quoting Marsh, he explained that forest-clearing had desiccated the once-spongy soil and dried up these sources of boyhood diversions. A year later, the *New England Farmer* announced that forest preservation was claiming "great attention" and, in the 1850s and 1860s, before and after Marsh's major work on the subject, editorials were making dire predictions based on their assessment of forest destruction. Farmers everywhere, according to one article, noticed a "diminution of water in [their] ... own neighborhoods." It was the forest that maintained the streams, anchored the soils to the hillsides, kept the atmosphere

---

[2] Henry Savage, Jr., and Elizabeth J. Savage, *André and François-André Michaux* (Charlottesville, 1986), p. 355; David Lowenthal, *George Perkins Marsh: Prophet of Conservation* (Seattle, 2000), p. 275.

moist, protected the land from desiccating winds, and charged the air with electricity.[3] In articles like these, Marsh's ecological principles rang like a tocsin through Vermont and across the East.

Marsh's warnings, as the story goes, coupled with a new appreciation for wilderness encouraged by Romantics such as Ralph Waldo Emerson, James Fenimore Cooper, Henry David Thoreau, and Thomas Cole, set the stage for the conservation movement at the turn of the century. However, as historian Richard Grove writes, Marsh and the Romantics "have been so securely elevated to a pantheon of conservationist prophets as to discourage the proper investigation of . . . their earlier . . . counterparts."[4] As Grove intimates, the rapid dissemination of Marsh's ideas almost immediately after the Rutland address suggests that others had been busy preparing this fertile soil. In 1872, the *New England Farmer* reported a "wide-spread public impression" that forest-clearing affected the climate unfavorably. Listing the sources of this impression, the editor failed to mention Marsh but drew on earlier works by Samuel Williams, Alexander von Humboldt, John William Draper, and Noah Webster.[5] As an 1864 review pointed out, the main thought in *Man and Nature* was not new; it was simply "brought out so forcibly, and illustrated by such encyclopedic learning, that it has the power of novelty."[6] In fact, the conservation message that seemed to spring into being in Rutland in 1847 was grounded in observations on nature going back more than half a century.

Conservation and Natural History

Concern over wood shortages can be found in some of the earliest colonial records and, although this had little of the ecological insight found in Marsh's work, it highlighted the forest in the pursuit of natural history.

---

[3] Marcus Hall, *Earth Repair: A Transatlantic History of Environmental Restoration* (Charlottesville, 2005), pp. 21–22; F. Holbrook, *New England Farmer* 1 (September 1, 1848): p. 302; *New England Farmer* 1 (April 14, 1849): p. 139. See *New England Farmer* 1 (September 1, 1848): p. 302; ibid., 2 (March 2, 1850): p. 76; ibid., January 28, 1871; *Maine Farmer*, August 25, October 24, 1864; July 22, 1871; *Thirteenth Annual Report of the Secretary of the Maine Board of Agriculture, 1868* (Augusta, 1868), pp. 114–16; *Tenth Annual Report of the Secretary of the Maine Board of Agriculture, 1865* (Augusta, 1865), pp. 71–103; *Burlington Free Press*, November 7, 1866; May 8, 1869; December 24, 1870.

[4] Richard H. Grove, *Green Imperialism: Colonial Expansion, Tropical Island Edens, and the Origins of Environmentalism, 1600–1860* (New York, 1995), p. 2.

[5] *New England Farmer*, October 19, 1872.

[6] Review of *Man and Nature* in Hall, *Earth Repair*, pp. 31–2.

Writing to his friends, Jared Eliot and Benjamin Franklin, John Bartram noted an "approaching distress on ye account of our want of timber for fencing & indeed many of our necessary uses" and proposed replanting abandoned fields with red cedar. Again, his line of reasoning was not ecological, but it demonstrated that Bartram could put his vast botanical knowledge to practical conservation uses. No other tree would grow so well on different soils, he insisted, "for upon our sandy beaches,...they grow as thick as possible.... They will grow well in high gravelly or clay soil, in rich or poor, or even upon a rock, if there be but half a foot of sand or earth upon it."[7] In other instances, he turned this knowledge into an ecological argument. Soils in the forested lands were light and soft and absorbed rainwater like a sponge, he observed. When the hillsides were denuded, rains scoured off this loam, "tear[ing] ye surface" and leaving the brooks running "black with mud." The "coarse sand" beneath the loam washed down from the hills and impoverished the fields below.[8] Peter Kalm collected similar expressions of economic and ecological concern in the 1750s. Fuel-wood prices were rising, his informants told him, and the streams that once powered sawmills and gristmills were drying up, a condition they attributed to the "extirpation of great forests" in the vicinity. Nevertheless, Kalm observed, farmers continued to pasture their cattle in the young growth and hack down the older trees for fuel and fencing. Agriculturalist John Mitchell repeated these observations in 1775 and suggested laws to conserve both public and private forests; and, in 1798, the Massachusetts Agricultural Society and its county affiliates began offering premiums to encourage farmers to replant old fields and beautify towns and roads with trees. These incentives garnered few takers because agricultural societies were still comparatively new and their authority weak among ordinary farmers; but, in subsequent decades, their influence grew and their conservation message began to take hold, particularly as demand for wood in adjacent cities rose.[9]

---

[7] John Bartram to Jared Eliot, February 12, 1753; Bartram to Benjamin Franklin, ca. 1748, Edmund Berkeley and Dorothy Smith Berkeley, *The Correspondence of John Bartram, 1734–1777* (Gainesville, 1992), pp. 295–7, 342. See Bartram to Peter Collinson, July 1739 in ibid., p. 121.

[8] John Bartram to Jared Eliot, Spring 1751, Berkeley and Berkeley, *Correspondence of John Bartram*, pp. 322–3.

[9] Peter Kalm, *Travels into North America, Containing Its Natural History, and a Circumstantial Account of Its Plantations and Agriculture in General*, John R. Foster (trans.) (Warrington, England, 1753–1771), I, pp. 92–3, 134; ibid., Vol. 2, pp. 135–6; John Mitchell and Arthur Young, *American Husbandry: Containing an Account of the Soil, Climate, Production of the British Colonies in North-America and the West-Indies*

These concerns grew stronger after the turn of the century when French botanist François-André Michaux introduced the concept of arboriculture to American readers. Michaux's *Silva* was translated into English by Augustus L. Hillhouse in 1819 and, a year later, William Maclure purchased the remaining Hillhouse volumes and sold them at a reduced price. Later, he acquired Michaux's original copper plates and reprinted the book in a cheaper format.[10] Michaux did not condemn forest destruction outright but, after explaining the importance of each species, he suggested means of propagating the most valuable, and he expressed alarm at the loss of white pine in the North, cypress in the South, and the hardwoods that were felled to fuel tanneries, potteries, brick kilns, distilleries, and salt evaporators: "When the period arrives that it is necessary in the United States, as in Europe, to renew the forests," he wrote, "the American forester will find among the oaks, the walnuts, and the ashes, many species... deserving of his care." The conservation message was muted, but the act of naming and prioritizing trees was an important beginning.[11]

Michaux and Kalm, having been sent to America to find tree species suitable for their homelands, wrote against a backdrop of rising European interest in forestry. France began a systematic program of state forestry under Louis XIV and Colbert in the late eighteenth century, and Frederick the Great began regulating wood use and forest-cutting in Prussia a century later. Sweden, Denmark, Spain, and Portugal also regulated forest-cutting, as did civil engineers and foresters in the mountainous parts of Europe, where the erosive effects of deforestation were well understood. Other influences came from European overseas colonial administrators, where absolutist regimes allowed even more comprehensive responses to tropical deforestation. Although these systems were inappropriate for America, with its huge forest stock and decentralized government, observers could see the value in some form of conservation.[12]

(London, 1775), pp. 83–4; *Massachusetts Agricultural Repository and Journal* 5 (No. 1, 1818): pp. 32–40. See *The Agriculture of Massachusetts, as Shown in Returns of the Agricultural Societies, 1853* (Boston, 1854), p. 117; Thomas Allen, *An Historical Sketch of the County of Berkshire and the Town of Pittsfield* (Boston, 1808), pp. 3–4; Noah Webster, *An Address, Delivered Before the Hampshire, Franklin, and Hampden Agricultural Society* (Northampton, 1818), p. 16.

[10] *North American Review*, n.s., 59 (July 1844): pp. 190–1.

[11] *North American Review*, n.s., 44 (April 1837): p. 335; Jacob Richard Schramm, "Influence – Past and Present – of François-André Michaux on Forestry and Forest Research in America," American Philosophical Society (hereafter APS) *Proceedings* 101 (No. 4, 1957): pp. 337–8.

[12] Bernhard E. Fernow, *A Brief History of Forestry in Europe, the United States, and Other Countries* (Toronto, 1911), pp. 51–2, 106, 125, 203, 216, 219–20; *Massachusetts*

Sensitive to events in Europe, naturalists expressed concern about the depletion of eastern America's forests.[13] Although only a few proposed regulating forest use, most described in detail the value of the trees they listed. "Around us and under our feet," William D. Williamson wrote in his natural history of Maine, "are various qualities of matter, which are, by discriminating knowledge and skillful management, wrought into articles of most extensive use and exquisite beauty." Confident that everything in nature was useful in some fashion, Williamson described the commercial properties of each tree species in the state: white ash for barrels, oars, handspikes, handles, and frames; black ash for baskets and brooms; birch for canoes; and black birch, with its fine grain and high polish, for household furniture.[14] Susan Fenimore Cooper repeated Williamson's appreciation for wood: "Our fields are divided by wooden fences; wooden bridges cross our rivers; our village streets and highways are being paved with wood; the engines that carry us on our way by land and by water are fed with wood; the rural dwellings within and without, their walls, their floors, stairways, and roofs are almost wholly of wood; and in this neighborhood the fires that burn on our household hearths are entirely the gift of the living forest."[15]

Benjamin Silliman, editor of the *American Journal of Science*, expressed concern that steamboats threatened the forests along the Ohio and Mississippi Rivers, and another editor attributed the "denuded hillsides" of New England to "the vast amount of fuel" consumed by steam locomotives. Scientists added other concerns. The loss of this magnificent natural laboratory would leave huge gaps in the scientific record, according to Daniel Drake; settlers would soon sweep aside the native trees, stop up the rivers, level the hills, and fill the valleys. Before this, he advised, "a portrait should be taken, that our children may contemplate the primitive physiognomy of their native land, and feast their eyes on its virgin charms." Two years later, his colleague, Samuel Hildreth,

---

Agricultural Repository and Journal 5 (Number 1, 1818), p. 34; *North American Review*, n.s., 35 (October 1832): p. 415; Grove, *Green Imperialism*, pp. 1, 7; Hall, *Earth Repair*, p. 31.

[13] *North American Review*, n.s., 44 (April 1837): pp. 339, 346–7, 357, 416; ibid., n.s., 58 (April 1844): pp. 327–9; *The Naturalist* 1 (November 1831): p. 349. See *American Journal of Science* 20 (No. 1, 1831): p. 133; *New England Farmer* 2 (March 2, 1850): p. 76; *Thirteenth Annual Report of the Secretary of the Maine Board of Agriculture, 1868* (Augusta, 1868), pp. 114–16.

[14] William D. Williamson, *The History of the State of Maine from its First Discovery, A.D. 1602, to the Separation, A.D. 1820, Inclusive* (Hallowell, 1839), Vol. 1, pp. 118–19, 174.

[15] Susan Fenimore Cooper, *Rural Hours* (New York, 1850), p. 215.

expressed similar concerns about the Muskingum Valley, once "clothed with immense forests of the most beautiful trees." Fires set by Indians cleared away the underbrush and gave this forest a "noble and enchanting appearance," he added; when the fires were checked, the woodlands quickly filled with brush, "converting these once beautiful forests into a rude and tasteless wilderness."[16] Farmers and loggers continued their assault on the forest but, by 1830, scientific and aesthetic arguments for conservation were mounting and in the popular press, "a few timid voices began to call for conservation," historian T. D. Seymour Bassett noted. As early as 1835, a correspondent to the *Maine Farmer* complained about settlers who "cut down all the timber, and . . . set fire to the whole, and thus throw up all the vegetable matter which has been accumulating for nearly six thousand years, more or less, in an hour, to manure the stars, if they are capable of being manured by smoke." It would seem, Robert Barclay Allardice concluded in 1842, "a matter of serious importance that the destruction of land . . . should be prevented."[17]

In 1842, the year of Allardice's conservation pronouncement and five years before Marsh's Rutland County address, Ebenezer Emmons entered a note of concern into the massive natural history survey of New York. The state's northern highlands, he pointed out, contained a "great extent of arable lands," yet the forests that clothed these highland soils were important as well because they ensured "a constant and regular supply of water" for the rivers below. Anticipating by forty years the New York constitutional amendment that created the Adirondack Forest Preserve and guaranteed the hills would remain "forever wild," Emmons pointed out that the Hudson River originated "wholly under the shadow of [these] forests, wild and uncultivated." His argument, although somewhat hesitant, summarized the growing concern over forest destruction in the scientific literature of the 1840s:

If now those forests were to be replaced by pastures or open fields of any description, the quantity of rain which now falls would be materially diminished,

---

[16] Daniel Drake, *Discourse on the History, Character, and Prospects of the West* (Gainesville, 1955 [1834]), p. 17; S. P. Hildreth, *American Journal of Science* 29 (1836): pp. 14–15, 46–7. See Zadock Thompson, *Natural History of Vermont: An Address Delivered at Boston, Before the Boston Society of Natural History* (Burlington, 1850), pp. 18–20; *American Journal of Science* 10 (February 1826): 2; ibid., 10 (No. 2, 1826): p. 317; ibid., n.s., 13 (1852): p. 397.

[17] Nathan Hoskins in T. D. Seymour Bassett, "Urban Penetration of Rural Vermont, 1840–80," Doctoral dissertation, Harvard University, 1952, pp. 16–17; *Maine Farmer* 3 (December 4, 1835): p. 346; Robert Barclay Allardice, *Agricultural Tour in the United States and Upper Canada* (Edinburgh, 1842), pp. 140–1.

especially during midsummer; or if it should not be diminished, the evaporation from the surface would be greatly increased, so that the result would remain the same under either condition. Less will flow in the natural channels, and the supply for navigation may be so far diminished as to prevent, or if not prevent, greatly impede the navigation, and interfere with its employment for moving machinery, or the various purposes to which water is applied.[18]

Many earlier scientists considered forest-clearing a complement to evolutionary naturalism; understanding why the same observable facts now led to such different conclusions helps explain the origins of conservation thought in America.

Proto-Ecological Debates

Clarence Glacken, writing in 1967, noted these concerns in the scientific literature but pronounced them sporadic and contradictory. In fact, he saw American science in a moment of transition.[19] In 1831, Constantine Rafinesque composed a series of essays on Pennsylvania trees that reflects the shift in thinking taking place at the time. In one essay written for the *Saturday Evening Post*, he described the cypress as a tree of great commercial value, important to the economy of man, but also necessary to the economy of nature. Cypress shed their leaves annually, he noted, building up the soil and changing the dank swamps it inhabited into seasonal wetlands and, finally, into meadows. Where earlier naturalists might have seen advantage in clearing away these dark cypress forests, Rafinesque declared his faith in the benefits of the standing trees.[20] Rafinesque was among a growing number of naturalists who looked at nature's interconnections as a lesson in conservation.

This transition in thinking affected some long-standing convictions about the relation between forests and other aspects of the natural world. Early scientists reasoned that because trees drew water out of the ground and exhaled it through their leaves, clearing forests would increase the flow of streams and springs. Robert Munro found northern New York

---

[18] Ebenezer Emmons, *Report of the Survey of the Second Geological District in Natural History of New-York, Part 4, Geology* (Albany, 1842–43), p. 13.

[19] Clarence J. Glacken, *Traces on the Rhodian Shore: Nature and Culture in Western Thought from Ancient Times to the End of the Eighteenth Century* (Berkeley, 1969), p. 686.

[20] Constantine Rafinesque, "Account of the Largest Tree Near Philadelphia" [for the *Saturday Evening Post*], n.d. (ca. May 1831), Constantine Rafinesque Papers, APS.

"indifferently watered" in 1804, but he expected this to change with land-clearing. Later naturalists challenged this view of hydrology. Forests, some thought, actually prevented desiccation by shading the ground, making the soil more absorbent, and charging the atmosphere with electricity, which brought rain.[21] In the Mediterranean Basin, Timothy Flint argued in 1833, rivers that once flowed freely had "dried up with the destruction of the forests" and, in his own time and place, springs and streams had disappeared, "now that the verdant screen from the Sun's rays is no more." Zadock Thompson argued that streams dried up because farmers had removed the leaves, limbs, and logs that held back their waters and recommended small upstream dams as a remedy, but others were less optimistic.[22] Daniel Drake predicted in 1815 that hot, dry western prairie winds would spread eastward as Ohio's forests were destroyed, drying the air and soil; and a writer in *North American Review* embellished his thoughts a year later: "When the ... forests are destroyed ... the *arid* south-west [winds] will then pass over the country, withering and suffocating like a sirocco. . . . The rivers [will] . . . become torrents, impetuous and destructive in winter and presenting only beds of sand in summer." The correspondent proposed a solution: "The Government should select some spots from whence the most important streams originate, and mark out a certain portion of contiguous territory, never to be alienated or stripped of its forests. This would at once provide perpetual supplies of timber, and protect the precious fountains of the rivers."[23]

Naturalists also reassessed the theory that forest-clearing would produce a warmer climate. The assumption was difficult to test because weather records were not particularly accurate. Thermometers had existed since the 1790s, but they were rare in the backcountry, and they

[21] Robert Munro, *A Description of the Genesee Country* (New York, 1804), pp. 8–9. See Samuel Williams, *The Natural and Civil History of Vermont* (Burlington, 1809), Vol. 1, pp. 90–1; Grove, *Green Imperialism*, pp. 156–7; *Georgick Papers for 1809, Consisting of Letters and Extracts Communicated to the Massachusetts Society for Promoting Agriculture* (Boston, 1809): p. 43.

[22] Timothy Flint, *Lectures upon Natural History, Geology, Chemistry, the Application of Steam, and Interesting Discoveries in the Arts* (Boston, 1833), pp. 246–8; Zadock Thompson, *History of Vermont, Natural, Civil, and Statistical* (Burlington, 1842), Vol, 1, p. 4. See J. Hector St. John de Crèvecoeur, *Letters from an American Farmer and Sketches of Eighteenth-Century America*, Albert E. Stone (ed.) (New York, 1986 [c. 1782]), pp. 285–6.

[23] Daniel Drake, *Natural and Statistical View, Or Picture of Cincinnati and the Miami Country* (Cincinnati, 1815): pp. 101–10; Daniel Drake, *Systematic Treatise, Historical, Etiological, and Practical, on the Principal Diseases of the Interior Valley of North America* (Cincinnati, 1850), p. 450; *North American Review* 3 (July 1816): pp. 225–6.

varied greatly in quality, making comparisons difficult. Nor did their owners keep records systematically. And, even where records existed, weather
patterns were complicated and confusing.[24] Timothy Flint thought that
New England climates alone would require a lifetime of study, and Benjamin Rush described Philadelphia as a "compound of all other climates
in the world," having "the damps and glooms of Britain in the spring,
the scorching rays of Africa in summer, the mild temperature of Italy in
June, the cold and snow of Norway, and the ice of Holland in the winter, somewhat of the storms of the west Indies at every season, and the
capricious winds and fluctuating weather of Great Britain throughout the
year." Summers were too cold one year and too hot the next, and these
"anomalous instances of inequality," as Jeremy Belknap called them,
reduced the debate over climate warming to speculation and opinion.
It was, Thaddeus Harris concluded, "impossible to speak with philosophical accuracy" on the subject. According to Rush, better housing
and clothing, heartier crops, and surfaced roads made cold weather less
inconvenient and left the impression that America was growing warmer.[25]

An important figure in this debate was Noah Webster, who challenged
the use of biblical and classical literature to support the notion that the
Mediterranean had grown warmer when Europe was cleared of its forests.
Biblical passages that described frost and cold simply recorded unusual
events, just as modern chronicles included remarkable weather in any
region. The mountains of Syria and Judea were still covered with snow
every winter, and frost was not unusual elsewhere. There was, he concluded, "too much generalizing out of particularly cold winters in the past,
and particularly warm winters in the present." Forest-clearing did bring
changes, Webster thought, but not necessarily improvements. Denuded

---

[24] Cadwallader Colden to James Alexander, January 7, 1735, Miscellaneous Collection,
APS. See Drake, *Systematic Treatise,* p. 453; Zadock Thompson, *Geography and Geol-
ogy of Vermont* (Burlington, 1848), p. 79; James Rodger Fleming, *Meteorology in
America, 1800–1770* (Baltimore, 1990), p. 12.

[25] Timothy Flint, *The United States and the Other Divisions of the American Continent*
(Cincinnati, 1832), Vol. 2, pp. 5–6; Benjamin Rush in Constantin Francois Chasseboeuf,
comte de Volney, *A View of the Soil and Climate of the United States* (Philadelphia,
1804), p. 114; Rush in James Mease, *Geological Account of the United States* (Philadelphia, 1807), p. 107; Jeremy Belknap, *History of New-Hampshire* (Dover, 1812), Vol. 3,
p. 20; Thaddeus Mason Harris, *The Journal of a Tour into the Territory Northwest of
the Mountains* (Boston, 1805), pp. 99–100. See Joseph Scott, *A Geographical Description of Pennsylvania* (Philadelphia, 1806), p. 17; Williams, *Natural and Civil History of
Vermont,* p. 70.

of trees and exposed to the wind, the earth absorbed more heat in summer and more cold in winter, making temperatures more extreme. In cleared country, winter snows would alternate with heavy rain, and the ground would freeze and thaw as the weather became more irregular. Snows had been deeper in the early days, as the old settlers remembered, but "it was not the *degree*, but the *steadiness* of the cold which produced this effect."[26] Samuel Williams noted that before settlement, the climate had been "uniform and regular." At his writing in 1809, spring temperatures gyrated between cold and hot in patterns that were "extremely injurious to vegetation." Residents of the lower Mississippi Valley told James Mease in 1807 that the climate was getting colder rather than warmer and, in 1818, westerner Caleb Atwater predicted that forest-clearing in Ohio would bring the northern winter winds farther south, spreading frigid air through the Valley. Bird migrations were already changing, and settlers were experiencing more rheumatism and pleurisy.[27]

In his three-volume *Natural, Statistical, and Civil History of the State of New-York*, published in 1829, James McCauley sorted through the various commentaries on climate and forests and attempted some conclusions. Like so many midcentury naturalists, he was ambivalent about the benefits of clearing. In earlier times, he reasoned, the highland forests retained a "cold dense air" that drifted into the settlements below, bringing cooler winters and later springs. As these forests were cleared, the cold abated and farmers reported more midwinter thaws and earlier springs. However, in summer the sun desiccated the earth on the open land, drawing the moisture from the ground and the air. Brooks were diminishing and dews and rains becoming less copious. McCauley included pages of testimony on the amount of snow, ice, and rain in various parts of the state, seeking perspective on this complex issue. Although some

---

[26] Noah Webster in Connecticut Academy of Arts and Sciences *Memoirs* 1 (Part 1, 1810): pp. 1–8, 11, 13, 19, 21, 30–1, 42–5. See Samuel Forry, *The Climate of the United States and Its Endemic Influences* (New York, 1842), p. 97; William Currie, *An Historical Account of the Climates and Diseases of the United States of America* (Philadelphia, 1792), p. 93; William B. Meyer, *Americans and Their Weather* (New York, 2000), pp. 4, 62–3; Gilbert Chinard, "Eighteenth-Century Theories on America as a Human Habitat," *APS Proceedings* 91 (February 1947): p. 46; James Rodger Fleming, *Historical Perspectives on Climate Change* (New York, 1998), p. 45.

[27] Williams, *Natural and Civil History of Vermont*, pp. 79–80; Mease, *Geological Account*, p. 106; Caleb Atwater in *American Journal of Science* 1 (1818): pp. 278–80, 282–3. See Francis Hall, *Travels in Canada, and the United States, in 1816 and 1817* (Boston, 1818), p. 149.

correspondents seemed to exaggerate, he was certain that changes had occurred. Whether this was for better or worse, he refused to say.[28]

Uncertainties like these clouded the debate over climate melioration. Benjamin Rush, at first convinced that the climate was warming, recanted when Philadelphia experienced a series of severe winters. While some still argued that deforestation brought a warmer and more salubrious climate, others pointed out that Asia, cultivated and treeless, was colder than the heavily forested Pacific Coast of America.[29] In 1842, army surgeon Samuel Forry argued in his massive *Climate of the United States and Its Endemic Influences* that seasons were becoming less equitable, but he questioned the possibility that human action alone was responsible. For more than three thousand years, he noted, eastern Mediterranean farmers had grown figs and pomegranates in the same place, and the cultivation of olives in France had proceeded no farther north than in ancient times. Neither records kept at the western Army posts nor floral calendars dating back to 1722 suggested long-term changes in America.[30] To this, Charles Lyell added a global perspective. When large land masses were concentrated in tropical regions, the sun beating on these equatorial surfaces elevated temperatures around the world. As the continents drifted toward the poles, global temperatures cooled. Lyell acknowledged the importance of local circumstances but, like Forry, he considered a continent's configuration and its relation to the sea and the prevailing winds far more important. In his influential *Principles of Geology*, he questioned the relation between forests and climate, convinced that nature operated according to more profound laws of equilibrium.[31]

By 1850, Drake had accepted Forry's conclusion that settlement had not changed the climate of the West, but he went on to say that an "immense proportion" of the Ohio Valley was still forested, and the effects he conjectured in 1815 might still lay in the future. Yet, whereas

[28] James McCauley, *The Natural, Statistical, and Civil History of the State of New-York* (Albany, 1829), Vol. 1, pp. 365, 368, 370-2, 376-7, 396, 398-9.

[29] Benjamin Rush in Volney, *View of the Soil and Climate of the United States*, p. 216; Benjamin Vaughan, "Weather," Vaughan Papers 4, No. 81 APS; "Climate and Agriculture" in ibid.; Timothy Dwight, *Travels in New England and New York*, Barbara Miller Solomon and Patricia M. King (eds.), (Cambridge, 1969), pp. 38-9, 40-2, 44; *American Journal of Science* 20 (No. 1, 1831): pp. 130-1.

[30] Forry, *Climate of the United States*, pp. 27, 96, 99; Forry in *American Journal of Science* 47 (October 1844): pp. 216, 227-9, 237-8. See Forry in Fleming, *Historical Perspectives on Climate Change*, pp. 48-9.

[31] Charles Lyell, *Principles of Geology* (Boston, 1842), Vol. 1, pp. 162-3, 180; ibid., Vol. 3, pp. 254-5, 257, 259.

Drake, Forry, and McCauley were mixed in their estimates of these changes, others were growing more pessimistic. It was certain, John Haywood of Tennessee wrote, "that the cold seasons are now advancing, and have been for twenty years and more...., [and] that the winters are now longer and more severe."[32] Samuel P. Hildreth wrote in 1848 that Ohio's deforested landscape offered no protection from the "rays of the summer sun and ... the cold blasts of winter" and, consequently, winters were growing colder and summers hotter. According to an 1857 New York publication, it was "universally conceded that the winters of the Northern States are colder now than they were thirty and forty years ago" when a thick belt of woodland "broke the force of the winter and spring winds."[33]

A naturalist's description of western Pennsylvania in 1837 illustrates the direction this debate was taking. The country he surveyed was potentially fertile, but farmers, he thought, would find the soils impossibly wet and "cold." This would change as more settlers moved into the area: "Where the forests are removed, the earth becomes sufficiently dry for all the purposes of agriculture, and for good permanent roads." Yet, this alteration left him uneasy. By shading the ground, trees moderated temperature extremes and, like mountains, they could "call ... down humidity from the clouds." Deforestation would intensify summer heats, diminish the rainfall, and reduce the stream flow. Perhaps, Samuel Williams resolved, forests should be cleared in the valleys, where lands were "wet and miry," but left on the mountains, where trees were necessary to anchor the soil to the slopes. Naturalists were growing more sophisticated in understanding the effects of deforestation and more concerned about the role of trees in the balance of nature.[34]

In the Cosmos publication written in 1870, Alexander von Humboldt declared the pleasant notion that deforestation improved America's climate "generally discredited." Yet, despite Lyell's Olympian view and Humboldt's dismissal of the whole debate, the idea that forests were part of the balance of nature had been imprinted in the popular mind. Taken up by the rural press, it added proto-ecological considerations to

---

[32] Drake, *Systematic Treatise*, p. 478; John Haywood, *The Natural and Aboriginal History of the Tennessee* (Nashville, 1823), pp. 65–6.

[33] Samuel P. Hildreth in John Warfield Simpson, *Visions of Paradise: Glimpses of Our Landscape's Legacy* (Berkeley, 1999), p. 33; *American Agriculturist* 16 (February 1857): p. 32.

[34] Anon. in *American Journal of Science* 31 (January 1837): p. 38; Williams, *Natural and Civil History of Vermont*, pp. 34–5.

arguments based on the forests' economic value. Scientists never gained consensus on the effects of deforestation but, like the Pennsylvania naturalist, they grew more cautious about the costs and benefits of disrupting nature's balance. Although these influences were not clearly understood, they remained a core component of the conservation message that emerged at the end of the century.[35]

Forests and Health

The debate over forests and disease followed a similar pattern. At the beginning of the century, most naturalists saw forests and swamps as the most significant source of fevers in frontier America. By midcentury, some were looking to the human causes for frontier diseases and, once again, challenging the theory of melioration. The improvements of greatest concern were water impoundments. Observers noted that Connecticut River towns, once among the healthiest in New England, became fever-ridden when dams blocked the river and its tributaries. Canals between the Ohio River and the Great Lakes similarly increased the incidence of disease, and the dams on Pennsylvania's French Creek, built in 1832–4, proved so deleterious that in 1843, nearby residents destroyed them.[36] In a long essay complaining about the impact of mill dams on agricultural property, Edmund Ruffin challenged the idea that forests and wetlands were inherently unhealthy. "When our ancestors first reached this shore, nearly the whole country was in a state of nature. . . . The streams had not been obstructed by the cutting down of trees across their beds, . . . no dams had obstructed the free and regular course of the streams. . . . The soil not having been cultivated, was not exposed to be washed away by the rains into the river. The waters . . . were therefore generally clear, instead of being generally muddy. . . . In this former state of things, there could have been existing but few sources of malaria."[37] Soils in the cleared lands washed into the streams and collected above the millponds, expanding the miasmatic marshes and swamps and, as the ponds filled, dams were elevated, increasing the water surface, the atmospheric moisture, and the miasmas.

[35] Alexander Humboldt, *Cosmos: A Sketch of a Physical Description of the Universe* (New York, 1870), pp. 103–4; Humboldt in Fleming, *Historical Perspectives on Climate Change*, pp. 49–50. See Forry, *Climate of the United States*, pp. 92, 99, 102; *American Journal of Science* 19 (No. 1, 1831): 291–2.

[36] Drake, *Systematic Treatise*, pp. 280–1, 285, 405; Dwight, *Travels*, pp. 235–6; *American Journal of Science* 11 (No. 2, 1826): p. 226.

[37] Edmund Ruffin, *Essays and Notes on Agriculture* (Richmond, 1855), pp. 295–6, 322–4, 331–2.

These circumstances, he thought, explained "why a particular neighborhood might formerly have been healthy,... and why it might gradually have become very unhealthy." Ruffin's argument was essentially conservative – God made free-flowing streams, so they must be healthy – but it was also sound conservationist thinking.[38]

Pointing to experiments with plants and oxygen made by Joseph Priestly in the 1760s, naturalists found other reasons to value trees. According to Edward A. Holyoke, trees were "grand corrector[s] of those impurities which might otherwise so far increase as to contaminate the whole mass of the atmosphere," a point Harvard botanist, Benjamin Waterhouse, elaborated on in 1811:

Ask the woodsman for what a tree was made – he will tell you to bear nuts; to be cut into boards; to burn, to keep him warm, and to cook his victuals. Ask the naturalist, and he will tell you that they are an important, nay indispensable link in the chain of human existence; insomuch that were the... Legislator of nature to cause every vegetable on earth at once to be annihilated, the atmospheric air would directly become a putrid mass of every thing that is noxious, and man, and other terrestrial animals of similar construction, would soon turn into a mortified lump of corruption.

Far from harmful, lush vegetation was a providential compensation that maintained the atmospheric balance of nature: "Wherever corruption reigns, nature begins to put forth a vigorous vegetation." This was one of the "beautiful adjustments," Timothy Flint thought, by which nature preserved the "happy equipoise" in organic life.[39]

The most ambitious attempt to assess these forest influences was Daniel Drake's *Systematic Treatise, Historical, Etiological, and Practical, on the Principal Diseases of the Interior Valley of North America*, published in 1850. For nearly three decades, Drake traveled between the Alleghenies and the Rockies gathering information on the West and, with this, he

---

[38] Ruffin, *Essays and Notes*, pp. 331–3. See Glacken, *Traces on the Rhodian Shore*, pp. 686, 693; *Philadelphia Medical and Physical Journal*, Part 1, Vol. 1 (1804): p. 8; Connecticut Academy of Arts and Sciences *Memoirs* 1 (Part 1, 1810): pp. 131–4.

[39] Edward A. Holyoke in American Academy of Arts and Sciences *Memoirs* 2 (No. 1, 1793), pp. 72–4; Manasseh Cutler to Edward Wigglesworth, February 14, 1783, in William Parker Cutler and Julia Perkins Cutler, *Life, Journals, and Correspondence of Rev. Manasseh Cutler, LL.D, by His Grandchildren* (Cincinnati, 1888), Vol. 2, pp. 213–14; Benjamin Waterhouse, *The Botanist; Being the Botanical Part of a Course of Lectures on Natural History* (Boston, 1811), pp. 155, 158; Flint, *Lectures upon Natural History*, pp. 130, 132, 212. See Samuel Mitchill to Henry E. Mühlenberg, October 24, 1796, Henry E. Mühlenberg Manuscripts, Pennsylvania Historical Society (hereafter PHS); Forry, *Climate of the United States*, p. 128; Grove, *Green Imperialism*, p. 159.

compiled a brief natural, social, moral, and disease history of each town.
Only a few years before the *Systematic Treatise* was published, William
Budd and John Snow introduced a germ theory of disease that gained
credibility over the next decade. Thus, Drake's work stood as the last
great compendium of general environmental causes of disease in America
and, indeed, one of the most ambitious environmentalist interpretations
in American history.[40]

Drake began with a detailed "hydrographical map" drawn by federal cartographer, D. P. Whiting. Largely devoid of civil divisions, it was
designed to highlight his conviction that climate, water, elevation, surficial strata, soil structure, wind direction, and forest cover determined
the hygienic constitution of a landscape. In each section, he described the
geological structure, which in turn determined the soils, the hydrology,
the forests, and the civil history of the region. North of the Ohio was a
land of transitional and secondary strata and thick drift deposits, with
countless seasonal brooks and ponds. From this topography emerged a
dangerous combination of deep organic soils, summer heat, and moisture.
The land immediately to the south of the Ohio was limestone, with rivers
coursing through steep-sided ravines containing little alluvial bottom-
land. South of the Cumberland Plateau, luxuriant vegetation and intense
heats nurtured "animalcules and microscopic plants" and enhanced the
"electrical perturbations" in the atmosphere. On this medical bedrock,
Drake added layers of social habits based on ethnic, race, and regional
variables; population density; and occupational, recreational, intellectual,
and moral patterns. These, in turn, induced variations in clothing, lodg-
ing, bathing practices, housing, diet, and drink. Finally, he described the
inner nature of the body, including pathologies for several diseases.[41] If,
indeed, these conditions were everywhere the same, medical conditions
would be uniform across the West. Differences revealed the connection
between disease and environment.[42]

Despite his enormous research, Drake's conclusions were tentative.
Trees, he noted, could be malignant or healthy, depending on species,

---

[40] S. D. Gross, *A Discourse on the Life, Character, and Services of Daniel Drake, M.D.*
(Louisville, 1853), pp. 52–54; Daniel Drake, *Pioneer Life in Kentucky*, Charles D. Drake
(ed.) (Cincinnati, 1870), p. xxxix; Drake, *Systematic Treatise*, p. 257.

[41] Drake, *Systematic Treatise*, pp. 260–2, 658, 676, 679, 696, 709–12; Daniel Drake
in APS *Transactions* 2, new series (1825), p. 258; Drake, *Pioneer Life in Kentucky*,
p. xxxviii.

[42] Drake, *Systematic Treatise*, pp. vii, 2–3.

location, and the state of cultivation around them. Upland pines were "chiefly resinous" and thus "little disposed to ... fermentation." Nor were swamps uniformly unhealthy. The fevers in the Genesee area had, by the time he wrote, "greatly abated," despite the marshes fringing the lakes. In the oldest settlements, millponds were numerous but the organic matter washed into them had "long since, by cultivation, been thoroughly exposed to the action of the air, rains, and sun." Groves of trees could provide a buffer against swamp miasmas, helping to "arrest the spread of that gaseous agent, whatever it may be, which is said to be the true cause of the Fever."[43]

Writing in 1789, Hugh Williamson had been certain that land-clearing would improve the country's health.[44] Nineteen years later, James Mease noted the uncertainty that clouded this conviction: "Whilst one condemns the air of woodland as destructive to life and health, another celebrates it as containing *nutritive* particles." Circumstances, he concluded, were too varied to provide firm conclusions. Belknap argued in 1812 that vapors from New England's resinous trees imparted a "balsamic quality" favorable to health, even in the uncultivated regions, and John Melish thought Georgia's upcountry healthy for the same reason. Like Mease, Timothy Flint pondered the huge body of literature on forests, climate, hydrology, and disease and found no easy answers.

> If our climate was originally too humid, cutting down the forests has so far ameliorated it, as it has clearly tended to render the air drier and rains less frequent. Yet it is a fact, attested, as it seems to me, beyond all question, that the primitive settlers, who reared their cabins under the shade of the unbroken forest, were healthier than their successors, who lived in the cleared fields.... In various portions of the Ohio Valley, the air has become decidedly more salubrious, since the country has been opened to the sun and air. In other districts of the West, as along the lower courses of the Mississippi and Red River, the reverse has decidedly been the case.[45]

Daniel Drake's detailed study of forest and disease in the West brought no resolution to this debate, but gone was the assurance that leveling the forest would improve the quality of life in the towns and cities of the West.

[43] Drake, *Systematic Treatise*, pp. 402–3, 252, 710, 720–1.
[44] Hugh Williamson in *APS Publications* 1 (1789), pp. 344–5.
[45] Mease, *Geological Account*, p. 85; Belknap, *History of New-Hampshire*, p. 172; John Melish, *A Description of the British Possessions in North America* (Philadelphia, 1812), pp. 34–5; Flint, *Lectures upon Natural History*, pp. 245–6.

Crisis and Society in the East

Why was forest destruction, once considered a means of improving nature, so hotly debated by the middle of the century? The answer lies as much in a series of social changes taking place in the eastern farmlands as in the new theories offered about forests in the balance of nature. Agriculture occupied a special place in the vision of national destiny, and expansion of the agrarian frontier fueled a sense of optimism regarding the effects of forest-clearing. New Hampshire's Daniel Lancaster opened his 1845 history of Gilmanton by inviting the reader to stand with him on a promontory and imagine the land before European settlement: "as far as the eye could reach," the reader would see "nothing but dense forests and deep ravines, with no cultivated spot to relieve the monotony of the scene." When the settler appeared, the reader would behold "the trackless wilderness as by magic changed into countless well cultivated farms, and instead of wild beasts that roam the forest, the hills are covered with the joyful flocks and herds." Nature in Lancaster's saga was an untilled garden, laid out "with great benevolence and design" to nourish just this final end.[46]

Although Lancaster's vision of improving nature remained at the heart of the national narrative, by the time he wrote, scientists were beginning to question the path from forest to fruitful field, in part because they questioned the perception that agriculture in the Northeast was properly consummating this narrative. In the early decades of the century, naturalists and agricultural improvers saw the region advancing through stages to the consummation Lancaster saw in the valley of the Connecticut. Although this expectation was borne out in many places, other sections of the East betrayed startling instances of retrogression and abandonment. When settlers first cleared away the northeastern forests, they found a "rich and fine soil before them, lying as loose between the trees as the best bed in a garden." Here, the stages of frontier development began, but in many parts of the Northeast, it faltered when settlers failed to husband these gifts of providence.[47] John Mitchell pointed out as early as 1755 that farming methods throughout the Northeast were "miserable," reasoning that farmers were seduced by the specter of endless virgin soil. In 1795, the duc de la Rochefoucauld-Liancourt predicted that these destructive

---

[46] Daniel Lancaster, *The History of Gilmanton* (Gilmanton, 1845), pp. 13–14.
[47] Kalm, *Travels into North America*, Vol. 2, pp. 192–4.

methods would drive farmers out of New England once the Mississippi Basin – then under French control – was opened to agriculture.[48]

During la Rochefoucauld's time, agrarian reformers urged farmers to read English agricultural manuals but, as Samuel Deane pointed out, these were impractical for a region "so differently circumstanced." In America, land was cheap, the climate colder and more variable, and the insects more destructive. The American pioneer was but the "veriest lilliputian" in a vast forest; the balance of forces was different and the farmer approached nature in different ways. Where Europeans husbanded their soils, Americans conserved their labor. They owned more land and paid fewer taxes; their farms were distant from markets; and their prices were low. Under such conditions, the "finished modes of agriculture" practiced in older countries were unworkable. American farmers would have to work out their own destiny, Deane thought, in concert with their own natural circumstances.[49]

For these reasons, farmers were slow to take up the message of soil conservation and, in the second decade of the century, La Rochefoucauld's predictions were beginning to bear out. In 1816, eastern farmers suffered an uncommonly cold spring followed by a summer of repeated frost and snow. The following spring was again chilly, and seed for wheat, rye, and corn was scarce. The "year without a summer" shook the confidence of the eastern farmer; over the next two decades, the Northeast reached the bottom of an economic cycle.[50] Sheep grazing, induced by high wool tariffs in 1828, kept the East prosperous for a time, but western wool production and lower tariffs undercut this industry and doomed many local spinning, weaving, and fulling mills. Large-scale factory production undercut the village mills, shops, foundries, ironworks,

---

[48] Mitchell and Young, *American Husbandry*, pp. 126–7, 129, 167; Francois Alexandre Liancourt, sur de La Rochefoucault, *Travels Through the United States of North America, the Country of the Iroquois, and Upper Canada, in the Years 1795, 1796, and 1797* (London, 1799), Vol. 2, p. 182.

[49] Samuel Deane, *The New-England Farmer; Or, Georgical Dictionary* (Worcester, 1790), pp. 2–3; John Shaw, *A Ramble Through the United States, Canada, and the West* (London, 1856), pp. 47–8; Thomas Green Fessenden, *The Complete Farmer and Rural Economist* (Boston, 1835), pp. 6–7.

[50] Joseph Whipple, *A Geographical View of the District of Maine* (Bangor, 1816), p. 41; Bradbury, *Travels in the Interior of America*, p. 296; Ernest L. Bogart, *Peacham: The Story of a Vermont Hill Town* (Montpelier, 1948), p. 314; Harold Fisher Wilson, *The Hill Country of Northern New England: Its Social and Economic History, 1790–1930* (New York, 1936), p. 60; Frank M. Bryan, "Vermont: The Politics of Ruralism," Doctoral dissertation, University of Connecticut, 1970, pp. ix, 26, 60–1.

and starch factories that provided local employment options for landless young people. The opening of the Erie Canal in 1825, the extension of steam navigation on western waters in the same decade, the beginnings of rail transport, the placer gold strikes in the far west in the late 1840s, and urban growth along the eastern seaboard augmented the demographic drain from the northeastern uplands, where the nomadic instinct lingered among a people who had settled this land only a generation or two earlier.[51]

In a labor-intensive agrarian economy dependent on family members for farm and domestic work, out-migration and farm stagnation were mutually reinforcing. The loss of sons and daughters was mitigated to some degree by factory-made cloth and labor-saving cultivators; seed drills; and reaping, threshing, and mowing machines; but semi-subsistent farmers on marginal lands had no choice but to use traditional tools in their mixed-farming strategies. Here, family labor remained indispensable to the success of the farm and, as city lights and western soils drew off the younger generation, upland farmers faced a crisis.[52] Rising equipment prices, crop failures, declines in wool and grain markets, and western competition combined to bring a halt to land-extensive agricultural practices in the eastern states.

Out-migration startled observers bent on documenting the rise of civilization in America. David Thomas remarked that the abandoned farms of western Pennsylvania filled him with "melancholy reflections." The nearby Ohio River, he thought, acted like the drain in a great sink, sucking the population and the vitality out of the upper basin.[53] America was becoming a land of two wildernesses: the western states where civilization had yet to smooth over the raw edges of frontier life, and the Atlantic states, where abandonment left an equally troubling landscape of untended fields and orchards and empty farmhouses. There were some who pointed out that abandonment occurred mostly in the remote and rocky backcountry, where owners wisely traded hardscrabble farms for

---

[51] Bryan, "Vermont," pp. ix, 26, 60–1; Wilson, *Hill Country*, pp. ix, 26, 60, 78–9, 81–2; Williamson, *History of the State of Maine*, Vol. 2, pp. 665–6; Bassett, "Urban Penetration of Rural Vermont," pp. 2–3; Bittinger, *History of Haverhill*, pp. 310–11; Bogart, *Peacham*, pp. 311, 314, 350; *Eighteenth Annual Report of the Secretary of the Maine Board of Agriculture, 1873* (Augusta, 1873), pp. 15, 18; *Maine Farmer*, October 24, 1874.

[52] Bogart, *Peacham*, p. 313.

[53] David Thomas, *Travels Through the Western Country in the Summer of 1816* (Auburn, 1819), pp. 41, 48–9.

new prospects out West.[54] Those on better land near transportation arteries prospered as nearby cities fueled markets for sweet corn, garden crops, and dairy products. Still, the mood was far from sanguine. Viewing these changes in symbolic terms, commentators were left uncertain about the trajectory of the agrarian republic. Some blamed outside forces – "sharpers and swindlers . . . flooding us with foreign productions, implements, machines, &c." – and others, the character flaws in a generation no longer content with the "humble, toilsome, and laborious" life their forebears led.[55] As the wave of agrarian optimism passed beyond the Appalachians, the once-independent eastern farmers faced a new reality of interregional markets, long-term mortgages, confusing production choices, and limited natural fertility. Here, in this new competitive environment, nature seemed less kind. Horace Greeley commented on the number of diseased and dying apple, peach, cherry, and plum orchards and attributed this condition to the "reckless slaughter" of insectivorous birds and the destruction of forests that checked the frosty northeast winds. Ravaging insects were everywhere, farmers complained. Eastern farmlands appeared to have been drained of their natural energies.[56]

Reform and the Forest

Reformers responded to these various challenges by advancing methods of draining, fencing, manuring, fallowing, and rotating to reinvigorate the land. The old form of cultivation had "had its day," and the means of pursuing it – abundant land, virgin soils, and unending forests – no longer existed in the East. Those who formerly exerted their labor "upon a large field," Rodolphus Dickinson wrote, would have to find new ways of growing more crops on less land.[57] Farmers would adapt over time,

---

[54] Whipple, *Geographical View of the District of Maine*, pp. 11–12, 41; Greenleaf, *Statistical View of the District of Maine*, pp. 174–6.

[55] Paul Glenn Munyon, *A Reassessment of New England Agriculture in the Last Thirty Years of the Nineteenth Century: New Hampshire, A Case Study* (New York, 1978), pp. 18–19, 47, 50–2; *Eighteenth Annual Report of the Secretary of the Maine Board of Agriculture, 1873* (Augusta, 1873), p. 13; Bassett, "Urban Penetration of Rural Vermont," pp. 2–3; Wilson, *Hill Country*, pp. 66, 68; *New England Farmer* 5 (January 1853): pp. 13, 46–7.

[56] Horace Greeley in *Burlington Daily Free Press*, November 7, 1866; *Fourteenth Annual Report of the Secretary of the Maine Board of Agriculture, 1869* (Augusta, 1870), p. 77.

[57] *The Farmer's Monthly Visitor*, 4 (September 30, 1842): p. 127; Dickinson, *Geographical and Statistical View of Massachusetts*, p. 8; *New England Farmer* 1 (March 17, 1849): p. 100; Allardice, *Agricultural Tour*, pp. 136–8, 140–1; Alexander Coventry, *Address*

but a "fatalistic inertia" slowed the process, and to draw attention to the need for change, reformers highlighted the mistakes that lay behind the dramatic population drain from the hill country. "A parcel of ground is stony, and it is in consequence half tilled, if tilled at all.... Brush is suffered to grow along the fences and around stumps, monopolizing too great a share of the field. A little spring... is suffered to saturate and spoil the land... for rods around it, when a little draining would make it the most productive parcel upon the farm."[58] The degree to which farmers were actually skinning their soil is difficult to determine because demographic, economic, and environmental pressures operated in a variety of ways across the Northeast. According to historian Harold Wilson, there was "no evidence to show that the hill-country soils had any less plant food [at midcentury] than they possessed when first cultivated." Yet, the perception painted by zealous reformers remained strong: Farmers had tipped the natural balance by taking more from the land than they gave back. A natural richness "preserved for ages by the existence of timber" had been squandered.[59]

Whereas farm reformers dwelled on the mistakes of the past, the rural press concentrated on the scenes of "desolation and ruin" that out-migrants left behind. A farm-journal contributor surveyed the abandoned lands in his own neighborhood and shifted seamlessly from demographic jeremiad to environmental declension:

Near this summit, four or five families resided in our boyhood.... but scarcely as much of their old buildings as a cellar-hole now remains. A short distance at the northeast, a district of farmers then existed, in which there were boys and girls enough to fill an ordinary country school house, that is now without an inhabitant.... Their farms have become pastures and wood lots, or bare ledges, from which the thin soil that once covered them has been washed by the mountain

to the Agricultural Society of the County of Oneida (Utica, 1819), p. 19; William H. Seward, "Introduction," in James E. De Kay, Zoology of New-York, or the New-York Fauna (Albany, 1842), p. 127; Henry Colman, Agriculture of the United States: An Address Delivered 14th April, 1841, Before the American Institute in New York (Boston, 1840), p. 10.

58 American Agriculturist 16 (June 1857): p. 131; Fessenden, Complete Farmer, p. 6. See Colman, Agriculture of the United States, p. 9; George Tibbits, Address, Delivered Before the Rensselaer Agricultural Society... October 13, 1819 (Troy, 1819), p. 7.

59 Wilson, Hill Country, p. 123; Webster, Address, Delivered Before the Hampshire, Franklin, and Hampden Agricultural Society, pp. 7, 11, 13; Crèvecoeur, Letters from an American Farmer, pp. 353–4; Allardice, Agricultural Tour, pp. 42, 138–9; Colman, Agriculture of the United States, p. 18; Jesse Buel, The Farmer's Companion: Essays on the Principles and Practice of American Husbandry (Boston, 1840), pp. 21–2, 45–52; Burlington Free Press, May 20, 1854.

torrent, or blown off by the mountain winds. Square rods – almost acres – of the bald rock are now exposed, where the reaper once laid heavy gavels of wheat or other grain, and where cattle and sheep were 'up to their eyes in clover.'[60]

Faced with scenes like these, farmers too grew critical of forest destruction, and their moralistic pronouncements about lands too hastily cleared fit neatly into the prevailing scientific debate on trees in the balance of nature.[61]

The arrival of the locomotive, with its huge demands for fuel wood, ties, and construction timber, linked these nascent conservation concerns to a variety of anxieties about the new order in the Northeast, including western competition and displacement of local artisans, merchants, and manufacturers.[62] At the same time, railroads connected farm districts to metropolitan fuel and lumber markets and transformed the upland forests into a cash crop, stimulating interest in reforestation. Anticipating a rising demand for timber and cordwood, the rural press began publishing articles on yields, cutting rotations, and soil types suitable for various forest species, drawing much of this information from farmers who submitted reports on their experiments.[63] Good land under proper care would yield twenty cords per acre in twenty years, one New Englander concluded – a return more profitable than dragging a plow through thin soils "in quest of a rye harvest that will scarcely repay the expense of cultivation."[64] Healthy forests offered future generations an economic return and provided a variety of ecological benefits as they grew to merchantable size. In 1846, German traveler, Frederick Ludwig Georg von Raumer, noted that the "practice of burning down the trees, which the first settler found

---

[60] *New England Farmer*, January 28, 1871; *Eighteenth Annual Report of the Secretary of the Maine Board of Agriculture, 1873* (Augusta, 1873), pp. 6–8.

[61] *Tenth Annual Report of the Secretary of the Maine Board of Agriculture, 1865* (Augusta, 1865), p. 71.

[62] Wilson, *Hill Country*, pp. 44–5.

[63] John M. Weeks in *New England Farmer* 2 (March 2, 1850): p. 76; Benjamin Silliman in *American Journal of Science* 19 (No. 1, 1831): p. 1. See *New England Farmer* 3 (January 4, 1851): pp. 9–10; ibid., 1 (March 17, 1849): p. 100; ibid., 1 (December 9, 1848): pp. 1–2; ibid., 1 (March 31, 1849): p. 130; ibid., 2 (March 2, 1850): p. 76; ibid., 3 (January 4, 1851): pp. 9–10; *The Farmer's Monthly Visitor* 4 (April 30, 1842), p. 51; *Report on the Agriculture of Massachusetts, 1841* (Boston, 1841), pp. 390–1; Webster, *Address, Delivered Before the Hampshire, Franklin, and Hampden Agricultural Society*, p. 16; J. Bailey Moore, *History of the Town of Candia* (Manchester, 1893), p. 273; Lyman Simpson Hayes, *History of the Town of Rockingham, Vermont* (Bellows Falls, 1907), p. 92.

[64] William Blanchard, *The Farmer's Monthly Visitor* 4 (April 30, 1842): p. 51. See ibid., 4 (September 30, 1842): p. 127; *New England Farmer* 1 (December 9, 1848): pp. 1–2, 5.

necessary, is constantly diminishing; since . . . the formerly worthless timber . . . [has] increas[ed in] . . . value."[65]

Woodlot management was part of a broad reform spirit aimed at
improving the economics and aesthetics of rural life. Reformers encouraged tree-planting along the roads and in the yards for shade, shelter, and
ornamentation. "Let the tree and shrub that spring up . . . naturally [along
the roadside] be cultivated, and fruit and shade trees fill up the waste
places," one advised. In this way, "the whole face of the country may
present a pleasing and cultivated aspect, and the traveller's eye rest contin-
ually on an ever-varying picture."[66] Trees planted for beauty and protection transformed "an unattractive village" into a picture of rural charm.[67]

Reaching Consensus on Conservation

In 1831, the *Naturalist*, a popular scientific journal published in Boston,
surveyed the emerging consensus about the role of the forest in the well-
being of the nation:

Independent of ornamenting the earth and of furnishing us with timber and
fuel, forests arrest the progress of impetuous and dangerous winds; maintain
the temperature of the air; diminish extreme cold, and regulate intense heat;
oppose the formation of ice, and shelter the earth from the scorching rays of
the sun; produce an abundance of water in the streams, and impose a barrier
to washing away or undermining their banks; preserve and enrich the soil on
hills and mountains; discharge the electricity of the atmosphere, and serve as
laboratories for purifying the air we breathe.[68]

The assessment suggests a degree of careful thinking about the limits of
expansion and the role of the forest in the maturing agrarian landscape.
By the middle of the century, most scientists agreed that when trees
disappeared, as a *North American Review* essayist concluded, "the earth
suffers."[69]

---

[65] Frederick Ludwig Georg von Raumer, *America and the American People*, William
W. Turner (trans.) (New York, 1846), p. 20. See Lowenthal, *George Perkins Marsh*,
pp. 281, 297.

[66] *Sixth Annual Report of the Secretary of the Maine Board of Agriculture, 1861* (Augusta,
1861), pp. 34–7; *Eleventh Annual Report of the Secretary of the Maine Board of Agriculture, 1866* (Augusta, 1866), pp. 17, 19. See Buel, *Farmer's Companion*, p. 253.

[67] *Eleventh Annual Report of the Secretary of the Maine Board of Agriculture, 1866*
(Augusta, 1866), pp. 17–19; *Vermont Watchman and Journal*, May 7, 1879.

[68] *The Naturalist* 1 (November 1831): pp. 349–50.

[69] *North American Review*, n.s., 35 (October 1832): pp. 410–11, 416–17. See Thompson,
Natural History of Vermont, pp. 18–19; Flint, *Lectures upon Natural History*,
pp. 248–9; Williams, *Natural and Civil History of Vermont*, pp. 96–7.

In 1846, fifteen years after the *Naturalist* article and a year before George Perkins Marsh's talk to the Rutland Agricultural Society, George Barrell Emerson composed an essay on the importance of forests for his *Report on the Trees and Shrubs Growing Naturally in the Forests of Massachusetts*. The Massachusetts agricultural societies had issued a premium for planting trees on barren lands a few years earlier, and Emerson's report encouraged farmers to take up these prizes. In pulling together his scientific and agrarian concerns, he tapped into a debate naturalists had begun more than a half-century earlier about how each element in the natural landscape – mountain, river, and forest – fit together as a whole.

Emerson opened his argument with an homage to the pioneer spirit. Drawing on images like those used by Daniel Lancaster in his history of Gilmanton, he noted that in earlier times, "the smoke from the Indian's wigwam rose only at distant intervals" across an almost uninterrupted forest. However, at this point he eulogized the forest rather than the pioneer: "Now, those old woods are every where falling. The axe has made ... wanton and terrible havoc. ... The new settler clears in a year more acres than he can cultivate in ten, and destroys at a single burning many a winter's fuel, which would better be kept in reserve for his grandchildren." One might suppose that frugal Yankee landowners would consider carefully the felling of an oak brought to perfection "by the slow lapse of fifty or a hundred years" but, in fact, they proved monumentally improvident. Drawing on the natural history of the integrated landscape, he spoke for the trees.[70]

He had begun his research by questioning farmers, mechanics, shipwrights, millwrights, and factory owners about the importance of wood in the Massachusetts economy. Local trees were used in almost every industry in the state, from ships to cabinets and brooms. Households needed thirteen or fourteen cords each year, and railroads demanded thousands more for fuel. Farmers required oak, maple, birch, hickory, and hornbeam for moldboards, scythes, wagons, yokes, oxbows, tool handles, and levers. Wagon and carriage makers used white oak for spokes and frames, elm for hubs, and bass for panels.[71] Farmers and manufacturers could, of course, import their wood from other states and, thus, his economic arguments might have fallen on deaf ears. However, trees were also important to the New England landscape. No country destitute of trees,

---

[70] George Barrell Emerson, *A Report on the Trees and Shrubs Growing Naturally in the Forests of Massachusetts* (Boston, 1846), pp. 2, 58, 61, 65, 87, 113; *North American Review*, n.s., 66 (January 1848): pp. 192, 195.

[71] George B. Emerson in *North American Review*, n.s., 66 (January 1848): p. 198; Emerson, *Report on the Trees and Shrubs*, pp. 12–13, 15–17, 129.

he pointed out, could be considered beautiful; the striking feature of the Berkshire Hills was their ancient forests, just as the hickories and oaks of Brookline and Roxbury enriched those towns. Massachusetts citizens were fortunate in having a wide selection of native trees, and each species had its own shape and cycle of budding and flowering, so that together they added a pleasing variety to any landscape. Emerson praised the oak: standing alone, it "throws out its mighty arms with an air of force and grandeur, which have made it every where to be considered the fittest emblem of strength and power of resistance."[72] Trees were essential to the image and identity of New England.

They were also important to the balance of nature. They equalized temperatures, dispersed the violent winter winds, and softened the climate, protecting inhabitants "from the extremes of cold and heat, dryness and humidity." Their fallen leaves manured the pastures, and their roots aerated the soils and prevented erosion. Trees extracted minerals, moisture, and carbonic acid and returned these nutrients to the land through their death and decay. They conducted electricity between the clouds and the earth, enhancing "the vital powers of plants, and leading the clouds to discharge their contents."[73] Emerson's treatise ended with a call for reforestation on lands not fit for tillage. While the trees were growing to harvest-size, they would enrich the soil, meliorate the climate, and beautify the countryside. And, when mature, they would provide fuel for the home and income for the farmer. Emerson provided detailed instructions for planting in various soils and proposed that the state purchase "worthless lands" and replant them to demonstrate the benefits of reforestation. His publication, he hoped, would begin a discussion of the "great and important study of the history and management of forest trees," and even as he wrote, he saw signs that the destructive practices of the pioneering era were "giving way to better views."[74]

Joining the Threads of American Conservation

Reflecting in 1883 on New Hampshire's long battle with thin soils and uneven ground, F. H. Bartlett made an observation that would have been

---

[72] Emerson, *Report on the Trees and Shrubs*, pp. 7–9, 36, 121.

[73] Emerson, *Report on the Trees and Shrubs*, pp. 3–6, 30; *North American Review*, n.s., 66 (January 1848): p. 193.

[74] George B. Emerson in *North American Review*, n.s., 66 (January 1848): pp. 196–8; Emerson, "Cultivation of Forest Trees," Essex Agricultural Society, *Transactions for 1847* (Danvers, 1847): pp. 78–81; Emerson, *Report on the Trees and Shrubs*, pp. 2, 35–6.

anathema in the first half of the century: "I do not regret the decline of farming in the Granite state. Its only excuse for struggling so long was that the true agricultural part of the country was ... out of easy reach [of markets]. ... I would rather take the knowledge that the times have forced upon us and act on it, and substitute forestry for husbandry. If nature will not cooperate with us to raise corn and wheat and cattle, let us follow in her lead and raise forests of pine and spruce and hemlock, and maple and birch and ash and oak." By Bartlett's day, this was a common sentiment in the rural press, and Bartlett's neighbors, surveying the "wintry blasts" that chilled the barren hilltops of New Hampshire, probably accepted his remark with a certain equanimity. An earlier generation had been guided by an expansionary agrarian ideology and a conviction that transforming forests into fruitful fields was the summa of evolutionary naturalism. Conditioned by a long history of shifting from crop to crop in a changing competitive situation, many like Bartlett were willing to yield their battle with the forest that returned so persistently to each abandoned field.[75]

In a cultural context of anxiety and change, farm reformers echoed the scientific consensus that forests offered important practical, aesthetic, and ecological advantages.[76] In its 1848 *Proceedings*, the Essex Agricultural Society recapitulated Emerson's remarks and added other ecological considerations.

The mildness of our climate, the purity of the air we breathe, the life and freshness of our water, the plentifulness of refreshing showers, the fulness of the out-gushing springs, the beauty of our scenery, the number and variety of the beautiful songsters of the woods, the facility of raising many of the tender plants, flowers, and fruits, the perfection even of the apples, pears, and peaches ... are all to a lesser or greater extent connected with the success of this enterprise. ... We can take no more wise and sure course, than to cover our hills, ornament our plains, and fill our valleys with a rich proportion and pleasing varieties of the forest trees.[77]

Other farm publications echoed these arguments. Without the forests, the hills would "no longer yield to the ... valleys below the fertilizing elements which used to descend from decaying vegetation with the showers or the melting snows of spring," and the vigor of the land would waste away.[78] Every drought brought a wave of commentary about the loss

[75] F. H. Bartlett in *Granite Monthly* 6 (September 1883): p. 380.

[76] Essex Agricultural Society, *Transactions for 1848* (Danvers, 1848): p. 17.

[77] Essex Agricultural Society, *Transactions for 1847*, p. 102.

[78] *Vermont Watchman and State Journal*, May 10, 1882. See ibid., May 27, 1882; *New England Farmer*, October 19, 1872.

of forests.[79] "The electrical rain-bearing clouds that approach from the westward, as they come within this dry atmosphere, are absorbed and dissipated before their watery contents can reach the earth," a Maine farmer complained in 1869, "while the clouds just [to the] north . . . float on over a better wooded district and yield copious rainfall." Springs were drying up and wells were failing. Winter brought more rain than snow, leaving the soils impoverished and the sawmills and gristmills without power.[80] The Maine Board of Agriculture determined that landscapes should be around 40 percent wooded in order "to maintain an equilibrium in nature."[81] Farmers, farm reformers, and scientists moved toward agreement on a conservation message for America.

In 1864, the year Marsh published *Man and Nature*, a farm editor wrote that "in some older portions of the country the process of restoring is already in progress." Trees were a profitable crop, the *New England Farmer* pointed out, but there were also good scientific reasons for planting them.

Year by year, as the roots penetrate deeper and spread wider beneath the surface of the earth, the air is allowed to penetrate to produce its decomposing effects. The rootlets slowly break up the coarser parts of the soil and extract from them their essential food, and the leaves, by means of the action of heat and light upon them, transform, in their mysterious way, these substances into the materials of which the plant is composed. And as these leaves annually fall to the earth and finally decay, plant food is prepared to be again taken into the tree.[82]

Forests prevented soil erosion, rendered the climate moist, and acted like an "enormous sponge" to conserve water in streams and brooks.[83] Farmers responded to the midcentury crisis in agriculture in a variety of ways, not the least being a reevaluation of the relation between rural society and its forest surroundings. It was not totally ironic, then, that Marsh's *Man and Nature* appeared at a point in time when the forests of the Northeast were beginning to reclaim the fields and pastures abandoned

---

[79] *Maine Farmer*, January 6, 1872. See ibid., January 27, 1872; *New England Farmer*, June 17, 1871.

[80] *Maine Farmer*, September 13, 1873; *Burlington Free Press* in *Rural Vermonter*, October 15, 1886; *New England Farmer*, October 19, 1872.

[81] *Fourteenth Annual Report of the Secretary of the Maine Board of Agriculture, 1869* (Augusta, 1870), p. 82; *Thirteenth Annual Report of the Secretary of the Maine Board of Agriculture, 1868* (Augusta, 1868), p. 94.

[82] *New England Farmer*, June 17, 1871. See *Burlington Free Press*, March 16, 1864.

[83] *New England Farmer* 1 (March 17, 1849): p. 100; 1 (April 14, 1849): p. 139; *Maine Farmer*, December 20, 1873; *Vermont Watchman and State Journal*, January 3, 1883; *Burlington Free Press*, July 30, 1883.

in the quest for better lands out west.[84] The book's reception owed much to Marsh's persuasive ecological genius, but historical events leading up to its publication were equally important: the awesome destruction of the trans-Appalachian forest in the sweep of a single generation; the acute sensitivity to the balance of nature among scientists and lay readers; and the closing of the agricultural frontier in the Northeast, with its social dislocations and cultural anxieties. These were the cultural threads woven into the late-nineteenth-century conservation movement.

To these rural concerns, Romantics added a plea for the aesthetic and symbolic importance of the forest. In 1832, Daniel J. Browne rewrote François-André Michaux's *Sylva* in popular form and added new sections on ornamental trees. One of the most influential tracts on horticulture in America, Browne's publication mixed the impulse to improve and the need to conserve into a new American pastorale. "The business of cultivating trees . . . is not one that can be wholly left to nature," he opined; it was by the "glory of such improvements, that man . . . improves the face of nature, and nature in its turn acknowledges the obligation by softening, purifying, and exalting the feelings of man."[85] Browne's celebration came at a time when trees were becoming essential ingredients in the American landscape. According to the *North American Review*, they served as "landmarks" for the memory, generating pride in place and promoting interest in public improvements. Old World pyramids and castles were relics of ancient superstition and barbarity; America's majestic forests were emblems of republican strength and vigor.[86] Susan Fenimore Cooper elaborated this cultural argument in her own celebration of nature and place. "Several noble pines, old friends and favorites, had been felled unknown to us during the winter," she remarked in her *Rural Hours*, leaving only a forlorn assemblage of "unsightly stumps and . . . chips." She noted a "sort of tradition in the village" that forest-cutting affected the climate, but her own bereavement rested on more intimate terms. Their disappearance, she thought, disrupted a familiar balance of field and forest and diminished the spirit of the landscape.

---

[84] *The Farmer's Monthly Visitor* 4 (September 30, 1842): p. 127; *New England Farmer* 1 (March 17, 1849): p. 100; Tibbits, *Address, Delivered Before the Renssalaer Agricultural Society*, p. 7; *Thirteenth Annual Report of the Secretary of the Maine Board of Agriculture, 1868* (Augusta, 1868), p. 117.

[85] D[aniel] J. Browne, *The Trees of America; Native and Foreign* (New York, 1846), pp. vii–viii; *North American Review*, n.s., 35 (October 1832): p. 418.

[86] *North American Review*, n.s., 35 (October 1832): pp. 337–9, 401–3, 409–10; ibid., n.s., 66 (January 1848): p. 205.

"Their rude simplicity of outline, the erect, unbending trunks, their stern, changeless character, and their scanty drapery of foliage" completed the cultural integration of the neighborhood. Trees were important to the balance of nature, but to Cooper, they were also a stand against the commercial temper of the times.

There is . . . something in the care of trees which rises above the common labors of husbandry, and speaks of a generous mind. We expect to wear the fleece from our flocks, to drink the milk from our herds, to feed upon the fruits of our fields; but in planting a young wood, in preserving a fine grove, a noble tree, we look beyond ourselves to the band of household friends, to our neighbors – ay, to the passing wayfarer and stranger who will share with us the pleasure they give, and it becomes a grateful reflection that long after we are gone, those trees will continue a good to our fellow-creatures for more years . . . than we can tell.[87]

The treatment of trees reflected the soul of America.

The second half of the century saw a number of state laws designed to encourage tree-planting and provide protection for the remaining forest. Using long quotes from Marsh, in January 1869, the Maine Board of Agriculture presented a memorial to the state government on the "expediency of inaugurating a State policy encouraging the preservation and production of forest trees." The board proposed premiums for planting trees along highways and in abandoned fields. If nature was restored, it urged, the "brooks and springs would flow again as they used to do in the days of our grandfathers, and everybody would be the richer for it in purse and peace of mind."[88] In 1872, Nebraska editor J. Sterling Morton founded Arbor Day and, in the following years, others began calling for similar celebrations in their own states. In 1884, Vermont's legislature adopted a resolution directing the governor "to inquire into the subject of the forests . . . and . . . their protection." The resulting commission sent circulars to every town in the state requesting information about their forests and, from this, it gauged the losses to fuel and lumber against the gains in forest regeneration. Asked about changes in the land, Vermont's older inhabitants, with "scarcely an exception," responded that "the water supply is year by year failing."[89]

---

[87] Cooper, *Rural Hours*, pp. 13, 16, 192–3, 213, 217, 235.

[88] *Fourteenth Annual Report of the Secretary of the Maine Board of Agriculture, 1869* (Augusta, 1870), pp. 65, 68, 77, 84–5. See *Patrons' Rural*, February 27, 1885.

[89] *Burlington Daily Free Press*, November 7, 1884. See ibid., April 2, 1883, April 22, September 19, 1884; *Rural Vermonter*, October 22, 1886; John C. Gray, *Essays: Agricultural and Literary* (Boston, 1856), pp. 83–4.

Activities like these began to bear fruit in the last decades of the century. In August 1873, New York physician, Franklin B. Hough, presented a paper before the American Association for the Advancement of Science (AAAS) in Portland, Maine, titled "On the Duty of Governments in the Preservation of Forests." Hough reiterated Marsh's lessons from the ancient world and predicted, like Marsh, that this was a fate that awaited America. "The presence of stately ruins in solitary deserts is conclusive proof that great climatic changes have taken place within the period of human history," Hough began. "We cannot account for the changes... except by ascribing them to the improvement acts of man, in destroying the trees and plants which once clothed the surface, and sheltered it from the sun and the winds." As superintendent of New York's 1856 and 1866 censuses, Hough had grown concerned about the state's diminishing forest reserves and, like other scientists of his generation, he equated this with the failure of springs, wells, and brooks and the "increasing difficulties of procuring water to supply canals for navigation, and... cities."[90] Lobbied by the AAAS, in 1876 Congress appointed Hough as special forestry agent in the Department of Agriculture, commissioned to study the forest situation in America. Hough became head of the department's new Division of Forestry in 1882, and his *Report upon Forestry*, a classic in the American conservation tradition, reiterated a number of points scientists had been making for decades about the importance of forests in the well-being of the nation.

In 1875, a year before Hough began his famous report, lumbermen, landscape designers, and arboriculturists joined together in Chicago to found the American Forestry Association (AFA), laying the foundations for private initiatives in forest conservation. In 1882, a similar group convened a Forestry Congress in Cincinnati and, later that year, in Montreal. Although much of the information in the papers presented at the congress was drawn from European forestry sources, the sense of alarm that triggered the congress was decidedly homegrown.[91] The closing decade of the century was a seedtime for American conservation, beginning with the establishment of the first federal forest reserves under the Forest Reserve Act of 1891. The conservation movement flowered after the turn of the century under the dynamic leadership of President Theodore Roosevelt

[90] Franklin Hough, "On the Duty of Governments in the Preservation of Forests," American Association for the Advancement of Science *Proceedings* (August 1873): pp. 1–2.
[91] *Burlington Free Press*, September 19, 1884; *Vermont Watchman and State Journal*, November 22, 1882.

and Chief U.S. Forester Gifford Pinchot, and although these powerful personalities directed the movement and inspired the nation, they drew on a scientific legacy that had been gestating for decades.

The roots of American conservation penetrate deep into the scientific debates of the early nineteenth century, the American Romantic movement, and the agrarian reforms of the 1860s and 1870s. How the average American understood these influences cannot be ascertained easily on a national scale, but hints in the northeastern agricultural press suggest that the message was indeed before the public in the middle of the century. In 1857, a correspondent to the *American Agriculturalist* voiced his concerns about the role of the forest in the balance of nature. He drew together the various threads of conservation concern then running through the agricultural and scientific press and wove a picture of rural life threatened by the disappearance of the forests. "In this season of the year, when the woodman's axe is ringing through all our forests, prostrating millions of trees," he wrote, "it is a timely subject of inquiry, What is to be the result of this wholesale demolition?" Beginning with the economic importance of wood, the essayist went on to address the broader concerns beginning to play across the rural Northeast: Coming generations would "lament the bleak and naked hills, and cry out against us for despoiling them of their chief beauty," he admonished. Forests exerted a "beneficial influence upon the climate"; they sheltered crops and villages from the frigid winds of the north, and they ensured against drought and desiccation: "Remove old trees, but touch the young with a sparing hand. Clear up your valleys, but do not strip bare the hill tops. Leave groups and single trees here and there in your pastures, both for the comfort of your flocks and herds, and for the beauty of the landscape." It was "universally conceded," he wrote, that winters were becoming colder and the weather more disagreeable.[92]

Did this New York farmer happen upon a copy of Marsh's 1847 address? Did he read Ebenezer Emmons's warning in the multivolume *Natural History of New-York* or George B. Emerson's erudite summary of ecological arguments in the Massachusetts report? Or were his ruminations drawn simply from a lifetime of careful observation? Nearly a century after the Vermont court's judgment on the Barton River flood, New Hampshire historian A. N. Somers offered a similar warning about precipitous changes in the landscape: "Now that the country has been so largely denuded of its forests, there is less humidity in the air, and all plant

[92] *American Agriculturist* 16 (February 1857): p. 32.

life suffers loss. The lakes and streams are much smaller than formerly." He verified his claim by reference to the "oldest residents of the town."[93] Like the New York correspondent, these old folks might have read their Marsh, but there are numerous other possibilities in the scientific and reform literature of the time. Here among the "oldest residents" was a reservoir of conservation reform, tapping perhaps the writings of Marsh but also drawing more deeply from the naturalist tradition and the agonizing choices made by rural people about the fate of the farm in eastern North America.

[93] A. N. Somers, *History of Lancaster, New Hampshire* (Concord, 1899), p. 284.

Conclusion

Completing a comprehensive natural history of America was one of the great achievements of nineteenth-century American science. This was accomplished in tandem with an equally momentous historical development, as settlers flooded into the trans-Appalachian West and transformed this wooded basin into a landscape of fields, meadows, pastures, and towns. The convergence of these two events brought the first comprehensive expressions of conservation thought in America.

The modern argument for conservation, based on a full range of practical, ecological, and aesthetic considerations, emerged out of a unique set of circumstances in early nineteenth-century natural science. The study of nature began in America when a few curious and eccentric explorers ventured west of the seacoast settlements in search of "undescript" species. To describe a wilderness of daunting size and complexity, they narrowed their focus of inquiry to a single interpretative question: How was this vast, inchoate landscape to be made useful to a rising American civilization? They built their natural history on this practical inquiry, but out of their firsthand observations came a much more expansive understanding of nature. Like most wilderness travelers, they saw elements of Eden in this new country and, like most Americans, they extolled its virtues passionately. Their exotic and sometimes fanciful descriptions won them a broad audience and, unlike Europe's more erudite and gentlemanly scientists, they encouraged this attention. Their Edenic and enthusiastic popular tone began the process of romanticizing America's natural landscapes.

The resulting natural history was formulated at a time when classical and Christian ideas of harmony and balance held currency in all scientific circles. Convinced that each species occupied an ordained place in a benevolent universe, naturalists applied the logic of purpose and perfect adaptation to the plants and animals they discovered, fusing antiquity and the empirical method into a surprisingly modern understanding of ecological relations. This they honed as they prepared instructions for the European gardeners who received the specimens they sent abroad. Naturalists carefully noted the soil, exposure, drainage, and nutrients necessary for transplanting their species and, in this way, became practiced at describing the environmental context for the plants they discovered. Colonial natural history was filtered through a practical lens, but even here it is possible to see signs of the ecological consciousness that emerged in the next century.

This consciousness was nurtured in the field-research methods used by a number of these early naturalists. In the years before the advent of convenient overland transportation, most traveled by foot, horseback, or canoe on a vaguely planned scientific ramble through the West. With equal enthusiasm, they observed and described virtually every natural curiosity in this transect – plant, animal, or mineral – and they allowed their imaginations to range across disciplinary boundaries in quest of affinities among them. To comprehend this diversity, they adopted the travel journal as a platform for scientific discourse. Compiled into a narrative, their daily entries accommodated a wide-ranging scientific curiosity that combined their love of the wilds with a precise record of observation. This flexible and fluid chronicle format allowed them to connect their observations into a system. Where their taxonomies separated and isolated specimens, their travel narratives arranged them into a holistic perspective.

Naturalists observed on many levels – scientific, aesthetic, moral, even theological; they included sound, smell, and even taste as part of the investigative method. This open and receptive consciousness gave their descriptions a tactile and sensual quality that drew the reader into the natural world. This approach reflected the nineteenth-century celebration of the curious mind: the explorer who found every aspect of nature worthy of scientific inspection, who valued the general over the specific, and who thought in symbolic as well as concrete terms. Engaged in the leisurely process of observing and recording, the curious naturalist found time to mull over the question of purpose and to fit the object of observation into nature's larger plan. This was the investigative exercise that gave nineteenth-century natural history its philosophical tone and revealed the ecological links in the web of nature. Narrative rendering, unbridled curiosity, and a capacity to imagine as well as to analyze – these were the hallmarks of nineteenth-century natural history. Even though the naturalists' ramble was a brief episode in the history of American science, it left its stamp. Subsequent nature-writers wedded this narrative rendering to a Thoreauvian literary presentation and extended its influence to the present day.

Applying this methodology, naturalists inspected the geological structure of America and interpreted its history as a progressive unfolding of divine creation. This providential and unutterably ancient framework added texture and historical drama to the natural landscape and provided inspiration for the American sublime. Reasoning upward from the geological strata, they imagined mountains, rivers, and forests linked systemically and dynamically by hydrological cycles, nutrient flows, and kinetic energies. Like these integrated landscape features, the world of animals, insects, and birds coalesced as a balanced and harmonious system. The idea of a tightly knit and perfected system of relations – the balance of nature – provided ecological justification for conservation thinking and offered a moral argument for protecting wild species. Each creature was an expression of God's perfect plan, and this made thoughtless destruction of birds, animals, trees, or, indeed, whole functioning natural landscapes a form of desecration.

These unique forms of exploration, deduction, and description helped shape the emerging Romantic movement. Interested in reaching a broad readership, American naturalists appealed to myth, curiosity, nostalgia, and aesthetic appreciation and, notwithstanding the tension between science and religion, they invented a rich devotional language to explain their emotional connection to nature. Writers, poets, and artists working in the Romantic tradition found these descriptions useful in their search for beauty and inspiration in natural forms. This fusion of perspectives – scientific and romantic – gave American landscapes transcendent meaning and positioned nature at the center of the American identity. At a time when male naturalists were beginning to draw narrow disciplinary boundaries around their work, female naturalists extended this practice of expansive and expressive nature-writing. Appealing to the beauty and morality in nature's harmonies, the latter completed the task of romanticizing American natural history.

Settlement of the trans-Appalachian West challenged the evolutionary vision of the nineteenth-century naturalist. In theory, the pioneering family conformed to the logic of evolutionary naturalism by improving the earth and clearing away the forest. This, naturalists thought, would warm the climate and ameliorate the conditions that gave rise to dangerous diseases. On closer inspection, however, naturalists discovered a different trajectory in the scarred lands and blackened forests left in the wake of the pioneer. Settlers might be instruments of progress, but their avaricious destruction of nature seemed at odds with the understanding of natural dynamics that scientists were developing in these same decades. Given pause by the ruined forests of the West and the abandoned farms of the East, naturalists reconsidered the idea of improving nature. Whereas this reassessment was inspired in part by the wide-ranging critique of deforestation offered in George Perkins Marsh's *Man and Nature*, it also reflected the results of a long scientific debate over nature's ecological designs. Scientists never gained complete consensus on the effects of unabated land-clearing, but they grew cautious about proclaiming its benefits for the integrated landscapes they pieced together in their narratives. Well before publication of *Man and Nature*, scientists, farm reformers, and Romantics had compiled a long list of practical, ecological, and aesthetic arguments against forest destruction.

This conservation perspective emerged out of a unique scientific culture that encouraged broad-based inquiry into the aesthetic, ethical, and theological implications of each scientific discovery. As American natural history adopted more rigid disciplinary boundaries in the second half of the nineteenth century, these holistic constructions became somewhat passé. Yet, they left a powerful legacy. The conservation movement that coalesced at the end of the century was nurtured on thoughts about the balance of nature, the sublimity of the untilled landscape, and the intrinsic worth of every living creature. These rich and suggestive perspectives generated a spirited defense of nature that transcended its original scientific matrix. It remains, today, the philosophic grounding for the spirit of conservation in America.

Index